THE ILLEGAL DANCE

Memories of a Young Bolivian Woman in London

Vicky Borda Oviedo

Copyright © 2016 Vicky Borda Oviedo
All rights reserved.

ISBN: 1539343847
ISBN 13: 9781539343844

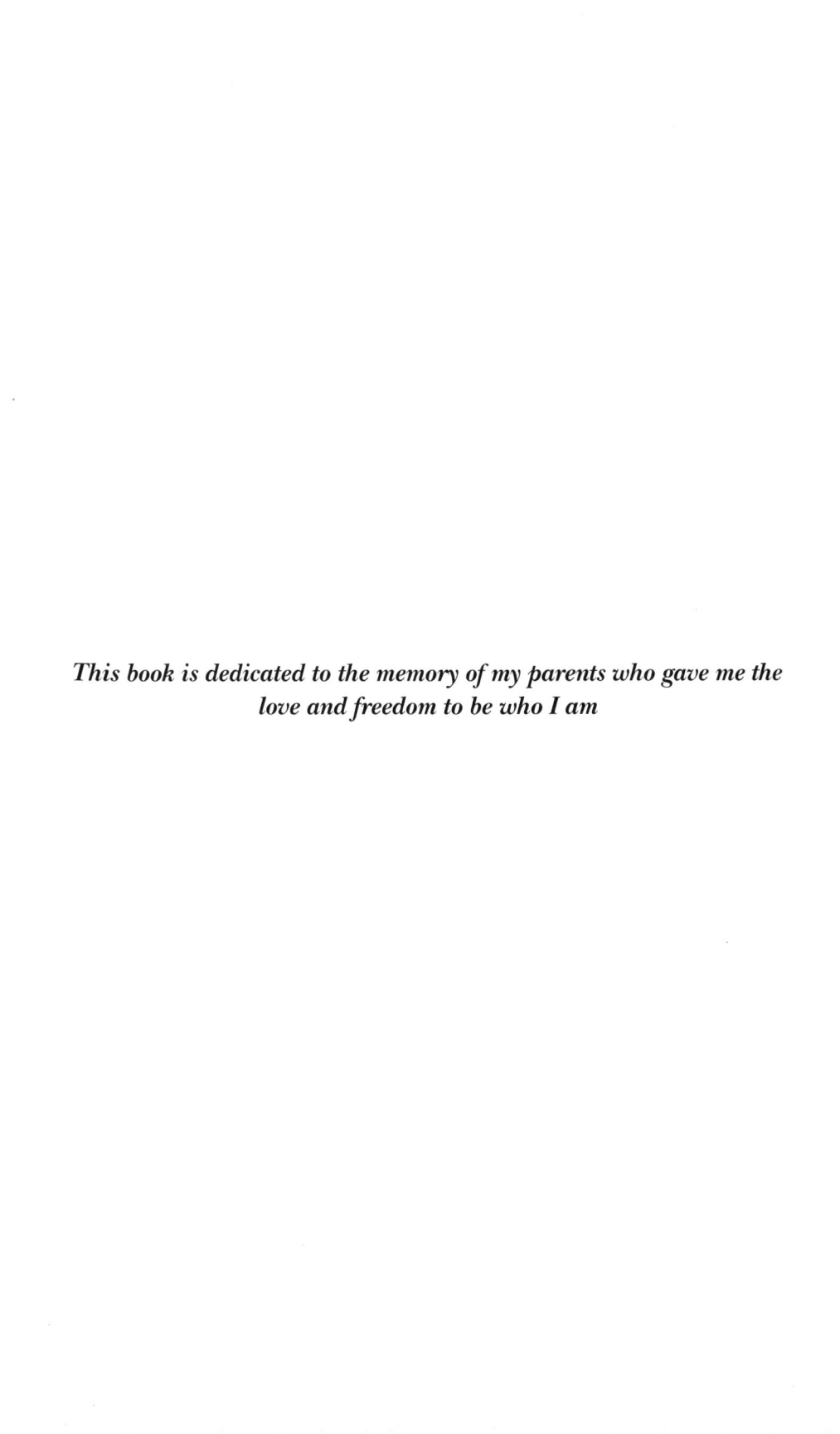

*This book is dedicated to the memory of my parents who gave me the
love and freedom to be who I am*

ACKNOWLEDGEMENTS

Completing this book has been a huge challenge, partly because I wrote it in English, a language that I will never be able to speak or write perfectly, but thanks to the unconditional support of my husband Richard who understood my madness for so many years, this book has been possible.

My friends Peter Neil, David and Connie Freeman, Hazel Shandor and Dr. Martin Parry, were the first to read the manuscript when it was still in its embryonic stage. Their advice helped enormously, and I thank them very much.

I wrote the Spanish version long after the English one and in doing so I discovered the magic in expressing myself in my own language. It encouraged and helped me to finish the book in both versions simultaneously. This arduous and slow work has been possible also thanks to my former classmate Dr. Elizabeth Velasco, who read the manuscript with great interest and enthusiastically pushed me towards publication. I also appreciate the help given me by my dear old friend Hugo Dorado Revilla whom I met by chance in the street in La Paz. I told him about my project, he offered to read the first draft, and on doing so he encouraged me to publish it. I thank my dear friend Cris Cortez, who after reading the draft shared his most intimate experiences of life in Bolivia and London.

My gratitude also goes to the writer Giancarla Quiroga for having read and corrected the manuscript more than once. I appreciate her concerns and advice about the content. Finally I thank all those friends and family who, with their voices of encouragement expressed their desire to read the finished book and this helped me to bring it all to an end at last.

__Any money made from this story will be for the children in need in Bolivia__

CHAPTER ONE

"Single means you are brave enough to face the glorious unknown of the unaccompanied journey"

Mandy Hale

"You are very welcome to the United Kingdom," ended the card I received from a fellow Bolivian I had not yet met. The words United Kingdom sounded fascinating, intriguing and mysterious to me; at just nineteen years old I felt like Alice going to Wonderland. But was I really going to a wonderful kingdom, or was it just the sumptuous name that attracted me?

It was a sunny afternoon in August 1980, when I arrived in London. I came by train from Malmö, Sweden, a quiet, cold and well organised city where some of my family lived as political refugees. When the train finally stopped at the platform at Victoria station I felt both excited and apprehensive. Passengers hurried off the train and began moving in all directions. Some of them only carried briefcases, but others were laden with heavy suitcases, like mine.

Somehow I managed to get out of the train, struggling with my cumbersome luggage, trying not to trip over it while my handbag was falling off my left shoulder insistently. I was due to meet a Bolivian man at the station, even though I was three hours late. I had been delayed in Dover, a coastal town in Kent in the south east of England that faced France; the train having been detained in the port for passport control checks. The customs officers wanted to ask me about the purpose of my visit to London. They were not happy with my unintelligible answers, so they had asked me to get off the train for what turned out to be more unsuccessful questioning at the immigration office. After about three hours they had exhausted their lines of enquiry and, as they could not find anybody who could speak Spanish to act as an interpreter, they gave me a one month visa and let me take the next train to London.

Although I was relieved to find out I could continue my journey, I was also terrified on my arrival in London to realise that Froilan, the man who I was supposed to meet, was not at Victoria station. This was a problem; I didn't know him and I had never seen him before, even in a photo. It would have been difficult to find him in this busy station even had I arrived on time. Perhaps Froilan would have recognised me, as he had met my father in Bolivia a few months earlier when he went for treatment at Dad's dental surgery. Froilan had told him that he lived and worked in London as a mechanical engineer. My father was delighted to meet somebody based in London and told Froilan that he was planning to send me to study in the U.K. Froilan had kindly offered to help me if I came to London one day. My father took Froilan's address and sent it to me in Malmö. A few weeks before leaving Sweden, I wrote Froilan a letter and he replied by return

The Illegal Dance

of post saying he would be at Victoria station to meet me. That was all I knew about him; I had his address, but no contact telephone number.

Bit by bit I pushed my wheel-less suitcase from the platform to the main arrivals hall in the station. I had read that years earlier, during the two World Wars, Victoria had been bombed heavily by the Germans as it had been one of the stations where trains had left for France carrying soldiers to war. Some of these soldiers came back to England wounded while others never came back at all. But by the time I arrived in 1980, there was of course no evidence of bomb damage; too many years had passed since then. Instead, the arrivals hall was a jumble of people of every colour, creed and nationality. It looked as if everybody in the world had made an appointment to meet there. The station had an effervescent atmosphere; people appeared and disappeared like small champagne bubbles. Coffee shops, food shops and even clothes shops were dotted around the main hall. There were many doors in the hall, too, some of them leading to offices and others to exits to the outside world. This terminus was totally different to the sleepy train station in Malmö.

Feeling lost, anxious and totally disorientated, I stood in the middle of the busy hall without knowing which direction to take. I could hardly speak any English to ask for directions and my heavy suitcase was also a problem. I began to think how unprepared I was for this trip. Suddenly a man caught my eye; he was coming towards me with a big smile on his face. He was short, slightly bald and wearing a brown suit with a white open shirt without a tie. "This could be Froilan," I thought, feeling relieved. Bolivian men are generally short and dress very casually if they are not at work, but as he came closer to me I realised he was too old to be Froilan, perhaps in his late sixties. As a matter of fact, I wasn't even sure how old Froilan was. I had never asked my father about his age and he never mentioned it either, but I imagined him as a younger man. He approached me and started talking to me. "Duyunedyelp?" *"Que? Como dijo?"* I asked in Spanish. He tried again. "Duyunedyelp? Me, taxi!" "Maybe he's a taxi driver," I thought, so I said "Taxi?" "Yes", he replied, indicating with his hand that I should go with him. He picked up my big suitcase and began to walk in front of me.

I started to follow him, but then remembered I needed to change money. "Stop, stop," I said. "Money, me money change!" I had 1000 US dollars that my father had given me in Bolivia and 1000 kronor that my cousin René had lent me. "Oh! Givmtyu money, change." He indicated with hand movements that he could change it for me. I reached for my purse in my handbag and opened it to get some money and give to him. "All, all," he said. I was just about to give him all my cash when he mentioned "mother". I think he must have said that his mother was waiting for him in his car; he would take her home first and then take me wherever I wanted to go afterwards. I looked at him, still holding the money in my hand. He seemed too old to have a mother. Then I remembered my Uncle Hector's parting words to me in Sweden. "You are too young to go on your own to London; it is a very dangerous city. I won't let you go unless your father sends me a letter authorising me to do so."

At around that time we heard in the news about a serial killer called "the Yorkshire Ripper", a man who murdered thirteen women, most of them prostitutes. I didn't know where Yorkshire was, but this man could easily have been him or some other killer. Suddenly I woke up to the situation and decided to get out of it. I was just about to give all my cash to a man who I had just met. I put my money back in my handbag, picked up my suitcase quickly and walked away from him as fast as my heavy luggage would allow me. I left the man behind, still trying to convince me that he only wanted to help me. I walked rapidly towards an exit door and on to the street without looking back. I carried on walking, until I saw a queue of people in front of me carrying their luggage, then I saw lots of black cars. "They must be the taxis," I thought. Further away there were also those beautiful red double-decker buses that I used to see in English films and on my right across the road, I saw a "Bureau de Change". "Great, I've got everything I need here", I thought feeling relieved. I just needed to get some change and get in one of those black taxis.

I handed the taxi driver Froilan's address that I had written on a piece of paper. He nodded his head in a positive way meaning he knew where it was. I smiled back and got into the taxi. I was relieved that the driver knew where he was going. At that time I didn't know that London taxi drivers have to study for at least three years to learn the city streets, a process called "the Knowledge of London." In Bolivia anybody with a car can work as a taxi driver. In times of economic crisis, like in the eighties, even professional people had to do this.

During my journey to Froilan's place I could appreciate how beautiful and interesting London was. The buildings were so different to Bolivia; a mixture of modern and classic styles showed a rich architectural heritage. My enthusiasm grew even more when we passed by an amazing park in the middle of the city. "That's Hyde Park", the taxi driver said, looking at me through the driving mirror. I had no words to express my excitement; I was overwhelmed to see so much greenery. This was totally different to the arid scenery of La Paz. "This city looks really interesting and colourful and it must be great fun to live here", I thought.

The taxi driver dropped me at Birchington Road in Kilburn, where Froilan lived. After paying the driver I went to the front door of the house. There was a note on the door that said, "Press Once." "Those crazy, precise English," I thought as I rang the bell eleven times. A few minutes later a tall, angry looking, scruffy blonde guy opened the front door of this Victorian house. He did not look very happy and not very Bolivian either. I asked him in my bad English, "Mr Rodriguez here?" "No, he is not here," he said. I asked him again. "He live here?" "Yes," he replied, but he is not here at the moment." "Me come in?" I asked. "No, sorry, I'm going out", he said. "Bag here, me come later." "Ok, you can leave your bag," he replied and allowed me to put the suitcase in the entrance hall. But before he closed the door he pointed at the note, and showing me with his finger how, he pressed the bell only once. "Ok?" he made sure I understood. I then realised that the word "once" meant only one and not eleven as in Spanish.

I went for a walk around the area for an hour or so, making sure I did not get lost. It was a marvellous afternoon; the sky was clear without the threat of rain. I was told that London was famous for its torrential and unexpected downpours, but that afternoon I was pleasantly surprised with the mild weather. However, the streets around Kilburn were dirty with uncollected rubbish dumped everywhere as there was a food market nearby. London looked like a busy city full of people, whereas Malmö gave me the impression that there were not enough people to dirty the streets. It was so clinically clean and silent. Malmö in the evenings felt like aliens from another planet had landed and taken everybody away, leaving the houses empty with the lights on.

The dirty streets and the market in Kilburn High Road reminded me of Bolivia, where people sell things everywhere, due to a lack of conventional jobs. In fact the whole country sometimes feels like it is a big market. The Kilburn streets looked real to me and it gave me a feeling of belonging.

I went back to the house an hour later. I noticed that all the buildings looked alike, apart from the walls being painted with different colours. This time I rang the bell only once, so as not to annoy anybody. I was lucky, Froilan, the guy from Bolivia, opened the door. I was so pleased to see him I gave him a big hug as though I had known him for ever. He was pleased to see me, too. He said he had waited at Victoria station on the right platform for about an hour, but then had given up, thinking that immigration had not let me into the country.

Froilan was tall, dark and good looking, but more than anything he seemed very nice and friendly. He did not invite me inside the house and, picking up my suitcase he took me out straight away. "You are going to stay at a friend's flat until we find you a place to live permanently and a job". I was delighted and grateful for the arrangement. We went to his car, which was parked in front of the house. It was small, white, very old and dirty. He explained on the way to their house that his friends were a married couple. The guy was from Santa Cruz de la Sierra, a city in the east of Bolivia, and she was from Galicia in Spain. They had a four-year-old son and lived in Ladbroke Grove, part of the west London Borough of Kensington.

We arrived about twenty minutes later. The area was dull and the houses were built like a line of boxes put together, looking all the same but without any architectural features. The buildings were very simplistic and practical; they were even painted the same colour, similar to Malmö's buildings, especially the one in which my relatives lived. I found out later that Froilan's friends rented their flat from the council; it was on the first floor. The entrance to the building was gloomy, the walls painted with graffiti. The Spanish girl opened the door. She was young and attractive, but did not seem particularly friendly. The flat was not very spacious. It had a narrow corridor, two bedrooms on one side, with a bathroom on the other. There was a small sitting room with a brown, patterned carpet and empty walls, with no bookshelves or paintings.

The furniture was basic, comprising a small sofa and a television. In the middle of the sitting room there was an ironing board next to a plastic basket full of unironed clothes. In the kitchen they had a table with four chairs. The flat did not inspire me or make me feel welcome; it looked like they were not expecting me. I could not help comparing it to my parents' house in Bolivia. My mum was always so house proud, her home always being very neat. In her living room, the carpet colour would match the sofas. There were always flowers on the table, paintings on the walls, and ornaments and photos of the family on the shelves. When we had visitors she made sure her house was spick and span. I also thought of my relatives in Sweden. Their sitting room had shelves full of books and paintings by famous Argentinian writers and artists, many of them close friends of my Uncle Hector such as Rodolfo Kusch, Haroldo Conti, Mario Benedetti, Ricardo Rojo, Julio Cortázar, Ricardo Carpani and Ponciano Cárdenas.

This flat had no books, no spirit; it was dull and cold. It seemed to me that the furniture had been bought without any thought, without respecting the space or thinking that the colour schemes may affect their souls. It did not come across as a happy flat. A small boy came running to see the visitors; he was half naked, wearing only a T-shirt. His mother explained that he was potty training. There was also an old lady sitting on the sofa. She was from Bolivia and the mother of Juan, the guy from Santa Cruz. She was visiting the family from abroad and was also new in town.

An hour later, Juan arrived home from work. He was a small chubby man, very cheerful, friendly and funny, always joking, although it seemed that his jokes did not amuse his wife. She never smiled and did not seem happy with all of us there. However, Juan seemed to be enjoying the crowded flat. "Let's have dinner", he suggested, taking some pots from the kitchen cupboards and in no time at all he had prepared a delicious Bolivian meal.

The five of us sat down around the small kitchen table to eat. Through the window, I could see trains passing by from time to time. The noise of the railway was loud and disturbing. I could not avoid having mixed feelings. On the one hand I felt lonely, in a big and dangerous city, on the other hand I felt excited by the unpredictability of my situation. I was curious and impatient to see what London had to offer me.

We spent the evening talking mainly about Bolivia. Juan's mother went on and on about people from my area in the west of the country. People in the east of Bolivia, like her, call us the *collas*; she blamed us for all the burglaries in her town. We were the lazy ones, the dirty ones, the ones who did not like to work. According to her, Santa Cruz would be a better place without the *collas*. From time to time Juan told his mother off for her constant attack on us and reminded her I was from the west. "Mum", he said. "Ana is from La Paz, she is a *colla*, don't say things like that." At first she apologised to me, but after a while she would remember once more something bad that the *collas* had done in her town and start up again. I found this amusing; I just laughed at her funny stories. It was clear in my mind that she was a narrow minded old lady. We call people from the east of Bolivia, "*cambas*". There is constant rivalry between the two parts of the country.

During the evening I also tried to get to know my new friend, Froilan. I noticed that his Spanish was poor; he seemed incapable of holding an interesting conversation or giving a well-argued opinion. I began to wonder whether or not he really was an engineer, as he had told my father.

At about one in the morning it was time to go to bed. Froilan left to go home but promised to come back the next day at midday to take me out to see the city. Maria, Juan's Spanish wife, arranged a bed for me on the floor of the sitting room. The old lady and her grandson slept in the one bedroom and the couple went to bed in the other one.

I lay down on my bed waiting for everyone to retire to their bedrooms so that I could use the bathroom. After about an hour

I could still hear the sound of people walking between the corridor and the bathroom. Suddenly I noticed the door of my room opened slightly, and then it closed again. "Oh God!" I thought this must be Juan, who had waited until his wife had gone to sleep before coming to try it on with me. Men from Santa Cruz are well known in Bolivia for being womanisers. I had heard so many stories of unfaithful husbands who had seduced a family friend or even the wife's best friend. I also had the feeling that he and his wife were not very happy together. She rarely smiled and seemed angry all the time. She was constantly screaming at her child when he didn't tell her when he wanted to do wee-wee.

I remembered something that happened when I was living in Sweden. My brother and I had gone to Stockholm to visit his friend, a Brazilian guy. We stayed in his flat for the weekend. The first night we stayed at his place I slept in the friend's bedroom. The Brazilian guy and my brother slept in the other room, but in the middle of the night I woke up to find the friend trying to get into my bed. I hardly knew the guy; that evening was the first time I had ever met him. I was outraged by his behaviour, so I told him to go away in no uncertain terms. Thank God he left immediately, but the next day he hardly spoke to me.

Now these memories kept coming into my head, I felt worried and frightened that Juan was trying to get into my room. "What do I do?" I thought to myself. "I have to be in this flat for a week at least until I find myself a place to live. If Juan comes in, do I scream? His wife would probably kick me out of the house straight away. What do I do, what do I do?"

I tried to organise my thoughts, hoping that Juan would change his mind and not come back again. However, a few minutes later the door opened again, this time even more widely. I decided to confront him, whatever the consequences; I couldn't let him take advantage of me just like that. There was an armchair on my right hand side, so he could not see if I was asleep or awake. I noticed a hand pulling a small stool to keep the door open; I sat up to face him, and there he was in front of me. When he came closer, though, I realised it was not Juan; it was a very big black man. His big, white eyes looked at me in disbelief.

I started shouting, "*Ladrón! Ladrón!*" Everybody came out of their bedrooms very quickly. I think my screams could have been heard two streets away. The man had entered the building through the bathroom window and left all the doors of the flat open to make a quick escape. All the noises I had heard were from this man carrying out a burglary. Juan and I ran after him all the way down the street. I don't know why we did that. The burglar disappeared in no time at all. We walked to the main road, looking for a public telephone to call the police to report the burglary.

About fifteen minutes later the police arrived. They asked questions and tried to find out if he had stolen anything. In my opinion there was nothing of value to steal in the flat. The old lady from Bolivia came out of her room groggy, alarmed and concerned. She asked her son to tell the police that the burglar must have been a *colla*. Juan lost his cool and shouted at her angrily, "we are in London, Mum, not Bolivia. Shut up, shut up please, enough is enough. Stop the *colla* thing!" I honestly didn't care if the man was a burglar just so long as it was not Juan.

CHAPTER TWO

"It is necessary to learn what you need, not just what you want"

Paulo Coelho

The next day, I woke up to the cries of the little boy, David. I imagined he had wet himself again and his mum had smacked him on his bare bum like she had the night before a couple of times. He came running into the sitting room where I was sleeping, trying to escape from his mum; I pretended I was still asleep. When he saw me lying on my bed on the floor he came and stopped just above me. He was naked from the waist down and stood there looking down at me quietly in a position that seemed like he was just about to pee all over me. "Boo!" I went, jumping out of the bed and he ran out of the room, laughing. I looked at my watch; it was time to get up. After rolling up my bed to make more space in the sitting room, I went to the bathroom to have a quick wash and get dressed.

At around ten we all sat down in the kitchen for breakfast, talking about the night before. Juan's wife changed her attitude; she became more friendly and talkative. Juan's mum was nicer and more humble. She stopped talking about the *colla* thing. They all seemed more pleasant to me that morning. Perhaps they felt a bit guilty that my first night in London should have started with such a commotion.

At around midday the bell rang. Surely it was Froilan coming to pick me up as we had agreed; I got up quickly from my chair to get ready. The family was still in the kitchen, talking and laughing. While in the bathroom I could hear them telling Froilan everything that had happened the night before. I could also hear Froilan's concerns. "Oh my God, poor Ana, she must have been terrified to see a black man in front of her." A few minutes later I was all made up ready to go and with a big smile on my face. I think I confused him a little as he was probably expecting a traumatised girl ready to return to Sweden straight away. He looked at me in surprise and appeared a bit confused. I felt he wanted to say something to me, but nothing came out from his lips. "Hi Froilan, you've probably heard it all by now," I said to him. "Oh poor you, what a night you've had!" he said very sympathetically. Before I had the chance to answer Juan began to tell him about his mum saying that the burglar must have been a *colla*. We all laughed.

I saw the sun coming through the kitchen window. It seemed a very nice day and the only thing I wanted was to get out of the flat and forget all about the night before. "Well, I'd better take this young lady out to see London," Froilan said. I picked up my handbag on the way out and noticed that Froilan looked very smart. He was wearing an impeccably ironed white shirt and tailored trousers. He was indeed an attractive man.

As we left the apartment building I saw that just across the road there was a garage full of those famous red buses. Further down the road was a red telephone box. "This must have been the public telephone we used to call the police the night before," I thought. The colourful buses, telephone boxes and black cabs gave the city a particular charm.

We drove towards central London, passing through Notting Hill Gate. I was amazed to see more foreign-looking people than white English in the streets, which was totally the opposite to what I had seen in Sweden. There seemed to be a cosmopolitan friendliness everywhere; something like the whole world belongs to you and you belong to it. I asked Froilan if these people were tourists or whether they lived in London. He replied that most of them probably lived in London. I was happy to hear that because when living in Sweden I had felt more like an outsider. There were not many foreigners there, so people like me stood out. I noticed there were lots of black people, too. I thought about Bolivia, recalling there were not many black people in the cities. Due to this fact it was a custom to pinch one's arm or somebody else's and say "lucky" whenever we saw a black person in the streets. If I had to do this in this city I would soon be bruised all over! Most of the black people in Bolivia lived in the countryside, not far from La Paz in a village called Tocaña, in the Yungas and, unlike London, there are very few foreigners anyway.

All around me was new, different and exciting. I was really pleased to have come to London, a true metropolis. I was bubbly, laughing, making jokes and asking lots of questions; I could not hide my excitement. Froilan did not talk very much; he was just quietly observing my enjoyment. We passed an exclusive area that he told me was Holland Park. The houses were very beautiful; most of them looked palatial, expensive and well maintained. It was undoubtedly a very wealthy area. Later on, Froilan suggested that we should visit Windsor to see the castle.

Once we arrived in the town, we made straight for Windsor Castle. I was overwhelmed by its grandeur and romantic feel. I noticed a bronze statue of Queen Victoria at the entrance to the castle. I imagined her wearing a long smart dress, wandering in the beautiful gardens or holding parties in lavishly decorated rooms. I had no words to express my astonishment, but I thought to myself, "my God, there's a lot of money in this country!" Walking around the State Rooms, I felt insignificant and only too conscious that I was from an insignificant country too. Then I recalled a story that I heard when I was at school. In 1868, the incumbent Bolivian dictator General Mariano Melgarejo invited the British Ambassador to a meeting to discuss the advisability of signing a treaty between the two countries, but the British authorities declined the proposal. The angry dictator had the ambassador tied on to a donkey, facing backwards and paraded him around the main square in La Paz. The ambassador fled home and told Queen Victoria of the outrage. "Where on Earth is Bolivia?" asked the Queen, demanding a map. When one was brought to her, she took a pen, scratched a cross on Bolivia and declared, "Bolivia no longer exists!"

I came back to the present when a familiar language caught my attention. A group of noisy Spanish speaking people greeted us. There were two middle aged couples and a young man who, it turned out, were all friends of Froilan; they were surprised to see him in Windsor.

We were introduced; Doña Asuncion and Agustin, her husband and the young man called Pedro was Doña Asuncion's son, who had arrived the previous day from Argentina. The other couple were Francisco, from Spain and his wife Alegria from Bolivia. The two couples had been living in England for more or less ten years. Francisco and Alegria lived in Windsor. Pedro was in his late twenties and was in London to study, like myself.

Asuncion was a small chubby lady with dyed bright orange hair, probably in her early fifties. She was the funniest of the whole group, often telling jokes and making fun of everybody including the castle guards. She was dancing in front of them to make them laugh. She was a very inquisitive lady, wanting to know everything. She asked me endless questions about my family, and my life growing up in Bolivia. She also told me all about herself and her children, and about how she came with her husband to work in London as cleaners in hospitals or as kitchen assistants. Her life seemed fascinating and happy.

The couple living in Windsor were also very friendly. Alegria was also in her fifties. A very petite lady with a long, unfashionable hairstyle that was totally unsuitable for her age and height. She and her husband worked in a restaurant and also did cleaning jobs. Alegria's husband, Francisco was not a typical Spanish man, loud and brash; he was quiet and gentle.

The Windsor couple invited us all to have something to eat at their home. The house was small but inviting. While Francisco and Alegria prepared the meal, the rest of us got into conversation with Pedro, who appeared to be an intelligent young man with an excellent sense of humour. He was a skilful magician and amused us all with his tricks. Until recently, Pedro had been a student in Argentina, but his mother discovered he was spending more time with girls than studying, so she decided to bring him to London to finish university under her supervision. Doña Asuncion also had a daughter in Bolivia, who worked in a bank.

My niggling doubts about Froilan began to be confirmed that evening. I did not believe he was a university graduate, as he had told my father. Unlike Pedro, he was not really a very educated man. We ate a delicious dinner and had drinks in the garden. The day passed very quickly and it was soon time to go. I had had a lovely time, especially with Doña Asuncion. We said goodbye, and Froilan and I left. It didn't occur to me at the time to ask them for their contact number or address, a decision that I would come to regret later on.

The Illegal Dance

The following morning I met Froilan again. He brought the newspaper with him, so we could start job hunting. We sat down in the kitchen with a cup of tea amid the noise of David's screams and his mum telling him off constantly. We agreed that the best thing for me to look for was a live in au pair position with an English family, which would mean that I would do some housework to get pocket money, but would also have time off to attend English classes. He chose a few advertisements and we went to the red telephone box near the flat to make the calls. I began to realise how dependent I was becoming on this guy and it made me feel uncomfortable. He was doing everything for me. As well as making all the telephone calls and speaking on my behalf, he had to drive me to the advertisers' places, introduce me, be my interpreter and try to convince them that I was the right person for the job. This exercise proved more complicated than I had first thought because as soon as they realised that I could not speak English or understand the language, they did not want to hire me.

The whole week passed without any luck. Although Froilan was positive and encouraging, I was beginning to get worried. There were a lot of factors to take into consideration. I did not want to abuse the generosity of the family who were kindly putting me up, especially as they had to cater for another visitor, Juan's mother and the flat was very small. I felt that I was imposing on their hospitality and it was not fair. Another problem was that Froilan had to start his job the following week. He explained to me that he worked shifts, one week in the morning and one week at night.

So during the following week he met me in the early evenings, but by the time we had looked through the newspapers and made the calls, most of the jobs had been taken. While waiting for Froilan I would play with David and talk to Juan's mother, who looked after the boy while Maria, his mother, worked. Juan's mother was so simple minded it was difficult to have a conversation with her. We had nothing in common, except for the fact that we both came from Bolivia.

One day she told me that she was not very happy with her Spanish daughter-in-law, Maria. Apparently the whole family went to Bolivia with the intention of living there permanently, but Maria hated everything about the country. She disliked Santa Cruz, the city where they came from, the food, the house and the people; nothing in Bolivia was good enough for her. It was no wonder she was unfriendly towards me when I first arrived as I was also from Bolivia.

I was bored waiting all morning for Froilan to come round, but I was not brave enough to go out on my own. Even though he took me out a few times, Froilan never taught me how to use the Underground or how the bus routes worked and I was too complacent to ask.

By the end of my second week in London I had a breakthrough; the Owens family wanted to see me. We made an appointment for Friday evening. The place was in Chepstow Villas, not far from where I was staying and was a lovely three storey house, totally different to my Bolivian friends' flat. It was tastefully decorated with a combination of what I later discovered were French and English styles. The sitting room had a big mirror above the fireplaces, on top of which were lovely dried flowers and some photos of the family. On both sides of the fireplace were shelves filled with books. The room had a large table in the middle covered with architectural magazines. There were two round tables on either side of a big cream coloured sofa, each with a beautiful lamp on it. The walls were covered with modern paintings, which made the room look very welcoming.

On first acquaintance, the family seemed friendly enough. They were young, perhaps in their late thirties. He was an English architect and she was French. They had three lovely boys. The oldest one was seven years old, the middle one about five and the baby was only seven months.

We sat down on the sofa to discuss the details of the job. The main part of my duties was to help with the children after school. I would have time to study in the mornings, from nine thirty until midday and two days free on Saturday and Sunday. My wages were fifteen pounds per week, with room and meals provided. The duties and schedule seemed straightforward. The couple did not seem worried that my English was practically non-existent; they wanted me to start straight away. There was an English language school ten minutes' walk away from the house. It all seemed too good to be true.

Froilan and I left their house feeling great. I was due to move in on Sunday evening, so I could start my work on Monday morning. Froilan seemed to be more relaxed and communicative. We were both relieved that I had found a placement with a good family; it promised to be an interesting experience for me and a great opportunity to learn English.

The Saturday before I started work, we went sightseeing again. We took photos of Buckingham Palace, Tower Bridge and the Houses of Parliament. I was so impressed with the splendour and elegance of it all. There was no doubt that this was a city built for kings and queens; it was magical and full of mystery. The contrast from one area to another was also remarkable. On the one hand, there were the beautiful buildings both old and new and on the other hand, I felt I was visiting a developing country in some of the markets, where people would sell their products or second hand clothes in the street. But somehow the whole picture blended wonderfully.

On Sunday, after helping my Bolivian friends to tidy up their flat, I packed my bags and got ready to leave. I must have looked nervous or preoccupied because Juan held my shoulder and said, "don't worry, girl, as long as you learn to say "please", "thank you" and "sorry" as many times as possible, you will be fine." This sounded funny but later on I learned that English people are very polite and use these words a lot. In fact an old lady once told me that one night she got up to go to the bathroom in the dark, collided with the door and apologised to it, saying, "sorry". Froilan came to pick me up in the late afternoon and drove me to what was going to be my new home.

It was about six in the evening when we arrived at the house. Mr Owen opened the door and took my suitcase inside. He did not engage in any conversation with my friend so I had the feeling they were busy. I thanked Froilan as we said our goodbyes, and he replied, "I will come on Saturday to take you out."

Once in the house, Mr Owen guided me upstairs to my room on the second floor. The room was well appointed, with a decent view of the back garden. Placed near the window was a single bed, a bedside table and a small wardrobe; the other side of the room housed storage units full of children's toys. There was a bathroom next to my room for me to use. Mr Owen also showed me where the children slept. A second bedroom had an *en suite* bathroom; it was for the two older boys. There was also a single bedroom, which was for the baby.

Mr Owen asked me to come down to the kitchen where they were having their dinner. I went downstairs and sat with them at the table. They tried to make conversation, but I didn't understand what they were saying. As they had to pay attention to their children, it didn't matter anyway. I felt uncomfortable; I didn't know what to do or what to say, so I just sat there watching the children and smiling at them. The children looked tired; the middle boy didn't want to eat his dinner, the older one ate quickly so he could watch television for another half an hour and the baby was being fed so he could soon be put to bed. I ate a little, but was so nervous I didn't feel hungry at all.

Mrs Owen took the baby upstairs to bed while her husband helped the five-year-old to finish his dinner. I got up to clear the table but he stopped me. "Tomorrow, tomorrow", he said. I sat down again, but he indicated I could go to my room and relax.

I needed to be alone to gather my thoughts and come to terms with the fact that from now on I was going to live in an English home that was so different to my home in Bolivia. I also wanted to write a letter to my parents to tell them how I was and to give them my new address, so they could send me money to pay for my school fees. By seven thirty the three children were in bed, sleeping. This was not common practice in Bolivia. Children usually stay up late, playing and if they were from poor families they were either working with their parents or at home by themselves until late. I used to see this in La Paz if I came out of the movies with my parents late at night; the children would be selling sweets outside the cinema.

At around ten at night the baby woke up and started crying, incessantly. I waited for a while to see if either of his parents would come to see him, but they didn't. I got up and went out of my bedroom thinking that maybe they hadn't heard him. I was on the landing when Mr Owen came upstairs. He managed to communicate to me that they were listening to him via a monitor. He thanked me and sent me to bed again. I went back to my room. The child stopped crying for five minutes and then started up again. He cried and cried and cried. I don't know how long this went on, perhaps not long but it was torture for me. I could not sleep; I did not understand why the parents didn't go to him.

I waited a while, but eventually I got up again. This time I was determined to go to him. As I was about to enter his room, his mother stopped me. She said that the baby was fine and that I shouldn't worry. We both went into the room to check. His poor little face was red with so much crying. She made sure he was not wet or hungry and checked the room temperature. Then she said, "everything's fine, let's go". We both left the room, she went downstairs to her bedroom and I went to mine. The child started to cry again straight away.

I could not believe it. I held my head in my hands. "What are they doing?" I thought. "Why do they let him cry so much?" I didn't know what to do. I opened the window and stuck my head out. I didn't want to listen to the baby's distress anymore. The poor thing cried until he fell asleep. I thought this was a barbaric way to discipline him, but it worked. The following two nights, they used the same system until he settled into his routine.

The next morning the two older children woke up around six o'clock. Jean-Paul was the older boy and Damian the younger. They came to my room to play with their toys. I lay in my bed for another half an hour, watching them. In the beginning they were shy and tried not to make any noise but that didn't last very long. They started arguing about one of the toys and the noise became louder and louder. I felt like asking them to shut up because I was still sleeping, but I had to think twice. I was not in my own house, and these boys were not my children.

A while later their mother came upstairs to wash them and get them ready for breakfast. I was getting dressed when she asked me to hurry up. She wanted me to see how I should help the children get ready for school. Then we all went downstairs for breakfast. Later on, Mrs Owen took them to school. She asked me to watch the baby while she was away.

Twenty minutes later she came back. She asked me to come upstairs with the baby to show me how to change nappies. While she was getting things ready in the bathroom I was holding the baby in my weak and inexperienced arms. The little boy was so heavy and active that at one point he almost fell out of my arms. She noticed my incompetence and took him away from me, looking rather irritated.

During the days that followed I would make mistake after mistake; like putting a nappy on the wrong way round and the baby's clothes would end up wet. I would forget to use the rash cream on his bottom and the next day he would get blisters on his backside. This task was new to me because in Bolivia in those days we didn't have proper nappies. Mothers had to make nappies themselves from towels or flannels and wash them by hand, because very few people had washing machines. Some well off families paid women a few pesos for washing clothes by hand, but the poor who couldn't afford it or did not have the time to wash the flannels, would often leave their children dirty for long periods, having to tolerate their suffering from the rashes on their bottoms.

My grandfather, who was a chemist, invented a treatment for this type of condition. It was made from cod liver oil and zinc oxide, because the pharmaceutical companies didn't export these types of ointments to Bolivia. My father called it "the sacred cream" for its wonderful healing properties and it has been used by the parents of all the children in my family.

A young, smiling Filipina called Mutia also worked at the Owens' house as a cleaner. She worked all week for four hours a day and had another job in the afternoons, cleaning for another French lady who was married to a Peruvian man. One day she came crying to the house and told Mrs Owen that she had been sacked from her job. Apparently the couple, who were Christians like Mutia, found out that she was not giving a tithe of ten per cent of her earnings to the church she was attending because she was helping her family in the Philippines. I was surprised when I heard this. "Love the Lord your God with all your heart, with all your soul, with all your mind" (Matthew 22:37), but surely it didn't say with your money, too?

One day Mrs Owen asked me to put all the dirty plates into the dishwasher. By mistake I put "Fairy Liquid" into the machine instead of dishwasher detergent. Minutes later there were bubbles everywhere. It took the dishwasher three or four attempts to wash the dishes, as there was so much detergent that had to be cleared. She was not pleased at all with what I had done.

Every day at around two in the afternoon I took the children to a private park near her house in Kensington Park Road to play for two hours. She put the park gate key in my pocket and made me hold the baby's pram with both hands. One of the children would be on my right and the other on my left, and the three of us pushing the pram would walk to the park. I was amazed to learn that they had their own key to the park. I thought that parks were for everyone. Did they have to pay for this? This would never have occurred in Bolivia. At four o'clock it was teatime, after which the children were allowed to watch television for one hour until six in the evening when they had to get ready for bed.

One afternoon I went to the park with the children and on the way back home I experienced a frightening incident. There were four steps to get to the front door of the house from the street. I pushed the pram up the steps and put my hand in my pocket to take out the keys for opening the front door. As I was about to go inside, the pram started to roll back down the steps. I tried to grab it, but it was too late; it crashed on to the pavement with the baby inside. The child started crying and crying. I quickly picked the baby up to calm him down. Thank God the parents were not at home!

We went into the house, had some tea and the children watched television while I got the baby ready for bed. A few minutes later the parents arrived. "Is everything all right?" they asked. "Yes," I replied. I was not going to tell them what had happened. The baby was fine; he hadn't been hurt as he was well protected inside the pram. He had also stopped crying, so I thought there was nothing to report. But as soon as the older boy saw his parents he told them everything. His mother was furious with me and demanded that I explain exactly what had happened. "It's ok, it's ok," I said. I had no English words to explain anything else. She picked up the baby from his bed immediately and rushed him to the doctor. An hour later she came back and told me that the doctor thought the child was fine but, just in case, he was going for an X-ray the next day.

From my perspective, this was making a big fuss over a small incident. When I was five years old, I remember falling from the first floor on to the patio at my grandmother's house in Oruro. I went down like a sack of potatoes from the top of the open stairs. I remember some of the episode, like my father trying to make me come round by giving me the kiss of life; the doctors around me in hospital and not being able to cry or speak. I was in and out of consciousness for a while. I didn't break anything, but it seems that the fall had damaged my optic nerve, resulting in permanent loss of vision in my left eye. So I suppose Mr and Mrs Owen were right in being alarmed, although from my point of view this was a minor accident.

One morning while the children were at school Mrs Owen asked me to iron her shirts. I did four of them and hung them in her wardrobe. Later on she came up to me with the shirts, and threw them at me angrily. "Is this the way you iron?" she shouted. I looked at her in shock because I thought I had done a good job. She screamed in a language I didn't understand, but I guessed she said that no man would marry me if I couldn't iron properly. She left the shirts on the ironing board and ordered me to do them again and this time properly.

I thought about my maid in Bolivia and the times I didn't like her ironing. I would put the clothes back in the basket for her to iron again, but I would not have shouted at her. My parents wouldn't have allowed me to, but I'm sure other Bolivians would have reacted in the same way as Mrs Owen. I felt like crying with frustration as I didn't think I could do any better than I had already done. I realised I didn't know how to iron properly. As soon as I had finished one side of the shirt the other would get creased. It took me forever to do it again and it was still not perfect. Years later, my Spanish friend Yolanda showed me a technique of how to iron shirts in two minutes. By the end of the week I was exhausted; nothing I did was good enough for Mrs Owen. She would ask me to do each task over again and constantly shouted and screamed at me. "Don't do that! Hurry up! Be careful with the baby!"

On the Friday afternoon I asked if I could go out for a couple of hours. I felt I needed to see Juan, his wife, his mum and little David. Although we didn't have much in common, we did at least share the Spanish language. I wanted to talk about anything, to energise myself. I needed to have a few hours away from the Owen family. I wanted to hear Juan's jokes to cheer me up. I bought a small present for David and went to visit them.

It was around six in the evening when I left the house. On the way out Mrs Owen said something to me, showing me her watch. I thought she was trying to tell me not to come back too late, like my mum used to do every time I went out. When I came back, as I was approaching the house, I saw Mr and Mrs Owen standing outside waiting for me, their faces distorted with rage. I looked at my watch, it was only eight thirty in the evening, which I thought was not very late, but she pointed her finger at her watch. "Oh God, what have I done now?" I thought. I didn't understand what the problem was until we got into the house and her husband showed me two theatre tickets. She must have asked me to come back early to stay with the children, so they could go out, but I had not understood. The Owens had missed their night out, as it was too late for them to go to the theatre by then; I said I was sorry.

I went up to my room feeling angry with myself for not being able to understand them. I lay down on my bed thinking about my country and how we treat the servants there. We don't always treat them well; on the contrary, we are often not very tolerant at all. I thought about some friends I had who were not very nice to their servants. "This stupid Indian doesn't know anything", they would shout, when perhaps one of the problems was the same as mine, they didn't understand the Spanish language properly and that they were also living in a house with a different culture.

Many of the indigenous people in my country speak their native languages: Aymara, Quechua, Guarani and other languages, depending on where in Bolivia they come from. Spanish would be the second language for many of them and some would not speak it at all. I also thought of the long hours the servants worked and how badly they were paid. They would usually start at seven in the morning and often wouldn't finish until ten at night. I heard many times that their bosses didn't pay them their full salaries and they were sometimes physically, emotionally, or sexually abused. Servants in Bolivia would never sit down to have their meal with the rest of the family; they ate in the kitchen.

I also thought about my own behaviour. Maybe I was unaware of treating servants badly because it is so normal to be less than courteous towards them, although my parents did not allow us to be rude. In my country we tend to take indigenous people for granted. Some of them have no choice but to work in any conditions since it is so difficult to get a job. At least I had a choice, I could always go back home; I didn't have to be a maid. I spent hours thinking about all the women who worked for us. I fell asleep trying to remember their names, the way they looked and the reasons why they left.

The next day was Saturday; at about midday Froilan came to take me out. Mr and Mrs Owen invited him in, saying that they had to talk. We all sat down in the sitting room. By the expressions on their faces, their body language and the tone of their voices I knew I was in trouble. I could see my friend trying to reason with them, but eventually Froilan got up and walked towards the door. I followed, and we left the house.

Once in his car he looked at me with disappointment and in a very judgemental way he said, "they are not happy with you, they don't want you anymore". I looked at him in silence; I was angry for letting him down as well as myself. I didn't know what to do or what to say. Where would I go? I didn't want to go back to Juan's house again. I knew I hadn't done the job properly, but it was mainly because I had never done it before. I had never cleaned in my parents' house, I had never ironed anything; I had only been to school, that's all I had done in Bolivia. My mother sent me once to learn how to sew clothes at a sewing school where my cousins were also learning, and they were very good at it. But me, I couldn't sew anything; my cousins had to do it for me! They helped me all the time, partly because they didn't want me to spoil the good quality material that my mother had bought for me. My cousins were experts at everything to do with housework. They could bake delicious cakes, they were wonderful cooks and they could also make their own dresses. They were very skilful girls. My mother was always trying to teach me to bake cakes but I couldn't learn how to cook properly; she used to say to me all frustrated, "it seems that you have two left hands!"

I remember one day my boyfriend came to visit me. Mum invited him in for a cup of tea and a piece of cake. "It's really delicious", he said, "did you make it?" Before I had the opportunity to answer my mum replied, "yes, she made it". She probably thought the more domesticated I was, the better husband I would find. The last time I had tried to bake a cake was with my cousin Eliana. We put all the ingredients into a blender to be mixed but, stupidly I put a spoon inside the machine while it was switched on to check if the paste was thick enough. The spoon touched the blade and broke the glass container. All the paste, mixed with pieces of glass, went all over the place; the walls and the floor were covered in paste. Eliana said we should hide the blender so my mother wouldn't see it until we had bought a new one. But I didn't have much money. So I suggested I should pay a visit to a friend who was a lawyer to borrow the money. The next day I went to his office and told him what had happened. He said I should not worry and he was going to lend me the fifty bolivianos to buy the new blender. A few weeks later I returned to his office to pay him back and he said, "oh darling, it doesn't matter, if you give me a little kiss you don't have to pay me." I glared at him furiously, put the money on his desk and ran out.

Another time my parents were away. I invited my two cousins and their boyfriends for lunch. My plan was to cook something nice and simple so I went to do the shopping. On my return I realised I had locked myself out of the house, so I asked the porter to send for a locksmith. At about midday my guests arrived, but I was still outside with all my shopping waiting for the man to open the door. When we finally got in, my cousins did all the cooking so we could eat on time. My hopes of learning how to cook and showing off my skills were put off for another day yet again.

When I went to live in Sweden I thought it would be a good place to learn how to cook as I had more time. Whenever I went to visit my brother, José, at his university accommodation we would play darts in the kitchen, which he used to share with other students. The rule was the one who lost would do the cooking. I always lost, but never cooked. My brother would change the rules to avoid any disaster. It was always safer for me to just do the washing up.

Froilan broke into my thoughts and said to me, "I asked Mr and Mrs Owen if you could stay one more week with them and they agreed. This will give us time to look for another job and give them time to find somebody else."

"Thanks, Froilan," I said, embarrassed but relieved.

CHAPTER THREE

"My grandmother came from Africa to bring up the liberator Bolivar, who gratefully freed my nation"

Felipe Maldonado Ochoa
La Saya de Coroico

My arrival in London came after a long and tortuous journey. I had left Bolivia in May 1980. I was sent to Sweden to stay with Uncle Hector, my father's older brother, and his wife, Aunt Betty, my mum's older sister. They used to say that the two brothers married two sisters in order to have only one mother-in-law! In spite of their joke, they always praised my grandmother, of whom they were very fond.

Uncle Hector and his family went to live in Buenos Aires, Argentina in 1971 as political refugees, running away from the brutal military dictator, Hugo Banzer Suárez. This tyrant ruled

Bolivia with an iron fist from 1971 to 1978. During the time of his regime, around five hundred people were killed, three thousand were arrested and thousands more were exiled. The worst incident was the so-called Massacre of the Valley in January 1974, when around two hundred Indian peasant farmers were killed by the army as they protested against price rises.

A few years later, in January 1977, Uncle Hector and his family had to escape again to neutral Sweden, but this time it was from the murderous Argentinian military regime of Jorge Videla. Thousands of labour leaders, students, workers, clergymen, scientists, doctors and political party leaders disappeared while Videla was in power. The then popular President of Bolivia, Juan José Torres who was in exile in Argentina was kidnapped and killed by death squads of the Videla Government. Many writer friends of Uncle Hector disappeared too, such as Haroldo Conti. Others ended up in exile, like Humberto Constantini and Ricardo Carpani. From the mid-1970s until the late 1980s, Operation Condor ruled South America. This was a criminal and clandestine organisation controlled at governmental level, in many countries, because of the fear of the spread of communism. Brutal dictatorial regimes violated human rights and terrible atrocities were committed in many South American countries.

When they were young, Uncle Hector and my father were involved in politics, which resulted in both of them spending time in prison or in exile. Uncle Hector, who was a well-educated man and a poet, kept on believing that it was somehow possible to change things through politics in Bolivia. He was one of the founders of the Bolivian Socialist Party-1 and a Member of Parliament for many years.

Uncle Hector and my father were born in Sucre, the capital, a beautiful city set in a valley surrounded by low mountains. It is very much a Spanish town, with narrow streets, churches and white houses reflecting its Andalusian culture. Later on, their family moved to Oruro, a mining city on the Altiplano that lies a short distance east of the Chilean border. It was here where Uncle Hector and my dad met their wives. Uncle Hector was working for my grandfather René at his business. One cold and windy afternoon, Hector approached Grandpa with some news. "Don René, I've got something to tell you, I got married this morning." "Congratulations, who is the lucky lady?" my grandfather asked. "Your daughter, Don René!" he replied without hesitation. "Oh dear!" my grandfather replied distressed. "It will have to be me who breaks this news to her mother."

My father also had a story about his marriage and remembered with pride the details of what happened. Mum had chosen a very nice church, but far from where they lived. When they went to ask the priest about the possibility of marrying in that church, he explained that they had to marry in the area where they lived. He said if they wanted to change churches they had to get permission from the Bishop. My father was very upset about such a stupid rule and pleaded with the priest to marry them in the church that my mother liked. But the priest insisted that without authorisation from the Bishop this would not be possible. My father then got very angry and told the priest, "Father, if you don't marry us here I will have to steal my girlfriend and live with her unmarried, and you will be committing a sin for allowing this to happen!" The poor priest was so alarmed by my father's threat that he agreed to marry them in his church immediately. They didn't have a big party; as a matter of fact, they only invited close relatives to their wedding, perhaps no more than six people. Instead, they saved all their money and went for one year on honeymoon to Argentina. But, about eight months later, my mother became pregnant with me and they decided to return to Bolivia to be near her mother for the birth of their first child. A year later, my brother José was born and still later on my younger brother Marcelo.

The Illegal Dance

My grandparents on my father's side were born in Potosí, a mining town with enormous silver deposits. By the sixteenth century this city had become one of the richest in the world, with a population in those days exceeding two hundred thousand people. During the period of Spanish colonisation, it was from Potosí that most of the silver was shipped to Spain and from there to the rest of Europe. According to official records forty five thousand tons of pure silver were mined from Cerro Rico (Rich Mountain) in Potosí from 1556 to 1783. Of this total, seven thousand tons went to the Spanish monarchy. The human cost of this was the death of about eight million indigenous and African slaves, not only from brutal labour conditions, hunger and illness, but also from mercury poisoning due to the refining process.

In his book, The Roots of a Nation, Angola Maconde writes that the Spanish conquistadors made a request to the Crown in Madrid in 1608 to allow the importation of one thousand five hundred to two thousand slaves from Africa every year to compensate for the diminishing indigenous labour force. An estimated total of thirty thousand African slaves were taken to Potosí throughout the colonial era to work as *"acémilas humanas"* (human mules). But the mines of Cerro Rico were situated in the high regions of the Andes, with heights of more than four thousand three hundred metres above sea level. The acclimatisation of these slaves from the lowlands was difficult. The researcher Hernán Criales Alcazar tells us that genetically the Africans were not prepared for such conditions so this saved them from going down the mines; instead they were sent to work in the mills where the work was less arduous. They minted the silver coins that financed economic growth throughout Europe during the seventeenth century.

Due to the high death rate a black slave in Potosi cost more than in other countries. A slave could be sold for thirty times what was paid in Africa. In Cuba, the price was from eighty to a hundred pesos, in Potosí one slave cost from four hundred and fifty to seven hundred pesos. Criales Alcázar claims that Potosí in the seventeenth and eighteenth century was the slave city of the world. Later on, in the nineteenth century, with the reduction of the amount of ore from the mines and the difficulties of living in a very cold climate, their owners transferred them to the warmer areas of the country, including the Yungas in the department of La Paz, where they worked on farms, cultivating coca and citrus fruits among other crops.

The mountain continues to be mined for silver to this day. Due to poor working conditions and mainly a lack of protective equipment against constant dust inhalation, the miners still have a short life expectancy; most of them contract silicosis. Even now, children begin working in the mines from the age of fourteen. Years ago they started as young as five or six.

My grandmother Victorina was only sixteen years old when she got married. Soon afterwards, the young couple moved to Sucre, where Uncle Hector and my father were born. A few years later, in 1932, the Chaco War started. The Chaco War was the result of a dispute over a region called the Chaco Boreal, which lies between Bolivia and Paraguay. It was one of the bloodiest conflicts ever fought in South America. Nearly one hundred thousand men died during three years of war. During this time, Bolivia's political leaders forced many indigenous people into military service, during which many died of hunger, thirst, snakebite, or disease rather than gunshot wounds. Paraguay eventually claimed victory over Bolivia, firmly establishing most of the Chaco Boreal as part of Paraguay.

At the beginning of the Chaco War, both of these South American nations already felt vulnerable as previous conflicts had severely weakened them. Bolivia had lost its coastline to Chile in the Pacific War (1879-1883). Paraguay had lost more than half of its territory during the Triple Alliance War (1865-1870) with the lost land being divided between Brazil and Argentina. As a result, Paraguay and Bolivia both felt the need to regain territory lost in these previous wars. To keep most of the Chaco Boreal would have meant for Bolivia a way out to the Atlantic Ocean through the Paraguay River via Argentina. However, Paraguay was clearly not prepared to lose any more of its territory. It is said that the Chaco War was also encouraged by two companies interested in the oil found in the region. A British company, Royal Dutch Shell supported Paraguay and the American Standard Oil Company, which was already extracting oil from Villa Montes in eastern Bolivia, was supporting Bolivia.

My grandfather was called up for military service, leaving his young wife and two small children. My grandmother worked as a court secretary after completing a short course in typewriting, to be able to support her two boys. My father always remembered his mother as an audacious, humanitarian and courageous woman, who was an experienced horse rider. In those days, ladies only rode a horse side saddle. When my father and uncle were a bit older, she would take them to visit her landowner relatives, where she passed her time helping and healing the peasants whose health problems were ignored by her well off family. She used all her knowledge of herbal medicine to help the disadvantaged indigenous people; for this reason they called her "*Mamá Médica.*" Later in life, she suffered a long and painful illness, cancer of the uterus, for which she would only take aspirin. My brave grandmother never believed in taking any medicines for the sake of taking them, and strong painkillers such as morphine were out of the question. She died aged just fifty.

After his military service, my grandfather, Ernesto, studied biochemistry and pharmacy at the University Mayor Real and Pontificia of San Francisco Xavier in Sucre. This university was founded in 1624, long before Harvard, by the mandate of the then Spanish King, Philip IV. This granted Sucre its first touch of education and gave it a cosmopolitan feel. It was one of the most prestigious universities in the country. From the moment he started studying, my grandfather stood out as an excellent student. During his professional life as a pharmacist, he became well known for his intelligence and decency. He would not accept mediocrity; he was a man of principle and would defend his point of view with conviction.

He was a city man, not liking the countryside. He didn't like music, never danced or drank alcohol. His only pleasure in life apart from working was his books. He read everything he could; he was an erudite, cultured man. My father described him as a very strict and vigorous person. He remembered being told of one occasion when Ernesto was travelling from Oruro to La Paz. While waiting on the platform for the train to arrive, a lady approached my grandfather and asked him if he would take a letter to one of her sons. Ernesto put his hand in his waistcoat pocket, handed her a few coins and replied emphatically, "my dear lady, I am not a postman. Please take these coins and send your letter through the post office!"

Before my father got married, his father sent him back from Oruro to Sucre to study dentistry. Dad always remembers his father's advice before taking the train. "Young man there are only three things you have to do. The first one is to study, the second one is to study and the third one is to study!" "That's all I did," Dad remembered with a smile on his face. "When studying, I even memorised the page numbers of the book I was using and wrote it down when answering an exam question."

When I was seventeen years old, I wrote my grandfather a letter inviting him to my graduation. I was living at that time in La Paz and he was living in Oruro. Two weeks later the post arrived with a letter addressed to me; it was his reply. I went running to show my father the letter; I was so excited to know whether my grandfather was coming to my graduation or not. When I opened the envelope I stared in disbelief. He had sent me back my own letter with corrections in red ink pointing out all my spelling and grammatical mistakes. He also enclosed some instructions about how to write private, business, diplomatic and commercial letters. I felt so embarrassed, especially as he did not mention whether or not he was coming to my graduation. He probably thought I was not yet ready to graduate from high school!

In 1985, while living in London, I went back to visit my parents in La Paz. My grandfather was also there; he had come to La Paz to receive an award for fifty years of professional service. I offered to take him to the ceremony. He was delighted and proud to be escorted by his young granddaughter. After the awarding of medals the party started with the sounds of a terrific band called "La Swing Bali." Although I knew he was not a dancer, I asked if he wanted to dance. He immediately said, "yes, why not?" but his salsa steps soon turned into marching movements; my grandfather couldn't dance at all. But we still enjoyed the party until the early hours of the morning. The next day my father knocked on my bedroom door in an agitated state to tell me there was something wrong with my grandfather. It was eleven o'clock and he was still not up. This was very strange because he was always up at six in the morning with an open book on his desk, yet that morning he was lying in his bed like a dead body. I jumped out of bed thinking he may have passed away during the night, but when we went to wake him up we realised that he was still fast asleep in his bed. The dancing at the party the previous night had taken its toll.

At the age of seventy, he gave a lecture on nuclear physics at the University in Oruro. The last time I saw him was a year later, just before I returned to London. I went to Oruro to visit him and say goodbye. He was sitting on his roof terrace studying English.

His pronunciation wasn't very good, but he had learned a wide vocabulary and amazed me with his knowledge of English grammar. He died when he was ninety three years old, surrounded by the three children from his second marriage.

My maternal grandparents were born in Tupiza, in the Department of Potosi. The locals called this town the jewel of Bolivia. Its charm lies in the surrounding countryside. The city is situated in the valley of the river Tupiza. The landscape is straight out of the Old West; it is the place where the North American outlaws, Butch Cassidy and the Sundance Kid were killed in 1908 after robbing the payroll from a tin mine in San Vicente. The Oscar winning film starring Paul Newman and Robert Redford tells the story of these two gang leaders who, despite being unable to speak Spanish, made many attempts to rob banks, until they were shot by the Bolivian authorities.

In 1918, my grandparents René and Elvira married while very young and had four children, three girls and a boy. My mother's father was a quiet man with a very dry sense of humour. He was loved and respected in the community, gaining the position of Mayor of Tupiza. A successful businessman, he used to import goods from Argentina to sell in Bolivia. His parents were wealthy landowners in Tupiza and they owned horses, which my grandfather learned to ride. One of his favourite sports was polo, in which he excelled; he was so good that he played for one of the most prestigious teams of that time, that of Carlos Victor Aramayo who was a Bolivian magnate owner of tin mines, including the one robbed by Butch and Sundance. My grandfather was also a keen and accomplished bridge player, as well as another card game called El Tresillo. Originating in Spain at the beginning of the seventeenth century, El Tresillo is called Rocambo in South America. It spread across Europe during the seventeenth and eighteenth centuries, becoming a very fashionable game. It enjoyed a position of prestige similar to that of bridge today.

My mum's mother also came from a well-to-do family. When I was little, my mother took me to visit my grandmother's house in Tupiza. It was on a big ranch divided into different sections. One of them had many fruit trees like peaches, apples and prickly pears. There was another area full of flowers and another with animals. I still remember her beautiful and expensive furniture which my mother told me years later had been imported from Argentina and Spain.

Because my grandmother was the only girl and the eldest of five children, from a very early age she had been prepared to become a dutiful housewife. Together with the two servants she was in charge of keeping the house in perfect order and looking after her younger brothers. She played the piano with a lot of skill and feeling. Her beauty and elegance were perhaps contributing factors in her marrying young and becoming a spoiled, bourgeois lady. In 1920 they moved to Oruro. This was the time when Bolivia's tin mining industry was flourishing, with ownership mainly in the hands of three powerful capitalists: Simon Patiño, Carlos Aramayo and the German, Moritz Hochschild.

The most well-known of these men was Simon Patiño. He controlled about fifty per cent of Bolivia's tin output. By the 1940s he controlled the entire international tin market and was one of the wealthiest men in the world. He was nicknamed the "King of Tin." Patiño is said to be the seventh richest person of all time. Once his wealth was secure in foreign banks, he purchased homes in London, Paris, New York and Buenos Aires, where he died. His son and heir, Antenor Patiño married Maria Cristina, the Duchess of Durcal and had two daughters. One of them was Isabella Patiño, who in 1954 married the Eton-educated young man James Goldsmith. Isabella Patiño died when giving birth to their first daughter, Isabella, who James Goldsmith won custody of. According to Goldsmith's obituary, the marriage provoked a famous conversation. "Nothing personal in this, Mr Goldsmith," said Antenor Patiño, "but in my family we do not marry Jews." Goldsmith replied, "true, Señor Patiño, but there have to be exceptions. You see, in my family, we do not marry Indians!"

In those days Oruro enjoyed an economic bonanza and my grandparents had a prosperous business. They lived in a huge, beautiful house with twelve bedrooms, two drawing rooms, two sitting rooms, four bathrooms and three kitchens. It had a garden full of cherry trees and a patio at the back of the house, but also a front garden and a garage. Their good fortune helped my grandmother's charitable work but, in contrast to my grandmother on my father's side, she didn't make direct contact with the poor. She always had a basket attached to a long cord on her balcony. Whenever someone rang the bell to ask for some second hand clothes, food, or money, she was ready to put something in the basket and lower it down to the beggar. Nobody would leave her house empty handed. She would then worry all day about the poor people she had helped. Also, as a good bourgeois lady, my grandmother enjoyed shopping trips abroad with her husband to places like Argentina, Chile and Spain. It was not very common in those days for Bolivians to travel abroad on holiday. She died at eighty three years old from a heart attack.

My grandfather used to remember with tenderness and in great detail the things my grandmother would say, and what they did together. For example, he once told me that the only time he lost horse riding competitions was when she was involved. In those days they used to play a game where the rider would carry a needle and cotton thread in their free hand and race to the other side of a field with it. The wives and girlfriends waiting for them there would receive it, ready to thread the cotton through the eye of the needle and return it to their respective rider husband or boyfriend. My grandmother never managed to insert the cotton thread quickly enough, so my grandfather would lose the competition every time she was involved. He would also remember one occasion on a cold day in Oruro when they went to the funeral of a friend. When leaving the cemetery, my grandmother sighed sadly and told my grandfather that when she died she didn't want to be buried there because it was too cold. On another occasion they were invited to a posh dinner and a delicious dessert of orange was served. But my grandmother with an innocence that distinguished her told the hostess, "your orange dessert was delicious, but if had tasted like apple I would have eaten it all." My grandfather died of a broken heart exactly one year after her death.

Uncle José was the oldest of my grandparent's children. He was a very good pianist too, and used to delight us when he was in the mood, with bolero and tango ballads. I remember him as a very elegant man, impeccably dressed always in a three-piece suit of English cashmere fabric and a bowler hat. He lived for ten years in Argentina with his Argentinian wife and their daughter before coming back to establish himself in Bolivia. He married years later for a second time to a very kind and gentle Bolivian lady who was his distant cousin.

Aunt Teresa was the youngest of the children. She married my mum's class mate, Julio, who became a successful mining engineer, holding down a prestigious job at one of the largest government mining companies, Comibol. During his time as an engineer he travelled between mines with his wife and five children in tow. They were the typical Bolivian couple. In times of bonanza they enjoyed life to the full, going to expensive social events, giving parties and buying presents. They spent money lavishly without thinking of tomorrow and they never used to hold back their generosity with friends and family.

In 1967 my family moved to La Paz. Located nearly four thousand metres above sea level, La Paz sits in a caldera surrounded by the Altiplano and is the legislative capital of Bolivia. "The city that touches the sky," is perhaps the best description. The year 1967 was also when revolutionary icon Che Guevara was murdered by the Bolivian army under the orders of General René Barrientos Ortuño, who was the President of Bolivia at the time. Barrientos Ortuño had been quoted as saying that he wanted to see Guevara's head exhibited on a spike in La Paz. Although this didn't happen, Guevara's attempted revolution was eventually put down by Bolivian troops with the help of the CIA. It was also the time when General Barrientos Ortuño sent his troops in the early hours of the morning to massacre the unsuspecting miners who were celebrating the traditional bonfires of San Juan. Women and children died that night. This dreadful punishment was meted out because the miners supported Che Guevara's guerrilla movement. Finally, Guevara was captured and killed in the schoolhouse at La Higuera, near Valle Grande in the Department of Santa Cruz.

At that time, my Uncle Hector had also moved to La Paz with his family. He was working as Member of Parliament for the opposition party against the Barrientos Ortuño dictatorship. He was accused by the government of having connections with the guerrilla movement. This accusation was false but, later, Uncle Hector had by chance met the wife of one of the guerrilla fighters. She was a young lady who had come to Bolivia from Argentina with her lawyer and two young daughters to try to see her husband Ciro Bustos, who at the time was in prison in Camiri, Santa Cruz, for being a guerrilla fighter. My uncle facilitated the visit and took the opportunity to send his book of poems to a famous French journalist, Régis Debray, who was being held in the same prison, accused of being one of Guevara's men. In 1970 Debray was released after a long international campaign. In 1981 he became one of President Mitterrand's advisers on foreign affairs. Years later Uncle Hector and Ciro Bustos met in Sweden by chance and later on with Debray in France.

The Illegal Dance

Once they had moved to La Paz, my Aunt Betty became very ill with ulcerative colitis. The doctors gave up hope because the drug sulfasalazine needed for her treatment was not available anywhere in South America. Thanks to my uncle's position, he called on the help of a friend who worked for the Bolivian Government. The drug was brought from Sweden and arrived at the hospital at the same time that the priest was giving her the last rites. Whatever it was that did the trick, religion or medicine, somehow she was saved that day. She remained weak in hospital for a time, but then lived for many years more. Coincidentally she died in Sweden, the place the famous drug came from.

My family lived in La Paz for about a year, in an area where the roads were not only unpaved, they were piles of earth. Our house was a long corridor of rooms, one after another. It had a little patio, maybe three metres square, that the sun lit partially for a couple of hours only in the early afternoon. The place was dark, cold, damp and unwelcoming. The older of my brothers and I were constantly ill, suffering from sore throats and colds. My parents enrolled us in a school near where we lived that turned out to be awful. The teachers and the other children were so aggressive that I often felt that I was walking on eggshells. Playing in the break time, I often ended up getting hurt. My brother and I couldn't make friends, so we ended up sticking together on our own. The teachers also used to hit the students if they did anything wrong; it was common practice in schools like ours. One day my father noticed that my brother José could not open his mouth wide enough to eat. José told him that his teacher had hit him so hard for some stupid mistake he had made that he was in pain every time he opened his mouth. Father was so furious he went to the school and warned the teacher that he would take drastic action if he ever touched his son again.

Early in the mornings, my father, my older brother and I would leave the house. He would drop us at school and then he would continue on his way in the hope of finding a job. Mum with my little brother would wait all day for Dad to arrive, generally with bad news. It was also hard for her to have her sister Betty in hospital while my mum looked after her teenage children. Life was often like that, as two brothers had married two sisters; they often helped each other out.

Those were difficult times for all of us. Dad wasn't working so didn't have enough money to pay the school fees; at the end of every month we were thrown out. Occasionally we would meet my cousins outside school after they also had been excluded for not paying fees. Although their father, Uncle Hector, was a Member of Parliament at the time and earning good money, for some reason he didn't pay either. Perhaps it was because the hospital fees for Aunt Betty were so high there was not enough money to go around. La Paz seemed to me to be a horrible, big city. It had too many hills and too many cars struggling up them. It also had too many people walking breathlessly up the roads, always angry and in a hurry. I missed the peaceful area where we used to live in Oruro; my grandmother's big house, and my lovely school.

My father came home one lunch time with some interesting news. While he was walking the streets looking for a job he met by chance an old friend from university. This friend was also a dentist, who worked at that time in a village situated a hundred kilometres from La Paz. After living there for about ten years he had decided to return to the capital, so he offered the job to my father. Dad was delighted, but he didn't have the cash to pay for the old fashioned dental equipment that his friend was to leave in the surgery. Fortunately his colleague was not in a hurry for the money and was happy to wait until Dad had made enough to pay for it.

At first Mum was not very impressed with the news. A village a hundred kilometres from La Paz did not sound like a good idea to her. Perhaps she wasn't happy because most villages in Bolivia were made up of a long street with a few adobe brick houses, a small church and maybe a school, often without desks and chairs for the children to sit on. This was far removed from the expectations of an urban middle class lady. The subtropical climate, particularly the insects, was another factor that put her off the idea. Mum listened quietly, which she often did when she wasn't sure what to say or do. Dad kept talking about this interesting opportunity, but my mother's silence was becoming uncomfortable. It wasn't a sign of approval or disapproval, more that she was afraid of the change. Dad sounded like he was determined to explore the opportunity further. Although he was looking for mum's approval, he had more or less made up his mind. He was going to see where this intriguing village was located as soon as possible, to find out whether he could work there and make a decent living.

CHAPTER FOUR

"The earth has music for those who listen"

George Santayana

Totally excited and overwhelmed by what he had seen, Dad returned to La Paz seven days later. He told my mother about the village over and over again, describing to her in great detail how fantastic it was and all the advantages of living in a subtropical climate. My father thought everything in the village was perfect. He had fallen completely in love with the place and could see nothing negative about it. Just two weeks later, our family was on its way to Coroico.

We started the journey by bus from La Paz, arriving fifty minutes later at a summit called La Cumbre, which is 4633 metres above sea level. The landscape of this area comprises awesome, rugged mountains that only support sparse vegetation at their peaks, which are often shrouded in cloud. From La Cumbre we descended into the clouds, travelling one thousand seven hundred metres down from the top in two hours. As we were driven through the swirling mist, the visibility reduced dramatically. Gradually, as we made our way through the blanket of cloud, we began to notice the edges of the elfin forest as the vegetation became more lush. A Chiguanco thrush wagged its tail by the roadside and a mountain caracara took off from the middle of the road. The driver slipped into low gear to control the bus as we emerged from the cloud into the Yungas, a transitional forest that lines the eastern slopes of the Andes.

My father had neglected to tell us that the road was not only extremely steep but was also narrow, barely wide enough to accommodate a vehicle. The edge of the road had a sheer drop of over one thousand metres; at least once a week a bus or lorry would go off with fatal results for all its passengers. We found out later that this route was known locally as the Death Road, nowadays notorious for being one of the most dangerous in the world. Many times during our descent, we would hear the brakes screech, desperately trying to hold the old heavy bus. It was the rainy season so the road was muddy and slippery. The driver had an assistant who was assigned the task of watching constantly for signs of approaching buses, trucks, or cars. When a vehicle was spotted, the assistant would warn the driver to start looking for the best possible passing place to park and wait for the arrival of the vehicle. The driver and his assistant knew the road so well that we sometimes waited for as long as fifteen minutes for a vehicle to reach us because they knew we would not find a wider space in time further down the mountain. In case the bus left the road during passing, all passengers had to get off.

The poor visibility due to the mist and cloud was another problem on this road. The driver would sound his horn constantly, which added more drama to the journey. *"La Cola del*

Diablo" (The Tail of the Devil) was the local name for an infamous narrow hairpin bend black spot where a man would stand all day giving signals to drivers. When he saw vehicles coming down the mountain from La Paz he would wave a red flag to any traffic coming up the road so they could stop at a safe passing point and wait for the descending vehicle. He was nicknamed "the human traffic light"; every driver who negotiated the corner successfully would give him one Bolivian peso as payment. I could see my poor mother stricken with fear, looking at the drop through the window when we reached the corner. The public bus was packed with people, mostly locals. On many occasions, the few tourists on the bus would stand up from their seats and scream with terror.

Bus companies in Bolivia typically sell more tickets to passengers than the number of seats available on the vehicle. People have to sit along the corridor on wooden stools provided by the company, or simply find a space on the floor. This makes moving along inside the bus impossible, so once you are in your seat there is no chance of stretching your legs during the journey unless the bus stops for everyone to get off. On the trip to Coroico my family was sitting near the back of the bus. My brothers and I felt sick the entire trip. There was not enough ventilation and no on-board toilet. The smell of cramped, sweaty people and their food was hard to bear.

About one kilometre before reaching our destination the bus stopped abruptly. I woke up to people screaming, "get out, get out!" We could see smoke coming from the front. An instant later, a fire had started in the engine, which meant that the fuel tank could explode at any minute. We tried to escape, but it was difficult to move with so many people and their bags everywhere. Everybody was panicking and screaming, all trying to get off the bus at the same time. I remember being stuck in my seat with my brother José next to me, and people clambering over us.

Eventually my father put an end to this hysteria by ordering all the passengers to keep calm and get off the bus in a disciplined manner. He spoke in a very loud, authoritative voice and, somehow, his intervention worked; people started to move and get to safety in a more sensible way. As we all got out, my father kept giving instructions to keep everybody calm.

When we finally managed to leave the bus, Dad told us to run as far away as possible. My mother and a fat woman, a *chola* (indigenous woman), with voluminous skirts got stuck in the doorway as they tried to leave the bus. Neither of them could move forward, also one of my mother's high stiletto heels got stuck in a hole in the floor of the bus. Eventually she threw herself off the vehicle leaving the offending shoe behind and the fat woman came off the bus soon after. Mum ran after us wearing only one shoe, my father followed on behind, holding my little brother Marcelo. Once he had made sure we were safe, he went back to the bus to see if he could help further. He found a blanket, which he used to cover the engine until the driver, his assistant and my father managed to put out the flames. Eventually our family completed our journey to Coroico on foot, carrying our luggage with us.

Having survived our dramatic journey over the Andes to my new childhood home, we soon adapted to life in the village. Coroico at that time was stunningly beautiful. The village was alive with colour throughout its long, narrow streets. Adobe brick houses with small balconies lined each side of the roads, bougainvillea flowers in different colours bloomed everywhere. Coroico resembled a tropical garden, with many kinds of vegetation: bananas, citrus fruits, coffee plants and the famous coca leaf plantations. In Bolivia, coca leaves have a variety of therapeutic uses. For example, people drink coca tea for indigestion or altitude sickness. Also, the majority of the indigenous population chew coca leaves at parties or to combat hunger and fatigue when they work. The coca leaf is also used for blessing ceremonies. Unfortunately, in modern times, some foreigners taught local people how to make the drug cocaine from this sacred leaf. Although the Bolivian Government has tried to reduce coca production in an attempt to eradicate cocaine, they are doomed to fail. Cocaine production will remain a problem as long as the huge demand for the drug in places such as North America and Europe continues.

Coroico's fauna is very rich; birds of all kinds live there. These include the red-headed turkey vulture, the black vulture, the blue-and-white swallow, the yellow-chested bananaquit, the tropical kingbird, the red-billed parrot and the saffron finch. Another striking feature of life in the village was the beauty of colourful butterflies that looked as though they were following us everywhere. Coroico was also home to many other different types of insect. One of the strangest and most beautiful of these was the *cocalero* (a bush cricket). For camouflage these creatures have evolved to look like the coca leaves in the plantations where they live.

One of the most common insects was a problem for us, the mosquitoes. In the first week after our arrival, my mother, my brother José, Marcelo and I were in the open market buying our first groceries, when suddenly José was bitten by one and his face became badly swollen. A local woman in the market came to his rescue straight away. She chewed coca and a mixture of other leaves before rubbing the paste on to his face. By the following day, José looked as though he had never been touched.

I was nine years old when I was taken to Coroico, my brother José was eight and Marcelo was three. Two days after we arrived in the village, my father took José and me to the primary school. It was a welcoming, mixed Catholic school run by Colombian nuns, who kept the building in perfect condition. The classrooms were spacious and comfortable; from the windows you could see wonderful mountain scenery, but also the Death Road that we had travelled down to reach the village. The school was surrounded by vegetation and we had plenty of space to run around. My parents were pleased that we were going to study in such a harmonious environment and that I didn't miss my other lovely school in Oruro, which was run by German Catholic nuns.

On my first day at my new school, my teacher sat me next to a black boy from Tocaña. Tocaña is a little village nearby, where the biggest Afro–Bolivian community lives. It was the first time I had come across a black person in my life. I had never seen black children in my previous schools. His name was Vincenti and he had a beautiful smile. He was wearing a red jumper and a white shirt that accentuated his looks. I sat next to him thinking he was really a very pretty boy. His lovely black eyes and beautiful white teeth lit up the class. During the breaks he would follow me everywhere timidly and gently until I gave in to his non-verbal insinuations to play. When it was time for snacks he would sit down next to me in the fields of the school and, without talking we ate, contemplating the scenery that was so familiar to him.

One day my mother realised that I was not eating my school snacks. She was not very happy about it because I was very thin and this was a constant worry for her. She was always taking me to doctors and giving me vitamins and extra food to help me to put on weight. When we lived in Oruro, at my mother's instruction, the nuns at my school would send me home in the middle of the morning to eat a small lunch, usually grilled liver, kidneys or an egg. My mother warned me that if I did not eat my food she would tell the teacher to make sure I did. As she seemed so serious and upset about the situation I decided to tell her the truth. It was Vincenti who was eating my snacks. From then on my mother had to add extra food to my packed lunch for Vincenti and myself.

I loved walking to school in the morning in the warm weather, accompanied by the sound of singing birds and the revitalising smell of the forest. The school was on the outskirts of the village. It was in Coroico that I noticed for the first time that some children went to school wearing the white school uniform without shoes. Other children wore homemade sandals cut from rubber tyres. These shoes may have been cheap and cheerful, but they didn't look comfortable at all. Many children walked long distances to get to school and some of them, like Vincenti, would not have eaten breakfast.

Many years later I went back to Coroico on holiday and I met my black friend by chance in the plaza. By then he was a grown man. "Hi Vincenti," I said as he was passing by. He looked at me and it took him a few minutes to recognise me. "Hello, hello," he said, with the same lovely smile he had when we were children. He sat down next to me and we talked for a while. I asked him what he was up to, hoping he would tell me he had finished secondary school. Unfortunately he had left education before reaching that stage and had gone to work on his father's land. He was proud to tell me, however, that he had bought a mule. When he asked me about myself, I could not bring myself to tell him I was living in Europe. For some reason I felt sad that I had enjoyed the opportunity to study and travel and that Vincenti had not.

One day at the school, a dancing competition for the children was organised and I decided to participate. They put us in couples and the first prize was a pack of notebooks and coloured pens. The only rule was that less skilful dancers were gradually eliminated. After a while, to my surprise, only myself, my partner and another couple were left. "My God, it seems we are going to win this dancing competition," I thought.

I was moving gracefully to the sound of the music, dancing the best I could with the help of my partner. My legs moved with a synchronized and gracious rhythm and my body was set free into a dream world. My partner was stomping rhythmically around me with short steps and this gave the dance strength and agility. I looked at the other couple. There, before me was a tall, thin, black girl, who was dancing without shoes. Her thin legs gave little, coordinated jumps; her long arms moved harmoniously in different positions as if she was trying to pull us all into her wild and unknown domain. Her slender, energetic body sometimes moved like a gentle butterfly, but at other times like a turkey vulture generating dust with the beat of her wings. Her partner was not as skilled as her but it didn't matter. In the end this undulating and natural movement gave them first prize in the competition. I was really impressed that she beat me even though she danced barefoot.

One of my activities after the end of a school day was running around outside trying to catch butterflies with a special net that my mother made for me. I also collected other insects and spiders, killed them and preserved them for my collection, which I still have to this day. My father had given me a kit for this, consisting of a box, formalin and a syringe. The procedure was as follows: I hunted the insects with my net, killed them by pinching the thorax and put them in the box to bring them home. Then they were injected with formalin to preserve them. Before the insect hardened, I stretched their legs or wings and pinned them out on polystyrene until they were dry. Finally, I framed and hung them on the wall.

One day I came home with a big spider, a tarantula that I had found at school. I caught it in the plastic bag where I kept my sandwiches. I had never seen such a lovely spider in all my life. When I got home with it to show my mother, she almost had a heart attack and ran out of the house screaming. My poor mother could not bear even a fly in the house, never mind a huge spider on her dinner table. My insect collections were the best; I hung them on the walls of the sitting room with great pride.

On another occasion I was playing in the outskirts of the village when I saw something fall out of a tree; it looked like a small bag. I got close to it to see what it was, when suddenly a snake began to uncoil. I was paralysed with fear. Fortunately the snake went off in the opposite direction. It was probably not venomous, but was big enough to scare anyone.

After school I also used to go to the cemetery to play with other children. Some of the older graves were partially open and we would dig the bones out to try to identify them. If they were, say, arms or legs, I would compare them with my own arms and legs. When my mother found out about my escapades she got very angry, disinfected me with alcohol and banned me from ever going to the cemetery again. Interestingly, I was never afraid of these human remains and oddly enough I lived next door to a cemetery in London. Perhaps I just liked quiet neighbours.

There was a fiesta that I loved when living in Coroico, it was called *Todos Santos* (All Saints). It was celebrated each year at the cemetery, where people who had a dead relative would prepare food that the deceased person had liked when they were alive. Everyone would go to the cemetery to celebrate, with music and dancing. I never missed that day.

We made many friends at school in a short space of time. All the children we befriended were lovely and happy to play with us. One day we were celebrating my brother José's birthday. My parents invited all his classmates to our house. At around five in the afternoon my mother was about to serve tea with José's birthday cake, but she realised there was a child missing; it was Tomas, a black boy. Mum went outside to check if he was trying to find our house. To her surprise, she found him sitting outside our front door on the pavement. The landlady had not allowed him into the house. She may have thought he had not been invited because of the colour of his skin. Whatever her logic, she had not let him in. I remember my mother being furious with her. We lived in the same house as the landlady, Doña Justa, a woman with a strange personality. She had a son who lived with her; he was in his late forties when we arrived in Coroico. Doña Justa would never allow him to go out with friends and he was certainly not allowed to have any girlfriends. Mother and son would do everything together, such as going out every afternoon for long walks in the country. They would take a rifle with them to shoot birds, which they would desiccate and hang up as trophies around their house. One day she saw a cat trying to catch the little birds in her garden. She picked up the rifle, took aim and killed the cat with one shot. They were also experts in making honey, which they would sell in a little shop at the front of the house. The store was depressing as the only things on sale were honey, candles and matches.

One day, we discovered that the son, Don Roni, had married a local girl in secret and fathered two children. No one knew if the children had come before the wedding or after but, whatever the order, Doña Justa did not allow him to live with his wife and children and they were not allowed to come near her house. Years later, the son died, leaving his ninety-year-old mother on her own. The stubborn old lady immediately sold her house to make sure her son's children would not inherit the home. Then she rented a room until she died aged one hundred years.

During the winter school holidays, Aunt Teresa, my mother's younger sister and my cousins would come all the way from Oruro to spend time with us. My brothers and I loved their visits because we used to go for long walks in the country or go swimming. Coroico has two big rivers, these are the Santa Barbara, about fifteen kilometres from the village and the Yolosa, which flows about ten kilometres away from Coroico by the side of the road to La Paz. One day my cousins Liz and Pepe, my brother José and I woke up early and walked through the fields down to the Santa Barbara. We spent the whole day swimming and playing in the river. Later in the afternoon we decided it was better to try to go home by car rather than walking as it was getting late. We managed to get a ride on a truck that was going towards Yolosa village. We worked out that if we could get to Yolosa it might be easy to get another truck to Coroico. It was around seven o'clock by the time we got to Yolosa. We waited there for about two hours, but there were no vehicles going towards Coroico. We decided to walk the ten kilometres to our village. It was dark, with no lights on the road and no moon or stars to guide us; just the lights of the fireflies and the noise of the bush crickets. We walked in the middle of the road to avoid snakes. My poor cousins who came from the city were petrified. In Coroico, my parents and Aunt Teresa were worried sick and desperate to find us. They knew the river had a strong current and that my cousins could not swim. By ten at night we were still not back. My father spoke to the colonel to borrow his car to begin a search. It was lucky that they chose the road to Yolosa first and they soon found us slowly making our way home. They were so relieved to see us alive and well that they forgot to tell us off.

Our lives in the village were full of incident. A few months after our arrival in Coroico, a fire started in a house across the road from us. At about noon one day, Francisca our neighbour was cooking lunch. Her three-year-old daughter Juanita was playing next to her and her four-month-old baby was asleep upstairs. Distracted by her toddler, Francisca picked up the wrong container and put gasoline into the frying pan rather than cooking oil. Fire spread quickly throughout the small building and Francisca ran out of the house leaving the children inside. The entire neighbourhood immediately tried to put the fire out with buckets of water. Francisca was screaming desperately, "my daughters, my daughters! Somebody help my daughters!" A man arrived with a big ladder, climbed up to the first floor balcony and managed to rescue the baby. The problem was that the girl,

The Illegal Dance

Juanita was still in the kitchen. My father was working at the time in his surgery next door. When he heard people screaming and shouting, he stopped work, came outside, got a blanket from somewhere, covered himself with it, and ran into the burning house to look for the little girl. Seconds later he came back with her in his arms. Unfortunately it was too late; the girl died a week later from a combination of her burns and the lack of specialised medical care in Coroico.

A year after the fire we moved to a large and beautiful house up the hill; it had a big patio and a fantastic wild garden in which to play. We shared the house with the owners, who had three children of our own age with whom we spent countless hours playing.

Our playmates' parents were a peculiar couple. Doña Serena was a kind and soft lady; she spent hours in the kitchen cooking before cleaning the pots, pans and cutlery meticulously until they shone. In the afternoon she would often busy herself mending clothes belonging to her husband or children. She was extremely short sighted, so whatever task she set out to achieve was a big effort for her. I never understood why she didn't own a pair of glasses. She always walked around the house staring at the ground to avoid stepping into something nasty. This made her look older than her true age. She never dressed up and never went out, not even to church. She must have been attractive when she was young because she had big, green eyes and the remains of a beautiful face. Don Nardo, her husband, was also attractive, but he was not a nice man. He often looked angry and was unpleasant in his behaviour to other people. He was a control freak who felt the need to be in charge of everything and everyone. He dressed smartly and looked much younger than his wife. He would go out shopping every day and run whatever other errands needed to be done. I think he was a clerk because he had a small office at the front of the house. In this room there was only a desk, two chairs and a small, old typewriter. I would often see him shuffling papers back and forth, pretending to be busy.

People gossiped that Don Nardo was having an affair with a neighbour who lived down the road; a small, fat, ugly, deformed woman. Although the rumours spread widely through the village, Doña Serena chose to ignore them. She would sometimes send her children to her to borrow sugar, rice or whatever was needed. The other woman would kindly supply the ingredients. Don Nardo had his own, impeccably clean bedroom while Doña Serena and the children slept in the other room, which doubled up as a dining area. It was odd for me to see this because my parents always slept together. Whenever we children wanted to sleep with Mum, my father would say, "sorry guys, but I married your mother so I could sleep with her."

My parents were happy living there, especially as most of the time my brother and I were either in the house or the wild garden so they knew where we were all the time. My mother started to learn to play the guitar with the best player in the village. She would spend whole afternoons practising while my father worked in his surgery.

A black woman called Pastusa was employed to help out with the housework. One day she became ill and was close to death. The local doctor thought it could be a tumour in her stomach but there was not much he could do about it. The village didn't have a hospital and almost no equipment to treat this kind of illness. My father volunteered to go to her house every day to give her a saline drip and some painkillers; it was about an hour's walk. Her family was so poor they could not afford to buy medicine. Another problem was that she couldn't visit the doctor's surgery because she was too weak to walk and her family didn't own any means of transport. As a last resort, her family brought an indigenous, traditional healer to the house. The healer recommended some plant-based medicines for Pastusa to take by mouth and

The Illegal Dance

some herbal heat packs for placing on her stomach. The family collected the herbs from within the area they lived. When they had treated Pastusa for a couple of days, she defaecated a ball of parasitic worms. She never had a tumour at all. My father continued to treat her for complications, which were tuberculosis and anaemia. We got to know her family well because, on many occasions, we all accompanied my father to see her. Once she had recovered completely she came back to work for us again.

Whenever black people got married in Coroico they would have beautiful parties. The bride and groom would dress in white and, after the church ceremony, they would ride a mule around the plaza while all the guests walked behind them throwing rice and confetti. It's a national custom that when Bolivians get married they have a godfather and a godmother, as well as legal witnesses. But only black people would compose songs as an act of appreciation for the godparents and dance for them all night. One of the songs that I remember goes like this:

> *It may be morning, it may be afternoon*
> *But I just happen to know and understand the goodwill of the godfather.*
> *It was Don Norton de la Torre the comforter of Coroico.*
> *Será buenos días, será buenas tardes*
> *Recién llegó de saber y comprender la nota del padrino.*
> *Había sido el Señor Norton de la Torre consolarío de Coroico.*

Although I was never invited to these weddings, I used to sneak into the parties. I would enjoy myself the whole day listening to the sounds of the drums and songs and watching the dancing. Then my father would find me and take me home, telling me that my mother had been looking for me all day. He would say that it was late in the evening and the partygoers were getting drunk. I had so many black friends at school that I began to speak and sing like them. They used a dialect to speak among themselves.

One afternoon the sweltering sun was beating down on the village. The birds had disappeared for their siesta and the inhabitants of Coroico sat uncomfortably in the shade of their front doors dozing open mouthed. I was with my school friends in the plaza when Pastusa's mother passed us by. I greeted her respectfully, "good morning, Mrs Sabana." One of my friends looked at me in disbelief and asked me why I had said "Mrs" when she was only a black woman. His reaction took me completely by surprise. I could not give him an answer as I was so angry; I just walked away in disgust. A year after this incident, the same friend went missing from school for a couple of days. Rumours spread that he had been badly beaten up by some local peasants who caught him stealing chickens from their fields. Whether or not the gossip was true, he died a few months later, perhaps as a result of his injuries. He was only nineteen years old.

When I was about thirteen I changed schools. The new secondary school was further away from the village. Although it was newly built, it was not as nice as my primary school and was not run by nuns. There was a tough man who worked as the headmaster's assistant. Every morning before going to class he would make us sing the Bolivian national anthem and then hit us with a stick if our uniform was dirty or if we didn't have a clean handkerchief. He couldn't complain about our footwear because the road to the school was unpaved, so our shoes were always covered in dust. Some students wore sandals for this reason. We were all afraid of him because he was very strict, but we did respect him.

It was very common for youngsters to study outside in the plaza or along the road early in the morning. Some of them would read outside their homes as they didn't live in comfortable houses. In many cases they lacked electricity and a large family might live in one room. Although we had enough space to study in our home, my parents allowed us to work outside with the rest of the children. They always encouraged us to mix with the kids in the village and join in with what they did.

Some mornings, instead of studying, we would play basketball. It was wonderful to get up early to exercise by playing sports before going to school. The serene, misty mornings gave us a sense of freedom and peace. It was the ideal time to reflect on and contemplate our simple life surrounded by an unspoilt and healthy landscape. It felt like we were being embraced by nature and that it was giving us its best; it was my favourite time of day. The village would be quiet before the buzz of the morning's activity and the sound of birdsong made for a gentle start to the day. We would meet in the plaza before heading for the sports field.

Every morning between five and six, the local butchers would slaughter a few cows by cutting their throats and leaving them to bleed. They made horrible painful noises before they died. I hated it, but it was difficult to avoid this unpleasant activity as the slaughterhouse was next to the sports field. However nasty the practice though, it also felt like this necessary human task was part of nature in a place like Coroico. Cockfighting was also practiced in the village, but we were forbidden to go and see such a thing by my father, who hated cruelty to animals.

Once I was settled in my secondary school, my father bought a small plot of land near the plaza and built a lovely three storey house. His surgery and the garage were situated at ground level and we all lived on the first and second floors. Dad was always busy. Apart from being a very good dentist, he was kind and friendly to everyone in the village. In those days, no one in Coroico and the local area owned a telephone to make an appointment. Patients travelled to the village, many of them by foot to see the doctor or dentist without having booked in advance. First come, first served was my dad's policy at work.

One Sunday morning, the American-born bishop of the village came to the dental surgery. As my father was very busy he politely asked the bishop to wait his turn. There were a few other patients in front of him in the queue. The bishop explained that he was in a hurry as he had a mass to attend. Dad replied, "I am very sorry Father, but these other people live far away and they came to the surgery before you, so I will see them before you." The bishop understood the rule and so didn't have any other option but to wait his turn. When my father eventually treated the bishop, he apologised for the delay and didn't charge him. An hour later the bishop sent Dad a box of wine and a card as a way of saying thank you.

Even though Dad was not a devout Catholic, he had an interesting relationship with the priests and nuns of the village. Although some of the nuns who lived in Coroico were in cloisters and so were not allowed to go out or receive visitors, they would often invite my parents for tea. The nuns would always encourage him to go to mass on Sundays, but this was my father's busiest day of the week. All the peasants living in the outskirts of Coroico would come to the village on Sundays to buy their weekly provisions and for medical attention. It was therefore impossible for him to go to mass.

There was another rule at my father's surgery. If any of his patients didn't have the cash to pay for their dental work, my father would still treat them and allow them to pay him whenever they had money to spare. Some of his patients would offer chickens, fruit, or coffee as payment, which Dad would accept. My father was always available for his patients at any time of day or night. He loved to work while listening to classical music, tangos, boleros or folk music, which he often recorded for patients if they asked him to do so. He would also assist the local doctor in the event of an accident or emergency, encouraging me to help the nurse with her duties. This experience taught me first aid skills and how to give injections.

By way of public entertainment, there were two cinemas in the village, one of which was a mobile van that screened movies to people in the open air. The van visited Coroico once a month. This venue showed films shot in black and white, but they were always of high quality. The cinema had only one projector, so there was always a short break while staff changed the movie reels. All the children would sit on the ground near the screen, clapping and cheering whenever something exciting happened in the movie. The adults would sit on the chairs they had brought for the evening. The other cinema was an indoor venue, which also had only one projector. This cinema screened films every weekend and, on occasion, during the week. Only rarely did it show good movies; on the whole, it offered audiences cheaply made Mexican films that my parents forbade us from seeing. Ever since my brother José and I were little and living in Oruro, we had loved the cinema. My parents would take us to films even though we were still drinking milk from the bottle. My brother and I would sit on our parents' laps and watch the movie until we fell asleep.

One day in the village the indoor cinema was showing The Good, the Bad and the Ugly, by the director Sergio Leone. My parents took me and my brothers to see it. At the entrance to the cinema the usherette stopped my brother José, who was eleven years old at the time to tell him, "I will only let you in this time because you are with your parents, but if you don't behave I will throw you out." My father was surprised by her threats and asked the woman what the problem was. She explained to him that my brother often came to the cinema, but when the house lights dimmed at the start of a film he would go around touching women's bums and breasts under the cover of darkness. My father tried not to laugh and promised the lady that he would not let José behave like that again.

Local people respected my dad; they would often request his advice or ask him to be a mediator in settling disputes. For example, people would consult him when they had arguments with their partners or marital problems. Once, Dad took the place of the father of a local boy and went with the young man to provide moral support when he was going to ask for his girlfriend's hand in marriage. The boy's name was Eraldo and his father had died. Eraldo told my father that the bride's family would be waiting for them the next day. Special occasions such as engagements are reasons for celebration in Bolivia and the family of the bride would often prepare a small party. The following day, my mum and dad dressed up for the visit to see the girl's family. Eraldo was punctual, and also well dressed. They walked all the way up the hill to where the girl lived. The three of them knocked, but no one came to open the front door. They kept knocking for a while, but it seemed that nobody was at home. Eventually my father asked Eraldo if he had told the family that they were coming that evening. He replied, "well, doctor, I didn't actually tell them, as I wanted this to be a surprise." "A surprise!? What do you mean by a surprise!? Does your girlfriend know you want to get married?" The guy replied with embarrassment, "no, I haven't told her either." He had assumed that if he went to the family with my parents, the girl would not feel able to refuse.

Eraldo was not an attractive man to look at, but he compensated for this by cracking jokes. People never knew whether or not to take him seriously. His mother used to work as a cook in one of the hotels, so occasionally after school he would go to help her by working as a waiter. We used to go sometimes to eat there and see him making fun of the tourists. He would give them a menu and once they chose what they wanted he would write everything down, but then he would shout at his mother, "lunch for five, Mum, please." There was no menu in that hotel; they only ever prepared one dish per day.

When people fell ill or had an accident in Coroico, it was often a problem as the village lacked a proper, well equipped hospital. The only medical facility was a small building with three rooms. At the request of local people, my parents helped to set up a committee to improve the local medical service. The other health professionals on the committee were the local doctor and a French scientist nicknamed *"Oui Oui"* by the locals, who was conducting research into tropical diseases. To raise money for a new medical facility, the committee organised parties, raffles and sold cooked food. They raised enough money to open a pharmacy, buy more beds and to add more treatment rooms to the medical centre. Doctor *"Oui Oui"* worked tirelessly on the campaign and, to show their gratitude, local people named the centre after him.

My family was really happy living in Coroico. Mum and Dad made many good friends, especially through the hours they spent in their spare time playing music. My father and his musician friends formed a group called the *Chuchuwasis* (a medicinal plant native to the Andes). They spent entire evenings singing and playing guitars and drums. My parents were often hosting parties and enjoying themselves.

There was only one problem with the area that made my mother unhappy, the Death Road. Almost everyone in the village had lost a family member to an accident on that road. There were incidents most weeks, sometimes involving a truck or bus, at other times a private car. Every so often, my father needed to travel to La Paz to buy resources for his dental practice. My mother would pray all day for my father's safe return. The Death Road haunted my mum to the point of trauma. She swore never to leave Coroico unless it was by air, in an aeroplane or helicopter.

CHAPTER FIVE

*"If you want to be a bird, fly. If you want to be a
maggot, crawl,
but don't cry when they crush you"*

Emiliano Zapata

The day after the London crisis meeting between Froilan and the Owens was a Sunday. At about nine thirty in the morning, I woke up to the noise of the family moving about downstairs. It sounded as though they were all getting ready to go out. The children didn't come to wake me as they were not allowed to play in my bedroom on Sundays so that I could sleep in a bit longer. I sat on my bed and looked out of the window. The weather looked foggy and gloomy and it seemed like rain was going to set in for the day. A sad and depressing feeling washed over me. The house was no longer a family home to me. I felt out of place and had no enthusiasm. Froilan was meant to phone me to go out, but I really didn't feel like seeing anybody or going anywhere. That huge, cold and unfamiliar house became my only refuge that Sunday and, especially knowing that I only had just a week to stay.

After a few hours the telephone rang; it was Froilan. He wanted to know what time we were going to meet up. I told him that I felt ill and wanted to stay in. He didn't sound happy about it, but said he would call me during the week. I put the phone down before lying back on my comfortable bed, but I couldn't go back to sleep. My mind was filled with reflections. "Maybe I should have stayed in Sweden," I thought, although I didn't like living there much. The weather was too cold, the language difficult to learn, but at least I had part of my family there.

I thought of those snowy days. We needed special clothes and shoes. We walked like robots in search of warmth. I remember once being outside when the weather turned particularly bad. I was caught in a snowstorm, buffeted by strong winds that moved even the trees sideways and I felt as though the wind was going to flatten me against a wall at any moment and cover me with snow. It was difficult to walk forward because of the blizzard. I was desperate to find a bus to take me home. The temperature must have been minus twenty degrees centigrade; every second that passed felt like an hour to me. My movements were getting harder; I thought I was going to freeze, standing out in the bitter cold waiting for the bus to arrive. But the fine white snow provided a wonderful landscape that soothed the merciless winter. It was only three in the afternoon, but being so far north, the starless night began, and with it my grief. Although Swedish buses are usually punctual, it seemed that this one was never going to arrive. There were other people waiting as well, but they didn't seem as concerned or as cold as me. I was well covered, but the wind and the falling snow hit me hard in the face. I tried to protect myself with my hands, but they and my feet seemed to have ceased to exist. I started to jump up and down, moving around to warm myself up to no great effect. Thankfully, the bus finally arrived and everyone waiting there let me on first. They must have thought I was a creature from the tropics; it was almost too much to bear.

Later that evening I spoke to my cousin René on the telephone. He said that the snow had almost entirely covered the house and his family were isolated. He could not open his front door. René's family were the only ones who lived in a house; as we lived in blocks of flats, snowdrifts were not a problem. The next day I woke up with a swollen face; my lips were twisted and one of my eyes was slightly closed. I went to the hospital; the specialist told me that I had suffered partial facial paralysis. He sent me to the physiotherapy department for treatment. After a few weeks I felt better, but from that day on I knew I could not live in Sweden for much longer.

As I lay on my bed that Sunday morning in London, I also thought about my cousin Eliana, who was my best friend. Married to a Bolivian guy, they had a beautiful daughter called Kantuta, of whom I was very fond. Eliana was a smart young lady and a woman of passion. She put all her energy into everything she did, following her heart more than her head. She was a dreamer; she loved reading, writing poems and discussing politics.

I liked going to her house, to see her and Kantuta. Eliana would read me quotes from books or poems that interested her and explain how this was relevant to Bolivian society and politics with great passion and detail. In her free time we would either window shop in town or go to a party. Eliana had lived with us in Coroico for a year to finish her A level equivalent examinations, as her parents were living in Argentina. During this time, she met her first husband to be. They later returned to Argentina and got married before the whole family moved to Sweden.

The Illegal Dance

My other cousin, Marcela, was a singer of Bolivian folk music, tangos and boleros. She spent most of her time touring Sweden, but sometimes she would perform gigs in countries like Germany, Denmark and Finland. She was often invited to sing at festivals, concerts and parties; we were sometimes able to tag along. She met a Bolivian musician with whom she had a beautiful daughter called Amankay. The whole family doted on Amankay; she was the youngest and naughtiest of the three children.

René was my oldest cousin. His first wife was an Argentinian lady with whom he had a son, called Waskar. They lived in Lund, which is a beautiful university town near Malmö. My youngest cousin, Rebeca, was still attending primary school at that time.

It was fun living in Sweden after all, especially as Lund was a very cultural place. My brother took me to concerts; rock, reggae, or blues, or to film festivals. The town was full of young people, so there were always parties going on and things to do.

One day my brother took me to a dinner party held at the university hall of residence where he lived. Swedish people are shy, so to meet new people they make up different games. On this occasion, they arranged a long table so that no one could sit near their friends. We were given numbers that matched a seating plan for the table. I ended up sitting far away from my brother. As I could neither speak Swedish nor English, the people sitting next to me felt cheated by not being able to communicate with me. My brother came over occasionally at the start of the evening to translate my Spanish, but he soon forgot about me once he had drunk a couple of glasses of wine.

I felt relieved when the dancing started, as it was easier to dance than talk. As a good, traditional Bolivian girl, I sat waiting for a boy to ask me to dance. Everyone got up to dance, either on their own or with whoever was nearby. It didn't matter if the music was a ballad, rock, reggae, pop or whatever; the movements were the same, arrhythmic and hopping everywhere. I waited and waited for a long time, but nobody invited me to dance. At last a tall guy came up to me, so I got up and started to dance with him. After a few minutes, however, he moved on to another girl for a while before moving on again. I felt embarrassed to be left on my own in the middle of the dance floor. I realised that I didn't fit in with this group of Nordic youngsters. Bolivian etiquette dictates that if a boy asks a girl to dance, he has to stay with her at least until the music finishes. I thought of Rafael, my boyfriend in Bolivia, he was so traditional he would not even allow me to dance with other boys. On another occasion, a Swedish guy invited me out for dinner. He picked me up from home in an expensive car and took me to a nice restaurant in Malmö. Although he behaved impeccably, he asked me to pay half the bill.

People in Sweden seemed more liberal than Bolivians. I was not used to so much informality. Relationships seemed to start easily, without the conventionalism I was used to. I felt out of place when I first arrived in the country, but I knew that I had to learn these customs if I wanted to enjoy myself; it was just a matter of time.

Sweden was a safe refuge. The country gave my cousins and their partners the opportunity to go to university. It also gave their parents the chance to live without the fear of having to escape from crazy dictators who would order anybody who didn't agree with them to be killed. My relatives were happy to live in a democratic, well organised country, but they always yearned to return home one day.

My reverie ended when I heard creaking noises in the Owens' house, as if somebody was slowly walking downstairs. I felt lonely and afraid in the empty London house, which seemed bigger without anyone at home. I stayed still in my room, blinking hard to stay alert. Nothing moved; I expected to hear more noise, more creaking noises, but the house fell silent again. I took a deep breath and I began to relax again. As I could not go back to sleep, my thoughts took me back to Bolivia.

In 1977, the year I met Rafael, a group of women and their children from the mines started a hunger strike against the military dictator Hugo Banzer Suárez. Later on, thousands of miners and a Spanish priest called Luis Espinal joined the strike. This forced the dictatorship to call an election. But the divisions and disagreements of all the political parties made it impossible for anyone to lead the country. During this period three elections were held, but no single party achieved a majority. Not even alliances of different political parties could break the deadlock. A succession of military coup d'états was Bolivia's political reality in those days. One of the shortest periods of power on record was that of Colonel Alberto Natush Busch. He stepped down after only two weeks in 1979 due to intense civilian opposition and limited military support. More than two hundred people died during his brief presidency. However Pedro Blanco Soto was President for only five days, being murdered by his opponents at aged thirty three in 1829.

An interim President called Lidia Gueiler Tejada was then appointed, promoted from her position of President of the Chamber of Deputies. She became the first woman President of Bolivia, governing from 1979 to 1980. When elections were finally called, Hernán Siles Zuazo, leader of the Democratic and Popular Unity (UDP) gained thirty eight per cent of the vote. Although it was not a majority, he was set to become the new democratic President in August 1980.

Although Uncle Hector was not then living in Bolivia, he was so well known and popular that he won a seat on the Chamber of Senators to represent his town, Oruro. The Socialist Party of which he was a member put his name forward in his absence. The whole family was delighted and everyone thought it was the right moment to go back home. Changes were happening fast in Bolivia and Hector and his wife Betty thought they had to be part of it, Betty being the most enthusiastic about the move. Even though she had begun to have a comfortable life in Sweden, she longed for a radical shift in Bolivian politics. She encouraged and celebrated her husband's hunger to contribute to that change. This was the time when I arrived in Sweden, when Uncle Hector was about to depart for Bolivia. A big farewell party was organised in a hall by all his friends in Malmö. Some of them were political refugees from other South American countries, such as Argentina, Uruguay and Chile. The whole family was invited to celebrate his happy return to Bolivia after so many years in exile. We came back home late, exhausted, but excited. His flight was scheduled for ten in the morning the next day.

We went to bed laughing and yawning, full of hopes and dreams, but at two in the morning the telephone rang. My uncle, who slept near the phone, took the call. He was soon wide awake, as it was Jorge Mansilla, a famous journalist known by his nickname Coco Manto; he was phoning from Mexico and was very agitated; "Hector, don't go to Bolivia!" he said. "There's been yet another coup, and Marcelo Quiroga Santa Cruz, the leader of the Socialist Party and candidate for the presidency has been killed, together with some union leaders." "Marcelo is dead!" my uncle exclaimed. We all felt like the whole house had collapsed, no more words came from Hector's mouth; he was probably in shock. My uncle was well known for his ability to talk for hours and speak on any subject without difficulty. But this time we could only hear him stuttering, trying in vain to say something. His son René took over the call and gleaned a little more information from the journalist.

This coup took place in July 1980, when the ruthless military dictator Luis Garcia Meza took over the country with the help of foreign collaborators and supported economically by Bolivian cocaine traffickers. This was the reason why the takeover was called

The Illegal Dance

the "Cocaine Coup." Luis Garcia Meza and his Minister of the Interior, Colonel Luis Arce Gómez, immediately sent paramilitary forces to the headquarters of the workers' union to shoot dead Marcelo Quiroga Santa Cruz and other union leaders in front of everybody. The victims had been holding a meeting to discuss how to resist the outrageous coup d'état. Later on it emerged that Quiroga Santa Cruz was taken injured, from the workers' headquarters to a military centre to be tortured to death.

For the rest of that night, we could not go back to sleep; the telephone would not stop ringing. Friends from all over Sweden called us trying to get more information or to give my uncle more up to date news. We also called my parents, who were very relieved to learn that Hector had not yet left Sweden. They strongly advised him not to come back. "People are phoning me trying to find out where you are," my father said to his brother. "But we don't know who they are as they won't leave their names. Don't you dare come back Hector; the situation is critical right now. We can hear gunfire out there, the noise of ambulance sirens and the sound of troops passing by in the street. We don't know how many more people have been killed or put in prison." My parents lived in the city centre and it was obvious that all this military activity was more evident there. Dad probably thought about what had happened in previous years in Bolivia, when other coups had taken place. Also in other countries like Chile and Argentina, where entire families were persecuted, tortured and killed. This coincided with the time Hector and his family were in political exile in Argentina; that is why they had to go to Sweden in exile. He was also worried because of what had happened in Bolivia even when we had democratic governments such as the one in 1952. Dad and Uncle Hector were actively involved with the Opposition at that time, so they were persecuted and tortured by members of the Nationalist Revolutionary Movement (MNR), a party that has held power in Bolivia many times over the years.

At that time my family lived in Oruro at my grandmother's house. The so called "Political Control" team within the MNR party would turn up unexpectedly at the house to look for my dad and Uncle Hector. Many times they escaped through the back door, often to hide from their pursuers with friends. Uncle Hector dyed his hair blonde so he would not be recognised so easily. If they were caught by the MNR, they would sometimes be taken and kept at police stations for days on end. Concentration camps were built by the MNR to keep their political opponents locked up and away from their supporters. There were two in Oruro, at Curahuara de Carangas and Unicia, plus Catavi in Potosi. Another was based on the Island of Koati (Isla de la Luna) at Lake Titicaca. They also built concentration camps in La Paz at Corocoro and in the Panóptico prison centre, where Hector was imprisoned a couple of times. As I was very young at the time, I don't remember much of those days from my direct experience, but Dad and Uncle Hector often talked about that period and the constant fear they felt when having to face the brutality of the MNR movement. Historians have compared this period in Bolivia with the Nazi period.

Then Dad spoke to me on the phone. "They have closed the University; there is nothing to do here at the moment, so stay over there for now and try to study something." My father's voice sounded worried and upset.

After speaking to Dad, Uncle Hector came to terms with the fact that he could not travel to Bolivia. He walked to the kitchen looking old, tired and helpless. He had always had a slight limp due to contracting poliomyelitis when he was a young boy, but that night it looked even more pronounced. He had to make a real effort to carry himself to the nearest chair. He sat down in the corner of the kitchen, as far away as possible from everybody; it seemed as though he wanted to be left alone for a while. He lit a cigarette with one hand and with the other began to play with a pen on the kitchen table that was lying on top of a newspaper crossword. He and Betty used to do the puzzle every morning while they were having their breakfast. They would compete with each other, but Hector would always praise my aunt's skill in solving the clues.

His face told a story of total desolation, frustration, anger and sadness. He may have been thinking about what his father told him when he was young. "Son, the only thing I want you to promise me is never to get involved in politics." Hector replied, "the only thing I can promise you is I will never to go to prison again as an innocent man." Hector was only nineteen years old when he was caught by members of the MNR taking blank paper to a printer which was going to be used to produce political leaflets. Although nothing was written on the paper, the authorities assumed, correctly, it was going to be used for propaganda, so they sent him to prison for nine months. He was sent to the concentration camp on the island of Koati, Lake Titicaca. At that time, he was the youngest of all the political prisoners.

Gradually, we began to sit down around him one by one without speaking, as we did not know what to say to comfort him. My aunt made coffee for everybody. With tears in his eyes Hector began to shout angrily, *"¡Qué cabrones; qué hijos de puta!"* (*"Bastards, sons of bitches"*). Without exchanging words, we knew he was referring to the murder of his friend Marcelo that had taken place during the coup, but none of us could say anything. He took off his glasses, cleaned them with a cloth and put them back on again. The smoke from his cigarette and the steam rising from the hot coffee made such a thick cloud that I could hardly see his face. A sip of coffee helped him regain his composure and he began to tell us about his comrade. "Bolivia doesn't give birth to men as talented as him every day, you know," he said, his voice cracking with emotion.

He started by telling us that he had first met Marcelo in 1966, when Hector was a Member of Parliament in the René Barrientos

Government. My uncle talked until the early hours of the morning about his friend's life in politics and achievements. Marcelo Quiroga Santa Cruz was a writer, dramatist, journalist, social commentator, university professor and socialist political leader. He was jailed by General René Barrientos for his denunciation of the "San Juan Massacre" in 1967, when dozens of miners were murdered by the army in the Bolivian highlands. In 1969, the new President Alfredo Ovando, a defector who pretended to be a populist, appointed him as Minister of Mining and Energy. Marcelo then asked Hector and other political allies to join his team to carry out the nationalisation of Bolivian concerns owned by the U.S. based Gulf Oil Company. This turned Marcelo into a national celebrity, but he was soon forced out of office by conservative forces who did not consider him a friend of the military.

In 1971 Marcelo, my uncle and their allies formed the "Socialist Party-1" in Bolivia. While they were in exile during the long years of the Hugo Bánzer Suarez dictatorship my uncle and Marcelo met up in Argentina. For their own safety, they soon parted again, Hector emigrating to Sweden and Marcelo to Mexico. Thinking the political climate was sufficiently safe, Marcelo returned to Bolivia in 1978 in order to participate in the presidential elections. He soon became the most visible and popular opposition spokesman. From his seat in Congress, he led efforts to bring former dictator, Hugo Bánzer to trial on charges of gross human rights violations and economic mismanagement. "This was probably the reason why they killed him," said Hector, sadly.

Uncle Hector went on to summarise what had happened throughout Bolivia's history up to that time. He said that two things had characterised the country's political system ever since independence in 1825 when Simón Bolívar became Head of State. Firstly, the governments were typified by an elite class of white men or mixed race mestizos who ran the country with their

The Illegal Dance

own version of democracy. They did not take into consideration the different cultures in Bolivia and they had a complete lack of vision with respect to the country's natural resources. Secondly, there was Bolivia's tendency to have a series of dictatorships following military coup d'états. Since 1841 it has endured about two hundred of them. I wondered that night if this was enough for Bolivia to have an entry in the Guinness Book of Records as the country with the most dictatorships. We listened to Hector's views on the political situation of Bolivia until sunrise. It may be that spilling out his opinions to us that night helped him to cope with the idea that he was not going back to his country for a long time and the realisation that he was never going to see his friend Marcelo again.

From about ten in the morning, the phone started to ring incessantly and people came over to visit him. All his friends at the farewell party from the previous night had already heard news of the coup on the radio. They came round to share their grief for the country and their respects for Hector's dead comrade. Hector's friends also wanted to make sense of what was going on in Bolivia and felt my uncle might have some insight. Throughout the day my aunt, my cousins and I prepared coffee and snacks for all the visitors. It felt as if we were hosting a wake after a funeral, but without the dead body. I still wonder how terrible the assassination must have been for Marcelo's wife and young family. Over thirty years later, none of the bodies of the people executed in the union building have ever been found.

The next day I made a call to Bolivia to my boyfriend, Rafael, who had been a member of the Socialist Party-1. I wanted to know how he was coping with the situation. One of his sisters answered the phone; she said he was fine, but not at home. I didn't want to ask any further questions in case the telephone line was tapped. I thanked her calmly and put down the receiver, relieved to learn that Rafael was alive and well at least.

A few weeks after the coup, a new wave of political refugees began to arrive in Sweden, all with terrible stories of the horrors taking place in Bolivia. Amongst them was the leader of the women who started the hunger strikes. The country was now in a state of curfew, with many people being imprisoned, tortured and killed by the government.

My uncle felt restless and wanted to do something positive about the crisis. He held various meetings with friends exiled from Argentina, Uruguay and Bolivia. They called themselves the "South Cone Group." The members of the group decided to travel around the continent to denounce the Bolivian coup d'état to important and influential political leaders in European countries. They wanted assurance from European governments that they would apply political and economic pressure on the undemocratic and brutal regime in Bolivia. The group contacted Pierre Schori, the Swedish Minister of External Affairs in Stockholm, who agreed to meet them to discuss possible sanctions. At that time, Olof Palme was the leader of the Social Democratic Party and the Prime Minister of Sweden. The South Cone Group invited me to travel with them since I was on holiday. It was a good opportunity to see Stockholm, one of the most beautiful of European capitals.

We travelled by car, six people in one vehicle, so the journey was uncomfortable. During the long trip the group members discussed South American politics from every angle. It was then that I discovered I was travelling with the top leaders of the *Tupamaros* (also known as the National Revolutionary Movement (MNL), an urban guerrilla left-wing organisation in Uruguay) and with the leaders of the *Montoneros* (or Peronist Movement), another urban left-wing guerrilla group active in Argentina. Both groups were formed during the 1960s and 1970s. I learned during the journey that Bolivia was not a special case when it came to political unrest; most political history in South America

The Illegal Dance

is full of bloody coups and corrupt military dictators who were desperately afraid of any opposition forces that would threaten their power. Dictators were particularly severe on groups and individuals who held socialist views. Until that moment, I had not known much about the disastrous political situations in many South American countries, not only Bolivia. The South Cone Group held a few meetings in Stockholm with high level politicians before we returned to Malmö a few days later.

Soon after the Stockholm excursion, Hector, Betty and the rest of the group headed for Holland, where they met representatives of workers' unions. In France they met Francois Mitterrand, who was leader of the Socialist Party at that time; in Spain, they saw Felipe González, who was then the leader of the Socialist Workers Party. Eventually the international outcry against the coup, instigated in part by the South Cone Group, the political refugees who left Bolivia and even the U.S.A. that did not approve of drug trafficking, forced García Meza's resignation from the Bolivian presidency in August 1981. Unfortunately, García Meza was superseded in office by the equally repressive leader, General Celso Torrelio.

García Meza left the country in August 1981 for exile in Brazil; in 1995 he was extradited back to Bolivia to face trial. He was convicted of serious human rights violations and was sent to prison for 30 years. His main collaborator in the dictatorship, Colonel Arce Gómez, was extradited to the U.S.A., where he was jailed for drug trafficking. In 2010 Gomez was sent back to Bolivia to face trial on charges of human rights violations. Both leaders of this infamous, repressive regime are now held in a maximum security prison.

The military rulers thought that replacing a brutal dictator with a less vicious one would calm the political situation down, but their scheme did not work out as planned. The other major problem was the shattered state of the Bolivian economy.

Torrelio's regime lasted only until July 1982, a total of ten months. Guido Vildoso, another military officer, replaced Torrelio in office, but the new interim leader had no option but to accept the results of the 1980 presidential election when Hernán Siles Zuazo won. Vildoso agreed to restore him as the constitutional President of Bolivia and, if only to avoid the possibility of civil war breaking out, Siles Zuazo took charge of a fragile democracy in October 1982. A few weeks later my Uncle Hector finally returned to Bolivia to take up his new job as the first Socialist Party-1 Senator. This was the beginning of a democratic period for Bolivia, which was soon replicated in other South American states: Argentina (1983), Uruguay (1985), Brazil (1985), Paraguay (1989) and Chile (1990).

CHAPTER SIX

"If you focus on results you will never change, but if you focus on change you will get results"

Jack Dixon

It was while I was living in Sweden that my father wrote me sending Froilan's address in London suggesting I go to England to study English. It sounded like a good idea at the time, but now I was here in London in a house where I was not wanted, in the middle of an accusing silence, feeling sorry for myself, feeling abandoned to my fate. I was asking myself what to do. That Sunday reflecting on my life in Sweden, in Bolivia and now on my future in England, negative thoughts seized me. I felt anguish that resulted in an uneven pounding of my heart; I felt anxiety and despair and I noticed that my hands were sweating and my forehead perspired. I felt fear, that fear you feel when you think you are losing control of your actions. I thought long and hard on what to do with myself and how to cope with my situation; I had to identify my options. To run defeated all the way back to Bolivia seemed a good choice. But another might be to begin again from zero and fight in an arduous and unknown land, but for this to happen I had to first face my doubts and insecurities. After a long self-criticism I started to calm down, I breathed in and expelled air almost with pleasure. Gradually my heart stopped beating quickly and with an almost involuntary reaction I decided what to do. I jumped out of bed and taking advantage of the family not being at home, I began the process of vindication. I wanted to prove to myself I could do it.

I started in my bedroom at noon and by mid-afternoon I had exhausted myself cleaning the whole house from top to bottom. I thought of Hector's words to me before I left Sweden, "I hope you know what "au pair" means. Well, you are going to be working as a servant, so you may as well prepare yourself for it." He also told me that I spent too long in front of the mirror doing my makeup or arranging my long hair. "You mustn't look too pretty," he said, "or you might find it difficult to find a job as an au pair." He also noticed I was always wearing high heels. "You won't go very far on those shoes," he said. I thought he was probably right, so I decided to change. There would be no more long hair, no more makeup and no more high heels while I was working.

The following day before I started work I went to a small Italian hairdressing salon near the house. I told the hairdresser to cut my hair as short as he could. "Short?" he asked. "Yes, very short," I replied. Twenty minutes later I had almost none left; my long wavy hair was gone. "Bella, bella," the Italian guy said; he probably thought he had misunderstood what I wanted and made a mistake. I looked like I was coming out of a concentration camp, but he tried to convince me that my new haircut suited me. "You look bella, bella," he repeated.

The Illegal Dance

I went back to the house, expecting a comment from Mrs Owen, but she ignored the change and set me to work straight away. The rest of the day and the following days passed uneventfully. I worked hard that week, always trying to be as attentive to the family as possible. From time to time I would see girls coming to the house for an interview, but none of them needed a translator like I did when I first met the family, so I assumed they all spoke good English. They all seemed like very nice girls and I wondered which one would take my place. By the end of the week I had packed my belongings in preparation to go.

On Saturday morning Froilan came to pick me up. I was in my room when Mrs Owen called me to let me know that he was waiting for me at the front door. I picked up my luggage and went slowly downstairs as if in my subconscious I did not want to leave the house. I saw that Mrs Owen and Froilan were having a cordial conversation. She seemed to be in a good mood. Froilan looked at me with a big smile and said, "Mrs Owen wants you to stay. She thinks you have improved and wants to give you another chance." I looked at her for confirmation and she nodded her head. I said, "thank you, Mrs Owen." I felt like a little girl after she has done her homework, waiting for her teacher's permission to let her play. I admit I was relieved not to have to start looking for another job.

The following week I received a cheque from my father. This was money for school fees, so I went to enrol for my English classes straight away. The lessons were for three hours from nine in the morning onwards, but Mrs Owen wanted me to be at the house at around noon, so I had to leave class half an hour early to be able to start work on time. Although I had to miss the end of my lessons, I didn't mind as the important thing for me at that time was to have a job and a place to live.

A few weeks later Mrs Owen sacked her cleaner, the Filipina who used to come three days a week. I had to take on the extra work myself as well as look after the three children. It was a struggle to finish everything on time, so I would leave the ironing until everyone was asleep because I was so slow at it.

Some of my tasks were easy. I remember one day it was the birthday of one of the boys. I found it interesting to see how the family celebrated the event. Mrs Owen sent invitations to all the children in her son's class, specifying the time of the party as between three to five in the afternoon. All the parents arrived with their children punctually and collected them at the exact time indicated on the invitation. This would never happen in Bolivia. If you invite people to come at three o'clock they generally arrive at least an hour late. I don't know the reason for this, it's just Bolivian culture; we love to make people wait. It may be a way of showing how important and busy people are. During the party the children had jelly, cakes and juice all served on plastic plates and cups, so it was easy to clear up. I put them all in the rubbish bin. I didn't have to do any washing up. By six pm I had cleaned everything and by seven in the evening the children were in bed. The precision with which Mrs Owen arranged her household was amazing.

In Bolivia we tend to complicate things more than we should. Even children's parties become a big issue. We put in enormous effort. We prepare everything weeks in advance; bake cakes and biscuits, and make small baskets for the children to carry things home. Children's parties can go on until nine in the evening, as parents join in. It's not unusual for dinner to be served.

After a few months, I realised I was spending most of my time cleaning, cooking, ironing and looking after the children; I was not doing much studying. On one occasion I wanted to chat with Mrs Owen in English, so I went downstairs after all the housework was done to ask her something to do with my homework. This was my way of trying to get to know her better as well as improve my language skills. She rejected me completely saying, "look it up in the dictionary." A few weeks later I had to sit an English exam. The teacher told me I had to stay until noon to complete the test. I asked him to write a note to Mrs Owen asking for her permission for me to stay longer in class for that day only. When she read the note she said, "I'm sorry, but that was not our arrangement." I was angry with her for being so rigid and intolerant.

One Saturday when Froilan came to pick me up Mrs Owen told him I could have the next week off in exchange for working full time the week after that. She wanted me to help with the children and the cleaning at the family's cottage in the countryside. Her mum was to come for a visit from France, so the whole family wanted to take a week's break. I was happy to do it although it meant I would miss a week from school. The following Monday, as I was leaving her home to attend my class, Mrs Owen asked if I wanted to babysit three evenings that week for extra cash. I said, ok, it was no problem. I was going be back at seven in the evening.

I returned to the house at the allotted time that evening and the couple went out. At around eleven thirty at night when they returned home, I decided to go to bed. As I went up to my room, Mrs Owen followed me to ask what I was doing. "You have to go now," she said. I didn't understand what she meant. "To go now? It's almost midnight!" I said, showing her my watch. "I'm sorry, but babysitting is only for a few hours," she replied. She had not made it clear to Froilan and me that I could not stay at the house during my week off. "No problem, Mrs Owen. No money for me," I said, thinking that she didn't want to pay for extra time.

Her husband came upstairs, trying to be helpful, as he seemed to have understood perfectly the misunderstanding. He asked her to let me stay. "Absolutely not! I've already changed the sheets for my mother; she is staying in her room." She was adamant. "It's not a problem, I change sheets tomorrow." I tried to explain that I could put my old sheets back on the bed. Her husband suggested gently that I could sleep in the sitting room, but she was having none of it. "No way, the rules are that babysitters do not stay overnight." I had to get dressed to leave. There was nothing her husband or I could say to convince her that it was too late for me to find somewhere to sleep at that time. As I was leaving, I was amazed to hear her say, "I'll see you on Wednesday evening," before she closed the front door.

I left the house feeling numb. I could not find a reasonable explanation for her behaviour. My father told me that English people were kind, disciplined, punctual and honest. I thought she may have acted the way she did because she was not English, but this was not a legitimate excuse. The fact that her husband tried to persuade her to let me stay may have annoyed her even more. He did not seem to have a say in the matter.

Westbourne Grove at night was a busy place. Many shops and bars were open. I was not sure whether this was a good or a bad thing, but it all felt pretty threatening to me. At about one in the morning, I took the number 28 bus to Kilburn where Froilan lived. When I got there I rang the bell but nobody answered the door. I knew he was working his night shift but I was hoping someone else would open the door; unfortunately, no one was awake.

It was the middle of September, so the night was beginning to get cold. I sat down on the front stairs for a while but no one came except for a few people passing by returning from a night out. I walked the street a few times to keep myself busy and warm. There were lots of drunks trying to get home in one piece. They would walk a bit and then stop, trying to keep themselves upright. From time to time they held themselves against a wall for support before moving forward again. I was not afraid of these drunks as they were in no fit state to attack me. If they did come near me, I could push them away from me easily. My peace of mind was not helped, however, by the occasional sound of the siren of a police car. At about two in the morning it began to rain and I started to worry about being out on the street all night. I decided to try to get into one of the cars that were parked on both sides of the street. I tried one by one to open every car in the street. Finally I was lucky and found one with a door unlocked. I got inside just as the rain got heavier. I shivered with cold and fear. I sat in the car hoping the owner would not appear until dawn, but I had to be prepared for someone turning up at any moment. I could not fall asleep as I could not risk being woken up by someone attacking me or by the police arresting me for trying to steal a car. It rained intermittently all night, so people ignored me in the car in their rush to get home as quickly as possible. In the middle of the night I felt desperate to go to the toilet, a feeling that worsened the colder it got. My frayed nerves didn't help either. The closer it got to daybreak the quieter the street became, so my confidence grew that no one would come to the car. I had already begun to relax when around six in the morning I saw Froilan returning home.

I jumped out of the car. He held his head in disbelief and anger when he saw me and I told him what had happened. We went to the top floor of the house where Froilan had his bedroom. It was the first time I had been to his place. The room was large, containing a single bed, two bedside tables, a big table, one small wardrobe and two armchairs. The kitchen was next door and the bathroom, which he had to share with the other tenants, was one floor down. I was surprised that he lived in such basic conditions, but at that moment I didn't care; I was in good hands and that was all that mattered.

"Do you want a cup of tea?" he asked me, seeing that I was still shivering with cold. "Yes, please," I replied, before going downstairs to the toilet. We drank our tea saying nothing to each other. I don't know whether he was too tired to talk, or too cross with me for invading his privacy. Froilan put the armchairs together to build a makeshift bed for me. This was one occasion when I was glad to be small, as I fitted the space like a glove. He lay down on his bed fully dressed and went to sleep straight away.

We woke up at around noon. Froilan took a quick shower before asking me if I wanted one myself. I declined as, before I had gone to sleep, I had noticed that the bathroom was dirty and I didn't want to go near it. I just wanted to go back to the Owens' house. During breakfast Froilan was quiet and thoughtful. After a long silence he said, "you are not going back to see the Owen family ever again. I will collect your stuff today and find you another job." He sounded irritated and angry, so I didn't want to argue with him. Frolian's decision seemed right. I stayed silent and just did as he said.

CHAPTER SEVEN

"Kisses that come laughing, then crying, go away, and in them goes away the life that never again will be"

Miguel de Unamuno

My mother's vow not to leave Coroico unless it was by plane or helicopter, was of course a pipe dream. There was neither an airport nor a suitable field in which to land within easy reach of the village. My father therefore travelled to the capital to buy a vehicle appropriate for the Death Road. He bought a Volkswagen minibus to take us to the city from time to time.

The Death Road did not lose any of its ability to instil fear into my family. On one occasion Dad was driving us all in the new car from La Paz to Coroico; my brothers and I had fallen asleep in the back. We were travelling slowly down the road into the deep, cloudy forest; it was raining and visibility was poor. Suddenly I was woken up by my mother's screams and the screeching sound produced by the brakes of our car trying to avoid a head on collision. I sat up straight on the back seat, from where I could see the frightened face of the other driver, who was climbing the ascent from Coroico in a truck. Both vehicles stopped abruptly, facing each other and almost touching. There was a panicked silence and it took them a few minutes to act. Dad and the truck driver got out on to the road to assess the situation and decide which of them had to give way by driving backwards.

The rules of the road clearly stated that the driver travelling uphill had the right of way. We were going downhill, but my father told the other driver that the road was very narrow. It was also muddy and slippery, as it had been raining all day. He argued that it would be easier for the truck driver to drive backwards to find a passing point, but the other man disagreed. He said that he had too much of a load on board his truck and he would have to drive back too far to find a passing area.

Dad was determined not to give in. He must have thought it was more dangerous for him to drive backwards as he was not as experienced as regular lorry drivers at steering a vehicle on that awful road. The argument went on until Dad got angry and shouted at him, "yes, your truck is loaded, but only with dead chickens! I have three children with me." Coroico had lots of chicken farms at that time, so trips to La Paz with poultry deliveries were a regular occurrence. Eventually the other driver gave in and reversed his truck back down the road. We followed him slowly, until we reached a safe passing point. The truck stopped at the edge of the precipice, while Dad drove our minibus past triumphantly. Suddenly we felt a jolt as the Volkswagen fell into a roadside ditch. Our brand new vehicle was damaged. The truck driver drove off, smiling. We were stuck in the ditch for hours, waiting for help to arrive. My mother soon realised that it made no difference whether she travelled in my father's car or by bus;

the risk remained the same. Over the years she became as fatalistic as the rest of the local people.

One wonderful, sunny morning at school, I was staring distractedly out of the window at infinite nature, admiring the thick, verdant, remote mountains that surrounded us. I was lost in thought rather than paying attention to the teacher. From a distance the Death Road looked like a solitary, long, thin, and sleepy snake. Suddenly I was horrified to see a truck drive off the edge of the mountain; it rolled down raising dust. I shouted out, "oh my God! Look!" This attracted everybody's attention. We all ran out of the school, towards the site of the accident. When we arrived at the scene, the driver and his assistant were lying dead with broken bottles and money everywhere. Later, someone told us that the truck driver had been transporting fizzy drinks to deliver to the shops in Coroico. It seemed that the driver had misjudged the space available for another vehicle to pass by. I shivered at the thought of my family nearly suffering the same fate a few months earlier when my father drove us back from La Paz.

Even though the Death Road was so lethal, local people organised daredevil car racing competitions on it at least once every two years. This festival was a popular event for spectators. We would prepare picnics and sit in the hills along the road under the shadow of a coffee or banana tree, waiting for the winning driver to arrive. It was not unusual for participants not to arrive, having driven over the edge to their deaths in the valley far below. The Death Road also had a tragic history with visitors. Many tourists would travel to Coroico over the mountain pass, attracted by the stunning scenery. Occasionally they too would fall victim to this fearful route. One morning we heard that a Swiss family had driven down the road towards Caranavi, another village nearby. But they didn't make their destination as they drove off the edge. Local peasants managed to free them from the car and took them to the clinic at Coroico for medical attention. The father was dead on arrival; the mother and their two children were badly injured. The doctor decided that it was better to take the survivors to La Paz as the village did not have the appropriate facilities. Unfortunately there was no ambulance to transport the injured people to the city safely. A local man kindly offered to take the Swiss family to La Paz in his truck. A further problem was finding a coffin big enough for the body of the dead foreigner. The local coffins were too small, as they were made for Bolivian people; it took a few days to construct one large enough. The body was left in the only available place, which was the patio of the small health centre, but as the weather was very hot, the corpse began to decompose, producing a terrible smell.

Every day after school I would play in the dusty countryside, unearth skeletons in the cemetery, or swim in the cold, clear river. At dusk the sound of church bells would tell us that it was time for God. The church was situated in the main plaza, next to the town hall, and mass was held every evening. In the town hall was the local radio station which had its speakers in strategic positions around the village. After mass, soft, romantic melodies would be played on air. For one peso people could dedicate a song to a loved one, perhaps to commemorate a special occasion like a birthday or Mother's Day. The radio station also announced weddings, funerals, and the names of debtors yet to pay their creditors.

On Saturdays at noon, busloads of people would arrive in the village from La Paz. Some passengers were tourists; others were locals living or studying in the city, who travelled home to spend the weekend or their break from college in Coroico. In the evenings after mass, local young people would hang out in the square, hoping to meet the new faces. Its high palms, beautiful gardens and the mellow music from the radio station created a romantic atmosphere. Wearing high heels and colourful dresses the local girls would stroll around the plaza, flirting and moving their bodies gracefully in time with the music. The boys would sit in the square acting macho. They would whistle or shout out compliments as the girls passed by. This courtship ritual would go on night after night until eventually one of the boys would have the courage to talk to a girl and invite her to sit with him. If romance blossomed, couples would sit in the centre of the plaza where tropical plants served as cover making it more romantic and less visible to prying eyes. Couples could hold hands and steal a kiss without anybody seeing.

Life in the village was fun for us young people, but the local standard of education was poor. The region had only state schools and it seemed that the staff would come and go as they pleased; there was no continuity of teaching. My parents were so concerned they decided to send José to school in La Paz. He was only thirteen years old when he was sent to a strict Catholic boarding school called Domingo Savio. Many years later I found out that my brother had been intensely homesick and hated being separated from his family at such an early age. A year after José started boarding, Dad bought a three bedroom apartment in an excellent neighbourhood in central La Paz. In 1975, two years after my brother first left Coroico, the whole family moved to the city. Dad set up his dental clinic in the Plaza Murillo, next to the Congress building and Presidential Palace. He worked in La Paz during the week then travelled to Coroico to attend to his busy clinic every weekend. The flat in La Paz was comfortable to live in and tastefully decorated, but we children felt like caged birds. The city did not have many parks or playing fields, nor were there rivers in which to swim. There was not even a cemetery within easy reach. La Paz was a big city; expensive, cold, isolating and unfriendly. We would spend hours looking through the apartment's windows, staring at the traffic and people passing by below.

When the school term was about to start for José's third year, Dad took him to be re-enrolled. The headmaster, who was a very serious minded priest, told my father that José was a troublemaker and unless his behaviour improved he was not going to be accepted in the school again. My father was at a loss for words when he heard this. He looked at my brother expecting an apology and hoping that the headmaster's complaint would encourage him to behave himself. José's reaction was the opposite of my father's wishes; he stood up from his chair and in a defiant tone told the headmaster to accept him without imposing any conditions. The headmaster replied that he was sorry but the condition was clear, José had to behave himself. He refused to cooperate, and walked out of the school that very moment. Dad followed his son out of the building, visibly upset. José had been expelled from one of the best schools in La Paz. He now had only one option, to attend a state school, which was precisely what my father had wanted to avoid.

State schools, which are free in Bolivia, did not have a good reputation in the mid-1970s. Typically, they lacked discipline, the standard of education was poor in general and there was no guarantee on leaving the school of securing a place at university. José was a very intelligent boy, so my father didn't want him to waste his talents or get involved with the wrong crowd. As a last resort, Dad wrote a letter to Uncle Hector to explain the situation. A few months later, at the age of fifteen, José was sent to continue his education in Sweden.

My younger brother Marcelo had no such problems getting into a good school in La Paz. He was at the beginning of his time in primary education, so he was starting with a clean slate as far as the authorities were concerned.

I was just about to turn sixteen years old when we moved to La Paz. It was difficult to find a suitable school for me because I had not been a particularly good student when I was living in

The Illegal Dance

Coroico, as was clearly shown by my grades. José was in a class below me, but he would complain to my mother that I would repeat aloud the text I was reading many times over. "Mum, I know her lessons already just by her constant repetition," he would say. Eventually he would get so annoyed that he would tell me to shut up.

Every Catholic school where my parents tried to enrol me refused to consider my application as my grades were so low. The rules of this type of school were that you had to be an able student, unless you started at primary level so you could be moulded to the demands of the school. Also the parents had to be Catholics, and they had to have enough money to pay the high fees. My parents had these requirements; the only problem was the low grades. So my poor school results meant I had no chance of securing a place at a private school. My parents got ever more anxious as time passed, with only a few days left to be enrolled at any of the best schools in La Paz, I was yet to be accepted.

One morning my father woke up with a crazy idea. First he discussed with my mother which school they wanted me to attend. Once this had been agreed on, my father went out to make a call from a public telephone, as we had no phone at the time. He pretended to be Monseigneur Manning, the Bishop of Coroico who had sent my Dad the case of wine. Impersonating the bishop, he recommended me without reservation to the head of the school, a lovely Spanish nun. Monseigneur Manning was from the U.S.A., so Dad had to speak with an American accent and as the Bishop was such a well-known Catholic authority, the nuns could not refuse the request. An hour later, I had enrolled as a pupil at the school, with the proviso that I had to catch up with the other students in all subjects.

The two storey school building was an impressive colonial sight, its long corridors making a square with high ceiling classrooms along them. The college was well equipped, including language and chemistry laboratories, a music room with grand piano, and an onsite church where we would say our daily prayers. The school also boasted a basketball court, a volleyball field and three recreation yards. At the far edge of these playgrounds, there was a long line of shrubs that served as a wall separating my new college from another one. The neighbouring college accepted girls from low income families. Students from the two schools never mixed. Years later, after I had left school, I read an article in a Bolivian newspaper about a feud between parents and students from both schools. This row erupted because the authorities joined the schools together and decreed that the combined school would enrol children from all backgrounds. The well off parents from my school could not accept that such a prestigious educational sanctuary was to merge with a college that catered for undesirable, working class students. Even now, many years later, some of my school friends feel disgusted that the two socially different schools are now one.

My first day at my new college, Le Sacré Coeur, was a daunting experience. I felt totally alone, insecure and ignored. Nobody came to welcome me as a new student as they had at my old school in the village. The girls were quite snobbish, involved in their own little worlds without the slightest curiosity about others. The girls' Spanish was fluent and sophisticated. I felt compelled to make every effort to speak like them as I remembered how my Dad would correct me all the time when we lived in Coroico, especially when I used the village accent or the black community's dialect. The girls were fashionable, lively and bright. Although we wore white uniforms to school, most of the girls wore high heels and used make up. As the school was run by French nuns, some of the students spoke fluent French, or even English.

All the teachers were strict, they rarely smiled and took their jobs extremely seriously. The history teacher often started her lessons with an oral test. She would choose one of us at random to stand in front of the class to be bombarded with questions about the subject. Whenever I was chosen for this ordeal, I always felt that after my performance I was going to be shot by firing squad. The teacher was excellent, but I always struggled to remember important historical dates, or the names, achievements and failures of Bolivian presidents. Even with coaching from my cousin Eliana, learning historical facts remained out of my reach.

In chemistry lessons, my class would often use the laboratory for practical sessions. We would perform experiments to explore phenomena such as osmosis or mix substances in test tubes to learn about chemical reactions, which often resulted in changes of colour or gas being produced. Smoke would often pour out of the test tubes. Our language teachers would give us long lists of vocabulary and phrases to memorise, which we then had to recite in class. As we learned this material like parrots, I never really understood what we were saying. We sang the French national anthem better than the Bolivian one and we sang this French song in chorus:

Alouette, gentille Alouette
Alouette, je te plumerai la tête
Et la tête, et la tête Alouette, Alouette

The music teacher was Gilberto Rojas, a well-known Bolivian composer. We would sing along with his beautiful piano playing. Although I come from a family of musicians, my singing skills were non-existent. It all seemed too much for me to learn. My father soon began to pay for me to have extra tuition in the evenings in all subjects, to help me keep up with the demands of the school.

During breaks from lessons, I would try to join in conversation with other girls, who were always in small groups. I wanted to integrate myself and make friends by exploring topics of common interest, but I remained unattached to any particular group. The girls' conversations were mostly about boys and dating. Other girls would talk casually about their first sexual encounters. Some of them already had boyfriends; others claimed they only dated foreigners with exotic and difficult to pronounce names, such as Smith, Schneeberger or Curland. The girls with foreign surnames would proudly discuss their European origins, to give themselves a glamorous air and enhance their class and status among their peers. Some of them had already experienced smoking cigarettes or drinking alcohol. The responsible ones would criticise those who pretended to be more adventurous and gave them lessons in spirituality, morality and virginity. Some of the girls were superficial and with an air of superiority; other girls were easy going, friendly and kind. On the whole, we were just a bunch of fun girls.

Every now and then I would see nuns walking along the corridors, making sure things were in perfect order. They were particularly concerned about how the girls wore their school uniforms, especially the length of their skirts. If they found someone who was breaking the rules, they would be furious with her and undo the stitching on the spot to make the skirt the required length. The teacher of religious studies, Father Andrew, would make us feel guilty about being young women. He would accuse us of tempting the devil with our sinful thoughts and body language. He would tell us in a husky voice, "men use women to satisfy their wicked desires," which would make us wish that we hadn't been born. I never liked this teacher, but he was typical of the priests I met. They all seemed so close to God, but so far from real people's lives.

My first conversation with a priest was in the confessional box at church, when I was at primary school; I was eight-years-old, preparing for my first communion. While waiting for confession, along with other girls, I tried to remember my sins, but none came to mind. I wasn't sure whether lying to my mother about eating the snacks she packed for my school lunch was a sin or not. So I decided to make up some evil things that sounded wicked. When I was called to the confessional box, the old priest asked me if I had any sins. After I had replied, "yes, Father," he said, "well, tell me your sins, child." I started by saying, "Father, I have been a bad girl." "What did you do wrong?" he asked. I then got a bit scared about telling lies, so I began to mumble words with no meaning and no sins came from my lips. The priest said, "don't be afraid, God will forgive you." "Yes, Father," I replied, but then I muttered something that even I didn't understand. Before I could say anything else, the priest sent me away to pray six Hail Marys. He sounded annoyed with me for wasting his time. Thinking in retrospect I wonder what sort of sins a priest expected an eight year old girl to have committed.

One day at my new school in La Paz, the physical education teacher didn't turn up for work. We heard that the nuns had sacked her because they found out she was gay, and was suspected of having a relationship with a pupil. My school was so strict and conservative that the topic of homosexuality was never discussed. Under no circumstances could a Catholic school condone the gay lifestyle. Many years later, after I had left school, I heard on the grapevine that one headmistress of the college, a Spanish nun, had returned to Spain and got married. She may have tired of the Catholic mentality and its draconian rules.

I started school in La Paz at the same time as a girl from Beni, the northern, tropical region of Bolivia. As she was such a good student in her village, she had won a scholarship to be educated at a privileged school in the capital. Unfortunately, her excellent grades were not enough to help her get on with her classmates. Nobody talked to her, cared about her, or helped her to integrate. We all ignored her, myself included. In my defence, I was also fighting for survival at school. The girl was always on her own, until one day halfway through the school year, she disappeared and we never heard from her again. Her lack of confidence, her social status and perhaps her plain physical appearance, contributed to her being ignored by us. Other newcomers were treated differently if they were tall, blonde and physically attractive. We would be friendly to these girls, making them feel at home. Everyone would make a fuss of them. Such students didn't leave the school unexpectedly and are in our graduation photos.

Years later I met a girl who also studied at my school and she told me, "there were two girls who came from outside the capital; one of them was from Beni and she didn't survive at the school. The other one was from Coroico and she survived; she was very funny." I let her know that the Coroico girl was me and that to survive in that school one had to have a strong sense of humour.

When it came to our graduation ceremony the girls in my class had specific plans for how it was to be celebrated. Some of them wanted to have a very expensive party at the best nightclub in La Paz followed by a trip to Florida to visit Disney World. Other girls wanted to mark the occasion with a spiritual ceremony complete with formal dress code and religious celebration. When the school year came to an end, we only had enough money for a formal party in an expensive club in La Paz. We had to abandon the idea of travelling to Florida. But feeling we should still go somewhere, I came up with the idea of Coroico. My classmates didn't take me seriously at first. "Coroico?" they asked. "Where the hell is that?" Everyone knew about Disney World, but they were clueless when it came to Coroico. After a few weeks, the girls came to realise that a trip to Coroico was an interesting idea after all. Two weeks later we were heading towards the village where I grew up. On arrival, my friends from my old school received us with great warmth. Sports competitions, parties and serenades in the evenings were organised in our honour. The girls from La Paz had the opportunity to see another side to life. Disney World was completely forgotten and thirty years later my classmates still remember their wonderful trip to Coroico.

After my graduation in 1976, my father took me to Buenos Aires as a reward for successfully completing my A levels. My visit to Argentina was my first trip abroad. When I returned to La Paz, I found out that I had been accepted to study medicine at the Higher University of San Andres; I was eighteen years old. After seeing so many dead and injured people during my time living in Coroico, I thought medicine was a good choice. My parents were delighted about my decision and bought me a Toyota Celica as a present; a two door sports car that was both trendy and fast. I took some driving lessons before getting my licence. I was soon driving up and down the hills of La Paz. In Bolivia, it's easy to get a driving licence if you know someone working for the police. You simply fill in a form and pay a bribe; you don't need to pass a driving test. In England this is called "corruption," in Bolivia it's called "friendship." This is the way many things get done in my country.

I would take my cousin Liz with me on drives to practice my new skills. She was the only person who dared to risk her life travelling with me. Every time I took the car out of the garage I would crash it. Either I drove the car too fast or I was too slow to use the brakes in time.

When I was driving down the road one day, an ambulance sounded its siren to let me know it was trying to pass. Instead of staying calm, I zigzagged to the right and left of the road; I couldn't decide on which side of the road the ambulance should pass me. When it finally managed to overtake me the driver shouted obscenities. I was constantly being fined for my bad driving. I would park in the wrong place or stall the car when stopped on a hill waiting for traffic lights to turn green. Many times the car rolled backwards to crash into the vehicle behind me.

I was taking my mother and Aunt Teresa to a tea party one day. I was driving fast and didn't notice a dog running out from a house. Before I knew it I had hit the dog, and with a sharp scream it was killed instantly. I was very upset and told my father as soon as I got home. He called the police, told them about the accident and asked them what he should do next. The police officer said there was nothing to do unless the owners reported the incident. My father gave them his name and address, but we never heard from the owners of the dog.

Even with many years of driving experience, I still couldn't handle a car properly. Years later when my husband and I went to Brazil on a birdwatching trip, we hired a car in Rio de Janeiro to go to Itatiaia, a famous national park in the region where there are about four hundred species of bird. We drove to a small village outside the park one hot evening to enjoy a beer with local people. After a few hours in the bar, Alan asked me to drive back to the park as I had not been drinking alcohol. There was no traffic; we had the wide jungle road to ourselves. As we approached the park entrance, Alan asked me to stop for a moment, so he could look at a bird through his binoculars, which he carried everywhere. The bird was perched in a roadside tree, a few metres from us. "Look, it's a beautiful tropical screech-owl," he said. "An owl?" I replied in a worried tone of voice. "This will bring us bad luck." "Bad luck, what do you mean?" he asked, without taking his eyes off the bird. "We are superstitious in Bolivia and believe that owls bring bad luck. We shouldn't be looking at it," I said firmly. My husband ignored the warning completely and carried on observing the owl with great interest. "It's got fantastic big staring eyes and its wings have a wonderful brown, velvet colour," he said, looking at the owl as if it were the most magnificent creature he had ever seen. He felt the same when he saw a condor in Bolivia for the first time. "Look at it, please, it's a fantastic creature," he said, passing me the binoculars. I didn't want to look at the bird, which seemed to be patiently waiting as if it was a deity. I was adamant that owls bring bad luck. After a few minutes of looking intently at the bird, he resumed his sitting position in the car for us to get going. He said, "this is really good luck for me. This bird is great! Can we go now please?" He was delighted to have seen something memorable that evening as he asked me to start the car.

I turned on the engine and started to drive slowly. As I speeded up, I crashed the car into the only post standing by the side of the road. The front of the car was badly damaged. In a sarcastic but calm way, Alan asked me, "how did you manage to do that without even drinking a glass of wine, darling?" I couldn't believe my stupidity. How could I crash the car on such a wide road? We spent the next few days trying to get it fixed; going backwards and forwards from the police to the mechanic before we had to return the vehicle to the rental company, who were very unhappy. With or without the excuse of an owl, my driving was so dangerous I would probably have caused a fatal accident had I ever driven again.

During the winter holidays of 1978 my parents, my younger brother Marcelo and I went back to Coroico. We looked forward to our return to the village every year. It was the best place to go to escape the low temperatures of La Paz, which, situated at high altitude, would get very cold, especially at night. For my parents this was also a time for relaxation. Living in a busy city and travelling every weekend to Coroico was taking its toll on my father. For my brother and me, it was a good opportunity to meet up with old friends and run around the countryside.

One warm evening I went to meet a friend in the village square. She was an attractive girl from the Amazon part of Bolivia. Women from that region are often regarded as being sexy and charming. That balmy, relaxed evening the town felt calm and untroubled. No accidents had been reported that day from the

Death Road. People were strolling around the plaza or sitting and talking about the unimportant daily things; no one was in a rush. The only thing that made that evening stand out as unusual was the fact that no music was playing on the town hall radio. There had been an electricity cut so one could hear the loud courtship songs of the bush crickets.

I didn't attend mass that evening. In fact, my visits to church had become less frequent since I left school. Although my parents had a Catholic upbringing, they never forced us to follow Catholicism to the letter. They may have thought that we experienced enough exposure to church at school, or perhaps they didn't want us to follow a religion that was imposed on Bolivia by Spanish conquistadors. My father saw religion as a symbol of oppression; he wanted us to be free to make up our own minds. We never talked about God at home. We took the view that God was nature and nature was God; a kind of Pantheism, which unconsciously mirrored the indigenous Bolivian belief known as *Pachamama* (Mother Earth). My mother was the only one in our family who would follow the Catholic faith and go to church on Sundays. My father would sometimes wait for her after Mass in the plaza, reading his newspaper.

Back to that balmy evening in Coroico, the sky was dressed with shining stars as if it were a sign of celebration, perhaps announcing dry weather for the next day. My friend and I walked around slowly and casually, totally indifferent to the rest of the world. The noise of the bush crickets was even louder. We had noticed two boys in their twenties who began to follow us. They were dirty looking and dressed in soiled, casual clothes, obviously not interested in impressing anyone. Without hiding their curiosity, the boys approached us. "Hi," said one of them. "Hi," answered my friend, showing off her voluptuous figure. I was quite shy, so I only answered with a smile. We had not met these guys before, so I was concerned about where they came from. I was also worried about my parents' reaction, as they held conservative views when it came to meeting boys; they didn't like me talking to strangers. They were probably lurking somewhere nearby as they always made sure that everything was in order. As Coroico was a small village, everybody knew each other, so a new face always raised interest.

The boys introduced themselves as Rafael and Carlos. We sat down on one of the benches under a luxuriant palm tree. People say that palms are the symbol of victory, peace and fertility. That evening was certainly peaceful and most probably fertile too, because the ever louder noise of the bush crickets seemed to suggest success in attracting suitable mates. We talked trivialities for the rest of the evening. There was nothing special about these guys, apart from the fact they were both architecture students in La Paz and were camping in the outskirts of the village. They seemed more interested in us than we were in them.

After about an hour, my friend got bored, so she slowly got up from the bench. As I was about to do the same, the guy named Rafael spotted a ring I wore on my finger. It was a lovely gold ring with a beautiful aquamarine stone, a present from my parents on my fifteenth birthday. "What a lovely ring!" he said. "Thank you," I replied, proudly. "Can I have a better look at it?" he asked, leaning towards me. I extended my hand to him, so he could see the ring more clearly. He took it gently off my finger before placing it on one of his own. "It looks really nice on me," he said, showing me his long, thin fingers. He tried to get the ring off but couldn't. He tried again, but the ring was stuck on his little finger. "My ring, give me back my ring," I begged him, but he got up and walked away. "I'll see you here again tomorrow and I'll give it back to you then." His friend looked as surprised as I did, but saying nothing, he got up and followed Rafael in the direction of where they were camping. I was annoyed with myself. I had only just met this guy and yet I had to see him again the next day if I wanted my ring back. My friend tried to put me at ease by saying that I should not worry because we would get the ring back the next day. I returned home, hoping my parents wouldn't notice anything until the following night.

The next morning while having breakfast, my mother, who was a very observant woman, realised that I was not wearing my ring. She asked me where it was, thinking that I had lost it as I was often scatter brained. I had lost a ring on a previous occasion, which my mother had not forgotten. It was gold encrusted with diamonds and rubies which mum had lent me to go to a party a few years before. It probably fell off my finger while I was dancing. The ring had safely passed down three generations, having first belonged to my great-grandmother.

"Where is your ring, where is your ring?" she kept repeating. I had to tell her the truth; "I'm sorry mum, but the guy I was talking to last night borrowed it." My mother was outraged. "What! Borrowed it? What do you mean borrowed it? Have you gone mad, giving your ring to a stranger? Who is he? Where is he staying? How did you meet him?" In my anger and confusion I could not answer. I didn't know what to say, so I ran out of the house to look for the boy. I left my mother behind threatening to tell my father if I didn't get the ring back.

Although Coroico was a small place, I didn't know where to find the guy. I knew he was camping somewhere close with his friend, but I hadn't asked exactly where. I hoped they had changed their minds about camping and checked into a hotel. I searched the hotels first, but with no success. Undeterred, I walked down the road in the direction of my old school, carrying on to the outskirts of the village on the road to Yolosa. They were not there either.

Finally, I decided to go up the hill towards the cemetery. On the way, I walked passed a place called *El Chawi*, a small, little used spring with only a trickle of water. It was as if nature had

had enough of generating the source of life as nobody took any interest in it. I stopped there for a few minutes, as it was a hot, dry day, I felt exhausted and had a terrible headache. In the rush to get out of the house, I had put on the wrong shoes, they were not the right ones to be wearing to search the countryside for two strangers; my feet hurt and I could hardly walk. Sweat ran down my forehead. I was dehydrated, feeling dizzy, and panting with thirst. So I went to drink some water from the spring and wet my sweaty face. Suddenly I remembered the local legend. "If you drink the water from *El Chawi*, you will stay in Coroico forever." I felt a pang of anxiety; I couldn't stay in Coroico, I had to go back to La Paz to become a doctor. I promised myself however, that one day I would come back to drink water from the spring and stay in the village forever. Without taking a drop, I carried on walking in search of the boys, without success. Later in the afternoon, I went back home, feeling worn out and upset. I thought Rafael had probably gone back to La Paz with my ring and I wouldn't see him again.

At dinnertime, my parents kept very quiet. This was an ominous sign that my father knew about the ring. My mum and dad could never keep secrets; they would tell each other everything. Dad didn't make any comment, as he always avoided arguments while we were eating. I wasn't hungry; I didn't want to eat anything that evening, but going without food may have made things worse at this sensitive moment, so I ate something. I wanted to get out of the house again and find that boy as soon as I could.

While we were eating I heard the church bells ring for Mass. I thought about going to church that evening to pray for the safe return of my ring. I knew, however, that if I got up from the table before everyone else had finished dinner, my father would have become even angrier. I swallowed my food very quickly without enjoying it. As soon as I could, I excused myself from the table, saying I was going to the square. As I left the house, I heard my Dad said, "we will be there soon."

I ran out of the house hoping to see Rafael where we had met the night before. I crossed the road in a hurry and, a short distance away, I saw a guy sitting in the same place we were the night before. He was sitting cross legged, with one of his arms outstretched along the back of the bench in a comfortable and confident manner. I couldn't believe what I saw; it was him, Rafael. "Hi," I said, with a big smile. "Can I have my ring back please?" "Hi," he replied, moving slightly to the right, inviting me to sit down next to him. I sat down hoping I would get the ring back, before asking again, "please will you give me my ring?" He still had the ring on his little finger, but he gave no sign of giving it back. He smiled at me mockingly, as if enjoying my agony. He seemed totally in charge of the situation, he was using the ring to keep me sitting next to him for as long as he wanted.

Raphael held my hand and stroked it. "Let me read your future," he said. He looked at the palm of my hand and compared it to his own, as if he was trying to find some mysterious connection. "You have a very interesting hand," he said. Suddenly my parents appeared in front of us from nowhere. I hadn't seen them coming as I was almost hypnotised by this guy. Before I could make the necessary introductions, Rafael got up from the bench to introduce himself. My father was not remotely interested in making his acquaintance.

"Where is the ring?" he demanded. Without saying anything that might upset my father even more, Rafael immediately took the ring off his finger and put it on one of mine. Dad ordered me to go home immediately. I couldn't argue with him, so I stood up from the bench. As I was about to go, I could see that Rafael seemed confused about the situation. However he looked me straight in the eyes and asked me to meet him again in the same place the next day. Rafael's behaviour surprised both me and my parents, but we walked away from him without saying a word.

We met the following day and for the rest of the holiday. Sometimes my girlfriend and Carlos would come along with us, but most of the time it was just Rafael and me. My parents didn't take to my new friend; nobody knew anything about him. This was not my father's idea of a holiday for me. He would have preferred me to be running around the fields catching butterflies, or even playing in the cemetery looking for open graves, rather than spending time with boys. Father saw me as his carefree little girl and he wanted to keep me that way as long as he could. He was so protective that he would stop the boys from coming near me with one fierce look. Boys were afraid of him, so they had to ask for his permission to take me out. My new friend had a strong personality for his age and my father's feelings didn't seem to bother him too much.

Raphael was twenty two years old, but acted as if he were older. I liked him because he was different; he was a bit of a philosopher. He would analyse everything from the life of an ant, to the dreams and hardships of a native Bolivian peasant. "Nobody cares about these people," he would say. "In Europe, dogs are treated better than them; their owners even clean up their mess behind them, collecting it in little bags." In those days we were living under the dictatorship of Hugo Banzer Suárez and death was common for anyone who dared to speak out against it and even more so if they were peasants. Rafael would sit for hours in the countryside trying to guess what the peasants' thoughts and feelings were. "For us, they are just ignorant Indians and that is all they are," he would say with sadness.

He loved poetry too. He would read or recite Pablo Neruda's verses to me. Rafael would write poems himself; poems which describe the hardships of the indigenous people and the miners who lived in deplorable conditions and died young due to lung disease. He was an interesting young man: well read, intelligent and sensitive. He would talk about all the injustices that happened in Bolivia, injustices that I had also noticed, but was not able to express as well as he did; or perhaps it was because I thought that things that could not be changed might as well be accepted. Raphael was more optimistic. "One day, sooner or later, things will have to change in this country," he would say.

Finally the holiday came to an end and we both had to return to La Paz. On our last evening in Coroico, Rafael and I were sitting in the plaza. The full moon made it feel like a magic night, full of romance and it seemed an important moment in both our lives. In the background, gentle and nostalgic melodies were drifting on the air from the town hall radio. In Bolivia, people hold different views about the meaning of a full moon. Some say it is a sign of death and rebirth. Others believe it signifies a time for healing, creativity and psychic energy. I associated that evening with the hope of fulfilling dreams and desires; the birth of a new life ahead of me, or just being aware of change. Whatever the meaning of that full moon was, that evening was divine. There was no need for words, just our presence was enough. We were enjoying watching people strolling around the plaza; perhaps some of them were also savouring one of their last evenings in Coroico.

At about ten o'clock my parents joined us to remind me it was time to go home. "Can you stay a bit longer?" Rafael asked me. "I'm sorry, Rafael, but I can't," I said, sadly. I explained to him that my parents didn't like it if I stayed out late at night, especially if I was out with a stranger during a full moon. "People talk in a small village, Rafael," I said, "and my parents are highly respected here." "Can I see you again in La Paz, then?" he asked me as if he wanted to extend that evening forever. "Yes," I said, with a big smile on my face.

The Illegal Dance

We exchanged telephone numbers and as I was about to walk away, he stood up from the bench with a defiant attitude and said, "I will walk you home." We walked for a few minutes behind my parents. Just before we reached my house, he placed his lips gently on mine. Feeling elated and almost possessed by him, I said "good night," before stepping through the front door.

CHAPTER EIGHT

"When love is not madness, it is not love"

Pedro Calderón de la Barca

It is said that when one is in love every part of the body changes. The pupils of the eyes enlarge and one begins to be more aware of one's surroundings. Hormones move more swiftly through the blood, making one feel more radiant and attractive; you feel more alive and energised. Vivid dreams and butterflies in the stomach wake you up in the middle of the night and you are filled with new emotions, plans and purposes. There was no doubt I was in love. I felt my glowing face and pounding heart, every time I thought of Rafael's kiss. Everything around me seemed wonderful. La Paz was no longer a cold and unfamiliar city. It had transformed into a warm and exciting metropolis. I walked the streets that left me breathless before, with a smile on my lips. I could finally appreciate its diversity and incomparable beauty. For the first time I felt that this city was the place where I could live happily.

The day of our first date in La Paz arrived. I was very anxious especially because of the bad start we had had in Coroico with the ring incident. From my bedroom window I saw Rafael coming down towards my building. He was smartly dressed; it looked like he had made a special effort for this occasion. His moustache and neat, short beard made his manly face seem more seductive and mysterious. His rapid, proud walk signalled strength and self-confidence. He held a book under his arm, which gave me the impression that he wanted to look studious.

After a few minutes I heard the doorbell ringing. The maid opened the front door and came to my bedroom, to let me know that I had a visitor. While I was still getting ready, Mum went to talk to him. It was my parent's custom to entertain friends who came to visit me, to get to know them better. It was generally my father who would do the talking; on many occasions he would even ask me to invite them for dinner. My father had a saying: *"En la mesa y en la mesilla se conoce a la gentecilla."* ("At the table one always gets to know the riffraff"). This time, it was my mother who was doing the checking out because it was late in the afternoon and my father was still at work.

I looked at myself once more in the mirror, to make sure the clothes I was wearing were right for the occasion. I realised that afternoon for the first time that I was becoming just as concerned about my appearance as my mother was about hers. She was well known for being coquettish and very careful about the way she dressed. She was adept at combining colours and never went out for the evening without wearing the right jewellery. I was not sure about the clothes I was wearing, so I quickly changed into another outfit. I also made sure that my makeup and hair were perfect. I walked out towards the sitting room feeling nervous and excited at the same time, hoping I was not going to totter in my high heels. Rafael was sitting very comfortably on the large sofa, looking perfectly at ease; my mother perched on one of the armchairs, her small face reflecting a smile of acceptance. She seemed pleasantly surprised to see Rafael looking so well dressed, not scruffy like the first time she saw him in Coroico. Some people take pride in their appearance and, as my mother was one of them, she noticed these things.

"Hi Rafael," I said, shy and insecure, but pleased to see him again. "Hi," he replied, standing up to greet me with a kiss on my cheek. I sat down in one of the armchairs, hoping my mother would soon leave us alone, but she wasn't going anywhere. It seemed that she wanted to stay with us longer so she could work out the true intentions of my new friend. We felt watched by my mother and an awkward silence filled the room. Raphael and I didn't know what to say to each other for a while. Eventually he broke the ice by suggesting he and I could go to the cinema. I looked at my mother for her approval. "Yes, no problem," she said to my surprise. "As long as you bring her back as soon as the film is over." "Yes, of course," we answered in unison. We left the flat feeling flushed with excitement, as if we had got to the top of the mountain without making too much effort.

As I love dancing, the film I chose was Saturday Night Fever, starring John Travolta. Rafael accepted my choice happily, but made it clear that he was going to be the one who decided which films we saw in future. After this first date, he took me to see films that were largely forbidden in Bolivia at that time because they documented controversial facts about Bolivian society. The Courage of the People was one of many films by the Bolivian director, Jorge Sanjines. It showed the terrible slaughter that took place during one night in a Potosi tin mine called Siglo XX in 1967, when General Barrientos's Government tried to prevent a meeting of mine workers, factory workers and students who were supporting Che Guevara's brand of guerrilla warfare. The Main Enemy was another film by the same director. This was about the brutal exploitation of the peasantry by the ruling élite. There was a small non-profit cinema called *La Cinemateca* near the Plaza Murillo in La Paz. They specialised in showing alternative, contemporary, cultural films that were shot mostly in black and white. We became regular visitors to *La Cinemateca*; we rarely went to watch commercial Hollywood films.

Rafael was a privileged boy who came from a respectable middle class family that lived in a wealthy part of La Paz. His father was a prominent engineer, his mother a distinguished bourgeois lady. His sisters attended my school but Rafael had been sent to study in Chile, where he became interested in politics. While he was studying at university in Santiago, the military dictator Augusto Pinochet and his ruthless regime overthrew Salvador Allende's socialist government in a coup. Rafael had to return to Bolivia for his own safety. In those days, however, my country was also going through a very difficult time. In the four years from 1978-82, Bolivia was ruled by ten presidents, one of them, Alberto Natusch for two weeks only. This was the most unstable period in the country's history.

I heard about Pinochet for the first time from Rafael, but years later the Chilean dictator crossed my path in October 1998 when I was living in London. One afternoon, I had finished work and was walking towards Baker Street to take the Underground when I heard people chanting, "Death to Pinochet! Death to Pinochet!" I crossed the road to see what was going on. Among the crowd I spotted Roberto, a friend of mine from Chile. "Ana, Ana, come here," he called to me. "What's going on?" I asked. Roberto was very excited and said, "you won't believe this! Pinochet is in this exclusive and expensive clinic." It was the London Clinic in Devonshire Place, practically around the corner from where I was working. Apparently Pinochet, one of the cruellest men in

South American history was at the hospital for a back operation. But the Chilean ex-dictator was actually under arrest because a Spanish judge, Baltazar Garzón, had presented Britain with an extradition warrant for Pinochet to be put on trial in Spain for human rights abuses.

"Are you serious?" I asked him. I couldn't believe that Pinochet was practically next to the place where I worked. I thought of Rafael's stories about this monster. Roberto asked me if I could help them. "What do you want me to do?" I asked. "Just come here every day. We will be putting pressure on the British Government until this bastard goes to prison; this is our opportunity," he said, with enthusiasm.

Roberto was studying at the University of Santiago, Chile, when Pinochet's army raided his house at five in the morning one day and took him to prison. A few days later his girlfriend was also arrested. The couple were accused of being left-wing activists. Roberto spent two years in a Chilean jail. He survived physical and mental torture until, with the help of the Red Cross, he eventually left for England as a political refugee. Years later he found out that his girlfriend managed to escape from Chile but he didn't know where she had gone.

That unexpected afternoon I stayed with Roberto and the other people in the crowd shouting, "Death to Pinochet" for about an hour. I left the group with the promise that I would return to protest as often as I could.

I kept my word; during the time Pinochet spent in the London Clinic, I joined protests several times to show my support for the Chilean exiles. One day in March 1999, Roberto called me at work sounding very excited. His usual reason for calling was to invite me to a gig or festival, or to ask me to go dancing, but this time was different. "Meet me outside the House of Lords tomorrow at noon. I'll be there with a group of people, supporting the dictator's extradition," he said. "I'll be working tomorrow, I don't know if I'll be able to get away early." "You must come, you must come!" he insisted. "It's an important day for Chileans and all South Americans; the future of that murderous bastard will be decided tomorrow!" "Ok, I will do my best Roberto," I replied. Before we hung up, he added in a mysterious voice, "I have something else important to tell you when I see you." I didn't think much of it at the time, although his tone of voice was disconcerting. I thought it was probably to do with a concert or something like that. Roberto was a musician and he was often going to those kinds of events.

The next day I managed to leave work early and I rushed to the House of Lords as quickly as I could. I arrived about two hours after the protest had begun. The whole area was packed with people; on one side stood Pinochet's supporters, on the other, his opponents. "My God!" I thought, "I'll never find Roberto in this crowd!" I searched everywhere, before finally spotting my friend wearing a poncho, a brown hat, and playing his guitar.

A policeman helped me make my way through to the front, where I finally reached Roberto. He had almost lost his voice through all the shouting and singing. "Hi Ana, thanks for coming." "How are things going?" I asked. "We don't know anything yet, but it's just a matter of time," he replied, starting to sing without giving me more details. "Are these people all from Chile?" I asked him, looking at the crowd. "No, they've travelled from all over South America and Europe. Lots of expatriate Chileans are also here from many other countries," he said, proudly. I stayed for over an hour until I began to tire of standing up in my high heels. "I'm exhausted, Roberto. I don't think I'll be able to stay here much longer," I said to my over excited friend. Roberto insisted that I should not leave. "Don't go yet, please. You mustn't miss the final hearing. After this I'll treat you to a coffee; I have something to tell you."

I compromised by sitting on the ground to rest my aching feet while waiting for the House of Lords' ruling. After a few more minutes the good news was announced. It was decreed that Augusto Pinochet was not immune from prosecution on charges of genocide and could be put on trial in Spain. Everybody roared: "Victory for Chile, at last!" It was a moment of collective hysteria. We all sang and shouted with joy; a lot of people cried, too. Soon, Roberto and I left the group to find a coffee shop. We ordered hot drinks and sat down, feeling delighted but exhausted.

An increasing stream of people arrived at the coffee shop, and Roberto constantly got up to greet everyone. As he was a musician, many people in the South American community knew him. I was curious and impatient to find out the news he promised to tell me, so I asked him to ignore his friends for a while so that we could talk. "You're acting strangely," I said. "What's the matter?" "You won't believe this. Do you remember when we met for the first time and I told you about an ex-girlfriend I had in Chile?" "Yes, I remember," I said, recalling the occasion. We had met a year earlier at the birthday party of a mutual Chilean friend's one-year-old son. Roberto was at the party with his four-year-old daughter. When we got talking he was interested that I came from Bolivia, the country where his ex-wife was born. He had been married to a Bolivian woman for two years, but they separated when his daughter was only two years old. Although he mentioned his former wife briefly, he talked much more about his Chilean girlfriend. Roberto told me everything about how and why they had lost contact and his reasons for leaving Chile. We then shared a few sad stories about our countries so perhaps that was the reason why we became friends.

"She's here." "What do you mean she's here?", I asked, intrigued. "She is here in London and was in the crowd this afternoon," he added, smiling with the satisfaction of having kept his secret until that moment. "How do you know it was her?" I asked. "We met by chance two days ago at one of the Chilean meetings I've been organising to support Pinochet's extradition to Spain.

She came from Spain for the final hearing. She lives there with her husband and daughter. It was pure chance." I bombarded him with questions. "Is her husband from Chile? What does she look like? Has she changed a lot? Did you talk to each other? How did you feel when you saw her?" I couldn't stop asking him questions. I was living his story as if it was my own. He enjoyed seeing my curiosity and excitement. He told me they had arranged to meet again for coffee the next day. "Just the two of you?" I asked. "Yes, of course, but only for an hour." She was going shopping with friends, so they were to meet up at Bond Street station. I was amazed; I couldn't believe his story. It was Pinochet who triggered their separation and Pinochet who caused their reunion after so many years. We left the coffee shop talking about what might happen the next day. We joked about some possible outcomes before I said goodbye, wishing him luck.

After that day I saw Roberto a couple of times in salsa clubs, but he was always drunk and looking miserable. On many occasions either he didn't recognise me or pretended not to, so I did the same. We both avoided each other, but I didn't know why. Perhaps he didn't want to apologise for his drinking and maybe I didn't want to hear his painful story again.

About four years after the Pinochet protests in London, a girlfriend and I went to Ronnie Scott's Jazz Club. At the entrance to the club I bumped into Roberto. We couldn't ignore one another as we were facing each other. "Hi Roberto," I greeted him, pleased to see him. "Hi, Anita" he replied giving me a hug. While my friend went to collect the tickets we had reserved, we chatted. "Long time no see, where have you been?" "Busy working," he replied, casually. He looked good and was totally sober. "Are you coming dancing after the gig?" I asked, hoping he would say yes. "Of course, we'll see you upstairs later," he replied, enthusiastically. Ronnie Scott's had a salsa dancing club on the first floor, so after any jazz concert you could go upstairs to dance without having to pay extra.

We met up again later and danced until the club closed. It was then that he told me more about the girlfriend; how she had managed to leave Chile, after a traumatic time in prison. Their meeting in Bond Street had been very emotional, but they decided not to keep in touch for obvious reasons. However, two months previously, four years after they last saw each other, she contacted him again to say she had divorced her husband, who was also a Chilean refugee. I sensed that Roberto was beginning to have hope for the relationship again, so I asked him how he felt about the new situation. "Delighted, delighted!" he said laughing. But he had the same sad eyes now as he had when we first met, even though he was laughing.

Going back to my life in La Paz, my parents began to relax and cut the umbilical cord. I had more freedom to stay out late studying with friends, or having fun with them. My university commitments took up most of my time, anyway. This was the time when I met two former school friends again. Although we had not been close at school, we became friends now, as we were all studying medicine. These girls were both attractive and intelligent; they would always get the best grades and praise from the lecturers. I stuck to them like glue, hoping that their intelligence would be contagious and I would get that most desirable disease, the knowledge of medicine. The girls were good fun; we often went partying and enjoyed every minute of it.

At the same time my relationship with Rafael was becoming more serious. We saw each other almost every day and spoke on the phone for hours at night while we studied in our homes. When we were together we felt the hours passed faster and faster and the days were getting shorter and shorter. An inevitable and uncontrollable force was transforming our young, innocent love and taking over our private world. For us, holding hands, kissing and hugging were insufficient expressions of affection. We felt a vital need to share other forms of closeness and intimacy.

The Illegal Dance

I was eighteen years old when an unforeseen event changed my life. It was about seven in the evening when Rafael phoned me at home. "I want to see you immediately. Meet me in ten minutes outside your place!" he demanded. His voice sounded worried. "It's raining; don't you want to come in?" I asked. "No, I need to talk to you alone; it's urgent!" He probably didn't want to be interrupted by my parents, so I agreed to go down and meet him outside the building.

Trying to protect himself from the rain, he stood in a small entrance in front of my building. He was looking thoughtful, concerned, slightly stooped, and holding his books under his arm as he usually did. As soon as he saw me he straightened up. "Let's walk!" he said. It was a cold and rainy evening, not really one for walking, but I didn't argue, I just followed him.

We walked towards the local plaza, but before we got there he stopped and sat on a window ledge. Without saying anything, he produced an envelope from inside one of his books. He opened it, took out a piece of paper and handed it to me. I don't know if it was the rain that blurred my eyes or what I read that made me dizzy, but I couldn't see properly. I didn't understand what I was reading or perhaps didn't want to understand or accept that the piece of paper I was staring at was my pregnancy test results. I had missed my period a month before and had mentioned this to Rafael. He offered to take a urine sample to a laboratory and collect the results himself to avoid gossip and damage to my reputation.

I don't really recall how, when and where it all started. Perhaps it was already fated on the evening we met in Coroico, under the umbrella of that romantic palm tree, listening to the songs of the bush crickets. Or perhaps it was one of those cold, rainy nights in La Paz. Who knows? It actually didn't really matter. I just remembered how an intense desire for one another began to escalate as time passed. We made love everywhere we could; on the stairs of the building where I lived; in the garage where I kept my car; inside the car or his; or at the studio where Rafael use to retreat to draw and write poems. It was anywhere and everywhere with no awareness of time or place and without fear, without reproach. We breathed love, we ate love and we drank love, until the inevitable had to happen.

That evening the sky was crying over the unexpected news for which neither of us was prepared. Perhaps we had felt untouchable by God, by nature, or by life itself. Perhaps we felt that what we were doing wasn't ever going to culminate in the creation of life. Why hadn't we anticipated this and taken precautions? It is hard to know. This miscalculation must have been the product of our youth, or our total irresponsibility and ignorance, or even an unconscious desire to see the fruit of our love. I don't know and perhaps I will never know.

I looked at him, stunned, without questions and without answers. Silence crippled us; neither of us knew what to say or what to do. Raphael spoke at last, but his voice sounded more like a whisper, delicate and soft, as if he didn't want to hurt or damage me further by what he was about to say. "We are too young; we are both still students. I would love to marry you but...." I knew what was coming, so I didn't need to hear it. But I stayed there motionless with the rain mingling with my tears, knowing that Raphael was probably right. "Don't worry, I'll make sure everything is fine. I'll look for a surgeon to perform the abortion; I shall pay for the operation, so you don't have to worry about anything." He spoke as if he had worked it all out in his mind already while he was waiting for me outside my home.

Bolivia is a devoutly Catholic country, so this type of procedure was totally forbidden and illegal. Every abortion had to be carried out in secret and in those days cost a lot of money. However, the price came down if the operation was carried out by an unqualified person, such as a medical student or an untrained amateur. I once heard from my father about the daughter of a colleague who had had an abortion done by a quack; he had pierced the uterus and the girl bled to death. One common procedure used was with herbal abortifacients, but these could be risky with an incorrect dose.

"Please don't tell your parents anything," he said. We held each other for a few minutes in complete silence. I didn't feel fear, anger or guilt; I felt numb.

It soon proved impossible to keep our secret. On special occasions, such as Christmas or my birthday, Rafael would write letters or poems for me, which often referred to our lovemaking. I kept all his messages in a wooden box in my bedroom, together with any presents he gave me. A few days after we found out about my pregnancy, my mother found the box and read the correspondence. There was no point in coming up with false explanations or lies; our affair had been revealed in copious poetic notes, written by hand in meticulous detail.

His poems described everything we had done from the first time we began to explore each other's naked and abandoned bodies, tasting the juices of our excitement. Sometimes our lovemaking culminated in total penetration as a result of an overwhelming and unavoidable force which descended upon each of us, making us lose control of all those rigid rules on which we had been educated. At other times, we were satisfied to indulge in foreplay, like two dancing cranes, displaying our sexuality, but only stimulating our erotic senses and desires for the promise of more to come.

His poems and letters were incriminating evidence that proved my complete rejection of my puritanical, Catholic upbringing. I was no longer the sweet and innocent girl who ran around catching butterflies. Neither was I the respectable girl my parents had brought up with so much love and dedication. If the spiders I brought home in Coroico gave my mother heart palpitations, this revelation almost killed her.

She kept control of herself until my father came home, but then both of them confronted me with the full force of their anger and distress. My father was usually a happy and placid man who was not worried about anything. He was well-adjusted, always joking and looked on the bright side of life. He had a cool temperament and would always think before he acted; a man who would advise people in their moments of crisis or despair. This time, however, my father was a different person; an enraged man, possessed by disappointment and bitterness.

He struck me so hard with his hand, the blow destabilised me and I fell to the floor, where I got more beatings. "What have you done, what have you done?" He screamed with indignation, hitting me time and time again. I tried to protect myself, but it didn't help. In a blind rage he kept attacking me, pulling my hair and slapping my face. Finally, in a moment of sanity, his assault on me stopped. He probably realised that he might kill me if he carried on. He looked at my mother and said, "I knew it! I knew he was not to be trusted. I would rather sit in prison than see that bastard walking the streets!"

He went to his bedroom and opened the wardrobe, the mirror inside reflected his face distorted with anger. From one of the drawers he took out a gun, which a few weeks previously a family friend had tried to borrow in order to kill his wife. The man had come to our home one evening in total despair because his wife had run away with her lover, leaving him to look after their two little children. Dad had talked to him calmly and persuaded him not to do anything for the sake of the children; he refused to give him the gun.

There was no one to calm my father down. He put the pistol in his trouser pocket, threw on his jacket and left the flat. "I'm going to kill that bastard!" he hissed, closing the door before my mother had chance to stop him. Mum was a kind woman, an excellent mother, totally dedicated to her children. She was gentle and loving; even her voice sounded like a soft melody. But when she had to discipline us she was as hard as nails. She did not come to console me, or to see how badly I was hurt. Yes, she was crying too but unforgiving. What I had done was too much for them to comprehend. They didn't expect this from me. They had put all their energy into bringing up a decent girl. They gave me a great education that many other children never received. They gave my brothers and me a good, stable and loving home. They gave me everything I wanted; all I had to do was ask. How dare I repay them like this? My mother was mortified, crying inconsolably, saying how stupid I was to have ruined my life and my father's, too. I had never seen my parents so angry and upset before. Seeing my father like a wounded dog maltreated by his master hurt me more than the beating he gave me. I was ashamed to see my mother humiliated by the dishonour of her only daughter. For days afterwards I was confined to my bedroom; I was not allowed to go out or make any contact with Rafael. My parents hardly spoke to me; I would only come out of my bedroom for meals. I don't know if my little brother knew what was happening, or if my mother had simply told him to keep an eye on me, but every time I tried to use the telephone he would tell Mum.

One day I was left alone for a while, so I took the opportunity to call Rafael. I warned him that my father was going out to work every day with a gun in his pocket. The university where Rafael studied was on my father's way to work and I was getting more and more worried about his intentions. Dad was so furious that he was capable of anything at this stage. Rafael decided that the best thing to do was to come round to my house to talk to my parents and face up to the consequences of his actions. At around eight that evening he turned up and, surprisingly, my father didn't shoot him. They sat down in the living room for about three hours to discuss my future without involving me in the decisions. I was not allowed to participate in the meeting.

They never asked me what I wanted or how I felt about it. I had no say in the matter; I just had to obey.

In retrospect I don't think I knew what I wanted. Maybe this was because I wasn't asked, so I didn't even bother to think about what was best for me. I let them sort it all out. It was easier and less painful. I never knew until many years later what was really discussed that evening. A few days later I was taken to a private clinic for the abortion that was to terminate the life I was carrying in my uterus.

Everything happened quickly; an injection put me to sleep and then like magic my whole world went black. When I woke up my parents were sat at my bedside. Rafael occupied a chair in a corner of the room and in front of me was the surgeon. "You can go home any time you are ready, everything is fine," he said, feeling proud of his work. It was the perfect surgical procedure without causing any apparent lasting damage. I didn't answer him as I couldn't have cared less about my state of health; not waking up would also have been a good option. I waited for my parents and Rafael to make the decision about when to take me home.

Rafael was allowed to visit me the next day. He came with a bunch of flowers and a present. He was always so loving and kind to me, but also possessive and over protective, a bit like my father. I think there was a certain rivalry between them. He looked drawn and defeated that day, guilty to have put me in that situation. He didn't say anything; he just sat quietly on my bed holding my hand, his tearful, sad eyes saying more than any words he might have spoken. I am sure we both thought that one day we would have another opportunity to have a child.

CHAPTER NINE

*"Promise me you'll never forget me
because if I thought you would, I'd never leave"*

A. A. Milne

A month or two passed by without further incident. I went back to university and everything seemed to have reverted to normal. My parents didn't stop me seeing Rafael from time to time, which I greatly appreciated, but it was clear that from now on we were going to have to be more sensible. Rafael threw himself into his books and architectural drawings and I was just pleased that the whole ordeal had come to an end without more complications. Little did I know at the time that what was about to come was going to hit me even harder.

One day, my father came home from work in a cheerful mood. It was lunchtime, and we were sitting at the dinner table ready to eat when he took an envelope from his pocket. "This is for you," he said. I looked at it without any fear of more bad news. It came from Dad, so why should I be afraid? I opened the envelope and to my surprise, it contained a plane ticket to Sweden. "Sweden?" I asked in disbelief. "What I am going to do in Sweden?" I was angry because I had not been consulted about this at all. "You are going to study there," he said, very sure of what he was doing and certain it was the right thing for me. "What about university?" I asked him. "University is a waste of time in this country; you will never finish the course the way things are going. The political situation is deteriorating so quickly I can assure you that in a few months' time they will close it again." He was soon proved right. The constant instability in Bolivia was disrupting the educational system.

I wanted to ask him about Rafael, but didn't. To mention his name would have provoked a heated argument. But the distress on my face was too much for my father to ignore. "If you stay here you will end up getting married without doing anything with your life. At least you should travel before that happens," he said. It was so cleverly and carefully put that I could not refuse his offer.

Mum and I spent the next few days getting my documentation together. Two weeks before my departure, Rafael came to see me at home. I had not yet told him anything about Sweden because I was hoping that at the last minute something might happen to prevent me going at all. God knows what I expected, perhaps a coup d'état to prevent me leaving the country. But there were no changes, and I had to tell Rafael.

"I'm going to Sweden for a short holiday," I said to him as though Sweden was just around the corner. He didn't believe me at first, but when he saw the plane ticket he went mad; he demanded I destroy it. "Tear it up, tear it up, you are not going anywhere!" Then he rattled off questions. "Do you even know where Sweden is? Do you realise how far away it is? Have you even bothered to look in the atlas to see where they are sending you, you silly girl? Why are they sending you there? What about us?' He went on and on, feeling powerless and frustrated. He could not understand why my parents were doing this.

After a while he calmed down and tried to reason with me in a last attempt to make me see sense. "Listen," he said. "It is too dangerous for you over there; you are too young, too vulnerable to go to Europe. Don't go! We will get married as soon as I finish university, but don't go! What are you going to do with all those moronic Vikings anyway?" He mocked me, trying to convince me that Sweden was not a country for me and to make me react against my parents' authority, but I sat impassively and said nothing. It was easier to do what my parents wanted to avoid more problems. I promised him that I was going to go for no longer than a year. "A year goes quickly Rafael, I promise just one year," I said.

Before leaving, annoyed and irritated, he looked at me straight in my eyes and said, "I hope one day then, in Europe, you will learn how to say the word NO." He probably thought he had a girlfriend without a backbone; a stupid girl who would do whatever other people wanted her to. He was right, that was me and that was also the reason why going abroad was perhaps the right thing for me to do at the time. I didn't want to go, but this was my opportunity to learn to say "NO" somewhere else, away from the domineering, influence of both my parents and Rafael.

My departure was scheduled for the seventh of May. The flight was via Lima, Peru and then on to Switzerland, where my brother José would be waiting for me to continue on to Denmark by train and then across the Baltic Sea to Malmö, Sweden by boat. Nowadays there is an eight kilometre bridge carrying trains and road vehicles across the Oresund Strait.

My cousins and friends organised a farewell tea party for the Saturday before my departure. After tea, one of the girls came up with the brilliant idea of drinking some alcohol; we dug into her father's drinks cabinet to get some booze and the real party started then and there. We drank and drank and in less than an hour we could hardly walk or stand up. I felt that the room was going round and round. We were losing our balance while we danced and started slurring our speech; then our initial euphoria turned into sadness and depression. I remember being stuck in the toilet, vomiting everything I had in my stomach. One girl was sick in the bath and another one threw up in the sink; it was absolutely chaotic.

My cousin Lily, who was the most sensible and had never been drunk in her life, was lying on the floor. She had tried to keep her balance by holding on to the curtains, but they had come down on top on her. Cousin Lisa was crying on the sofa. There were broken glasses everywhere, and chairs overturned on the carpet. It was a disastrous scene that was also very funny. I was far too drunk to drive, so somebody called Rafael to come and pick us up. One by one he carried us to my car and ferried us home. He did a few round trips until everybody was safely transported back to their houses.

When he was driving me home, he stopped the car and tried to wake me up. "Ana, Ana, listen, I have something to tell you." I was too drunk to listen or care. I could hardly open my eyes, never mind have a conversation. He persisted, but I only heard words, "I … Lima … airport … tomorrow … wait …" These words didn't mean anything to me at the time. I just said, "yes, fine," without knowing what he was talking about. The next thing I remember is hearing my mother's voice when we got home. "Oh my God, oh my God, what happened?" she asked, probably thinking I had tried to commit suicide. Rafael was carrying me in his arms, my head hung to one side. "She is drunk," he said. He took me to my bed but before he left he whispered in my ear, "don't forget, just wait for me." As he was about to leave I started screaming, "don't go, don't leave me, don't leave me, please!" I think my screams and shouts could be heard out in the street. I didn't want to let him go. I got hold of his arm and I wouldn't let go. "No, no don't go, don't go. Don't leave me, please!" I was desperately screaming, hoping he would stay with me forever.

He managed to release himself from my grasp and left. The separation produced the most terrible agony. The effects of the alcohol had intensified and confused my feelings. I had the sensation of being torn apart. It was unbearable; every part of my body hurt. The memories of my abortion and my imminent departure had made me face my situation, one of total and awful pain. My poor mother didn't know what to do or say when she saw me in that state. There was nothing that could calm me down. I was in total despair emotionally; I didn't want anything but Rafael with me. Perhaps she began to think it was a mistake to send me away.

I had a terrible hangover the next day. I felt like an old rug; I could hardly lift myself from bed. My head was still going round in circles and I kept running to the toilet to vomit. None of the remedies my mother gave me helped. I had no memory of the night before; in fact, I wanted to forget everything, even the fact that I was alive. I slept almost all day. At around eight at night, my mother woke me up to have some dinner. I sat down on my bed to eat a bit and, with some food in my stomach, my memory came back. "Airport ... Lima ... wait," I tried to make sense of the words. I went back to sleep thinking about Rafael.

The next morning I woke up feeling better, but it was a cold day. La Paz is always cold and uncomfortable in the mornings. Outside, people were rushing to work, pedestrians crossing streets anywhere but at zebra crossings. The traffic was horrendous, chaotic and the noise of the car horns of frustrated drivers was typical of a disorganised, unsophisticated city. Bolivian drivers think that by sounding their horns incessantly, other cars will disappear, to leave the streets empty for them. My parents were also in a hurry that morning as they were taking me to the airport.

Throughout the journey my mother regaled me with travel advice, which I hardly paid attention to as Rafael's words were still in my mind. We got to El Alto, a city situated in the highlands on the periphery of La Paz. On my left I looked down to La Paz for the last time. I couldn't help but notice the magnificent Mount Illimani, dominating in the background. "I should have drunk water from *El Chawi* fountain and stayed in Coroico," I thought to myself. It was my first time travelling abroad on my own, so I felt uneasy.

We eventually got to El Alto airport. Farewells are usually sad, dramatic and stressful, and this goodbye was no exception. Mum was crying; Dad made sure I had all the correct documentation. I tried to reassure them and unconsciously reassured myself that everything would be fine. I walked for the first time towards that big machine with its arms open, waiting patiently to be filled with passengers. I sat down on the left side of the plane, hoping I would not panic and change my mind before it took off. Half an hour later we were in the air. I looked through the little window and Mount Illimani appeared again between the clouds. Its imperious look made me feel small, scared and defenceless. I shivered before its formidable appearance and asked for its forgiveness for deserting my beloved country. I asked for its blessing and protection, and promised the mountain that I was going to come back soon.

Two hours later we landed at Lima airport; I was not sure what to expect. I thought of Rafael's words again. "Wait for me," he had said, but he hadn't said where and for how long. I collected my luggage and walked towards the main hall, looking around hoping to see his familiar face. Lima was my stopover for a night before continuing my journey the next day. I thought of the lie I had told my mother to give her peace of mind. "I am

The Illegal Dance

going to stay at a friend's place in Lima." But that friend didn't exist. I sat down in the waiting room with only my luggage for company, thinking about Rafael. I gradually began to piece together what he had told me the evening he picked me up after my farewell party. "I couldn't stand saying goodbye to you in front of all your family, I will see you at Lima airport; I will try to get there somehow, just wait for me please." When Rafael and I lived in La Paz and arranged to meet somewhere, he would always say to me, "just wait for me please; I will come even if I am late." He would never let me down and would always turn up sooner or later.

Long hours passed and there was still no sign of him. There was no way to communicate with him as, in those days, we did not have mobile phones. I began to get anxious not knowing what to do. My thoughts went back to the evening I had drunk alcohol like no other time in my life. The evening I wanted to forget all about my sins and the sins of others. It was then that I realised for the first time that the only person who really mattered to me was Rafael. So I didn't care how long I had to wait. I sat patiently without a book or a magazine to help me kill the time. I remembered with a start that I had promised to call my parents as soon as I met my non-existent friend in Lima. But I didn't dare get up from my seat to look for a phone in case Rafael came and I wasn't in an obvious place. I wasn't sure whether he was coming on the next flight or by another means of transport. The place I was sitting seemed perfect as it was just in front of the main entrance. I could see clearly people coming in or going out, so I decided not to move. I watched carefully anyone who passed by, so I didn't miss him among the crowd.

After a long wait, maybe six hours, I saw someone coming towards me, the sun backlighting his outline, so I couldn't see his face properly from the front. As he got inside the airport main door I saw a virile young man covered in dust. At last, this was

Rafael, late as ever, but true to his promise. I ran towards him overwhelmed with joy.

"There is a taxi waiting for us outside." He guided me towards the car, picking up my luggage. "Quick, get in," he said. He told the driver to take us to any bed and breakfast. Happy and relieved to see me, he said, "I want to show you this city before it gets too dark."

While the taxi driver was looking for suitable accommodation, Rafael told me how he had travelled to Lima, feeling excited and proud of his heroic deed. "I left La Paz the next day after your farewell party and took a bus to Lake Titicaca. From there I took a steam boat to Puno; I slept on the bow of the boat. In Puno I took a bus to Juliaca and then another bus to Arequipa, where I slept one night. The next day, as early as I could, I took another bus to Lima bus station and then a taxi to the airport." "Why didn't you fly to Lima?" I asked, wondering why he had gone to all that trouble. "I didn't have enough money, so I took the cheapest route," he said. I had to admit it was a lovely gesture that reassured and nourished my spirit.

After a quick shower we went out looking for adventure, like two crazy lovers on a holiday to last forever. Rafael led the way to the sights of the city; we walked excitedly around the streets of Lima. We reached the place where the Spanish conquistadors had left their mark, in the old colonial part of the city. *La Plaza Mayor* or *Plaza de Armas* is where the Spanish forces of power and arrogance had clashed face to face. It is the place where the savage conqueror Francisco Pizarro met his death at the hands of one of his own kind, the Spaniard Diego de Almagro, who took over the rule of Peru. In the 17th century, *La Plaza Mayor* was also the location where the Spanish Inquisition chose to burn people they thought were witches or other heretics.

We were thrilled to be in a city that I had never seen before and to have a feeling of total freedom. Rafael was full of

The Illegal Dance

enthusiasm and ideas. "I want us to go to a restaurant to eat the famous Peruvian dish, ceviche, I want to show you the ocean tomorrow; I want to be the first person to see the sea with you," he said while we were having dinner. His impulsive attitude gave me the impression that he wanted to show me everything he could in one day so my ignorance wasn't so obvious when I arrived in Europe and that nothing that I was to do later in life was going to be more exciting or more important than these moments with him.

Bolivia lost its coastline in 1879 in a brutal war with Chile. The conflict started when Chile invaded Bolivian territory because Bolivia had imposed a tax on nitrate exported by the Antofagasta Nitrate Company, a Chilean concern. Chile claimed it had the right to twenty five years of exploiting the mineral tax free. At the time, Chile was going through a difficult economic period, the country being pressurised by Britain, which was also pressing a claim over the nitrate for fertilisers and explosives. Chile didn't accept the imposed tax, all diplomatic negotiations failed and the war started.

Ever since that time, most Bolivians have only seen the immense ocean in films. When I was at school, the teacher would make us draw or sing songs about the Pacific. People often say that you do not miss or wish for things that you never had. This may be so, but we Bolivians were once owners of part of the Pacific coast and it is difficult to give up what was once ours. For Rafael and me it was important to see the sea together.

That night we walked aimlessly through the noisy streets of Lima. A few days before there had been elections in Peru. The squares were filled with people, some expressing joy and others discontent about the winner, Fernando Belaunde. After we had absorbed the political atmosphere we returned to the hostel. There among the fragile silence in the dark room, we loved each other once more.

The next day we got up early and made our way towards the port of El Callao, not far from central Lima. We walked through the aristocratic area of Miraflores, where the famous writer Mario Vargas Llosa lived. We felt a refreshing breeze in that hot and humid climate as we approached the port. The infinite sea in front of me gave me a feeling of never ending life and love. Holding hands, we walked slowly along the path of a lonely rocky cliff. The immense Pacific Ocean looked abandoned and unkempt; it had a dirty foamy black mass around its edges. A solitary Peruvian pelican flew above us. Later in the afternoon we arrived at the airport. There was a group of Bolivian musicians called *Los Kjarkas* who were travelling on the same flight. We approached them to make friends; Rafael asked if they would look after me during the flight. It became clear that this was also their first trip abroad, so they were as anxious and afraid as I was. Years later, these musicians travelled the globe, becoming famous all over the world.

We had nothing left to say to each other; we had said it all. It was time for me to leave Rafael behind, but before passing the point of no return I gave him thirty letters I had written. They were all love letters in which I said how much I loved him, how much I wanted to be with him soon, again and forever. The letters begged him to wait for me and to never forget me. "Read one every day Rafael," I asked him. "By the time you have read them all, you will have received more from me," I said. We hugged and kissed each other for the last time. He was quiet, thoughtful, a slight disconcerting smile without words appeared on his lips. This time it was me who was putting on a brave face and doing the talking. "Wait for me Rafael please, just wait for me. I will be back soon," I said walking away from him.

CHAPTER TEN

"Things are never quite as scary when you've got a good friend"

Bill Watterson

Little did I know that my flight to Sweden would lead to such a difficult time in London. Two days after that miserable and wet night in the streets, I got a new job. Froilan and I used the same method as before. We bought a newspaper and made calls from a public phone to arrange interviews; this time the process seemed easier. Mr and Mrs Barton were an elderly couple who needed an au pair. They explained the terms and conditions of the job to Froilan over the phone and that they wanted to see me for an interview without delay. It sounded like the perfect job for me. There were no children and the couple were retired, which I hoped would mean I would have more time to study English and they would have time to talk to me so I could practise the language that I needed to learn so much. I got the job and moved in the next day. It was a magnificent place in Hampstead, one of the most expensive areas of London. On one side of Hampstead Lane, all the houses had large, well-kept front gardens, on the other side there was a huge wild area, Hampstead Heath. The locals called it the "Lung of London." This fantastic green space gave me the feeling of living in Coroico.

The house was detached and spacious. In the entrance hall a wooden staircase created a stunning centrepiece, with a tall wide window facing the back garden. It had two lovely, tastefully decorated sitting rooms. I saw myself enjoying a cup of tea in their English-style lounge, sitting in front of their elegant fireplace, appreciating their gold-plated mirror, which was situated above it, or sitting next to the French windows facing the garden. On the other side of the hall was a large kitchen diner and another big dining room, which was beautifully furnished with antiques. Sumptuous burgundy fitted carpet covered the floors, giving a warm and welcoming effect. Elegant lamps hanging from the ceilings matched perfectly the classic and aristocratic décor. Silver and crystal ornaments had been placed carefully on shelves; other pieces brought from China, Japan and India were positioned on top of expensive, stylish furniture around the house. The Bartons lived some distance from my school and I needed to take two buses to get to my class, but it didn't matter. I was delighted to have found a good job and a lovely place to live.

The first morning Mrs Barton and I got up at seven o'clock; she was going to show me how to prepare their breakfast. "We like to have porridge every morning," she stated, showing me how to do it. "You must make sure it is not too thick and not too watery either," she explained, while whisking the porridge. "In the meantime, you must place white bread in the toaster and put the kettle on for a cup of tea, so everything is ready at once."

She sounded very posh and a little bit bossy. "The tea pot must be prewarmed, then you must put the tea and the hot water in the pot and don't forget to cover it to keep it warm," she said, picking up a tea cosy that was hanging on a hook on one side of the kitchen. "When the porridge is ready, it goes in the bowls; the toast should be put in the toast holder, the butter and marmalade in the dishes and there you have it." She picked up the breakfast tray and placed it in my hands to take it upstairs to their bedroom. I wobbled a bit with the weight; it felt like my knees were going to give way, but I followed her upstairs, making sure not to drop anything on her beautiful carpet. For the rest of the morning she showed me how to clean the whole house, how to iron the clothes and explained to me the rules of the house in meticulous detail.

In the early evening on my return from school, I saw Mr Barton sitting in the small lounge. "Good evening, Mr Barton," I said, on my way in. "Hello, hello," he replied inviting me to watch television. I accepted his invitation and joined him. Although I was tired and had a headache, I hoped that this would be an opportunity to start practising my English. I sat down in front of him and he turned the volume down a little to talk to me. "How was school today young lady?" he said, cheerfully. "Good," I replied immediately. I then tried to say a bit more, but he didn't understand me. I repeated myself and he replied, "oh! I see, I see." He then said something I didn't understand, so he repeated it but I still didn't get his meaning. He tried to explain once more, but to no avail. Eventually he gave up and turned the volume of the television back up again. Unfortunately that was the end of our conversation.

The next day I got up sneezing and had a sore throat. I went downstairs to prepare their breakfast. A few minutes later I brought it all upstairs. Mrs Barton complained that the porridge was too thick, the tea too cold and the toast was burnt. She asked me politely, but firmly to do it all over again. At the second attempt she ate all her breakfast, but complained later that it was not as she expected. By the end of the day I felt even worse. I began to have chills, a runny nose and a throbbing headache. I decided not to go to school and went to bed straight after lunch. I woke up in the middle of the night to go to the toilet. All the house lights were off, everybody was sleeping. I walked to the loo, trying not to make any noise, shivering and feeling unwell. Without turning on the toilet lights I tried to pass water. A burning sensation got hold of me and made me double up in pain. I went back to bed, but immediately wanted to go to the toilet again. This time I felt the sharp pain again when passing urine. I spent all night going backwards and forwards from my bed to the toilet. I didn't have any tablets to take, not even paracetamol. I was still shivering and found a thick jumper in my luggage and put it on, but I was still feeling cold. I got up the next day in a really bad state and went down to the kitchen to prepare their breakfast, running from time to time to the toilet. Mrs Barton was not happy again; the porridge was too thick, so she came down to do it herself. I started to clean the house. Every movement was an effort and every attempt I made to do the job properly was making me feel worse. After finishing for the day I went to bed again, but could not sleep; there was constant pain in my bladder and I made frequent trips to the toilet.

In the middle of the afternoon Mr and Mrs Barton went out, so I made a quick telephone call to Sweden to ask my Aunt Betty what I should do. She recommended I drink camomile tea. "You probably have cystitis," she said. "What's that?" I asked, worried. "It's an infection of the bladder," she replied. "You sometimes get this if you use dirty toilets. It gets worse if the weather is cold." I didn't want to tell her I had spent a night in a car in the middle of London. I put the phone down and went to the kitchen to look for camomile tea, but there wasn't any. I didn't feel well enough

The Illegal Dance

to go out to look for some in a shop, so I called Froilan at his work. He didn't answer, so I left a message and went back to bed. That night I felt worse than the night before. The urgency to pass water was becoming more frequent and the burning and stinging sensations felt like electric shocks all over my body. My lower back started to hurt and I even felt pain in my scalp as I tried unsuccessfully to pee.

The next day was a Saturday. I hoped in vain that Froilan would return my call. My employers were expecting their son, Mark and daughter-in-law for lunch, so Mrs Barton was busy preparing it in the kitchen while I tried to help her. My backache limited my movements and I found it difficult to walk. I felt so unwell that lying down was the only thing I wanted to do. Mark and his wife arrived; it was time for lunch. The family were seated at the beautiful antique table in the dining room. Mrs Barton was with me in the kitchen, preparing the dishes when she asked me to pass her the pepper. I misunderstood her request and passed her the salt. She suddenly lost her temper and yelled, "the pepper, the pepper, the pepper!" Mrs Barton's cry for help sounded so desperate and full of frustration that Mark came running into the kitchen to pass her the pepper. He returned to the dining room and a few minutes later came back to the kitchen to invite me to eat with them. "No thanks, I'd rather eat in the kitchen," I excused myself in an agonised tone of voice. I didn't want to disturb their lunch with my constant need to get up to go to the toilet. "Are you ok?" he asked in Spanish, to my surprise. "Yes, I'm ok thanks," I replied in my mother tongue, with as much of a smile as I could muster.

I had my lunch alone, getting up when I needed to use the lavatory. Later on I helped them to clear away everything. While they sat in the living room for tea, I went into the garden, sat down on a comfortable wooden chair feeling the cold breeze of early autumn and the tender touch of a dying sun. I was suddenly in Coroico, walking down the road on my way to school catching strange insects for my collection, without pain, just free and happy. Suddenly I heard a Spanish voice with an English accent. "Are you ok, are you ok?" I opened my tired eyes from the sleepless night. The palms of my hands were sweating, but I was still feeling cold from my general sickness. "Are you ok?" Mark asked me again. "No, I don't feel well," I admitted. "I'm not surprised; you don't look at all well. You were talking in your sleep, I think you are a bit delirious," he said. "It must be a fever," I thought to myself. "Do you need any help? I'm going to town now if you want a lift anywhere I'm happy to take you," he said kindly. "Can you take me to my friend Froilan?" I asked him. "Yes, of course." A few minutes later Mark, his wife Carol and I went to Froilan's house in Kilburn. They left me at the front door and continued on their way. I rang the bell a couple of times, but there was no answer. After waiting a few minutes I realised I had made a terrible mistake in not asking them to take me to the hospital instead. It was a mistake that cost me dearly later.

I left Froilan a note to call me as soon as possible, went to a shop to get paracetamol and returned to the Bartons' house almost unable to stand upright. There was a pub called the Spaniards near the house. I thought to myself, "surely this bar must be Spanish." Thanks to the paracetamol I managed to sleep a little that night dreaming of beautiful and seductive girls dancing Flamenco and Sevillanas at the Spaniards pub.

The next day, Sunday, I waited all day for Froilan to call, but he didn't. Later that evening, I decided to go to the pub in the hope of meeting some Spanish people. "They may know of a doctor around this area," I thought, thinking of how easy it was for me to get medical help in Bolivia. My father would simply make a call and a doctor would come any time, day or night. However, if you are poor and live in the countryside there is no chance of receiving medical help, so many people die due to lack of medical attention.

The Illegal Dance

Every step I took was an effort; the pain in my bladder and lower back was making me walk very slowly. In addition, the symptoms of a bad cold were making me act very clumsily. I dragged myself towards the pub, hopeful that I would meet somebody who would help me. It wasn't a long walk, but it seemed like miles to me at the time. When I finally got there I realised it was full of English people, with neither Flamenco dancers nor Sevillanas in sight. I went back home to the Bartons', hoping that Froilan would soon call me. It was only years later that I found out that the Spaniards pub was built in the late 16th century as a country house for a Spanish ambassador.

The following day Mrs Barton asked me to call my friend as she seemed to have realised how ill and inefficient I was. She handed me the phone. "Call him, now!" she ordered, arrogantly. She became even more irritable when she found out that Froilan didn't reply. I left another voice message for him before continuing my duties. I retired later on to my bedroom, which was my only refuge. I wasn't going to be able to go to school that day or any other day if I didn't get well soon.

In the early evening a knock on my door from Mrs Barton got me out of bed. She had come to deliver a speech. From her tone of voice and the expression on her face I knew she was unhappy with me. She talked endlessly without making any gestures. Her hands and arms were passive and expressionless, not like Latin people who move the whole of their body when they have something to say. At that moment I knew my days were numbered in her house. I was not going to have any more cups of tea in her regal lounge, facing the garden. I nodded my head pretending to understand what she was saying, but my English was not yet good enough to get more than the gist of it.

The evening that followed was terrible. I began to have earache; I took my last paracetamol, but it didn't help. The dreadful pain extended all the way down to my jaws and teeth and my throat felt painful and dry. I felt dizzy, nauseous, and thirsty and could not even get out of bed; just my thoughts roamed the kitchen in search of water. The constant pain like electric shocks wouldn't let me get up to use the toilet. I folded a towel to use as a nappy and soon noticed blood in my urine. Nothing could keep me warm; I was fully dressed but still shivering.

I cried bitterly that night, like an orphan abandoned by her mother. I yearned for my parents to help me by passing me a hot drink or getting me a doctor. I must have dozed a little in the morning, as I remember dreaming that I was playing in the cemetery in Coroico. I dreamt that dead bodies came out of their graves to embrace me and, once I was in their arms, they tried to drag me into their tombs. I fought with them not to be buried alive, but they pulled me down into the ground. I felt the dry soil in my mouth and the bright sun blinding my eyes so badly that I couldn't see their faces. I tried to scream, but had no voice. I woke up suddenly to a knock on my door that sounded so loud I thought the house had collapsed.

The door opened wide to reveal Mrs Barton standing there in her dressing gown with her hair all over the place and a frown on her face. She looked grim and ugly and had a scar on her right cheek that I had not noticed before. Her bared teeth were stained with the coffee she had just drunk that morning. She spat out bits and pieces of porridge from her mouth as she screamed at me. Her tired, devil eyes, bulged out of their sockets and stared at me with hate. "Was she the corpse that was trying to bury me alive?" I thought, still feeling groggy and not completely awake. I didn't know what was going on; she didn't give me time to apologise for my failure to prepare breakfast. She opened the wardrobe, took out my suitcase and screamed furiously, "out, out, out!" I rose from the bed like a zombie and staggered around the room like a drunk, tripping over my clothes that were all over the floor. I picked them up and put them in my suitcase, together with other

The Illegal Dance

clothes that were lying on the bed. I felt very weak; the suitcase was too heavy for me to carry. By dragging the case along the floor, I managed to lug it downstairs. I dropped it near the front door and pleaded with Mrs Barton to let me come back for it later; she reluctantly agreed. I left the house struggling to get to the bus stop, but the overwhelming feeling of wanting to pee made me run into the bushes.

A few minutes later, a bus arrived to take me to Froilan's place. Hoping he would be home, I got on and travelled to Golders Green, from where I took another bus to Kilburn. To my surprise he was in; it must have been around ten in the morning. "Take me to hospital," I urged him, as soon as he opened the front door. He looked surprised, his eyes wide open, when he saw me outside his door begging for help, curled up like a foetus trying to stop myself passing water yet again. He didn't say anything but just ran upstairs to get his car keys and drove me to St Mary's Hospital as fast as he could. Neither of us spoke a word until we arrived. "Go straight to Casualty, they will look after you there," he said, in an uncaring voice. I thought that was it, this was the last I would see of Froilan; he didn't even say if he was coming back for me. I got out of the car and staggered into the hospital. Somebody at a desk asked me for my name, before I collapsed on the floor and lost consciousness.

I woke up in a bed with curtains around me. A doctor was taking my temperature, pulse and blood pressure. Froilan was also there; he must have felt guilty and come back to the hospital or maybe he just went to park his car. The doctor asked me a few questions, which Froilan translated. "We are going to take urine and blood samples before you go home," he said. A few minutes later a nurse came and did a number of tests. I lay down again and she inserted a drip into my left arm. "You are very dehydrated," she said, drying the tears from my eyes with a tissue. She also helped me to take a pill with some water. "Relax, you will soon feel better;" she comforted me with a lovely smile, her white teeth contrasting against her dark skin. I thanked her for her kindness and reassurance.

Of course I was dehydrated; I had been trying not to drink anything to avoid having to go to the toilet all the time. I learned later on that you have to drink at least one litre of water a day to increase the flow of urine to flush out bacterial infections.

"I'm sorry, I didn't think you were that ill," Froilan spoke, feeling guilty now. "Why didn't you call me back at the house?" I asked him. "I didn't think it was that important," he replied. For the first time I began to see I was probably becoming a burden to him. He had promised my father that he would help me, without realising just how much responsibility was involved. He must have thought I was a grown up, independent girl, which at that time I wasn't; it took me a few years to appreciate how immature I had been.

A few hours later, we left the hospital with all the doctor's prescriptions and recommendations. We went back to Froilan's home and he cooked me one of the most delicious chicken soups I had eaten in my life. After lunch, I went to sleep and Froilan went to collect my suitcase yet again; this time from the Bartons' house. Two days later I was feeling much better and I again asked Froilan to help me get another job. We bought the newspaper and he glanced at it quickly. "There is nothing interesting here for you," he told me. The following day was the same message; he didn't find any adverts for a job as an au pair. I felt he was beginning to lose interest in helping me.

One evening in October, we were having dinner in his kitchen. He was in a good mood, laughing and chatting away. He seemed to have forgotten he had to go to work. At around nine I reminded him of the time. He looked at his watch and rose from the chair to get ready to leave. "See you tomorrow morning," he said, putting on his jacket. "Bye," I replied from the kitchen while doing the washing up. He went downstairs and closed the front door. A few minutes later I heard him coming back again, running up the stairs, two steps at a time. I was still in the kitchen when he got in, appearing very troubled; he looked at me suspiciously. I asked him if he had forgotten something, but he didn't answer. He went into the bedroom and searched around. As he didn't find whatever he was looking for, he walked towards the wall and punched it hard a couple of times. I was astonished to see him like that. "What's wrong Froilan?" I asked, standing between the bedroom and the landing, holding a plate and a kitchen towel in my hands; he didn't answer. "Leave the kitchen as it is and get into the bedroom," he shouted at me furiously. I followed his instructions meekly, while watching his eyes that had changed inexplicably into a suspicious and angry stare. He locked me in the bedroom and left. I heard him running downstairs and slamming the front door.

Feeling upset by his attitude I went to sleep in my makeshift bed made out of the two armchairs. Around seven in the morning he came back to the house, unlocked the door and went straight to bed. I woke up soon afterwards and went downstairs. When I came back I heard him screaming, "where did you go, where did you go?" "I went to the toilet," I replied, innocently. He began to tear things apart furiously. He tore his sheets, papers and magazines, which were strewn on the floor near his bed. I giggled at his over-the-top reaction. It looked funny to see him acting like that, but then he starting saying things that didn't make sense to me; I got worried and went quiet. "This country is very dangerous. The man next door is a drunk and can hurt you, people are bad in this city, the police could come anytime," he said. I didn't know what he was talking about. I had never seen the man next door, apart from on the day I first arrived when he had opened the door. As a matter of fact I thought he had moved. Surely Froilan was overreacting, I went back to sleep without saying anything.

Later that morning I went to my school and forgot all about Froilan's strange outburst. In the early afternoon he met me at school, holding the newspaper. "There is nothing for you in here," he said. We didn't even make one call that day to look for a job. He looked depressed, annoyed and disinterested. We went back to his place and had dinner. Once again he went to work leaving me locked in the bedroom. I turned on the television to distract my thoughts. Barry Manilow was singing "Copacabana" in a concert. I imagined myself in a nightclub on an open boat on the River Thames, dressed in glittering clothes, dancing away to "her name is Lola," with the stars lighting up the dark sky and the party. I didn't want to be stuck in this miserable, lonely and degrading room with a man I did not understand. When he returned in the morning, before he went to sleep he locked the bedroom door again, so I couldn't go to school. In the afternoons, he would go out for a few hours leaving me locked in my bedroom.

One morning, I caught him off guard. I offered to go out to buy potatoes while he was making lunch. He agreed, but on my return he was waiting outside the house for me impatiently. "Where were you? It took you more than twenty minutes to get just this? Where did you go?" He questioned me relentlessly. The more he asked me the more nervous I got. The changes in his behaviour were pretty unpredictable. Although I felt it was important to talk to him about his attitude I didn't know how to start. There was a long silence during lunch until Froilan began to speak. "I'm very worried about you. What would I tell your father if anything happened to you?" he said. I listened quietly to everything he said, thinking he might be right; perhaps he was just concerned about my welfare. Suddenly, however, his explanation went too far when he suggested it would be better if I married him. "You would be safer and I would feel better; I could even buy you a sewing machine." I swallowed a whole piece of meat that was in my mouth without chewing it. What he was saying to me seemed hilarious. I felt like laughing out loud, but I controlled myself not wanting to antagonise him. "Sewing machine?" I thought. "What would I do with a sewing machine?" If only he knew I couldn't even sew a button on to a shirt. He made the offer sound as if the sewing machine was going to make me the luckiest bride in London. A slight smile on my lips almost betrayed me. Pulling myself together I replied, "I am too young to marry anyone right now, Froilan." I didn't want to tell him that if I ever married anybody it was going to be Rafael.

Later that day I asked him to take me to see Doña Asuncion, the lady we met at Windsor Castle. He refused to do so, saying that she didn't want to see me. "What about Juan and his Spanish wife? Why don't we go to visit them?" I asked him. "None of them want anything to do with you anymore," he said. I kept silent wondering whether this was true or whether he was just trying to intimidate me.

It was a week since I had left the Bartons' house; a week without any serious possibility of getting another job. Froilan was behaving more and more strangely as the days passed, especially when I asked him to help me to find another job. There is nothing for you was his constant excuse. Myself, impotence was all I felt; the impotence of not be able to speak the language, of not be able to make my own calls and impotence for being so dependent.

The following Sunday morning I asked Froilan if we could go out somewhere. To my surprise he agreed and we went to visit some of his friends who lived outside London. Froilan had told me they were another Bolivian/Spanish couple, who worked as housekeepers in a country farmhouse for a wealthy English family. He drove his old car through lovely English countryside; the fields were covered with litter-free and carefully managed vegetation, with small hills and slopes that look like waves. I was just beginning to relax when he said something that sent shivers down my spine. "I think you should know that the police are looking for me." "Looking for you, why?" I asked casually, trying not to sound worried. "Well, they think I've killed a woman," he replied. "Killed a woman?" I repeated back to him, trying to keep calm until I had all the facts. "Yes, the police think I killed a woman. I'm telling you this because I don't want you to hear it from other people," he said, convincingly. "Did you do it?" I asked him, shocked by this unexpected revelation. "I'm not sure." "You're not sure? What do you mean?" I replied, by now very concerned. "It wasn't just me; there were other guys, too. We were at a party, drinking." Then he told me the police followed him everywhere he went. "Can you give me more details of how, when and where this happened?" I asked, trying to get more information. But he didn't want to talk about it anymore. I was so overwhelmed by this that I stayed quiet for the rest of the trip. I was restless and felt inner despair that I could not express. When we arrived at his friends' place, I didn't know what to talk to them about. I had no idea how much his friends knew about this. My thoughts were in a muddle; I felt very stressed and worried about what Froilan had just told me. I tried to reassure myself by thinking that he didn't seem to be someone capable of killing anyone. I wondered why he had suddenly come out with all this. Was he trying to scare me? Was he trying to warn me about his dark side? What was his intention in telling me this story? It all seemed surreal and awful.

In the early evening we went back to London; we ate a snack and then he told me to get ready, as I was going out with him again. "Going out? Where?" I asked, bewildered. It was almost ten at night and I was exhausted with everything that had happened. "I'm going to work and you're coming with me," he said. "No, I don't want to go." I tried to resist, but he insisted I was going with him whether I liked it or not. "Bring the blanket that's on my bed and wear some warm clothes," he said, while he was getting himself ready to leave. I picked up the blanket and went down to the car without knowing where we were going and for how long. He drove a long way, until we arrived at a large, open area full of abandoned cars of every description. He stopped his car somewhere in the middle of this car cemetery and got out. "I'll be back soon," he said. "Where are you going?" I shouted at him, feeling quite frightened to be left alone in that place. "I'm going to work," he said. "Please don't leave me all on my own," I begged him. "I will be back soon." He slammed the door and walked away.

I watched Froilan disappear quickly into the dark, thick mist. "His office must be somewhere in that direction," I thought, because I could see a small light far away in the distance. "What sort of engineer could he be to work in a place like this? Perhaps Froilan was simply some kind of security guard who had tried to impress my father by saying he was an engineer," I said to myself. Many Bolivians behave like that, pretending to be something they are not. "I'm a nurse working at St Thomas' Hospital," a Bolivian girl once told me; I found out later she was a cleaner.

The night was pitch-black, cold and totally silent. There were lots of dark shadows and I felt frightened; there were no dogs barking to break the silence or foxes looking for food in the rubbish bins and howling at the moon. In fact there was no moon that night, nor any stars. I stayed still for a long time, not thinking of anything. I knew my situation was absurd and dangerous. I was afraid of being alone in this strange place. I was frightened of getting ill again with cystitis and I was scared of the dark for the first time in my life. I thought of my father to give me courage, he taught us not to be afraid of anything. I remembered one evening when I was young and living in Coroico, there was a tropical storm that made me think that God was punishing us. The sound of the thunder scared my mother. She got out of bed to start praying and lit some candles to the Saints. Dad got angry and told her to stop that nonsense. "Don't scare the children. It's just rain, which we badly needed anyway. It's been too dry lately; it hasn't rained for months. It's been so parched that the birds don't even sing anymore." Mum was afraid of everything and Dad would always pull her up about it. He wanted his children to grow up without fear, regardless of the seriousness of the situation. We found out later that the roof connecting two houses had collapsed due to that night's storm.

That night in the car park, like my mother I was terrified of the dark, but unlike her, I couldn't pray. No prayers came to my mind, just morbid thoughts. "What if it's true that he had killed a woman? What if he had brought me to this isolated place to kill me too? Maybe he's not working at all, but preparing to murder me?" I speculated on how he would kill me when he returned. "Would he strangle me with his bare hands or would he put a plastic bag over my head? The bag would be easier, as it wouldn't make too much mess. It wouldn't be a bloody death." My mind continued to race. "He might use the blanket he asked me to bring to wrap me in and then dump my body somewhere." This remote spot would be a good place; no one would hear my screams and pleas begging him not to kill me.

Nobody knew me in this country anyway; the Owens and the Bartons had probably forgotten all about me already. I had appeared in their lives suddenly and just as quickly disappeared. The few Bolivians I had met would ask him about me perhaps, but Froilan could simply tell them that I had gone back to Sweden. All these macabre and destructive thoughts rushed through my mind, feeding my fears and feelings of helplessness at not being able to do anything about my situation. My heart was beating fast. I was in a state of high alert, expecting anything at any moment. I didn't even feel cold anymore; on the contrary I was hot and sweaty. A wave of panic bathed my entire body. My rapid breathing was steaming up the car windows and this obstructed the view, making it even scarier and more difficult to see anything outside. Two hours passed with no sign of Froilan. I decided to walk towards the light in the distance, although it seemed far away and I wasn't sure if it was coming from inside the parking area or somewhere else. I got out of the car to assess the situation, but my fears started to take over again. "What if I walked all the way there and found nobody? What if there was somebody there and they tried to hurt me? What if I can't find the car again?" I regained my composure and made a conscious decision to stay where I was and wait no matter how long it took. I breathed in and out a couple of times to control my anxiety. Getting back in the car, I covered myself with the blanket and gathered my thoughts. The situation was ironic; Dad had put me into the hands of a guy we hardly knew in a foreign country and yet in Bolivia he was so protective. Dad was naive and gullible to have trusted this man to look after me.

Another long hour passed and Froilan still didn't come. The night was tedious and endless; I couldn't sleep. I felt bored and impatient, but no longer scared. I had become resigned to my fate, whatever was going to happen to me I hoped it would be soon. I had had enough of waiting, what will be will be. I got out of the car again to stretch my legs that had become numb. Looking up, I hoped to find a solution to my predicament; but the sky was empty and black and gave me no inspiration at all. I walked around the vehicle a couple of times aimlessly. There was nothing to do to distract my mind, just broken cars everywhere. I thought to myself I am sure some of these could be repaired. In Bolivia they would fix them and use them again, like they do with everything. We cannot afford to throw anything away; anything and everything can be repaired. I actually felt sorry for those abandoned cars that had been dumped without pity.

When I was in Havana, Cuba, years later I saw a lot of beautiful 1950s American cars that have practically disappeared from the U.S.A., but not from Cuba. They have been repaired a thousand times over, helping to make the city a romantic relic of the past. I also thought of Sweden; how people would throw away furniture that was almost new as they would always have plenty of money for replacements.

Doña Asuncion sprang to mind; how stupid I was. Why hadn't I asked her for her address when I first met her? She seemed like such a nice lady. I banged my head against the car with frustration. But in that scary and uncomfortable silence, although the sky was dark and empty, I experienced a sudden moment of clarity. I was determined that this was going to be the last night I spent with this lunatic who had said that England is a very dangerous country and then leaves me in a deserted scrapyard all night on my own. I got back to the car and planned my getaway. At about five in the morning Froilan came back; he didn't try to kill me after all, on the contrary he took me home safely. I had survived that lonely night.

The next day I got up and put a few things in my school bag. I noticed that Froilan had forgotten to lock the bedroom door. I left the house while he was sleeping. On the way to school I thought about Martha, a Colombian girl who used to come to my class sometimes, if she wasn't working. We were not good friends, but we would always say hello whenever we saw each other. Most of the South Americans I met in those days enrolled on an English course just to get a visa to stay in the country; they almost never attended classes as they were too busy working. "She might put me up at her place and help me find a job," I thought. If she was not there I was going to ask the secretary at the school to help me. I had enough money to stay in a hotel for a few days.

I got to school late for my class; unfortunately the Colombian girl was not there. The secretary was too busy to talk to me at that moment, she asked me to come back in the afternoon. On the way out I met two students from my class. One of them was an Iranian and the other a Polish boy. I asked them if they knew about any cheap accommodation near the school, but they didn't. The Iranian guy invited me to go with them to Hyde Park to have a snack. This was the huge park that I first saw the day I arrived in London. I agreed and we walked through the park, kicking the yellow autumn leaves lying on the damp grass. It began to rain gently and the day felt humid, cold and sad. We sat down on a bench to eat the sandwiches that we had bought on the way to the park. As the boys knew I was looking for cheap accommodation, the Iranian boy made me an offer in broken English. "You want to stay in my place is good, no problem for me." "Oh, thank you," I replied, thinking about it. After a long pause, I said to him in equally bad English, "I stay in your place, no sex for me!" He and the Polish boy roared with laughter. It came out really badly, but funny. I had just wanted to make clear that if I stayed in his place for one or two nights it was going to be just an arrangement without any attachments. The Iranian guy nodded his head and said, "yes, sex good, very good, sex no problem." We laughed, feeding the ducks in the Serpentine with the remains of our sandwiches and joking about sex.

I returned to the school to find the secretary. As I was going up the stairs I heard a man's voice speaking Spanish. "Hello, what a surprise!" he said. Oh God, it's Froilan, I thought. I looked up and couldn't believe my eyes. "Pedro!" I screamed. It was Doña Asuncion's son. "What are you doing here?" I asked, delighted to see him. "I study here," he replied. "What about you? What are you doing here?" "I study here, too!" We could not believe that we both were in the same English school and we had never seen each other during all this time. He was in the afternoon class and I was in the morning one when I used to work at the Owens' house. I asked him if I could come one day to visit his mum. "Of course, yes, let's go now," he said. "Now? Are you sure?" I asked him, concerned about what Doña Asuncion would think if I just appeared at her home without being invited. I was also worried about what Froilan had told me about her not wanting to see me. "Yes, absolutely, let's go now, we live very near." Princes Square was where Doña Asuncion lived. I was amazed that they lived so close to the Owen family and that we had never come across each other.

Pedro opened the door of a vibrant and happy place. The big bright room was very welcoming. I didn't see just a room with a few pieces of cheap furniture; I saw a comfortable, welcoming and wonderful home. She was there holding a dustpan in one hand and a brush in the other, probably just finishing her daily housework routine. "Hi Doña Asuncion," I greeted her a little embarrassed to have come without her knowing. "Oh my God, thank God you have come darling!" she said raising her eyes to heaven as though she had been praying for this day to come. She was as surprised and happy as I was. "I was hoping Froilan would bring you, but he told us you didn't want to come," she said. It was evident that Froilan didn't want us to meet again, for whatever strange reason we will never know.

We talked all afternoon about Froilan and the whole saga. She told me how worried she had been about me, ever since we had met at Windsor Castle. She thought I was too young and vulnerable to be with a man who had not been acting very sensibly lately. "I know him very well," she said recounting the time when she and her husband had arrived in England about ten years before. She had thought of Froilan as a nice, quiet boy. But his friends bullied him constantly and he began to develop certain phobias, such as thinking that his body had a peculiar smell or that people were talking about him all the time. He was constantly taking showers and changing his clothes. "I'm sure this affected him," she said, remembering how insecure he was when

The Illegal Dance

he was young. "He was always thinking that his friends and girlfriends were dishonest with him." She remembered that on one occasion Froilan had a fight with his cousin because he thought his cousin was going out with his girlfriend. Later on, he got more paranoid and was constantly talking about people and the police following him.

Doña Asuncion's stories about Froilan reminded me about one day when I was working as an au pair for the Owen family. Froilan took me to a park where he was going to play football. On the way we picked up a Bolivian boy from his home, who was also going to play. The guy was from a humble family; he was joking about the new shiny shoes he was wearing; he called them his "Sunday shoes." He told me he only had two pairs of shoes. One was the Sunday shoes which he played football with and the other pair was the one he wore from Monday to Saturday, when he wasn't playing football. Later that day Froilan commented that I shouldn't be too friendly with the boy as he was just a peasant. "You should not treat him as an equal. You are too approachable, too easy going," he said. "Don't be ridiculous," I replied angrily. "Nobody is better or worse than anybody else." At that time I didn't take much notice of this, but now, talking to Doña Asuncion, I began to think he had a serious inferiority complex as he also came from a humble family. When I told Asuncion about the story of him possibly killing a woman, she said she didn't think it was true, but she confessed that it had crossed her mind that he could have hurt me because he was known for having violent outbursts.

Doña Asuncion's home was one large, cheerful room where she would sleep, eat and do everything else. The room had two beds pushed together. On the left hand side was a big wardrobe, next to it a very small kitchenette; on the other side was a small shelf with a few books. There was also a television and a record player, a table in the middle of the room close to a big window facing the main road, with a couple of chairs; this was all she had. The bathroom and toilet were outside the room and had to be shared with other tenants. Doña Asuncion's home might have been small, but her heart was big. "Don't worry darling you will be ok, there are plenty of jobs for you. You will get one tomorrow, you'll see," she comforted me with her lovely, friendly attitude. "You will never see that man again, I will look after you from now on," she said without even knowing me really.

That evening, Doña Asuncion, her husband Agustin and Pedro took me to a bed and breakfast hotel in Leinster Square, Westbourne Grove. It was literally around the corner from their home. They left me in a single room making sure I locked my door properly. She promised me that Agustin was going to collect my luggage from Froilan's place the following day. She also reassured me that she was coming to meet me the following day after breakfast. I went to bed relieved and pleased to have finally met this lovely lady again. London wasn't as bad as I thought after all. That night I had no dreams, no worries and I slept like a log, feeling blessed for the first time in a while.

CHAPTER ELEVEN

"Desperation can make a person do surprising things"

Veronica Roth, Allegiant

Soon after I had moved to stay in the hotel, Doña Asuncion made friends with one of the chambermaids. She was Spanish and had been working there for a couple of months. "I've had enough of this disgusting place," she said one morning while cleaning the stairs. Doña Asuncion ignored her comments but made her promise to talk to the manager about me, so I could replace her when she left.

A week later I started my new job as a chambermaid. There were only two girls in charge of the cleaning, a Colombian called Samantha and me. The hotel was divided into two wings, each with about thirteen rooms and seven bathrooms. My job was to clean one side of the hotel and the Colombian girl the other;

it was a live in job. My basement room was very spacious with a small kitchenette/diner. It had a small window and a door to a patio facing the street where we left the hotel rubbish for collection. Samantha's room was on the first floor; it was very small, with no kitchenette, but had more light than mine.

As the job was so close to Doña Asuncion's home, I often visited her. She loved telling me stories about her life and her large family in Bolivia. Sometimes I would meet other Bolivians who came to visit her. They were also doing cleaning jobs like me. At weekends Asuncion's family would take me out to a Bolivian party, to visit a museum, or if the weather was good we would spend the day in one of the great London parks.

Doña Asuncion would sometimes come to see me at the hotel in the middle of the morning with a bowl of chicken soup. "Anita, I don't think you are eating well," she would say, looking concerned, at the same time taking the opportunity to show me how to clean the hotel rooms more quickly and efficiently. At other times she would come to my room and teach me how to cook. "It's easy Anita, very easy; this is how you do it!" She would pick up the few ingredients I had in my kitchenette and start preparing something for me.

It seemed there was nothing in life she couldn't do. I admired her good temperament, strength and determination. She worked very hard but somehow always had time to entertain people and have fun; she never complained of tiredness. Every Saturday we went to the trendy Portobello Road market to buy groceries, but first we would sneak into the shops. She loved buying things, especially jewellery and liked to show off the rings and earrings she had bought in Bolivia, making sure I knew the high prices she paid for them. Her philosophy was simple; money was to be spent, particularly if, like her, you worked hard for it.

In spite of the age difference Doña Asuncion became my best and only real friend in London. Her humour and vitality were contagious; we laughed all the time like two young girls, especially when the two of us were alone. Although her English was poor she always managed to interact with people, even if it took ages to make herself understood. Sometimes she would say things that led to much confusion. One day when she was leaving work she asked her boss to give her the sack. "No, Asuncion, I don't want to give you the sack, you are a very good worker, I want you to work for me, I like you very much, you are a nice and honest woman." But Doña Asuncion insisted that he should give her the sack. Finally she pointed to her jacket, which was hanging up too high for her to reach. She used the word "sack" because in Bolivia the word for jacket is *saco*.

Misunderstandings like this were a common feature of her life, even in Spanish. One day I went to her home for tea. Pedro arrived with a video that somebody had lent him. Doña Asuncion asked him if we could all watch it together, but he refused giving us different excuses. But she insisted on watching the film as it was a cold afternoon and there was nothing else to do. Eventually after so much persistence on her part Pedro had to confess that it was a porno film and not suitable for us to watch. Doña Asuncion, innocent soul, then gave her point of view. "There is nothing wrong with sex, it's the most natural thing in the world and we should never be embarrassed about it. It's better to have sex than to have wars." Sometimes she had a liberal way of seeing things, but other times she was conservative; she was unpredictable. "Ok, Mum, if that's what you want, we will watch it," Pedro replied. The three of us made ourselves comfortable in front of the television, and Pedro put the video on. When the film started to show explicit sex, her reaction was immediate. She flipped from calmness to anger and shouted at Pedro to turn it off. "Oh my God, oh my God, have you no shame in watching this revolting stuff? You have no respect for your mother, or this young lady!" Pedro and I burst out laughing about her sudden change of attitude. I don't think she realised how hardcore some porno films can be.

"I have met a nice Bolivian lady from La Paz," I told my parents in a letter to let them know that I was in good hands. They were worried sick about me. Mum and Dad wrote to me every other week and once a month they would send me money to pay my school fees, as the money I was paid by the hotel was only enough to pay for food and a few other essentials. As for Rafael, it was more than four months since I had heard from him, even though I wrote to him many times. International calls in those days were very expensive, so we hadn't spoken on the phone since I left Bolivia.

One day I decided to call him. There was a very nice manager and receptionist in the hotel called Mr Singh from Punjab in North West India. He was a Sikh by religion and wore a turban; he was always dressed in a suit and tie. His thick moustache and long white beard almost concealed his friendly smile and perfect straight white teeth. I approached him with the telephone number written on a piece of paper that he read carefully and confirmed out loud. "So, young lady you want to make a call to Bolivia." He dialled the number from the reception switchboard and seconds later, Rafael's voice, as if by magic, was in my ears. I hadn't heard him for such a long time and now it sounded as if he was just there right next to me. It felt like a gentle melody that was going to soothe my time in London. "Hello, hello, who is this?" he asked, probably guessing it was an international call. "It's me, Rafael, Ana," I replied, excitedly. "Hi, where are you calling from?" He sounded pleased to hear from me. "I'm still in London and I want to stay a bit longer. I want to learn English before I come back." There was silence on the line. I continued telling him all I had planned to say in three minutes of conversation. "Maybe you could come to visit me for a holiday?" I suggested. "I

The Illegal Dance

can't leave the university at the moment," he said, without leaving room for discussion. His voice sounded disturbed, but firm. "Is anything wrong?" I asked. "Well, I've met somebody else and it's serious," he said in an inflexible and determined voice. My lips started trembling and I ground my teeth as I tried to take in his words. I felt like somebody had thrown a bucket of cold water over me. I sat on the floor in reception and stayed there unable to make sense of what he was saying and unable to hold back my tears. I don't think I said anything. I just returned the phone to Mr Singh and stayed on the floor, crying.

A gentle hand on my shoulder brought me back to reality. It was Mr Singh telling me not to worry. "You will soon learn English, dear and then go back to Bolivia," he said, passing me some tissues. "I know you are missing your parents dear, but time passes quickly and I will teach you English if you like. Come to reception after school and I will help you with your homework, dear." He tried to console me, but I was so upset that I didn't see any point in learning English. "Learn English? What for?" I felt like saying to him. What was the point in me learning English? To talk to people I didn't even like? What did I need this language for? To clean those dirty toilets better? I felt so sad and abandoned that I began to think there was no point in anything, not even going back to Bolivia.

I cried without shame in front of Mr Singh, full of anger and frustration. "I should have never left Bolivia, I never should have parted with Rafael," I thought. I paid for my call, thanked him for his kindness and walked down into the basement room feeling totally alone. I began to notice that my room was in fact not very nice. It was dark and depressing without direct daylight although I had the small window facing outside. The dirty looking carpet and the smell of damp were more obvious than before; the white, cold neon light I had on all the time was bothering my eyes, but when I turned it off it was dark and gloomy. I lay down on my bed thinking how naive I had been to think that true love goes on forever; I felt humiliated and rejected. That night I cried and cried, my suffering had left me exhausted and I fell asleep; but at about four o'clock I woke up feeling anxious and started to think of Rafael and what he had told me on the phone. Rafael was a passionate young man and a dreamer and he probably felt the need to fill the emptiness that my departure had left him. Surely a loveless life of a person of that age is incomplete. I also thought that he could not leave his university studies or afford the journey to London.

I got up at six o'clock in the morning tired of thinking of Rafael and trying to understand why he had stopped loving me. I started to prepare the breakfast and the hours passed interspersed with happy memories of when I was with Rafael.

During the days that followed, I avoided staying in my depressing room, licking my wounds. Instead I would go for walks around Queensway. This was one of the most cosmopolitan streets in central London, full of shops and people. There were Indians selling exotic foods and souvenirs, Arab women covered in black gowns from head to foot, buying things or strolling slowly behind their husbands. You could smell delicious aromas coming from Chinese, Italian and Greek restaurants, or have a hot chocolate with tempting cakes in the Spanish coffee shop. In the pubs, this eclectic mix included Rastafarian men proudly showing off their long and ancient dreadlocks; well-dressed Englishmen and women drank beer and chatted to friends. I would walk up and down watching people from all over the world, all of them comfortable with their own individualities in a free and tolerant country. I would walk, looking in shop windows but seeing nothing, trying to keep my mind busy with things that didn't matter.

Sometimes after school I would go straight to see Doña Asuncion. At other times I would stop at the hotel reception for an English lesson with Mr Singh. One day during one of these

The Illegal Dance

lessons a young man came into the hotel. He was wearing thick glasses and his face was full of little scars, perhaps due to acne which hadn't healed properly. He bared crooked teeth and had a protruding chin. He wore a suit and was holding a briefcase; he looked like a proper businessman. Mr Singh whispered, "I want you to meet this nice boy. He is from Karachi, the financial capital of Pakistan; he is studying economics." Mr Singh greeted the guest effusively. "Hello Kalam, how was your day?" "Not too bad Mr Singh," replied the young man with a shy smile. "Are you going to go to the party on Saturday?" asked Mr Singh. "I don't know anything about it," Kalam replied. "Oh well, there is a party this Saturday downstairs in the breakfast room organised by some of the guests at the hotel," continued Mr Singh. The hotel was home to a lot of young refugees from Somalia, Ethiopia and Eritrea, escaping from wars and famine. There were also young English couples, most of them unemployed and on benefits waiting to be rehoused. Some of the hotel guests had apparently asked the owner if they could use the breakfast room to hold a party. "Take this young lady with you, Kalam; go together and enjoy yourselves." Mr Singh was organising my date with enthusiasm without giving the boy or myself a chance to refuse. Kalam's timid smile acknowledged me for the first time. "Do you want to go?" he asked me, almost forced by the circumstances. Before I had a chance to reply, Mr Singh said, "yes, dear, go, go and enjoy yourself!" Kalam had no option but to ask me to meet him on Saturday at eight in the evening at the front of the hotel. I asked Samantha, the Colombian girl, to come to the party too, but she was working until late that evening, so I asked Pedro to come along with me as well. It was my first party in London and it turned out to be very good. Pedro met an Irish girl who also lived in the hotel. Kalam and I tried to communicate, without much success, but we at least danced to pop and African music until the early hours of the morning.

Pedro's mum would often encourage me to go out and make more friends, but I was always too tired to go anywhere. Every time she asked Pedro to take me out he would say, "no, Mum, I am not taking Ana out with me. Don't even mention it. She always spoils the evening by complaining she is tired." Cleaning and going to school every day was more than enough for me, so I was happy to stay in or go to visit Pedro's mum instead.

One day, a few months after the hotel party, Doña Asuncion came to see me in my room. "Ana, I want to talk to you," she said looking serious and concerned. "I am rather worried about you. You are a very young and decent girl and you come from a good family. Your father is a respected doctor (he was a dentist) and I don't want anything bad to happen to you." She was frowning, which she always did when she wanted to be taken seriously. "What is the matter, Doña Asuncion?" I asked, a bit worried. "When Pedro comes to see you, you should not let him in every night. You cannot trust men, not even my son." "Pedro?" I asked, not being sure what she was talking about. "He doesn't come to see me every night, in fact he never comes," I assured her. "Well, if he doesn't come to see you where does he go then? He leaves home every evening saying he is going to visit you." "Oh! I know where he goes," I said to her. "He met an Irish girl at the party and he probably goes to see her every night. She lives here in the hotel," I said laughing and hoping to clear up the misunderstanding. "What a naughty boy, he's been deceiving me all this time!" she said, laughing with me.

Pedro had a plan. He wanted to take Karen, the Irish girl, to the coast, to Brighton for the weekend and he wanted Kalam and me to go along. So, a few days later, that weekend, we were on the train to Brighton, not knowing exactly what Pedro had in mind. During the journey I noticed that Pedro seemed a bit anxious about something and I asked him what was wrong. He would try to tell me, but then would change his mind again.

Eventually, just when we were about to arrive, he asked me to do him a big favour. "What is it?" I asked a little concerned, thinking he wanted money. "Well, when we get to the bed and breakfast in Brighton, can you tell Karen you want to sleep with Kalam and not share the room with her?" "What, are you mad?" I replied. "Please, Anita, help me out this time," Pedro continued. "You see, I want to sleep with Karen, but this won't happen unless you say you want to sleep with Kalam." "I'm sorry, Pedro, but no way am I sleeping with Kalam just to help you out," I said firmly. "You don't have to do anything with him, just share the room, please, please say yes." He begged me all the way to Brighton and promised to take me out dancing if I did what he wanted.

When we arrived at the bed and breakfast I was surprised when I heard myself saying to the receptionist that I wanted a double room for Kalam and me. Both Karen and Kalam looked at me in disbelief, but accepted my decision without arguing. I thought it was going to be difficult to make Kalam understand why I had done this, but it turned out that he was such a nice, well behaved boy that he didn't question my reasons or try anything on with me that night. That weekend was the beginning of a long relationship between Pedro and Karen.

After Brighton, Kalam and I continued our friendship. But I wondered why he had never tried to seduce me even though we spent a lot of time together. So one evening "curiosity killed the cat;" I tried to have sex with him. He refused and explained that in his culture and religion there is no physical relationship whatsoever before marriage. Perhaps this made me even more determined to break his rules, so I began to work on him. "Well," I said, gently trying to persuade him, "in my religion you do not have to have sex before marriage either, but some people still do it, of course and it's not a bad thing." Kalam looked at me thoughtfully and confused. "I have never done it before. I have never even had a girlfriend," he said, feeling embarrassed about his inadequacy. "It's ok," I said, kissing him gently on his lips and playing with his hair, so that he would give in to my advances. Slowly and lovingly I took off his glasses and placed them on the bedside table where a small lamp produced a dim and delicate light conducive to the moment. Then I unbuttoned his shirt and trousers, continually stroking his tense body all over, so he wouldn't change his mind. Excited by what I was doing, he gave in without any resistance, perhaps trying to convince himself that this had nothing to do with culture or religion, perhaps thinking it was an inevitable act at a certain age, or maybe he was thinking he had met the right girl who could be his wife. I myself didn't really know what I was trying to achieve. We became passionately involved in what was going to be for him possibly the first and most important sexual experience of his life. I felt in me, his strength, his agitation, his exaltation but also his inexperience. His movements began to increase as he was about to climax; I suddenly changed my mind and pushed him away. Rafael had come into my mind like a powerful ghost to haunt me. I felt stupid and angry for what I was doing. "Get out, get out!" I screamed wildly at him. "I'm sorry, Ana. What have I done wrong?" he said, with fear in his eyes, his hands grasping his crotch and his body undergoing inevitable orgasmic spasms. "No, you haven't done anything wrong, I just want you to go and leave me alone," I said without any explanation. "Please Ana, let me stay with you tonight," he asked me almost crying, but the more he pleaded, the more I hated him. I just wanted him out of my room and life forever. He eventually got dressed and left, leaving me angry and sick with regret. It was the first time I had tried to have sex since my relationship with Rafael; I realised I couldn't do it, as I didn't love the boy.

I never saw Kalam again. He not only left my room that night; he left the hotel, too. Mr Singh would often ask me if I had heard from him. I always replied that I hadn't and pretended I didn't know why he had left. Nobody in the hotel heard from him again; I think Mr Singh felt a bit let down that Kalam never said goodbye to him. Kalam had a part time job in an office while he was studying and although I had his work number, I neither called him nor gave the number to Mr Singh. Perhaps I was afraid Kalam might have told him how horrible I had been to him.

A year later, I felt that my English had improved enough for me to be able to explain to Kalam why I had behaved so badly, so I decided to contact him. Hoping he would still have the same work number, I called him. I had written down everything I wanted to say to avoid missing anything out. "Hi Kalam, this is Ana, I'm calling to apologise…." I got no further before the line went dead. He had put the phone down on me.

Mr Singh decided to go back to India because he felt old and tired. "I have worked since I was fourteen years old, dear and lived in this country for forty five years; now I need to retire," he said to me. During my English lessons with Mr Singh, he told me about his life both in Punjab and when he came to live in England for the first time. His parents worked in the fields, planting wheat; it was a very large and very poor family. Mr Singh had five brothers and two sisters. When he was only thirteen, his mother died of an undiagnosed illness. There were no doctors in his village. He believed it could have been a stomach infection, because she suffered greatly with stomach pains, diarrhoea and vomiting. Because his father could not look after so many children on his own, he decided to sell his young daughters into marriage; one was sixteen and the other fifteen. The men who married them were in their forties. His brothers remained working in the fields with his father. A friend of his father took Mr Singh to work for him in New Delhi in his fabric store. At sixteen, the same friend brought him to Slough, an industrial town near London, to open an Indian restaurant. But after working in the restaurant for almost ten years Mr Singh realised that his father's friend was exploiting him. The man paid him only fifty pounds a month for working twelve hours a day, six days a week. At the age of twenty six Mr Singh decided to go to London, where he started from scratch working in various hotels. He never married and returned to Punjab only once when his father died. He would often say, "I worked like a slave for so many years without enjoying myself, so I like to see people enjoying themselves without hurting anybody." Mr Singh was such a kind old man, everybody liked him. I think it was partly because he allowed all the guests of the hotel to do more or less what they wanted. Some of them even cooked in their rooms, such as one Indian family. There were five of them, living in room 10, which only had three single beds. They never allowed me in to clean it, but would half open the door for me to pass them the vacuum cleaner so they could do it themselves. Every time they opened the door the smell of curry would be so strong it made me take one step backwards. They spent most of their time indoors and when they went out they were always together like a small clan, wearing their saris and slippers even in winter.

In room 22 there was an attractive, skinny, black woman. I think she was a prostitute, as every time I went to clean her room she was sleeping with a different man. They never woke up while I was collecting the rubbish and cleaning the sink. She would only come down for breakfast when she didn't have a man to sleep with. One day I knocked on the door of room 23, but there was no answer; so I let myself in with my master key, only to see two men having sex. They didn't even notice me. I quickly closed the door again, feeling frightened. It was the first time in my life I had seen two men in bed together.

This seedy hotel was full of eccentrics, most of whom did nothing all day. There was a young, friendly English couple who were expecting their first child. They looked so callow and

The Illegal Dance

inexperienced that I wondered whether they would be capable of looking after it. This couple would tell me everything that was going on in the hotel. The problem was that they would talk and giggle at the same time, which made it almost impossible for me to understand what they were saying. In room 30 lived a very strange man, a total loner who seemed to be in a world of his own. I think he suffered from depression as sometimes he was talkative and on other occasions simply ignored everyone. He was very tall with curly red hair and freckles. His body looked like it was made of two people joined together. He had a small frame with long and languid arms and legs. It seemed that his clothes belonged to a shorter man. He walked and talked like a robot and never smiled, unless he heard me saying something in English. I don't know how he became my friend, but he would occasionally come down to my room for a cup of tea.

When Mr Singh was due to leave for India, the guests prepared a small farewell party for him. Following his departure, things at the hotel changed radically. A few days later he was replaced by an attractive Thai woman, who took up residence with her husband in Mr Singh's flat on the first floor. Our workload doubled and her relationship with the guests was distant; she was strict and unfriendly.

On one occasion, it must have been about one in the morning, I was almost asleep when I heard somebody knocking on my door. For a moment I became excited thinking it might be Rafael who had changed his mind and had decided to pay me a surprise visit. "Who is it?" I asked in Spanish. There was no answer, but the loud knocking continued. I dressed quickly and when I opened the door I almost collapsed. Two tall, well-built policemen stood in front of me. They were dressed in dark blue uniforms with high helmets. They looked distinguished, professional and serious. Ever since I began working at the hotel, I had been worried about the police because, although I was not in the country illegally, I didn't have a work permit yet. Every time immigration officers came to check if there were any illegal workers, Samantha and I would hide on the top floor until they left the building.

This reminds me of an incident many years later when I worked in a health club in London. An Australian woman had recently been appointed to be the manageress. She was efficient and hardworking, but made the mistake of sacking a couple of people who had worked there for a long time. Every day I went to work there was always an atmosphere of fear that one of us might be dismissed. After the sackings, somehow one of the staff, an Irish girl, found out that the Australian manageress didn't have a work permit. She called Immigration and within forty eight hours she was out of the country. I remember the day she was taken from her office in front of everybody. It may have been embarrassing for her, but I admit we were relieved when she had gone. She was escorted from the building by two men as big and strong as those I now had in front of me.

One of the policemen asked me if I worked at the hotel. There was no point in denying it. Somebody must have told them that I was one of the chambermaids and that's why they had come down to my room. "Yes, I do sir." I replied, resigned to being taken away. "I may as well surrender and pack my things," I thought. But to my surprise they were after somebody else. "Do you know John Beckett?" "No, I don't know him sir," I answered. Of course I knew him, he was a guest in the hotel and was staying in room 35 on the third floor, but for some reason I pretended not to know him. I didn't want to be involved in his arrest; it must have been self-preservation or I don't know what. "Where is the receptionist's flat?" one of the policemen asked. "I'll show you," I said, picking up my keys to go upstairs. As we passed through reception there were two men playing cards. They were probably the ones who let the policemen into the hotel and sent them to

The Illegal Dance

my room. We knocked at the receptionist's door, but she didn't open it. They persisted for a long time, without getting any answer from her. "We will be back tomorrow, early in the morning," they said leaving the hotel without any further questions.

The next day I got up early and went upstairs to John's room. I knocked on his door and he opened it half naked, looking rough and sleepy. His arms and chest were covered in tattoos and his teeth tinted yellow from excessive cigarette smoking. There were a few chicken bones in Kentucky Fried Chicken cartons. Empty bottles of beer and cigarette ends littered the floor. His room stank as much as he did. "Last night police look for you, police come back half an hour," I said to him. "Thanks, love," he said. He got dressed quickly and went down the stairs behind me. I led him into my room, so he wouldn't have to go out through the main hotel door. I opened the back door to the yard, which had a way out to the street. "Thanks, love," he said again before leaving. I never knew what this man had done. Was he a burglar, a rapist, a murderer? Why did I sympathise with this dirty looking man? I would never know. The police came back at seven sharp, but he had gone.

Samantha and I would meet up every morning in the kitchen to prepare breakfast for the hotel guests. One morning she came down an hour late and was very apologetic. "Sorry, I couldn't get up," she said. I knew she had another cleaning job in the evening which she didn't finish until nine. But that particular morning she looked really tired, fed up and apathetic. "We need to talk," she said while she made herself a cup of strong coffee. "I've got a new job and I won't be finishing until around two or three in the morning every day. I hope you don't mind if I come down to make the breakfast one hour later every day, but you can finish earlier and start cleaning upstairs. I will finish the washing up on my own," she said. "It sounds good to me," I replied, realising that this arrangement was going to give me enough time to have lunch before going to school instead of rushing without anything to eat.

For a few weeks everything was normal at the hotel; the new arrangement with Samantha was working out fine until something disturbing happened. I was a sound sleeper in those days and nothing would wake me up; but one night at about three in the morning I was disturbed by some terrible screams. "Help! Please help!" I sat bolt upright in bed. I was not sure whether I had been dreaming or if the screams were for real. I heard my name being called; the screams were coming from upstairs. "Ana, please help me! Someone's trying to get into my room, help me please!"

I quickly put on my shoes, picked up my keys and rushed out of the bedroom. Samantha's screams became louder as I was going up the stairs. "He wants to rape me, please help me!" I got to the reception area and saw three guys drinking beer and playing cards. Without saying anything to them I went up one floor more to Samantha's room and knocked on her door. "Samantha, are you ok?" "Call the police!" she said, crying.

I ran downstairs to the landing between reception and Samantha's floor. There was a public telephone and I tried to ring 999, but the line was dead. I went down one floor more to the reception room and started shouting at the men in bad English. "Who try to get Samantha's room? You see anybody?" They looked at me startled. "No, there is nobody around apart from us," they went back to their game, totally uninterested.

I went back upstairs to Samantha's room. She opened the door slightly and I tried to reassure her. "It's me, Ana. There's nobody out here." Finally, looking distressed, she let me in. "Somebody tried to get into my room, I swear to God. Somebody wanted to rape me!" she was sobbing inconsolably. Later on, I tried to tell the manageress about what had happened, but again she didn't open her door. I then suggested to Samantha that we should bring her mattress downstairs for her to sleep in my room.

The Illegal Dance

Samantha was in her late twenties and was a very good looking woman. She had long black hair, green eyes and a great figure. One day a man in the street had spotted her and offered her a job as a hostess in a club. She had to drink and dine with men who would pay lots of money to have the company of a pretty girl. She took the job but soon found out she hated it; but she felt she had to do it because she had come to London from Colombia saddled with huge debts and her meagre hotel pay was not going to help very much. For the next few months Samantha stayed with me in my room. This was not the perfect arrangement because she didn't come home until three in the morning every day and she always woke me up. She liked sleeping and listening to her tapes of religious sermons. Belonging to a Christian group, she never missed church and religious meetings on Sundays. Unfortunately, her faith did not fit in with her new life style and would have serious repercussions, as I would witness later.

Every night while listening to her religious sermons, she would carefully put on makeup and dress up in elegant and sexy clothes with high heels. She would cross herself three times and then leave the hotel to work as a hostess. The next day she would wake up looking drained and depressed. One day I suggested that we should buy an English course on tape between the two of us. "Samantha, the sooner we learn English the better. We might be able to get better jobs with more money if we speak the language," I said. "You are right, but to learn this bloody language will take me forever," she replied. Sounding defeated, she simply turned up the volume of her religious talks. I used to wonder how she managed to entertain men without speaking much English.

Samantha hated herself for working in that club. Sometimes she would come back to the hotel with stories about how her boss complained that she didn't encourage clients to spend more money on drinks. At other times she told me that men at the club would ask to take her to a hotel after work for her to sleep with them, offering her a fortune to do so. "I would never do that," she would say, but I sensed that sooner or later she might give in. One time she came back from work in an animated mood and woke me up as usual. "Anita, I have something to tell you," she said jumping up and down with excitement. I opened my eyes and saw Samantha smiling for the first time in ages. "What is it, why are you so happy?" "I met a very nice Spanish man at the club," she said. "Great, what happened?" "He's been coming to the club for the last few nights and always asks for me," she said describing in great detail what he looked like. "He's a real gentleman and has promised to get me out of the club and find me a decent job," she said enthusiastically.

Samantha and the Spanish man began to meet outside the club. He made good on his promise to get her a new job, a cashier in a Spanish restaurant. He even began to talk about marriage, which made Samantha very happy. The relationship seemed to be going well for a few months until one day her boss found out there was some money missing. He thought she had made a serious mistake with the restaurant accounts. She paid for the loss from her salary, but the following month, the same thing happened; she lost them money again. This time she was sacked. She didn't only lose her job but her relationship too; her boyfriend lost interest and left her. This was the start of her downfall. Samantha went into deep depression. It was sad to see such a young and attractive woman feel so worthless. It was a struggle every day for her to get up and do the cleaning job at the hotel. After work she would sleep all afternoon listening to the religious speeches. She started to hear noises and the feeling she was going to be raped returned to be a constant fear.

Sometimes after I returned from college I would find her crying and insisting that somebody had tried to get into my room to rape her. She had moved the furniture around to protect herself from intruders. Sometimes I would find the wardrobe, or the table near the door, which made it difficult for me to get in. She also hated being left on her own and she lost the will to go out unless it was to church. I was pretty sure the rape threats were in her imagination, but real to her. I didn't think she was making it up.

While I advised her to pull herself together, to go to school to learn English to get a better job, her religious friends advised her that she should go back to Colombia because her situation in London was affecting her mentally. She agreed and two days before flying back she asked me to go shopping with her. We went to a Marks & Spencer store where she bought some nice underwear. She paid for it, but as we were about to leave the shop she spotted something else she liked. "Oh, I love this jumper, but it's very expensive," she said, looking at the price tag. Without a moment's hesitation, she asked me to cover her as she thrust the jumper in the same plastic bag as the underwear and we left the shop. As soon as we got outside, two men in plain clothes stopped us and led us back into the store, to a private office; they called the police. While we waited for them to arrive they explained that they were security guards and why they had brought us into the office. "You took a jumper that you didn't pay for," they said. They searched our handbags to see if we had stolen anything else. Samantha and I were crying and kept repeating, "sorry, sorry!" I think they were the only words that came out of our mouths that humiliating day. They told us we had to wait for the police. I began to shake; I couldn't stop my knees knocking and my chin trembling. Samantha was crying and biting her nails.

About twenty minutes later, two policemen entered the office. The security guards explained to them what had happened, showing the evidence on a television screen. The police asked us if what they were saying was true and we agreed. They asked us a few more questions and wrote down everything we said. One of the policemen was aggressive; he was the only one to speak, as the other one just watched us quietly.

We couldn't stop crying. The policemen had to repeat simple questions many times over because our English was so limited. I think they read us our rights. Once they were satisfied with the information they had collected, they explained that because we had no official documentation on us they were going to take us home to get our passports before going to the local police station. They also told us we were going to be provided with a solicitor.

We left Marks & Spencer in a police car and were taken to the hotel where we lived. Samantha showed them her passport and her return flight ticket to Colombia. I showed them my passport too. "What are you doing in this country?" one of them asked me. "I am a student," I replied still sobbing. "How long do you want to stay in London?" the quiet policeman asked. "One year," I replied, drying my tears. They both looked at each other and said something.

The more aggressive one spoke to me slowly and calmly, "we are going to write a report to say it was Samantha who took the jumper. That is what we saw on the CCTV tape, but because she has her plane ticket to leave the U.K. in two days' time she won't need to go to court. We are just going to make sure she leaves the country. We won't take you with us to the police station. Is that ok?" he asked me. "Yes, thank you," I replied, very relieved. They asked Samantha to pack her bags immediately. They explained to her that she was going to be held in custody until the day of her flight. She did what they said and they all left a few minutes later in the police car. A few months later I received a card from Samantha saying she was happy and well in Colombia. She had a job and had met a local man to whom she was planning to get married. She still owed money to the bank but the debt was going to be paid off within a year between her and her boyfriend.

Two years later I was preparing for my first important English exam, the Cambridge First Certificate. The school I attended was in Hammersmith, so I used to go there every day by the Underground, generally packed with people. One afternoon I noticed a man looking at me intently; he was sitting in front of me. Every time I looked at him he smiled. I had the feeling I knew the man but I could not remember where I had met him. I tried to avoid his gaze by pretending I was reading my school text books but as soon as he had the opportunity he changed seats and sat next to me. "Hi Ivanna," he said. The sound of my full Christian name made me shiver. Most people I knew called me Ana. "How the hell does this stranger know my name?" I thought. I turned my head and saw the policeman who had arrested me in Marks & Spencer, this time in plain clothes. It was the quiet one, the officer who had asked me how long I was staying in the country. My God, I wanted to run a mile, but I stayed calm and forced myself to say hello to him. "Are you going to school?" he asked me. "Yes," I replied without giving him any more details, hoping he would stop questioning me again. "Are you ok?" he asked. "Yes," I replied, wondering if he was genuinely concerned about me.

Thankfully the train soon arrived at my station. "Goodbye," I said, but he followed me, trying to make conversation. I skipped up the stairs in the direction of the exit, but he kept pace behind me. I left the station and as I was about to cross the road, the traffic lights changed to green so we had to stop at the pedestrian crossing. "My name is Mark," he said. I didn't respond. "Don't be afraid of me, I'm not going to eat you," he said, smiling. I don't think I was afraid of him, more embarrassed due to how we had met; he knew too much about me. We crossed the road, and before we said goodbye, he asked if he could see me again. "No thank you," I said, but he insisted on meeting me for a coffee after school. That evening he told me he was the one who suggested to the other policeman to let me go. Two days later he waited for me in front of the school and took me for a drink in a pub and then he would be there a couple of days a week. Sometimes he would be dressed in plain clothes, at other times in police uniform. Sometimes we would go for a drink, sometimes he would just take me home and then go straight to work. He was indeed a very nice man, but I felt uneasy in his company, especially when my school friends made fun of me saying, "be careful with your police friend, he may want to lock you up for the night!" After a couple of dates, he realised I was not interested in him; I never saw him again.

CHAPTER TWELVE

"Monsters are real, and ghosts are real too. They live inside us, and sometimes, they win"

Stephen King

After Samantha had left the U.K., Doña Asuncion told me that two young girls had just arrived in London from Bolivia. One of them was called Mirta, the other Magdalena and they were looking for a job. I suggested that one of them could work at the hotel instead of Samantha. We asked the manageress and she made no objection. Mirta moved in straight away and started work. Problems soon arose with her attitude however. She had great difficulty in accepting that she was employed to do a cleaning job. Most of all, she hated serving breakfast to black guests. "I don't like black people," she would tell me, pulling faces without giving any reason for her feelings towards them. So it ended up with her in the kitchen preparing the breakfast while I served it. One day I refused to carry on with this arrangement. "I'll prepare breakfast today and you will serve it to the guests," I told her. I was determined that she was not going to get away with her prejudice anymore. So that morning having no choice but to do the job, she swanned around the dining room like a diva, with a haughty look on her face as though she was above everyone else. She was so sickened with her task that she warned me, "I don't want anybody in Bolivia to know what I am doing here. As a matter of fact, if we ever meet in Bolivia, you don't know me."

This girl reminds me of another Bolivian woman called Lisa I met in London some years later. I was going to see my family in Bolivia and Lisa brought a few presents for me to take to her relatives. She said to me, "somebody told my parents I'm working here as a cleaner. I asked my parents to host a party in your honour; all my family will be there. Please can you tell them I am not a cleaner." she said. She was furious when I told her that I was not going to alter the truth. She still gave me all the gifts to take to Bolivia, but the party was cancelled.

Days later, Pedro met Mirta in Bayswater. "Where are you going in such a hurry?" he asked. "I'm going to meet the musician Carlos Santana," she boasted, thinking that Pedro would believe her fantasy. Doña Asuncion, who had also noticed her strange behaviour, warned me to be careful in her company.

Over the years in London I met lots of snobbish Bolivian girls but Mirta was unique. A few days after her tantrum over serving breakfast, she came down to my room and said, "I'm very worried, my period hasn't come." "Don't worry, it may be the change of climate and food," I replied, trying to put her mind at ease. A few weeks later she told me again that she had not had her period. I offered to go with her to the doctor to have a checkup, but she didn't want to. Eventually she went to the pharmacy and asked to have a urine pregnancy test. Two days later she collected the results. To her amazement and mine the result was positive. "This can't be right, I haven't done anything; I have never been to bed with a man in my life!" she spoke with tears in her eyes. "Don't worry then, your period will come sooner or later; it must be a false alarm." But she was very worried. She asked me if she could get pregnant by swimming in a pool with her boyfriend. I wasn't sure if she was naïve or the whole thing was a joke. I gave her the benefit of the doubt and told her that I didn't think she could get pregnant while swimming. "What do you have to do to get pregnant?" she asked me. "Are you pulling my leg?" I replied, stomping out of the kitchen.

A week later, Mirta asked me to go with her to see a GP. There was a surgery around the corner from the hotel, so we made an appointment after work. She asked me if I would translate. Although my English wasn't at all good, she felt it was better than hers. "What can I do for you young ladies?" the doctor asked, sitting down at his desk ready to take notes. "Her period doesn't come," I replied. "How long?" he asked. "Three months," I said, showing three fingers of my left hand to make sure I was giving him the right information. "Has she had a pregnancy test?" the doctor asked. "Yes," I replied. Mirta passed him the result of the urine test. "Hmm! It's positive," he looked at us, waiting for some comment. We both kept quiet. "Doesn't she want this child?" the doctor asked. "She thinks she isn't pregnant," I said. "Well, let's examine her," he said asking her to take her shoes off and to lie on the couch. He was about to palpate her stomach and cervix, when she pushed his hand away and started shouting. "No touch please, no touch, I am virgin, I am virgin!" The doctor lost his cool with her and angrily pointed to the door. "If you are a virgin get out, don't waste my time!"

I would only meet Mirta at breakfast time, but one day she left a small note under my door that read, "I'm going to kill myself." I got really angry with her as she was putting me in an impossible position. I wasn't sure what to do. I went to talk to Doña Asuncion to see what she thought. "Ana, she is trying to intimidate you. Don't get involved; she is not a nice girl," she said, telling me how badly she had treated the other girl who had arrived with her. "They are supposed to be friends, but ever since they arrived in London Mirta doesn't want to talk to her and do you know why that is Ana? It's because Mirta's brother has a relationship with Magdalena's sister and Mirta thinks that she is not good enough for her brother." Doña Asuncion was kind and helpful to people, but if somebody abused her kindness or behaved stupidly she would cut off all communication completely.

I went back to the hotel and without thinking of the consequences I wrote Mirta a note which said, "Mirta, if you want to kill yourself please go ahead, but do it somewhere else, not in this hotel. I don't want to have to deal with the police." I put the note in an envelope and under her door. The next day I woke up early; I was worried. I was going to wait for her in the kitchen for an hour or so and then I was going to go up to her room with the master key. I thought I might find her lifeless body lying on the floor, but my fears fortunately did not come to reality. She came down for breakfast and began to work in a more cooperative way. After a few more months she left and that was the last I saw of her. But then I heard that Mirta had returned to Bolivia and her friend Magdalena was deported by immigration officials about six months after that.

The manageress at the hotel was getting ever more demanding. Nothing I did was good enough. One afternoon, I was about to go off duty. I was holding the vacuum cleaner in one hand and a bucket full of cleaning materials in the other. As I came down the stairs I saw the manageress deliberately throwing rubbish all over the floor of the reception room. At the same time, the owner of the hotel came in. I met them both at reception and she began to complain about me. "It's almost two and she still hasn't cleaned the reception room." "Liar, liar!" I heard myself screaming. Both of them turned towards me, surprised to see my reaction. "I cleaned it this morning, I saw you dirtying it just now," I said furiously. She tried to defend herself, but I didn't let her talk. Words were coming out of my mouth like bullets from a gun. I was shouting, ignoring the owner's demands to keep calm and trying to put an end to the argument. Finally he said, "hmm, I thought you couldn't speak English." It was then that I realised for the first time that my English had begun to improve. That day the manageress let it go, but later on it was a different matter.

A new girl called Gracia started to work at the hotel and because she was new, the manageress started to make demands on her. One morning she asked Gracia to clean the flat where she lived with her husband, but she refused to do it claiming it was not her job. A big argument broke out between them and from then on the manageress took a dislike to her too, which made our jobs more difficult. Later on we found out that she was trying to replace us with Thai girls.

Gracia came from Madrid; she was a young, tall, pretty girl. She had worked as a model while living in Spain and that was how she met the Spanish singer Julio Iglesias with whom she had a short relationship. When she came to London, she went to work as an au pair at the home of an English family to learn English. But her stay in that house didn't last very long. One day when she was alone with her boss, he tried to take advantage of her. Although occasionally I heard this type of story in my school, most of the girls working for English families had good experiences, especially if the school had arranged the job and accommodation.

It was the beginning of spring, and although still cold, the natural changes in the park were noticeable. Leaves were appearing, daffodils were out and birdsong was in evidence. The days were getting longer; a year had passed quickly. I had long forgotten my problems of the first few months and had settled into a routine that I didn't particularly like, but didn't hate either. It was a temporary situation that I took in my stride because I was young and I knew that sooner or later things were going to change. One evening I went to see Doña Asuncion as usual. She was alone; her husband was out and Pedro was at the University. In talking to her that evening I found out more about her and the reason why Pedro had left Argentina. She was only fifteen years old when she got married. She had two children by a husband who didn't face up to his responsibilities. She left him and worked at every job she could find to provide for her two children. Later on when her children were older she met her second husband, Agustin, with whom she came to England to work in the seventies. Bolivian migration to the U.K. began in the sixties either for economic reasons, as was the case for Doña Asuncion, or political problems. Labour was scarce in those days, which is why people from different parts of Latin America were recruited for domestic work. Asuncion sent Pedro to university in Argentina, but one day she went to visit him over there. It was then that she found out he was not studying but instead had made his girlfriend pregnant. She was furious, as most mothers would be, so she bought Pedro a ticket back to Bolivia immediately and then a month later she brought him to London. But Doña Asuncion never forgot about the pregnant girl. She made Pedro send her money throughout the pregnancy and when the baby was born she forced him to recognise the child as his son and to make sure they lacked for nothing.

After a few hours of talking to me while waiting for Pedro and her husband, she began to worry that her son wasn't home yet. At about eleven at night we heard someone knocking at the door. She opened it to find two men there. "We are looking for the mother of Pedro Alvares." "That's me," she said, in a friendly voice. She invited the men in and asked them if they were friends of Pedro. The men produced identification. "Police?" she exclaimed, very alarmed. "What's happened to my son?" "He's ok," the plain clothes officer replied, "but we want you to come with us to the police station and please bring his passport with you."

Poor Doña Asuncion; I had never seen her so distressed and confused. She was so nervous it took her some time to find Pedro's documentation. While she was looking for it she kept telling the police that her son was a good boy who wouldn't do anything wrong. Then she turned to talk to me in Spanish. "These men smell of alcohol Ana, they don't seem to be policemen on duty." The two men waited quietly until she finally found the passport. Before she left with them I asked her if she wanted me to come with her. "No Ana, go home. I will see you tomorrow," she said looking worried. I started walking quickly to the hotel when a tall scruffy black man approached me. "Hi," he said. "Hi," I replied, without stopping to look at him. "You live at the Pembridge Hotel, don't you?" he said. "Yes," I replied, wondering how he knew that as I had never seen him before. "My cousin lives there," he said; "she's in room 22." I didn't reply, but his cousin was the girl I thought was a prostitute.

The hotel was close by so I speeded up, trying to get away from him. When I arrived, I went in as quickly as possible. As I was about to close the door, he put his foot in the gap to stop me. He then forced his way into the hotel. I didn't look at him; I walked towards the basement without turning back, hoping he would go upstairs to his cousin's room, but to my surprise he didn't. He followed me downstairs and I began to get frightened. Disturbing thoughts went through my mind. I thought of Samantha and the man who tried to get into her room. "Was this the man who tried to rape her?" I thought. "What if he tries to force himself on me? Nobody would hear my screams down here." I was alone and I wasn't sure if Gracia, the Spanish girl was in her room.

I didn't know what to do. I thought about turning back towards reception and escaping out into the street, but he could have easily stopped me. I had my room keys in my hand and thought about running downstairs quickly to get into my room, but he was too close to me. I could almost feel his knees against me as we were going down the stairs. I felt a sense of overwhelming fear and uncertainty. I tried to work out why he was following me, while trying not to panic; I didn't have many options. A few more steps down and I would be in my room. I could hear his breathing and smell his body odour. My heart was thumping rapidly, almost uncontrollably. My hands were shaking and sweating. I could not put the key in the lock. I envisaged a struggle with the man, I saw myself hitting him, scratching him, kicking him and spitting in his face. I could hear my begging not to touch me, then my screams, and my inevitable defeat.

As I was about to open the door my father's words came to me, "you kill more people with kindness than with poison." I turned around to face the intruder, looking him straight in the eyes. "Thank you very much for coming with me here." He looked surprised, he moved backwards almost automatically. "What about a cup of coffee?" he asked, trying his luck. "I'm sorry, not tonight, very tired, tomorrow please," I said sweetly; he smiled. This made him seem less of a threat. I continued to talk gently and kindly. "Come down tomorrow morning at breakfast time," I said. "Come in through that side door." I pointed to the door to the yard next to my bedroom. "But come before eight before the manageress starts work." Of course I was hoping he would not turn up and I would never see him again but, if he did appear, I would be safe in the hotel dining room. "Ok, thank you," he replied. He went back upstairs, pleased with our arrangement.

The following evening I went to see Doña Asuncion to find out what had happened to Pedro. He was there at home with his mother and her husband Agustin, all sitting around the table, looking very serious. From the look on their faces it was clear things were bad. Pedro was often making jokes and having a laugh, but now he looked grim and thoughtful. Doña Asuncion got up to serve dinner with a troubled look on her face; Agustin looked helpless.

"What happened?" I asked, hoping that talking might relieve the tension. Pedro began, "I was arrested last night and charged with assaulting a police officer. I sat down in silence, looking at their faces. I was hoping one of them would give in and start laughing and it would turn out to be just a joke like so many times before. But Pedro continued seriously. "I was leaving the University with my friend Tico, the black guy from the Dominican Republic. We were walking towards Paddington Station, minding our own business, when a car stopped right next to us and two men got out. We stepped up our pace, but they soon caught up with us. I thought this was strange so I told Tico to run. The men ran after us and suddenly started punching without any warning. We had to defend ourselves and so we fought back. I managed to knock one of them down and started to beat him up. Tico was hitting the other one, when suddenly the one I was hitting shouted that he was a police officer and told me to stop. I stopped immediately, apologised and did exactly what he said. He handcuffed me and pushed me into the car. Tico followed, his face bleeding badly. Then they took us to Paddington Green Police Station."

Doña Asuncion interrupted him. "The worst thing is Ana, if he is convicted he will get a criminal record and he may have to leave the country; and what about his studies?" She began to weep. "Did you explain at the police station exactly what happened?" I asked Pedro. "Yes," he said, "but the policemen denied it. They said we started the fight." "I told you Ana, do you remember?" said Doña Asuncion. "Those police were drunk last night. You know Pedro is not a violent man. He has never been in trouble with the police before." She was angry and obviously concerned about what was going to happen to her son. "The worst thing of all is that they made Pedro sign a document to say that it was him who assaulted the policeman. He signed it so he could come home last night. The other boy didn't want to sign and stayed in the police station."

That evening after talking for hours about what had happened to Pedro, I sensed that Doña Asuncion was going to move heaven and earth to clear her son's name.

This reminds me of another incident years later when Coker, a Nigerian friend of mine, was at Waterloo station. He had bought his ticket in a hurry and was running towards his train which was just about to leave. Suddenly two policemen dressed in plain clothes ran after him and grabbed him. Coker, who was a strong, well-built man, beat both of them up very badly. Lots of people in the station got involved in restraining the enraged Coker who was furiously hitting the men. Finally, more police arrived and they handcuffed him. He was arrested and taken away to the police station. He was charged with assaulting two police officers. When the case went to court it was revealed that the whole thing was a complete misunderstanding. It turned out that after buying his train ticket, he had forgotten his change. The female clerk started shouting for him to come back. The two plain clothed policemen nearby assumed he had robbed her and without showing any identification, tried to stop him. Coker thought he was being attacked by two racists and defended himself. He was found not guilty.

CHAPTER THIRTEEN

"Happy is he who takes no offence at me"

Matthew 11:6

"Go back to Bolivia, Anita! What are you doing here? You've got everything over there and you don't need to work, unlike many of us. Go back to Bolivia, get married, have babies, you are a nice young girl!" This was Doña Asuncion's advice after I told her I had been dismissed from my job. I knew she was right. I had asked myself many times what on earth I was doing cleaning dirty toilets in London, and now that I had lost my job, I didn't even have toilets to clean. I lost my job because the manageress found out I was giving breakfast to the black guy who followed me that night although he was not a guest at the hotel. I was also providing extra bread and milk, without charge, to some of the guests, especially the African refugees. Mr Singh had known all about this but never said anything. Pedro and his mum used to call me the "milk woman" because I would also take a bottle for them sometimes.

I sat down quietly in Doña Asuncion's room, not knowing what to say or do. After a while of her trying to persuade me to go back to Bolivia, she changed her mind and told me that I shouldn't worry, she was going to help me find another job once more. "The first thing to do Anita, is look for a room for you. Ah! By the way, I've got a friend; her name is Maria from Galicia. She lives just around the corner in Kensington Gardens Square and she probably has a room to rent out. I'll take you there this afternoon and introduce you to her, but I warn you Anita, she doesn't like South Americans. Believe me, Ana, she has no time for them at all."

In the afternoon we went to Maria's place and on the way Doña Asuncion told me, "you won't believe this Anita, but she's in her late sixties and has never had sex in her life; she's a virgin! Don't you think that's amazing, not to ever have had sex? Sometimes I feel like sending her my dear husband to do her a favour!" Her joke made me cry with laughter; I had to stop walking and sit down on a window ledge so I wouldn't wet myself. Bolivians are generally good at cracking sex jokes, but they were Doña Asuncion's speciality. "How do you know she's still a virgin?" I asked, intrigued by her story. "She told me Anita, that she hates men; she only talks about her father. She says she never married anyone because she couldn't find a man as good and as kind as her father." Then Doña Asuncion turned to me and said, "Anita, honestly if you don't find yourself a boyfriend soon you'll end up like Maria, or even worse. You might end up like that mad tramp that walks around Bayswater collecting rubbish and pulling out her pubic hair! Ha, Ha, Ha."

Maria had a flat in the basement of a big terraced house. We went down the stairs and knocked on the door of her kitchen.

The Illegal Dance

She opened it with an unhappy and distrustful look on her face, as though she didn't want any visitors. "How are you Maria? Are you all right? I hope you haven't been working too hard today. You have to look after yourself, Maria, you're not getting any younger!" Doña Asuncion's greeting didn't give Maria the chance to close the door on us.

Maria eventually dropped her guard and relaxed a bit, but did not invite us in; she started to complain about how tired she was and how inconsiderate people were. "The Moors who live on the second floor are the worst." (Spanish people use the term Moor in a derogatory way. It is associated with people of Moroccan ethnicity living in Europe). "They are so dirty and noisy, they make me sick. They never leave the bathroom clean after they've used it," she said. Maria was the housekeeper of that three storey house and had worked there for almost twenty five years, ever since she came to London in her late thirties.

Eventually Doña Asuncion and I forced ourselves into Maria's flat. "Maria, this is Anita," she tried to introduce me to her, but she completely ignored my presence. Bolivians love to introduce a person with great reverence and by using their title but I didn't have one, so she used my father's credentials instead to impress Maria. This shows you come from a good respectable family; even if you are a crook, a title will usually help you. "Her father is a doctor, Maria," she said, even though Dad was a dentist. Interestingly, lawyers are also known by the title "doctor" in Bolivia. Doña Asuncion carried on with the introduction. "She is studying English; she is a very good girl, very quiet, very clean, Maria. She is looking for a cheap room; do you have anything for her? She can even help you with the cleaning. You look like you need some help, Maria." "Oh, for goodness sake woman, not at all!" said Maria. "I can do the cleaning myself. Besides I wouldn't trust anybody else with the cleaning." Maria was annoyed and not impressed at all with my background, so she continued talking about the cleaning in the house. "Every time I go on holiday to Galicia and leave somebody here, they don't do the job properly. I have to work even harder when I come back," she said, completely dismissing the idea of me helping her.

Eventually, after a couple of hours of talking about Maria's problems with the tenants and Doña Asuncion telling her how good I was, Maria admitted that there was a small room on the top floor available for me. But I was not allowed to bring any men to the house, especially South Americans or, even worse, blacks. "They are disgusting, disgusting!" she said, spitting the words out and shaking her head looking down at the floor. But then a few minutes later she remembered she knew a couple of "good" South Americans she liked: Martha, Monchi and another Colombian girl who used to live in the house. The list of good South Americans began to grow as she remembered that Doña Asuncion, her husband and son were also from South America.

The dirty, unkempt flat where this strange woman lived showed that Maria's strength was coming to an end. That evening, while talking to her, I discovered that she not only disliked South Americans and blacks, but also Arabs, Portuguese and so on. "Oh! And I don't like English women, they are too loose and have no respect for themselves, they go to bed with the first man they meet," she said. In fact she didn't like anybody. I couldn't help wondering why she was so hostile, bitter and resentful. Was it because she was lonely? Or was it just because she had endured a hard life in London? I wondered why she hadn't gone back to Galicia. I imagined her home town being nice with a warm climate with beautiful beaches, full of happy people strolling along the promenade. Although Spanish people tend to sound a bit loud to us South Americans, Maria sounded harsher than any Spanish person I had ever met.

The next day I moved into that small, narrow room at the top of the house and with time, Maria became friendlier. To my surprise I even found myself visiting her at her flat from time to time. I realised that her hostility was the product of her loneliness and ignorance. She had some relatives who occasionally went to see her but the visits were sporadic and one sided. They had a full life with their children, they went on holidays, they had plans for the future; they had things to talk about. Maria instead, had a very small world; a world where nothing interesting happened, just the cleaning of the house. Nobody took her to a cinema, the theatre or to a restaurant. Yes, she would go from time to time to Galicia, but she didn't feel at home over there either and would return to her routine. Her solitude was a bitter one; without love, without happiness, without history. Her tiredness was not only physical but also mental and because of this, the opinions she had about the people she met were unjust. My visits to her were short and usually she was the one who did the talking and about the same things. I don't know if this helped to comfort her, but I'm sure at least it distracted her.

One day, the same year, 1982, I met an Argentinian woman. "Have you heard the news?" she asked me, looking very worried. "No, I haven't heard any news. I've been very busy moving to my new place and looking for a job," I answered. "A war has broken out between the U.K. and Argentina!" "A war, why?" I asked doubtfully. I was not convinced that in my lifetime I would ever witness a war between a South American country and Britain. "It's to do with the sovereignty of the Malvinas Islands," she said, explaining to me all the historical antecedents of the islands.

The woman seemed to be upset about what was going on. "I'm also looking for a job and every time I say I'm from Argentina I don't get one," she said. "All I get is funny looks during the interview. "From now on I'm going to tell everybody that I'm Spanish, I advise you to do the same; don't tell anyone you're from South America." She was quite convinced that all South Americans were going to be the target of some kind of prejudice.

Luckily the Falklands War didn't last very long and I didn't have to pretend to be Spanish. British military forces crushed the invasion of the islands by Argentinian forces in only three months. The dictator Leopoldo Galtieri never imagined that both America and Chile would become allies with Britain. This war greatly helped secure the reputation of Margaret Thatcher, the Prime Minister, whose leadership approval rating at the time was very low due to her authoritarianism, economic policies and the reduction of expenditure on public services, such as health and education. Also, the unpopular and repressive military junta headed by Galtieri in Argentina was using the war to distract attention away from its human rights violations and the country's economic problems. But also the conflict aroused a sense of Argentinian patriotism and revulsion towards the colonial actions of the U.K. In the same year as the Falklands War an important change in Bolivian politics occurred. In 1982, the military dictatorship retreated and Hernán Siles Suazo became the constitutional president. So my Uncle Hector returned to Bolivia at last to take on his job as the first Senator of the Socialist Party for Oruro.

Soon after moving to my new home I found a job cleaning a luxurious apartment in Albert Hall Mansions, Kensington, next door to the Royal Albert Hall. The flat was owned by an Indian family. On my first day at work, Mrs Ahsen, a tall, fat and distinguished looking woman, asked me to move a big potted plant from one room to another. The pot was so heavy I thought I had broken my back when I heard cracking noises coming from my spine while trying to straighten myself up. Mrs Ahsen couldn't ignore the look of pain on my face and with a pat on my sore back she said to me with a strong Indian accent, "thank you dear, you are going to be a beautiful girl to us, but only if you work very hard." Then she took me to the kitchen and asked me to wash up two huge cooking pots. Each one was so big that half of me was inside the pot being splashed with curry while I cleaned it. The family used to cook a large amount of food, once a week. This was then frozen to last the rest of the week. The cooking day was my hardest day and I would leave the house exhausted and smelling of curry.

Mrs Ahsen had two sons who were both married and lived with their wives in this luxurious flat. It seems quite common for Indian families to live in clans, as in Bolivia, with all the family residing in one place around the mother or mother-in-law. The daughters-in-law were two beautiful girls who were so used to being waited on by servants that they couldn't even be bothered to go into another room to fetch their slippers; they had to call me. All day it was "pass me this, pass me that." The only thing they did for themselves was to go shopping and get ready for their husbands before they came back from work. I was running all day from one end of the mansion flat to the other, cleaning, ironing and getting things for them. I felt like I was one of the lower caste "untouchables," the so-called "Dalits" of India.

One day Mrs Ahsen asked me to come back in the evening to help with the washing up as they had an important guest. I got to the house on time, seven in the evening and the visitor was already in the sitting room. I went straight to the kitchen and the cook, who was also there for the day, told me that the guest was Muhammed Ali, the legendary boxer who was apparently in London on a short visit. I sneaked into the sitting room with the excuse of serving the aperitifs and saw him there laughing; a very attractive man. That day I learned that the Ahsen family were Muslims.

Another time, months later, I went to clean a flat in Sloane Square, Knightsbridge. The cleaning company who hired me told me that it was owned by the American actor Telly Savalas. I couldn't believe my luck, I was to meet Kojak, a character I used to idolise when living in Bolivia. He turned out to be a very charming man. I thought that London was a place where you could meet lots of celebrities and all manner of strange people.

I had been working with the Ahsen family for about a year. It was hard work and left me with no energy to study, so when the opportunity to change jobs arrived I took it. It was cleaning the South Kensington house of Mary Gilliatt, a famous writer and interior designer. She was a very elegant woman and married to a prominent surgeon. She was the first to make a TV series of interior decorating in the U.K. in 1979, called Home and Design. Mrs Gilliatt was a woman to be admired for her strict discipline, organisation and exquisite taste; virtues that made her a prominent and influential woman. Every morning when I arrived at her home she was impeccably dressed and at her desk writing her books; she had written forty three, not only on design but also architecture and food. In the afternoon she would work for her design company or attend numerous meetings or functions.

One day there was a power failure in the house. Before she left she arranged for an electrician to come and asked me to let him in and to make sure that the work was done up to her standards. At around midday two men came to the house. One was white in his late fifties and the other was a handsome black man in his early thirties. After finishing their work and making sure that everything was working perfectly, the white guy asked me if there was any chance of a nice strong cup of tea. "Yes, of course," I said as I remembered that it is a custom in England, due to the cold weather, to drink cups of tea all day long. I invited them in to the kitchen; the white man introduced himself as Fred and the black guy as Romi. Generally, I have found workmen in England to be talkative, outgoing and friendly in comparison with those in Bolivia who are shy and humble. They would never ask you for a cup of tea or even a glass of water, even if they were dying of thirst. Sometimes when I passed by a building site in London, a workman would say something funny like, "for you love, I would even wear a tie." But you also come across the rude ones, of course. Like the one who said, "every time I see you love, I want to nail you."

The two electricians who came to Mrs Gilliatt's house were very polite. They drank their tea and left, but a few minutes later the doorbell rang again; it was the black guy. "Have you forgotten something?" I asked him. "I hope you don't mind me saying this, but I think you are a very good looking woman. Can I take you out for a drink?" he said taking me totally by surprise. His beautiful black, sad eyes combined with his mischievous smile attracted me. I gave him my telephone number and a few days later he called me. We went out for a drink to a pub in central London and after the first glass of beer, he told me something totally unexpected. "I've been in prison for ten years for armed robbery." I misheard him and replied, "you have been in the army for ten years?" "No, in prison, for armed robbery," he repeated slowly to make sure I understood. I must have opened my eyes and mouth very wide, because he went, "shush," placing his finger on my mouth, and looking around, thinking perhaps I might shout it out loud. "At the moment I'm on parole; I've only been out four weeks," he said, looking at me with his titillating and penetrating sad eyes. I held my glass of Guinness tight, so as not to drop it. This was not exactly what I wanted to hear on my first date with this guy and I was not certain how to react. I suppose most people would have ended the evening with a quick escape, but my reaction surprised me. I wanted to know more about this thief and I listened to his story with great interest.

The whole thing had been planned for a year; Romi was twenty at the time. The other two guys involved were in their late thirties and as he was the youngest and the most inexperienced, they had recruited him to drive the car, to make a quick getaway. But the whole robbery went wrong even before it started. Apparently, before the job took place, one of the guys had a few drinks in the pub in the early afternoon and later had an argument with his girlfriend about another woman. Unfortunately, it seems, the girlfriend knew all about the robbery. Later that day, before the post office closed, the raid took place. But the police arrived on the scene a few minutes later and caught them red-handed. The gang thought the girlfriend tipped off the police, so they ended up in prison. I don't think Romi was particularly proud of what he had done, but for some reason he wanted me to know about it. After a few drinks, he took me home and before he left we arranged to see each other again.

The following weekend we went for a walk in a park. London has so many beautiful open green spaces where one can escape from the stressful daily life typical of a big city. That afternoon while strolling around enjoying the sweet aroma of the flowers, I felt curious to see how he lived. So I asked him to take me to his home. "Take you to my home?" he laughed. "Yes, what's wrong with that?" I said, pretending it was the most natural thing to go to a criminal's house. "No, I'm sorry I can't," he apologised. "I live with my mother and brothers at the moment." His refusal made me determined to see how a man like him lived in London. "Let's go," I said, "I would love to meet your family." He gave in and agreed to take me there the following Saturday.

Romi's home was in Brixton, south London. At the time, it was often referred to as the drugs capital of London. Brixton was, and remains, a multi-ethnic area with a predominance of Afro-Caribbeans. The place looked neglected and poor; the walls of the houses were covered with graffiti. Unemployed youngsters hung around aimlessly in groups, drinking beer, smoking and casually dropping cigarette ends everywhere. Hungry dogs sniffed around rubbish bins. From time to time loud reggae music would emerge from a car passing by. I found it a depressing, unloved area where it seemed that even the sun had forgotten to shine. It was nothing like central London with its lovely parks and stately buildings fit for kings and queens.

The Illegal Dance

It didn't surprise me that terrible riots broke out in Brixton a year later. Confrontation between police and much of the black community ended up with hundreds of people being injured on both sides. Over a hundred vehicles were burned, including police cars and many buildings were damaged.

We arrived at his home, which was a council flat near Brixton tube station. If I thought the council flat where the Spanish girl and the Bolivian guy lived when I had just arrived was run down and soulless, this was even more so. It was also smaller and felt claustrophobic, with furniture crammed into a small main room, which could have been the living room, the dining room or both. Two teenagers were watching football on TV. Romi introduced them as his brothers. They looked at me quite surprised. "Hi," said one of them but the other didn't bother and they went back to their football. My friend offered me a chair and went to the kitchen to tell his mum we had arrived. Ten minutes later she came in with two plates full of Caribbean food; plantain, rice and beans, which I couldn't eat because it was too spicy. She looked at me suspiciously, without saying a word, before retreating to the kitchen and closing the door. Romi ate in silence. I realised I had made a mistake by insisting on coming to Romi's home. From time to time his mum would open the kitchen door slightly to look at me and then close it again. I probably spelled trouble to her. I also noticed that Romi's brothers were talking in low voices. Everybody felt uncomfortable. We left the flat almost immediately after he had finished eating. He took me home and we arranged to see each other the following weekend. I had the feeling I was taking a dangerous path but the thrill of the unknown was intriguing.

During the following weekends Romi told me more about his life. He spoke about his childhood with much resentment; the need he had had to have a father around. He told me about the sacrifices his mother had made to bring him up. He told me about the disastrous relationships his mother had with his father and the fathers of his two younger brothers. The second brother was born when Romi was almost fifteen years old and the third brother two years later. He talked about the difficulties of living with two brothers he hardly knew because most of his youth he had spent in prison. Romi told me that his grandparents on his mother's side had come from Jamaica to England on the Windrush in the fifties to do the jobs that many English people didn't want to do. They went to Leeds, a city in West Yorkshire, in England, where there was a lot of industry, particularly wool. At first his mother's parents had left their three young daughters in Jamaica, but every year brought one to England. The youngest was Romi's mother, who arrived in Leeds when she was only fifteen years old. One night when the girl had just had her sixteenth birthday her father entered her room and told her that she was a big girl now and that he had to make her a woman. That night the father forced his daughter to have sex with him. The next day, the scared girl told her sisters what had happened, but the sisters told her not to be alarmed because the same thing had happened to them. At seventeen Romí's mother ran away from home and later on she met a man with whom she had her first child, Romi. The relationship didn't last more than a year and Romi's mother had to struggle to look after her child on her own.

It had been six weeks since I had met Romi. One Saturday we went to the cinema. When the film started he held my hand gently. His fingers moved softly and slowly as if he was savouring a female's hand that he hadn't touched for years. His caresses woke up in me an immeasurable pleasure and uncontrollable sexual desire. After the film, on the way home I saw a small, dark dead end street. Without warning I pulled him into the shadows and turned into a wild animal with large tentacles. I started kissing and fondling his beautiful, strong body. He was kissing me

The Illegal Dance

too but he was nervously trying to see if there was anybody coming. We were like two octopuses with our hands everywhere until finally he stopped my excitement before it was too late. I admit my behaviour that evening was somewhat unusual, but it seemed that from time to time something would trigger these sexual outbursts. Before, my victim had been a nice, respectable, shy boy from Pakistan; this time it was a man on parole. I just hoped my next conquest would not be a priest.

A few days after that incident, Romi called me. "I'm sorry, Ana, I like you very much, but I can't see you anymore. I'm on licence, so I can't make any mistakes." He probably thought I was a loose cannon and if he wasn't careful, we would both end up in prison. I suspect there had also been pressure put on him by his mother for some reason.

Years later I went back to Brixton to a Bob Dylan concert at Brixton Academy with my husband and friends. I was glad to see that the area had improved tremendously. It was becoming a more upmarket, gentrified place.

Back at the house where Maria, the Spanish woman, was the housekeeper, I met a lovely, quiet couple living in the room next to mine. She was a sweet English girl called Sandy in her early twenties; he was a Moroccan called Ali who was maybe ten years older. Sandy and Ali became my friends and we would go to a pub for a drink occasionally. Ali was a Muslim so he didn't drink alcohol and would not allow his wife to either, so we would just order soft drinks. Most of the time however, we would stay in, listening to music and trying to learn the lyrics of Bob Marley's reggae songs, which in those days were very popular. I liked Bob Marley because he sang about social injustice and I studied the lyrics to try to gain more vocabulary. My new friends would help me with my English and correct my pronunciation.

One day Sandy and I were alone. Her husband was out, although this was unusual as they were nearly always together because neither of them worked; they lived on social security. That day Sandy told me a sad and disturbing story. She had become pregnant by another man before she met Ali, but before the baby was born the father left her. When the baby was about four months old she met the handsome Ali. After a few months of a happy relationship, Ali asked her to marry him. She was delighted and began preparations for a small wedding. But her plans rapidly turned sour when he told her that she would have to give up the child for adoption.

Her story broke my heart because as she was so besotted with this Ali she agreed to his appalling, selfish demand. She put her baby up for adoption when he was eight months old. Tears fell, wetting her beautiful face and blurring her sad blue eyes as she told me this. A few months after their wedding, Ali asked her to sleep with a rich Arab for money and yet again she accepted. I could not believe that Ali could be so cruel, but she made me promise not to ever mention it in front of him because he was also violent towards her.

One evening a few months later, Sandy and I were preparing dinner in her room; the three of us often used to eat together. Ali was fixing my cooker, which wasn't working properly. After dinner I went back to my room as it was time for bed. It must have been around midnight when I heard some gentle and hesitant knocks on my door. "Who is it?" I asked, before opening the door. "It's Sandy," she said in a soft and fragile voice. I opened the door; she was in her nightdress and looked like a scared and lost puppy. "Ana, Ali wants you to come and have sex with him," she said, very distressed. "Did he hit you?" I asked. "Yes," she said nodding her head. "Tell him I didn't open the door and I must be asleep, we will talk tomorrow," I said. She nodded again and left. A few days later I met Sandy on the stairs. "Ali doesn't want us all to be friends anymore," she said. "Thank God!" I thought.

CHAPTER FOURTEEN

*"In the end, it's not going to matter
How many breaths you took, but
How many moments took your breath away"*

Shing Xiong

I would say that the U.K. is generally a peaceful, tolerant, diverse society; however, different forms of discrimination do exist. In 1981 a fire in a house in south London, deliberately started by racists resulted in the death of many young black people. Those guilty were never found and this was considered partly due to a lack of effort on behalf of the police. This event was the beginning of a series of violent protests and riots against the police by the residents of that area, mostly of Afro-Caribbean origin. In 1985, the shooting of the mother of a suspected armed criminal ended in another wave of riots that lasted days in the same area of south London. The police thought that the mother was protecting her son at her home and she was somehow shot and paralysed by a policeman who admitted responsibility but was later acquitted in court. That same year the death of a black boy in police custody was again the beginning of more unrest and violence. The young man, armed with a knife had robbed a couple in their home while they slept. Years later, a group of young white, racist thugs murdered Stephen Lawrence, an innocent black boy who was only nineteen years old whilst he was waiting for a bus in Eltham, south east London. The police investigation of the case was extremely poor, but thanks to the pressure of the family and the public, the criminals were eventually convicted and sentenced to life in prison, after twenty years of freedom. Following this case a government instigated public enquiry found that the Metropolitan Police were institutionally racist.

It is well known that the police in U.K. tend to pick on young black men. This might be due to the fact that there is a high level of rebellion and criminality among them due to lack of employment, deficiency of decent housing or broken homes. According to a parliamentary report 60% of black Caribbean youngsters live in single parent households, usually with their mothers. But going back to the case of Doña Asuncion's son Pedro, he and his family lived far from south London. I imagined that the police saw Pedro and his friend as two trouble making immigrants, or perhaps as Asuncion warned that night, the police really were drunk and looking for trouble with anyone. So after Pedro's incident, as I predicted, Doña Asuncion devoted all her time to solving her son's problem. She was occupied with English and Spanish solicitors and a host of other legal advisors. Then the day arrived when Pedro had to go to court. All her team were well prepared to fight his case which she was threatening to take to the High Court to get justice. But, on the day of the court hearing, the two policemen did not turn up and the trial was

The Illegal Dance

set for another day. At this second hearing, the police witnesses again failed to turn up. The judge then halted all proceedings and gave Pedro an apology and a ten pound fine. Pedro finished his university studies and then went to work for a company in Sweden before later moving to Spain.

Once Pedro had moved to Malaga, Doña Asuncion encouraged him to send for his child and the mother in Argentina to live with him. Not only that, she insisted that they must get married to give their child a stable home, even though Pedro didn't particularly want to. This was typical of Asuncion's strong character. But just as she was a woman with social rules, she was also a woman full of contradictions. From time to time she would say that she didn't like her daughter-in-law because she was not good enough for her son. She didn't refer to the intellectual part of it, because in fact the daughter-in-law was an educated woman, but rather to the social. "She's an *imilla*", she would say referring to her being an indigenous woman. Later on she would contradict herself and tell me, "Ana, I would much prefer that Pedro marries an Indian than a *gringa*." But she would also praise a white person's beauty. If she saw a pretty white girl she would immediately assume she was from a "good family". These contradictions were typical of her Catholic upbringing, because the concept of a good or a bad family only depends on skin colour and social status in Bolivia and this is reflected in the Catholic churches where one almost never sees statues or images of Indians or black saints. Saints are normally white and good looking. Except for a few of us, Bolivians generally think like Doña Asuncion.

Doña Asuncion and I both got new jobs and we ended up working together for the first time in a hotel in Paddington. She was employed to do the cooking and I worked as her assistant. The guests were mainly Arab men. It seemed like a straightforward task, but little did I know that serving dinner to a bunch of uncouth men was like throwing raw meat to a pack of wild dogs.

Their malicious behaviour and constant physical harassment made the job an absolute nightmare. I ended up locking myself in the kitchen and passing the food through the hatch.

After a few months of being exploited, Doña Asuncion was sacked for asking for a pay rise and I ended up working as a guide to a hotel guest. He was an old blind man from Saudi Arabia who wanted to take me with him to his country. Eventually, he had his eyes operated on successfully and went back to his country with his family.

I continued working here and there constantly trying to find a decent, well paid job, but each time I found one that I thought was interesting, something untoward would happen. One day I saw an advert for a cleaner in my usual newspaper, the Evening Standard. As my English was improving I was now making my own enquiries about jobs. An old man's voice answered my telephone call. "Yes dear, I'm looking for some help," he said, giving me his address in Old Compton Street, Soho.

It was a convenient location, in central London, near Piccadilly Circus. I went there straight away. A pleasant, bald, frail, little man with vivacious eyes opened the door to his apartment and introduced himself as a judge. He explained carefully all the duties that I was going to be taking over and he wanted me to start the job straight away; I agreed to come back the next day. It was a good job, especially as it gave me enough time to go to school for my English lessons in the afternoons. The old man said he still worked three days a week, but on the days he stayed at home I was to prepare lunch for him.

During the following weeks, when he stayed at home he told me he was interested in astrology. When he found out that I was born in January he began to call me Miss Capricorn and he said that January was the luckiest month of the year because it was the first month. He told me that people born in this month should consider themselves very fortunate as they were going to have a

The Illegal Dance

fulfilled life, with considerable wealth and love. He would also talk about spirits of which one was the spirit of his mother who, according to him, had left him a fortune.

Mr Judge was full of mysterious and intriguing stories. As time passed he began to tell me more about his parents. He said that his mother had been a lovely, aristocratic woman and his father was a successful merchant; both had been born in the early part of the twentieth century. They would often be invited to exclusive parties and mix with lords and ladies. "My mother wore lovely clothes and elegant jewellery… jewellery that I keep in a safe place," he said. "Where? Here in the flat?" I asked the little man. "Oh no dear! Not at all! It is all put away in a safety deposit box in the bank and one day I shall show it all to you, Miss Capricorn."

Jewellery has never been my cup of tea, I think because of the problems I had with it when I was younger in Bolivia. I soon lost the first ring my mother gave me, the gold one inlaid with diamonds and rubies, and I was punished for it. The second one caused me problems with my parents when Rafael took it from me. I was not really interested in seeing any aristocratic, expensive stuff, but the old man would bring it up in conversation every time we had lunch together. Every time he talked about it he said that the day we were to go to the bank to see the jewellery was coming soon.

I began to picture myself in a dark, secret cellar of a bank in the City, where safety deposit boxes full of gold and expensive jewellery were kept. I saw myself opening them and being dazzled by a strong, shining light coming straight out from inside the boxes. I fantasised about trying on diamond rings, too big for my slender fingers. I saw myself wearing valuable necklaces, too heavy and expensive to show off in everyday life. I imagined the little old man inviting me to take a piece of jewellery for myself and not knowing what to choose. I think my imagination was partly the product of those Donald Duck magazines that I used to read as a kid, featuring rich, mean, Uncle Scrooge McDuck.

So the time passed, and I would do the job the best I could. When the judge wasn't there I would clean the flat thoroughly and when he stayed for lunch I would prepare something special for him. During the meal he would carry on the conversation about the jewellery and the possibility of me inheriting the family heirlooms as I was as small, delicate and refined as his mother was. Finally, the day arrived when he said we were going to the bank. We had a quick lunch, just a bit of salmon and salad. He seemed excited and keen to show me all he had in that security box. He talked endlessly all morning; he made jokes and sang old songs. He hurried me up to get ready to go. He encouraged me to dress with the aim of going for dinner to a very good restaurant afterwards and me wearing some of the jewellery of his deceased mother. I quickly did the washing up and got myself ready when I heard him calling me from the sitting room. When I went to see what he wanted, he asked me to sit down next to him. "Miss Capricorn, I like you, I like you." This octogenarian, hungry for love, clutched my hand tightly and pleaded desperately to have sex with me. I quickly stood up, confused and upset; he had taken me completely by surprise. I said politely that I was not interested in sex and especially with him. The old man's face changed; he was terribly disappointed. He stood up from the sofa with difficulty and staggered out of the sitting room. We never went to see the famous jewellery. When I arrived at the flat the next day, he said he would be hiring my replacement the following day.

A few years later, I found myself in that same area of London, walking along Old Compton Street, near Ronnie Scott's Club, where I used to listen to jazz and go salsa dancing. When I saw the lights on in his flat, on impulse, I rang the bell. He answered through the intercom. "Hello, Mr Judge," I said. "This is Miss

Capricorn do you remember me?" "Hello, young lady. Come upstairs please," he said pleasantly. I went up to the third floor. He opened the front door of his small flat and let me in. He was friendly and in a good mood. He led me into the sitting room and introduced me to Miss Sagittarius from Croatia. She was a teenager with an angelic face and was sitting on the large sofa, most probably listening with great interest to the jewellery story.

After I lost my job with Mr Judge, I found myself another one as a chambermaid in a five star hotel in Notting Hill Gate. I started at seven in the morning preparing breakfast. The service had to be fast and efficient. There were usually five girls working in a team, but one day one of them was off sick. The hotel was full, and there was a large group of Italians leaving early that morning. There were two girls serving the guests and one of them was me. Another one was in charge of cooking traditional English breakfasts and the other one was doing the washing up.

That morning it seemed that all the guests came down for breakfast at the same time. All the tables were full and we were having difficulty coping. The guests were getting more and more frustrated and irritable. They all had to get to the airport on time for their flights and we were not serving them quickly enough. The scene was chaotic; the Italians were shouting at us demanding at least a cup of coffee before they left. The problem was that there were not enough clean dishes in the kitchen. The dish washing machine was out of order and the girl who was in charge of the washing up was too slow. She ignored our pleas for her to speed up. There was an Italian girl serving with me, trying to calm things down, talking to the guests in Italian. I collected more and more dirty dishes and piled them all up in the sink, I suggested to the dish washing girl that I should do the washing up instead, but she got angry and pushed me away with a hip movement.

Unfortunately, the pile of dirty plates fell to the floor with a crash; everything was broken; I lost my temper. I don't remember exactly what happened, but I do recall being on top of her, pulling her hair and hitting her everywhere. Her face and long neck bled from the scratches I inflicted on her. The other girls screamed and tried to get me off her, but I wouldn't let go. I carried on beating her up on the floor. Some of the guests got up from their tables and came to the kitchen to see what was happening. They tried unsuccessfully to separate us. The manageress was called and put an end to the fighting. She took me upstairs to reception, paid me for the day and fired me.

So I found myself in the streets looking for a job yet again. I needed some change to make telephone calls, so I went to a kiosk in Bond Street Station and asked the sales assistant to change a ten pound note. He refused to do it unless I bought something. So I bought a packet of biscuits and when I got the change, there were no small coins for the telephone. Once more I asked him, "please, please", if he could give me small change. He refused, claiming he was too busy.

I lost my temper again and began to destroy the shop. Sweets, biscuits and magazines went flying. The man tried to stop me, but I was blind with anger and nothing would stop me throwing things everywhere. The salesman held me by one of my hands in an attempt to stop my madness, but it didn't prevent me throwing things on the floor with the other one. He threatened to call the police, but nothing would stop me, not even the fact that the police could come anytime. I was lucky, the police never came to arrest me. These outbursts must have been the result of my working in stressful, unfulfilling and badly paid jobs while struggling to learn the language and being away from my family. I was also preparing for an important English exam. Then my mother announced she was coming to see me in London.

A few months before, I had asked my parents to send me some anti-burn cream because I had burnt my hand while cooking. This happened when I was working at the hotel in Notting

Hill Gate; I almost burned down the building. A saucepan full of oil caught fire and instead of covering it with the lid and letting it cool down on its own, I panicked. I lifted the burning pan to try and throw it on to the patio, but the burning oil spilt on my hand and over the lino, starting a fire. I managed to get the pan out to the patio and put out the burning floor, but the result was painful burns on my right hand and a big hole in the plastic lino. So, my mum decided to come to London to check up on me; there was nothing in the world that would persuade her otherwise, even though they couldn't really afford it. Terrible inflation had quickly followed the election of Hernán Siles Zuazo as President of Bolivia, after twenty years of dictatorship. The unions who helped him to achieve power paralysed the government with constant strikes. He did not receive support from the political parties or members of Congress and even Jaime Paz Zamora, his vice president, abandoned him.

In one of my parents' letters they had told me that it was becoming increasingly difficult to send me money. People withdrew their savings from the bank in big plastic bags and had to transport the money by taxi. It was cash without any value at all. International economists said it was the fourth largest hyperinflation ever recorded in the world. My parents, like many other Bolivians, lost a lot of money. A few years later my Uncle José, Mum's older brother, told me bitterly that he had saved enough money to go around Europe on holiday, but lost it all in this economic crisis. He never quite recovered from the blow; years later he would talk about the things he could have done if it had not been for that disastrous period.

Many months later when the economic situation in Bolivia had improved a little I designed a scheme to extend my student visa in London. My parents would send me a cheque for a thousand dollars every three months. I would photocopy it and together with my passport and the school enrolment receipt, I would send it to the Home Office. Once my visa had been extended, I would cash the cheque and send the money back to my parents. They would then send me another cheque for a thousand dollars three months later and I would repeat the procedure to renew my visa every three months. That is how I extended my visa as student in London. The same amount of money would go backwards and forwards for years.

I tried to find a bigger place to move to before my mum arrived, but accommodation in London was so expensive that this was almost impossible. I remember one of my English teachers saying, "accommodation is both a difficult word to spell and difficult to find in London!" So I decided to stay in my little room. Mum was surprised to see me living in such a tiny space. There was hardly enough room for one person, never mind two. Finding me in good health, however, was all that really mattered to her. A few weeks after she arrived in London my mother and I decided to travel by train around Europe. My brother José and his Swedish girlfriend joined us in France. It was nice to be able to show Mum the best of European culture and art. We visited museums, churches, parks, good restaurants and all the important places you see in films and magazines. We finished the tour in Sweden, where Mum stayed for a few months with her sister Betty before returning to Bolivia. I returned to London to sit my English exam.

As soon as I arrived Doña Asuncion told me she had a surprise for me. She had met a young Colombian man at her work and she wanted to introduce me to him. "Ana, you must meet this handsome boy," she said. "I know he's the type you like." The next day out of curiosity I went to meet her at work. She was the manageress of a large office building where this good looking guy called Fabio was also working as a cleaner. He welcomed me effusively with a friendly smile. His wild, Afro hairstyle, inquisitive eyes and good physique made him a very attractive young man indeed.

The Illegal Dance

"Yes, I like him," I thought to myself. But when I turned around there was a sex goddess standing just behind me. She was a tall, seductive woman with beautiful black, flirtatious eyes and a husky, sexy voice; the type of woman who would make anyone look twice. She paraded her dynamic and harmonious body like a catwalk model; she was a Colombian beauty. Unfortunately she was also Fabio's girlfriend. Fabio and Julia were a young, carefree and fun loving couple. We became friends immediately and, a few weeks later, Julia and I became flatmates, sharing a damp, cold and dark room in the basement of a house in Bayswater Road, near Notting Hill Gate tube station.

My salsa period started at that time. The three of us went dancing every weekend. Julia and Fabio were terrific dancers; we were unstoppable. After a long day of work we were exhausted, but it didn't matter; we went out in search of musical energy that appeased our tiredness. Sometimes Julia and I were already in bed when she would suggest going out to one of the salsa clubs. She didn't have to wait long for my answer; in less than ten minutes we would be out and about. There were plenty of places to choose from in those days; an old pub in Farringdon, a club in Brixton, the Base Club in Old Street, or Ronnie Scott's, were the right places for salsa dancing. "Don't Hit the Black Woman," by Joe Arroyo, "Lloraras," by Oscar de Leon, and "Cali Pachangero," by the Niche group were my favourite songs. My God we danced! We moved every tired muscle to the beat. The blessed salsa, saviour of our sanity; we danced all night without stopping. Salsa, dropped from heaven, you were like a cry of joy, like a passionate and seductive animal and like a tight and ardent embrace. You helped us cope with the stress of living in a cold, demanding and foreign country. You helped us forget that we had to work the next day at those miserable and poorly paid jobs. We would go to bed hugging your tunes, wake up listening to them and feeling your erotic movements and your harmony. You were far more enjoyable than the religious sermons I had to listen to when I shared a room with Samantha. Salsa became my religion; I had more energy, I felt better, looked better and didn't get into any more fights.

Living with Julia was never dull; people would often come and go from our room. On many occasions I would wake up in the night to go to the toilet and stumble over bodies asleep on the floor. They were often Colombian girls who had arrived in London to work. Julia would feel sorry for them and put them up in our little room. She was a lovely, caring and placid girl. Nothing bothered her; that was the reason why we had so many visitors. When living in Colombia she had become pregnant very young and due to lack of work in her country, she had left her young child with her mum and came to work in London. During my time in England, I saw this story repeated many times over. I have met many South Americans who had to leave their families at home to better themselves in countries like the U.K., other European countries or the U.S.A.

Fabio, like Julia, had been brought up with strong moral values. He remembered his mother as a very strong character. One day when he was a small boy she found him smoking a cigarette butt he had picked up in the street. She hit him so severely that he never smoked or drank alcohol in his life again. As he was leaving Colombia, his mother told him not to come back home unless he had a degree. I lived with Julia and a variety of in transit Colombian girls for about a year. My salsa steps were getting better, but my English was getting worse. I decided to move out and live on my own again to be able to have more chance to study. Julia also decided to move out of the little damp room. She had a Colombian friend to share a place with, but when we gave our notice to leave the Spanish owner refused to return our deposit. So Julia and her friend didn't have enough money to get decent accommodation and ended up in a place as bad as the

The Illegal Dance

one we had just left. Because I had a better paying job than Julia, the stolen deposit did not affect me as much as her.

My new place was fairly central, in Kilburn, in the north of London and I even had a garden, but loneliness hit me hard. When I lived with the Colombians I had somebody to talk to, somebody to share things with. Some of the girls would make me feel more fortunate than them because I didn't have economic problems, I didn't have a son or a daughter to worry about, I didn't have to send money home every month to help anyone and I didn't have any debts to pay; I was free of commitment. But now, it was just me, someone I could not deceive. I was aware of my shortcomings and my lack of strength. I was alone with just my memories and secrets about what had happened in Bolivia. The philosopher Jean-Paul Sartre said: "If you are lonely when you are alone, you are in bad company." Yes, I did not like my own company, and I had more time to think of Rafael and his abandonment. So, to pacify these feelings I spent most of my free time watching television. This was the best way to improve my English under the circumstances. The television sitcom Yes, Minister was my favourite series. Although I didn't understand much of it, I enjoyed watching the actors' facial expressions, especially that of the minister who was constantly being manipulated by his advisor. Top of the Pops on Thursday evenings was another of my usual programmes. Later on I became hooked on the comedy series To the Manor Born. I loved Penelope Keith, an actress who seemed the epitome of an upper class, strong English woman, unable to show emotions in public. I used to wonder if I would ever be able to speak English like her one day. Little did I know then that years later I would actually meet not only Penelope Keith but also the actor who played the minister.

I had been in England for three years, but I had minimal interaction with English people; I didn't know much about the locals; all I learned about them was through the television programmes

I was watching. I was beginning to realise that the British have a good sense of humour. One day I met an Englishman in his late forties who lived around the corner from me. Every time I passed by his home he would try to talk to me. In Bolivia if a guy is interested he may whistle at you in the street or pay compliments to make you feel good, such as "you look pretty today," or "I love your legs." But in London the commonest conversation to break the ice usually involves the weather. "What a lovely day," people say when the sun is shining, but if it is overcast or raining nobody talks to you.

Eventually my neighbour plucked up the courage to talk to me. He opened the conversation with standard remarks about the weather, before moving on to enquire which country I was from. When I told him I was Bolivian and spoke Spanish he asked me if I could help him to make a phone call to Spain. He had a holiday home there and wanted me to talk to the caretaker to give him some instructions concerning his flat. I made the call for him and in gratitude he invited me for dinner at a cheap restaurant in Kilburn. During the dinner I found out that he not only had houses in Spain and in Kilburn, but also in St John's Wood and Hampstead. He was well off financially and looking for a wife. Not very tactfully, he asked me if I was interested in getting to know him better. Although I was poor and lonely at the time I had no intention of getting married, so I showed no interest in him and went back to my solitary existence.

A few months later I met another English guy who was much younger. He took his dog for walks in the park early in the morning. One day as I was passing by the dog sniffed at me, so the man apologised. This was the start of a friendship. Ted and the dog often visited me with flowers and little presents. He worked as a builder, so his hands were rough. He smelt of cement and cigarettes, he was a chain smoker and drank twelve cups of coffee a day.

Christmas Eve arrived and Ted phoned me to make arrangements to meet up. "I've got a lovely present for you," he said. But the thought of having to spend Christmas with him, his dog, his cigarettes and drinking coffee made me tell him a lie. "Oh, I'm sorry, Ted, but I've been invited to a friend's place, Doña Asuncion. Do you remember, the lady I told you about?' He sounded disappointed and put the phone down straight away. I spent that Christmas on my own for the first time. I still remember how happy I felt being by myself; that day I began to appreciate my own company. I never saw Ted again.

After about ten months of living in Kilburn, I realised how much I missed my Colombian friends, especially Julia and Fabio. I found out that they were again looking for a new place to live. I spoke to the property owner I had met a few months earlier. He told me there was an empty studio flat in his Kilburn house, around the corner from me. I told him about my friends and he accepted on condition that only two girls moved in. A few days later, Julia and two other Colombian girls moved into the studio flat in Kilburn; every time the landlord came to collect the rent, one of the girls would hide under the bed.

That was how many of us immigrants lived, all in the same room, packed together, embracing our problems. We lived far from the fine, artistic, cultural and opulent London. We lived by cleaning offices, hotels and private houses. We lived accumulating insomnia, worries and sorrows. Many counted pennies and prayed that the little they earned would be enough to send to their children.

A few weeks after the three girls moved in, the relationship between Julia and Fabio came to an end. I was sorry about this because I liked Fabio and didn't think I was going to see him again, but a few months later he contacted me and we continued our friendship. Fabio was never short of women; in fact he was an extrovert and was good at attracting any girl he wanted. Since he was an excellent dancer he also had the ability to make you dance well, even if you were not an expert. I once took an English girlfriend dancing with us and after a few dances with him, she said, "blimey, he's good, isn't he? I almost had an orgasm when I was dancing with him!"

Going out dancing with Fabio guaranteed a good night. I remember once, he and I went out. The night club was full of people. I was enjoying the attention and appreciative looks from the men. I noticed two handsome guys looking at me from a corner of the dance floor. "This is my night," I thought. Even Fabio noticed them looking at us and began to tease me. When we finished dancing, they approached us. I felt flattered until I found out that they were after Fabio, not me.

During the winter of 1984, Fabio and I worked in a sauna at Swiss Cottage. It was run by a very nice Irishman and was open twenty four hours a day, seven days a week. It was of course, nothing like the saunas I visited in Sweden when I lived there. Swedish saunas were built in the middle of forests, usually on the edge of a lake. The lakes would be surrounded by tall, thin pine trees almost reaching the sun, with just a few rays of light penetrating the canopy. After roasting in the sauna, naked men and women would have an invigorating splash in the freezing lake. The love of naturism is a Swedish characteristic. The summer sun is so precious there that people would walk or lie down in the parks half naked, including the women.

The Swiss Cottage sauna was totally different, but it had its own charm. Apart from its location in an expensive part of London, it had a good atmosphere. It was small, friendly, totally unpretentious and attracted people of all kinds, including a fair share of celebrities. These included Dave Stewart from the Eurhythmics, Marti Pellow, the lead singer from Wet Wet Wet, the American singer-songwriter, Bobby Womack and the poet, Benjamin Zephaniah. Among the staff were several girls who were osteopathy students at the nearby college. There was even a young doctor who later on became, together with her husband, also a doctor, pioneers in integrative and preventative medicine in London.

That winter was of one of the worst since I had arrived in England. It snowed heavily and was bitterly cold. I found it difficult to heat my room. Many houses lacked central heating, relying instead on a meter system that needed fifty pence coins to make it work. It was like putting money in a piggy bank, the only difference being that you never got your money back. Meters were usually installed in rented accommodation, so landlords could make even more profit from their tenants. My landlord would regularly turn up with a key for the meter to collect the coins from the meter box. I used to look at him wondering how much extra he was making out of me, especially when my room was still cold. Fifty pence every hour, more or less was the amount I needed to keep my room warmish in winter.

I had a Spanish friend called Bonita who worked out how to cheat the electricity meter. She taught me how to slide a photographic negative through a gap in the meter to stop the disc from turning. This helped me financially for a while, until one day the landlord found no money in the meter. He quickly had it changed for a more modern one so I had to go back to paying again. Bonita came up with another way of slowing the meter using a magnet but I never got round to trying it.

On one particularly cold evening the meter was swallowing my fifty pence pieces very quickly but I still wasn't able to warm the place up. I was in bed well wrapped up, but still cold; it was snowing heavily outside. I was running out of coins, and I couldn't sleep properly. I felt cold in my head, my feet, and my hands. The cold would wake me up from time to time. I felt it getting through the cracks of the old window frame and door like a thin veil of death. "There are no more coins!" I jumped out of bed. "Tomorrow the landlord would find the meter full of coins and my frozen body too." I decided to risk trying to get to the sauna. I dressed up and went out looking for a taxi. I could hardly walk in the snow. Finally a taxi felt sorry for me and stopped, but had great difficulty getting to Swiss Cottage as the roads were icy and very slippery.

That evening the sauna was full of people who had got stuck on their way home due to the bad weather. The English are not as prepared as the Swedish when it comes to a snow storm. The Swedes combat the snow with sophisticated equipment and efficient workers. At dawn you would see snow ploughs rapidly clearing the streets, in England however, they do not have the right equipment, maybe because it doesn't often snow heavily.

I spent a sleepless but warm night at the sauna with a few friends who were working; the time went quickly. I was supposed to be on the afternoon shift at the sauna that day, but when I got home the telephone rang. It was the receptionist from the sauna, her voice sounding concerned, "Ana, don't come to work today; we are surrounded by police! The whole street is closed. We will call you later, but please don't come, something very serious has happened, I can't talk now." She hung up the phone as if she were being overheard.

A few days later I found out that one of the Colombian cleaners at the sauna had been arrested for being part of a major drug smuggling ring. Only days before this happened he had told me he had only one more month to work before he was going back to Colombia for good with his pregnant wife. Apparently the police had found a car full of cocaine parked in north London. It could have been his car, I'm not sure. I only know that he was involved in drug trafficking, together with some other people, English, Irish and Colombian. Early in the morning, minutes after I had left the building, the police had stormed the sauna to take everyone by surprise. They arrested a few people including the Colombian guy and a full investigation started. They interviewed all the staff and searched the entire premises for drugs using sniffer dogs.

As the police didn't find any evidence that was the end of the ordeal and the sauna was not closed down. But the Colombian cleaner and his pregnant wife went to jail. That morning the police also found two illegal immigrants working at the sauna. They were deported. It never occurred to the owner of the sauna that Fabio and I might be involved in drugs, even though we came from countries associated with cocaine. We continued working there for another year.

CHAPTER FIFTEEN

"You don't love someone for their looks, or their clothes, or for their fancy car, but because they sing a song only you can hear"

Oscar Wilde

Time passes quickly in cities like London; there is little time to stop and reflect. One just has to get on with things without looking back. In London you are always on the go, looking for and creating new opportunities. This way of life is totally different to how I remember it was in Bolivia, where time is less important, where one takes it lightly. In my country we have time to pause, time to hesitate, time to waste. Time in Bolivia doesn't cost money, it is taken for granted. We even have time to be late or not keep our appointments at all.

Five years had passed and life in London for me still felt like a puzzle to be solved but at the same time something worthwhile to be experienced. Despite the fact that I was having a great time, it sometimes felt as if London was dragging me more and more on to an unknown and lonely road from which it would be difficult to leave.

Some people lean on religion when things are not going well or when one feels the need to belong. At that time, I was no different, so I began to explore different faiths. I attended talks on Buddhism, Hinduism and Christianity. I met people who believed that chanting was a good way to turn your life around, or those who practised meditation to gain inner energy and others who assured me eternal happiness in heaven if I followed their Christian faith. I also read books on philosophy by writers like Bertrand Russell, Alan Watts and Jean-Paul Sartre. I was like many other youngsters trying to find the meaning of life in an overwhelming city. While religion and books might give some kind of comfort they don't necessarily solve the problems of everyday life and even more so when you feel trapped by the love for a man who does not love you. With him I had vitality, energy and direction. Now I was stagnating, not knowing what to do.

Dad suggested I study natural medicine. "It is the medicine of the future," he wrote in one of his letters, perhaps sensing I was going through a confused and indecisive period. He had studied medical anthropology and often talked to me about it. He wanted me to learn a natural way to treat the sick, taking into account culture and beliefs. He was probably right, it seemed an excellent idea, but this meant spending more time in London. Although my English had improved considerably, I was still having difficulty in getting a good, well-paid job. Returning to Bolivia was an attractive option, but so was the possibility of studying an academic subject. I decided to start a new, advanced course in English, hoping that this might open the door to a university education and a better future, although without permanent U.K. residence my chances were slim.

One day, I spotted an advert in the Evening Standard for a job as a live in receptionist. I called up immediately and, after a short conversation with one of the staff, I was given an appointment for a formal interview the next day at the Hill Hotel, in Notting Hill Gate. After a short meeting with the manageress, who was from Portugal, I was offered the post and told I could start straight away. It was a real victory to graduate from cleaning jobs.

On starting, I was shocked by one of the manageress's rules: no black guests were allowed in the hotel. This surprised me even more than the time my school friend in Coroico criticised me for referring to my black maid's mother as Mrs. I thought it was a ridiculous rule that was probably illegal, as we were living in a cosmopolitan, free city, where everybody had the right to stay wherever they wanted. Black people were everywhere and are part of a civilised society. The rule was also odd because the receptionist who worked the morning shift was black and I am not entirely white myself. I said nothing about this and just hoped that no black people would ever come to the hotel to challenge her rules.

A few months later a good looking blonde woman came to the hotel to book a double room for the weekend. I checked her in and a few hours later she came back with her partner, a black man. When the manageress saw him the next morning at breakfast she told me off for allowing him to stay. I explained that the white woman had come on her own to book the room, and I had no idea she was with a black man. It seemed absurd to me to make such a fuss about a person's skin colour, but I had to explain myself because I was afraid of losing my job. The manageress accepted my explanation and suggested I should be more careful in future. Out of curiosity I asked her why she was so adamant about not having black people in the hotel. "They don't pay their bills," she said. "Oh well, if that's the case I don't blame you," I replied. But I took the opportunity to try to make a deal with her to avoid more misunderstandings. I put it to her that if I made sure full payment was made when a black person booked a room, would it then be ok for them to stay? She thought about this for a moment and said, "I'm not sure, I will have to think about this. It's not me, you know, the guests don't like black people."

Years later I met a woman from Nicaragua who told me that the only thing she didn't like about London was that there were too many blacks. I have noticed over the years living in England that the most racist people are the foreigners, especially people who are not that white. The guests at the hotel were mainly from Portugal, Spain, Cyprus and Greece. A few English and Italians stayed from time to time.

My life as a student at the English school was going well. My better English made me more confident. I made new friends and enjoyed my time going out to pubs, parties, music festivals, concerts and taking short trips to other European countries, as well as around Britain, some of which were organised by the school.

At that time I hung around with a musician I first met at a reggae concert when I was living in Sweden. We had kept in touch and met up again in London. He played in the band of the Jamaican dub poet Linton Kwesi Johnson and would sometimes take me to watch their rehearsals. In my English class I met a sweet Swedish girl called Birgitta. We became good friends when she found out that I had lived in Sweden. She was even more impressed to know that I had met Linton Kwesi Johnson. We began to spend time together and go to reggae concerts. I also took the opportunity to practise the little Swedish I knew with her. Birgitta was a lively girl in her early twenties who loved the buzz and sophistication of London. The city was a novelty for her because she came from a little village in Sweden called Landskrona. She was working as an au pair near the hotel where I lived and worked.

One evening, we went to a pub where we met two English guys. They were much older than us but seemed nice, interesting and fun. We arranged to meet them again to go to a nightclub. The following weekend they picked us up from Birgitta's house smartly dressed wearing leather jackets and colourful shirts with their hair greased and swept back like Elvis Presley. It seemed that both of them were wearing the same aftershave because its strong jasmine smell permeated every corner of the car.

On the way to the club we stopped in Kensington High Street to pick up another friend of theirs. When we arrived at his place we were invited in for drinks and nibbles; his kitchen table was full of things to eat: cheese, olives and Spanish *chorizos*. He had even baked a wonderful chocolate cake that Birgitta and I gorged on. It seemed that the guy had gone to a lot of trouble to make us feel welcome. After a few glasses of wine, pieces of cake and more nibbles, we all left for the nightclub. The host sat next to the driver; the other guy, Birgitta and I were in the back.

Five minutes later, we were on Queensway when Birgitta grabbed my hand without explanation and told me in Swedish to get out of the car. A few seconds later we stopped at some traffic lights and she suddenly opened the door. Both of us jumped out, ran in the opposite direction and turned into a side street. We were running and still holding hands when we saw a car coming behind us. Birgitta panicked, "they're coming after us!" she exclaimed, pulling me down the stairs of a basement flat.

Although it was around eleven at night the lights of the flat were on. She rang the bell desperately and a woman holding a baby opened the door. Birgitta told her there were three men following us and she let us in; until then I hadn't understood what was going on. We sat down in her sitting room remaining silent for a few minutes. The woman was so engrossed in her television programme that she didn't bother to ask us any questions. Neither did I ask Birgitta why we had run away so abruptly leaving

The Illegal Dance

the three guys without an explanation. They probably thought we were a couple of lunatics. Ten minutes later we thanked the woman for her kindness and left her home as quickly as we had entered it. We were about twenty minutes away from the hotel where I lived so we decided to walk. Birgitta was anxious and panicky; she was constantly looking behind and running from time to time, especially when she saw a car coming in our direction. "What happened, why did we run away?" I asked her, totally oblivious. "Didn't you hear what they were saying?" "No, I didn't," I replied, surprised at my lack of perception. "The guy who made the cake told the man who was driving that the cake was made of hashish." "Hashish? What's that?" "It's a drug, a drug!" she repeated a couple of times, as if she was talking to a real idiot.

My knowledge of drugs was limited in those days because I had never been exposed to any kind of drug in Bolivia. I had heard of cocaine, marijuana and heroin, but I had never seen them; I had never heard of hashish, let alone that you could make such a delicious cake with it. It tasted so good that I could have easily finished off the whole cake all on my own.

"How many pieces of cake did you have?" I asked her. "Two," she said. "What about you?" "I had three," I replied, hoping that the wine and the cake together wouldn't affect my sanity. Birgitta sounded upset. "I got scared because I heard them talking about going somewhere else instead of going to the nightclub," she said. "They probably wanted to go to buy more drugs," I replied, wondering how on earth I had not understood their conversation. It may have been the wine and the hashish that slowed my brain down, or was it the fact that my English was still not good enough?

My problem was also that I often don't pay attention when people talk. I thought about my time at school in Bolivia, when my teacher would tell my mum, "she looks like she's listening in class, but when I ask her a question she doesn't know the answer.

Her mind is always somewhere else and that's the reason she doesn't learn as quickly as the rest of the students. She doesn't pay attention." I thought of my time at the University in Bolivia. While my friends had no difficulty in learning the subjects, I often struggled and needed regular private tuition. I thought of my friends Pedro and Fabio who had arrived in England at almost the same time as me. They had learned English very quickly and were already at university. Here I was, still trying to perfect the language. We arrived at the hotel disappointed with our frustrating night out. Birgitta stayed overnight in my room. While lying in bed in the dark next to her listening to the sound of her gentle, peaceful and innocent breathing, I asked myself how much more wary must I be in this city to keep safe?

Over the following months I developed a very good relationship with the Portuguese manageress and her cousin, who also worked and lived in the hotel. We used to go out from time to time. My new friends were not party girls, so we often went to Portuguese restaurants. I felt that my job at the hotel was one of the best things that had happened to me since my arrival in London. It was a friendly place, clean, safe and with decent people staying there. Many guests remained only a few days; others practically lived there because they had long term business in London. I had a lot of free time for my studies, because my work started at seven in the evening and finished at eight in the morning. At about midnight I usually went to bed because there was not much to do, but I had to be alert all night in case any of the guests needed assistance.

On one occasion, one of the guests had to check out early in the morning, so he asked me to wake him up at six o'clock. I made the wakeup call from reception at the time agreed. Half an hour later he left the hotel and I went back to my room, which was just in front of the reception area. I was lying fully dressed and awake on my bed when I heard footsteps in the reception area. I

The Illegal Dance

thought it may be another guest who had woken up early and was coming down to the lounge to watch the morning news on the television. I got up from the bed quickly to see if I could be of any help, but as I was about to open my door I heard a familiar noise. It was the sound of a door hinge. There was a small corridor in front of my room with a fire safety door that led to the reception area. This door would make a noise when it was opened. I was surprised by the sound as it was so early, and guests never used that door. Anyone who needed assistance would ring the bell at the reception desk. Just as I was about to see who was out there, I felt a gentle push on my door; it was as if somebody was trying to check whether or not it was open. A bloodcurdling feeling took hold of me. Luckily that morning, for some unknown reason, I had closed my door properly. This was unusual because I was always going in and out of my room, so I used to leave it unlocked. I stood there, frozen with fear, with my ear pressed up against the door, trying to work out what was going on.

I remembered with a jolt that I had forgotten to lock the front door properly when the last guest left. "This might be him," I thought; perhaps he had forgotten something. I was about to open my door when I heard the hinge creaking again accompanied by footsteps leaving the small corridor and walking towards reception. I stood perplexed and sure that the person on the other side of my door was not a guest but a stranger. I tried to call the police from my room, but the telephone line was dead. Stupidly I had forgotten to connect the switchboard to my bedroom. I felt impotent and furious. I stayed inside my room, listening carefully for movements of the stranger. I heard the sound of drawers in reception being opened and closed. It also appeared that he was trying to use the public telephone, which was in the entrance hall.

Every time I was on the verge of going out to see what was going on, I forced myself to stay in my room; I was frightened.

All the suspicious activity in the reception area took less than ten minutes, and then there was complete silence. I didn't feel brave enough to leave my room. I waited and waited to make sure there was nobody out there. Finally I opened the door slightly, feeling my heart beating strongly, afraid that I might be assaulted. Slowly and carefully I ventured out to find that the whole reception room had been ransacked; it was obvious we had been burgled.

The morning receptionist arrived a few minutes later and both of us woke the manageress with the bad news. "They stole the cash box and all the money from the public telephone!" she shouted furiously, after going through everything in detail. Then she turned on me, fuming, "you have made two mistakes," she said. "First of all you left the front door open, but you also left the cash box unattended before going back to your room." I couldn't deny it; I should have taken the cash box into my room for security. It was clear that the burglary was my entire fault. "Yes, I'm sorry," I replied, looking down at the floor, hoping not to antagonise her even more. "Didn't you hear anything?" she asked. "Yes, I heard everything," I said. "You did?" she looked at me, confused. "You heard everything from beginning to end, but didn't do anything about it? Why didn't you call the police, or call me?" she shouted at me.

This time I was really worried. I now had to tell her about my third mistake and one which might cost me my job. "I forgot to connect the outside line to my room." "You forgot to connect the outside line to your room?" she repeated in disbelief. "So you heard everything, you knew what was going on and you did nothing, absolutely nothing?" she said, looking at me totally bewildered, probably thinking that I was useless and didn't deserve to work there. The morning receptionist and the manageress's cousin looked at me in surprise. I had pretty much dug my own grave; I think the three of us were completely sure that it was my last day at the hotel. "I was too scared to confront the burglar, that's why I didn't leave my room," I said. "How much money has been stolen?" I asked her, ready to play my last card. "About three hundred pounds," she replied, slapping her thigh with her hand. "To be honest, for that amount of money not even you would have gone out to fight with the man," I said, totally resigned to losing my job but hoping she would understand enough to forgive me.

The manageress looked at the morning receptionist as though seeking advice on what to do with me. Then she looked at her cousin who was standing outside her room still in her pyjamas. Neither of them said a word. She looked at me again and said in a low voice, "you are right, it was sensible not to confront the burglar." We heard footsteps from one of the guests coming downstairs for breakfast, and the noise of the girls who had arrived to get things ready in the kitchen. The manageress bounced back to her normal cheerful self and said, "well, the boss is coming back in two weeks. Let's see what he says." Everything then went back to business as usual. For some reason the manageress didn't call the police; maybe because I didn't have a work permit. Later on we discussed at length who the burglar might have been. If the thief had been an opportunistic passer-by, he wouldn't have known that the front door wasn't locked properly. Also, whoever came in probably would have known there was not a man working on reception. The burglar also must have known that the door he pushed led to my room and that I used to leave it unlocked sometimes. We speculated that the burglar might have been a guest.

This reminds me of something that happened before I started working at this hotel. At the end of the same street there was another hotel called the Slavia. I worked there briefly as a receptionist, replacing a Chilean friend. The job was Saturdays and Sundays in the evening from six until eleven. The hotel had a porter who started just after eleven o'clock.

One Sunday evening all the guests were in their rooms, it must have been around eleven. I didn't have much to do on the reception desk, so I sat down in the lounge to watch television. I was alone and the place was all quiet. I must have dozed off, when I woke up suddenly to a strange noise. I opened my eyes and saw a man climbing in through the front window. "Help! Help!" I screamed desperately.

The man managed to get into the sitting room, and started to move towards me. I was petrified with fear and tried to get up and run, but I was rooted to the sofa as my legs would not respond. The man put his hand over my mouth to shut me up. I tried desperately to get away from him, but I was in such a panic I didn't really know what was going on. He started shaking me while I was screaming; I was trembling and sweating with terror at the same time. I vaguely remember hearing the television in the background and my name being called, "Ana, Ana."

After struggling with the man for a while I came to my senses and realised it was Miguel, the Spanish night porter, who had forgotten his keys. He had rung the bell for a long time and there was no answer, so he finally decided to get in through the window. I must have been so deeply asleep, that I didn't hear anything. It took me a while to fully wake up and see it was Miguel who was shaking me and trying to calm me down. By the time I had completely woken up I was surrounded by some of the guests who had heard my screams and had come out of their rooms to see what was going on.

Many years previously I had witnessed another burglary incident when I lived in Bolivia. I was staying at my cousins' house in La Paz. Their parents were away so we went to bed quite late. After about an hour we woke up to a peculiar noise coming from outside the house. It sounded like somebody was trying to cut the window pane. We were all frightened and didn't know what to do. My eldest cousin, Patricia, got up and turned on the lights in the bedroom and we waited in silence to find out if we were going to hear the strange noise again. Nothing happened for a while, so we went to sleep again leaving the lights on. When we got up to go to school the next day, we found the burglar in the front yard. He had fallen asleep probably waiting for the lights to go off and there he was peacefully sleeping in the sunshine.

Two weeks after the burglary at the Hill Hotel, I finally met the owner when he arrived with his wife from Portugal. The couple were elegantly dressed and had the unmistakeable airs and graces of wealthy people. From the moment they set foot in the hotel, work increased considerably. Telephone calls were constantly made to meet their demands for one thing or another, such as bookings for the theatre, tennis at Wimbledon and restaurant reservations. Mr Tavares was in his late forties and had studied for a business degree at the University of London, which was where he met his wife. They had started in the hotel and restaurant business together, both in Portugal and London. After ten years, they had many assets, even owning a boat.

A few days after their arrival, their friends began to drop in at the hotel. They all drove beautiful, expensive cars. The boss would work early in the morning for a couple of hours before his wife and friends would join him to go out. In the evenings they would often ask me to book a table for them at top West End restaurants and they would return to the hotel usually in the early hours of the morning.

One morning the manageress knocked on my door. "Ana, Mr Tavares wants to talk to you." "Do you know what it's about?" She shrugged her shoulders. "It's about the burglary, isn't it?" I asked her, feeling worried. "I have no idea," she replied without interest. I was really concerned by the prospect of the meeting and I kept asking myself what it could be; why does he want to see me? I walked towards Mr Tavares's office feeling the weight of my legs, too heavy to want to take me there. "Surely it's about the burglary, what else can it be?" I thought. "I will probably lose my job today. I don't think I made a good impression on him since the day he arrived. He and his wife hardly acknowledge me, or are they too busy with themselves and their friends? He's probably angry at me about the burglary and thinks I am inexperienced; perhaps too young to work as a receptionist until late at night or maybe he has even found out I don't have a work permit." All these thoughts went through my mind as I dragged my feet to his office.

I knocked very gently on Mr Tavares's door, almost hoping he would not hear so I would not have to talk to him. But a booming voice commanded, "come in!" This threw me totally. "My God! What am I going to do if I lose my job? I would lose my home too. Where would I go? I would have to start all over again and without permanent residence my status in the country is questionable." My heart stopped beating for a second or two.

I opened the door and slowly walked in. "Come in, come in, sit down," he said, without looking at me, still reading his newspaper as though my presence wasn't that important. I sat on the edge of the chair ready to get up any minute and run out of the room in tears. He continued to ignore me, totally immersed in his paper. I looked around the office trying to focus on something to distract my mind and hide my nervousness. After a minute or so he looked up to give me his full attention. He wore a white shirt, pink tie and a dark, expensive suit. He had thick reading glasses that made him appear very distinguished and also made it impossible for me to see his eyes properly and read his thoughts. His casual attitude made me even more nervous as it seemed to me as though he didn't care. I was prepared for what I thought he was about to say, "thank for your services, but we don't need you anymore."

He eventually spoke. "Do you know the guest in room 17?" I was so concerned about the burglary that I tried hard to remember who was staying in room 17 on that day. He continued, trying to refresh my memory. "I'm talking about the tall, overweight, English guy, my friend." "Oh yes, yes of course, one of your friends," I replied with relief, realising that he was talking about the current guest and not the possible burglar. "Yes, that's right, Mark, Mark Brown," he confirmed. "Well, he wants to take you out to dinner, but he is concerned you may refuse because you are working for me," he said. "I just want you to know that if you would like to go out with him, it's fine by me."

I looked at him, astonished, I had been expecting to be thrown out of the hotel that morning but instead here I was being offered a dinner invitation. "Ok, thank you sir," I replied, hoping I had heard correctly. "All right Ana, off you go, that's all for today." I left his office almost jumping with glee, not because of the invitation, but because I hadn't lost my precious job.

Two days later, the owner's friend, Mark asked me out and I accepted without hesitation. First we went for dinner to an expensive restaurant called Le Caprice and then dancing at Stringfellows nightclub. It was my first night out with a well off, sophisticated guy who treated me like a lady. When we came back to the hotel in the early hours of the morning after an enjoyable evening he asked me in a gentlemanly manner to join him the next day for lunch. "You are lovely, I had a fantastic evening. I would love to take you to a typical English pub in the countryside. It's near where I live." I was flattered by the attention and accepted again without any reservations and knowing I had the blessing of my boss.

The next morning, my day off, we met at ten at the hotel reception and drove out to the country in his stunning Peugeot sports car. It was a lovely summer day, a perfect day for a date. The car slid down the motorway smooth and fast, with its roof open. As we increased speed my heart jumped with excitement and the refreshing breeze felt like a gentle touch on my face. I felt like one of James Bond's girlfriends, beautiful, important, successful and appreciated. Beatles music played on the car radio and Mark hummed to the tunes, making it a joyful journey.

About two hours later we arrived in a pretty Oxfordshire village. It had a medieval church that in the old days must have been the most important building in the settlement. The old pub was close by; it had very low ceilings giving it a feeling of warmth and community. Outside the pub, hanging baskets were full of colourful Busy Lizzy flowers. People gathered outside in a relaxed Sunday mood, children running freely around the tables. The village streets were narrow with beautiful houses made of stone. The walls and porches of some of the houses were covered in honeysuckle or woodbine climbers; others had roses. After lunch in the pub he suggested retreating to his cottage for a cup of tea before we returned to London.

His home was pretty and comfortable with wooden beams in the ceilings and white walls throughout, giving the place its period character. The house also had a lovely, colourful garden, of which Mark seemed to be very proud. "I spend a lot of time in this garden at the weekends," he said picking up a few dead leaves to make it look even more green and tidy. He walked around smelling the fragrance of the flowers, purple foxgloves, common poppies and wild daffodils. I loved the look of it all, but a feeling of emptiness held me. I didn't feel I belonged in this place or was part of the beautiful scenery. I stood there not knowing what to say or do. I thought this might be due to my continuing lack of confidence with the English language. A deep melancholy for Bolivia engulfed my thoughts as I thought of Rafael and wished he was here instead of Mark. For years I had made the conscious decision to forget all about Rafael, but somehow it seemed that the peace and quiet of the countryside brought his memory back to me; Mark was a total stranger. All the excitement of the sports car, the lovely places we had been to the night before, being treated like a lady and all the attention paid to me felt meaningless. His cheerful character didn't fill in the periods of silence between us; silence that I hadn't noticed the night before.

"Are you ok?" Mark asked, probably sensing some kind of discomfort in me. "Let's go in," he suggested and we walked into his sitting room, where he put on the television. The film Fiddler on the Roof was on. "Oh," I suddenly reacted, "let's watch this film please." I was hoping it would dissipate my nostalgia. "Would you like a cup of tea?" he asked, showing no interest in the film. Before I could reply, he walked out of the room. A few minutes passed. I was waiting for Mark to come back with the tea, but instead I heard his voice calling me, "Ana, can you come upstairs please?" I got up from the comfortable sofa feeling annoyed and went to find Mark. I was engrossed in the movie and didn't want to miss it.

There was a spacious landing and three bedrooms around it. I heard his voice coming from one of them. I went in and he was there lying on the bed, on his side, facing the door, wearing a silk dressing gown. He looked as if he had just come out of the shower. "Come in please," he said with a lascivious leer. "Come, lie down next to me;" he indicated his king size bed. Mark had a rounded face, black hair and brown eyes. He was tall, sturdy and had a big, prominent belly. But when I saw him lying on his bed with only his robe as protection, he looked bigger and totally disproportionate; I felt small and helpless. I imagined myself slumped next to him like a sack of potatoes, without any feeling. He was so casual as if it was the most natural thing to do. "No, I'm sorry but I don't want to do this," I said and turned around to go back downstairs as quickly as possible.

I thought of what had happened a few years earlier, when I was working as a cleaner in central London at the house of a very rich Middle Eastern family. On that occasion the mother and her two children had gone out to the park while her husband stayed in and went upstairs to have a shower. I was cleaning the house when the telephone rang. "Ask who it is please," Mr Baghdadi shouted from the bathroom. "It's Mr Jalal," I replied, still holding the phone in my hand. "Tell him to call me in half an hour." I gave the message, put the phone down, and continued my job.

A few minutes later I heard him calling again. "Ana, can you come upstairs please?" But when I went up I noticed the door of the bathroom was open. "What did my friend say?" he asked, suddenly exposing himself to me. "He will call you later, sir," I replied, surprised to see him naked in front of me, with his penis fully erect. "Would you help me to shower please?" he asked me with the same vulpine look that I had just seen on Mark's face. I ran out of the house leaving the vacuum cleaner in the middle of the room, dirty dishes in the kitchen, unmade beds, clothes, toys and mess everywhere. I left Mr Baghdadi probably wondering what sort of explanation he was going to give his wife when she returned to see that everything was as she had left it.

In Mark's case, I couldn't run away as I didn't know how to get back to London. Minutes later he came down fully dressed, picked up his car keys from the table, and turned off the television. "Let's go," he said, abruptly. We left the house in an embarrassed silence. He drove as fast as he could to the nearest train station, let me out of the car and without saying a word accelerated away from me. During the journey back home, I felt mortified by what had happened. I couldn't believe he could have behaved like this. I remembered my parents telling me that Englishmen had the reputation of being perfect gentlemen. I tried to understand Mark's attitude and analyse the reason for his behaviour, but my anger and lack of experience at that time didn't help me to come up with any answers.

Years later I did work out a few possible reasons for Mark's actions. He may have been shy, not knowing how to let a relationship develop. When he realised he had made a big mistake he may have wanted to get rid of me as quickly as possible to avoid the need for explanations and apologies. Another possibility was that his behaviour may have been typical of a spoiled rich man who didn't get what he wanted, when he wanted and the way he wanted it. This would explain why he dumped me at the station two hours away from London. A third reason may have been that he thought he didn't have to make any effort because I was a foreigner.

This incident reminds me of another one, many years later when I was introduced to a very wealthy English guy in London. He invited me for dinner at his home in Richmond. After dinner he took pride in taking me on a tour around his house. Holding our glasses of wine, we went to the swimming pool, which was just outside his bedroom, then on to his fantastic, well equipped gym and sauna. The afternoon was warm and pleasant so we walked through his beautiful garden before ending up in the comfortable lounge, clearly decorated with a man's touch; the touch of a man who knew about the good things in life. In one corner were two Spanish guitars standing up in a supporting frame, as if they were two precious trophies won in an important guitar competition. "Do you play the guitar?" I asked him. "Yes," he said, picking one of them up. "I played once with Paco Lucia."

We sat down on his sofa and he began to play a romantic Latin tune. As he played his guitar he moved so close to me I thought he was going to kiss me. I became nervous and spilt red wine on his lovely cream sofa. He got up, irritated, put the guitar away and brought salt, white wine, talcum powder and some chemical sprays to clean the stains, and then he called a minicab to take me home. The romance had ended before it had begun.

I once met a man whom I really fancied but it took him a while to notice me. When he eventually did invite me out for dinner, I was so excited that in the week prior to our date, I spent lots of time and effort preparing myself for the great event. I bought myself a beautiful dress, with matching high heeled Karen Millen shoes and went to the hairdresser to have my hair cut and coloured. I also had a manicure and a pedicure; I was ready for action. However, the day before our date I woke up with terrible flu-like symptoms. I took all the remedies possible to shift it but, as time passed, I felt even worse. When the day we were to meet arrived I had to call him to apologise and cancel. "You are very unreliable," he said, putting the phone down. He never called me again.

Another time I met a guy who was keen on me, but after my bad experiences I was not that enthusiastic about having a relationship with him. However, he insisted we go out, which we did a couple of times. He lived outside London and he would come to town every weekend to see me. We arranged to meet one Saturday at my place, and I got myself ready for him, but he neither came nor called me. Thinking that something bad had happened to him, I phoned him. To my surprise he answered as though nothing had happened. "Hi, are you all right?" I asked. "Yes," he said, calmly. "I'm waiting for you, are you coming?" "Well, not really, I'm sorry," he said and kept silent. A second later he spoke again. "The thing is that every time I come to see you I get lost, and to find the right way takes me forever, so let's call it a day shall we?" he said, as if it didn't really matter. So, up to that point I had not had much luck where love was concerned.

After the long train trip from Oxfordshire I was back to my normal working life in the hotel and I forgot all about Mark. My boss and his wife returned to Portugal and the hotel resumed its normal routine. I was busy with various courses; I had started a module in bilingual skills with a specialisation in health and I was also attending short courses in complementary therapy.

One evening I was in the hotel watching the news with some guests from Cyprus, when suddenly I saw my former neighbour from La Paz on the television screen. "My neighbour! My neighbour! That man was my neighbour in Bolivia!" I shouted, all excited. The guests looked at me as if I was mad. One of them said, "that man can't be your neighbour, he's a Nazi, a war criminal, what are you talking about?" "I swear to God, he is my neighbour; he and his wife lived in the same building as me and he used to help my mother and I with our shopping when we met in the lift."

I tried to convince them that I used to know the man very well, that my aunt's flat was exactly above his and our apartment was on another floor further up. Some of them laughed at me, not believing a word of it, but one or two said, "he may be, he may be, you never know." But I was certain that the man on the news was Mr Altmann, a respectable old man and they were trying to convince me that the man who was to go on trial in France was not my neighbour, was not a respectable old man and in fact was Klaus Barbie, a war criminal.

The next day the news of Klaus Barbie, the SS Gestapo officer, was in all the English newspapers. I read in total disbelief how this man who I had seen as kind, helpful and respectable was in reality responsible for the torture and murder of more than 26,000 people, mainly French Jews. His victims included 44 children from an orphanage at Izieu, near Lyons, who he had sent to their deaths at Auschwitz.

I wanted to find out more about this monster and so I bought a book by Tom Bower called Klaus Barbie: Butcher of Lyons. I was appalled by what I learnt in the book about how American Intelligence employed him as a U.S. agent after World War II and protected him from prosecution by the French. I also discovered that by using his experience of counter-guerrilla warfare Barbie helped the CIA to capture and murder Che Guevara in Bolivia in 1967.

I also learned about the atrocities he carried out while he was living in Bolivia. For example, in the period 1971–8, he worked as a security adviser to the Bolivian dictator Hugo Banzer Suárez. He used the name Klaus Altmann in Bolivia when he worked as an interrogator and torturer during the Luis Garcia Meza narco-coup in 1980. This was the year Marcelo Quiroga and others were killed and when my Uncle Hector was about to return to Bolivia from exile. While reading about my neighbour, I thought about how naive Bolivians can be when it comes to foreigners, especially if they are white. We usually trust them and think they are all good people, while Europeans are more cautious and do not trust foreigners before getting to know them.

It was the democratic president, Hernán Siles Zuazo, who allowed the extradition of Klaus Barbie to France in 1983, but his trial did not start until May 1987. Years later, on one of our visits to my country, my Uncle Hector took my husband and I to have a coffee at Café La Paz, the place where politicians meet to discuss current affairs. We sat at the same table where Klaus Barbie used to sip his coffee every day as a free man.

By the end of 1987, I had decided to return to Bolivia. A few days before my departure I went to visit to Doña Asuncion who had moved into a bigger flat in Victoria. She was delighted to hear of my decision to go back and even suggested I buy myself a white wedding dress, because it was going to be in Bolivia where I would meet the right man.

I left her flat laughing about her plans for me and headed for the shops in Kensington High Street to buy presents for my family. It was a cold, dark afternoon in December; the stores were crammed with Christmas shoppers, frantically buying toys, clothes and any gadgets they could get their hands on. Colourful Christmas illuminations gave the streets a festive look. The sound of a steel drum played by a black Caribbean man outside the Underground station enhanced the scene along with people singing Christmas carols. However, traffic jams were delaying everybody and spoiling the party mood. Pedestrians in a rush were trying to get home after a long day's work and shopping.

The Illegal Dance

I spent time flitting from one shop to another and ended up in C&A. Suddenly two men stormed into the store and went straight for a till, demanding money. One of them pointed a handgun at the cashier. I hid myself about five metres away behind a pillar, popping my head out to see what was going on. There were some people wandering around completely unaware of what was happening. I saw the robbers taking a customer hostage and the three of them left the shop in a hurry. It all happened so quickly that everybody just stood in a dazed silence. Seconds later the shop alarm started ringing like crazy, making the situation more tense and real. Police cars with their loud sirens appeared outside from all directions, but I think the men managed to escape. The hostage, a pregnant woman, was released outside the shop in a state of shock. The rest of us inside were evacuated through a side door and I ran home without buying anything.

CHAPTER SIXTEEN

"It is said that no one truly knows a nation until one has been inside its jails. A nation should not be judged by how it treats its highest citizens, but its lowest ones"

Nelson Mandela

Waiting for my luggage to appear on the carousel in the small airport of El Alto, La Paz, seemed like an eternity, but when it finally arrived a couple of young boys jumped up to offer their services. "*Señorita le ayudo, yo le ayudo señorita por favor.*" (Miss, can I help you, can I help you please, Miss?) The airport didn't provide trolleys for passengers to carry their suitcases, so it was a good opportunity for youngsters to make a bit of money. One of them finally got the job and carried my bags the few metres to the arrivals hall where all my family were waiting, smiling and waving to me.

Paola, my cousin saw the boy with my bags and jokingly said, "Anita you'd better carry your luggage otherwise people will think that this boy is the one arriving from Europe and not you!" We all laughed at her sense of humour.

When I approached my parents and the rest of the family it became clear to me how much time had passed. The indelible traces of age were etched on their faces and my little brother Marcelo, was almost unrecognisable as he had grown into a man. The change was also noticeable in my aunties, uncles and cousins who had also come to welcome me home.

We drove towards the city in a long caravan of cars. The blue, unpolluted sky made a stark contrast with the unpainted brick houses, the rubbish in the streets and the general unkempt appearance of the place. La Paz seemed a strange city, appearing to sprout people and cars from every direction. Seven years before this mayhem would have felt totally normal to me, but on this day of my arrival I had ambivalent feelings. I wasn't prepared for the culture shock. Buses passed by playing loud music. Young boys who should have been at school worked as drivers' assistants, hanging from the buses shouting the destinations as loudly as they could, *"Plaza Murillo, San Francisco, El Prado, Zona Sur!"*

During the journey we passed through one of the food markets. The aroma of Bolivian cuisine triggered in me deep feelings of happiness at being home, but as we approached the main part of the city, *El Prado,* my joy began to recede. Street sellers were using the main thoroughfare to trade anything from suitcases, food and ghetto blasters. The noise of car horns, the constant shouting of the young people on the buses, the insipid, commercial music and horrendous traffic jams were eerie and unsettling. It was like entering an apocalyptic era, hard to bear. It also seemed that the number of beggars and children working in the streets had increased; I couldn't help feeling sad, ashamed and concerned. The altitude of three thousand six hundred and fifty metres above sea level also had an effect on me. I thought my head was going to explode. All these things had never bothered me before, now it all looked terribly chaotic and unpleasant.

Later on, bad news about my family came as a shock. My father had not worked for more than a year due to a stroke that had paralysed half of his body. Although I was assured he was now much better, he was suffering the aftermath of the illness. He was still not working and was living off his savings. All the letters I had received from him in London had been typed by my mother and signed by him. I was also told that my Aunt Teresa and Uncle Julio had lost their home and as my mother had already told me when she came to London, Uncle José had lost all his savings due to hyperinflation of the economy. This political and economic situation had forced President Hernán Siles Zuazo to give up power and call an election one year early. So when I arrived in Bolivia in 1987 we had a new president, Victor Paz Estenssoro.

Estenssoro had started his political career as leader of the Nationalist Revolutionary Movement (MNR) in 1941, and in 1952 he became President of Bolivia for the first time. His revolutionary movement was one of the most important and progressive political forces in the Latin America of the 20th century. All indigenous citizens were allowed to vote for the first time and there was agrarian reform and nationalisation of the tin mines.

I often wondered why Uncle Hector and my father had not joined the MNR party. Later on I discovered it was not a democratic movement at all. Although it was not a military organisation, its armed members used violence against their opponents, to the extent of building the concentration camps with torture chambers, such as the one in which Uncle Hector was imprisoned. History proved the MNR to be an opportunistic, authoritarian and vicious organisation.

In 1985 when Paz Estenssoro was re-elected for the fourth time, it was not with a majority of votes, but by Congress. During this period, radical privatisation policies took shape under the wing of the Minister of Planning, Gonzalo Sánchez de Lozada. He had lived most of his life in the U.S.A. and was influenced by extreme right-wing politics. Together, he and Paz Estenssoro implemented the so-called "economic shock therapy," after taking advice from the U.S. economist Jeffrey Sachs. I am sure the methods these astute politicians used to achieve their aims were fine, but I am at a loss to understand how an American academic with an economic vision from the developed world could possibly advise a developing country that was so different from the U.S.A.

These drastic measures cut inflation, but seriously damaged the domestic economy, especially small companies. This left my country worse off than before due to a rise in unemployment and fall in industrial output. The tin mines were closed due to a world decline in the price of tin and thirty thousand miners were sacked from their jobs. The Bolivian economy now copied that of the U.S.A., moving towards privatisation. As the foreign investment was mainly from the U.S.A., this opened the doors to U.S. control of Bolivia.

These policies resulted in a terrible increase in poverty. It threw more people out of work and on to the streets of the main cities. Many of them abandoned their rural areas and, in a desperate search for a job, settled chaotically in the peripheral areas of La Paz such as El Alto. Here there was no urban organisation and they began to sell anything and everything in order to survive; others became professional beggars. The working class and the middle class, as much as the indigenous people suffered during this time and many turned even more to religion for salvation; even cinemas became places for praying. An exodus of Bolivians to foreign countries followed.

In the U.K., something similar happened in 1983 during an economic recession. At the time the state owned coal mines were heavily subsidised by the government. Prime Minister Thatcher declared that because the coal industry was unproductive many mines would have to be closed. The result was a bitter strike which lasted one year. The National Union of Mineworkers eventually lost. Inevitably unemployment rose, and whole communities were destroyed; this was entirely in line with Thatcher's quote: "There is no such thing as society." Historians now believe that her agenda was the destruction of the U.K. unions in general, as she believed they had become too powerful. The much reduced coal mining industry was finally privatised in 1994.

After spending Christmas with my family, I was invited to a smart New Year's Eve party. It was at the house of a wealthy friend of my relatives. The first thing I saw when we arrived at the party was two luxury sports cars parked in the garage at the side of the house. Mr Rich who worked for customs, showed us his acquisitions proudly.

Something else that caught my attention was the gold chain hung around his neck. He was wearing a white shirt that was slightly open, showing off his hairy chest. His attractive wife, elegantly dressed, was receiving guests and making sure everything was running smoothly. The whole house was carpeted, which was unusual in those days in Bolivia. It was not something one would normally see because carpet was both expensive and impractical for dancing.

Family and friends were all in the living room when we arrived, and the party was in full swing. Everybody seemed to be enjoying themselves and the meticulous attention given by the hosts. At midnight the music stopped and the toasts began. In Spanish tradition, champagne and grapes were served just before the church bells began to ring in the New Year. We had to eat one grape with each stroke of the bell. Each grape represented a month of the coming year. The saying goes that the sweeter the grape, the better the month will be.

After the ringing of the church bells had signalled midnight, everybody began to wish each other happiness for the future.

The Illegal Dance

I approached one of the guests to wish him a happy New Year with a big hug, but politely and apologetically he refused me; he told me that he wanted to give his first hug to the one who had the most money. This was the owner of the house, of course. Everybody seemed to have the same idea because the queue to embrace the rich customs officer was long. Superstitious behaviour continued that evening with people even carrying empty suitcases up and down the stairs if they were hoping to travel to Europe in the New Year. The single young girls were changing their knickers for red ones in the toilet, because this meant the arrival of a new love. Others were counting money, so they wouldn't be short of it; it was amusing. When all the fuss ended, we were invited to sit at the table as it was dinner time.

As we were moving towards the dining room we heard loud screaming coming from upstairs. We rushed back to the living room from where we could see the bedrooms. A bedroom door was open and we could clearly see Mr Rich badly beating up his wife. She was screaming desperately, trying to get away from the vicious man. My Uncle Julio and others quickly went upstairs to separate the couple and calm the situation down. Unfortunately this incident ended the party and gradually all the guests left the house.

Bolivia and England have certain similarities. People in both countries are formal, ceremonial, and in many ways conventional. The character of the Bolivians is respectful and somewhat shy, as are the English unless, of course, they get drunk like the hooligans in England and Mr Rich in Bolivia. One particular characteristic common to the two countries is that the cup of tea at five in the afternoon is sacrosanct, especially in the cold areas of Bolivia.

A few days later I was invited to have a cup of tea at the house of a prominent lawyer to celebrate my arrival in Bolivia. He was married to a well-known writer and the distinguished couple later on became my cousins-in-law. When my mother and I arrived at the house I noticed that in one of the corners of the entrance hall there was a small round table and on the top of it an open notebook. "What's this for?" I asked Mum. "When we leave the house we have to write something in the notebook," she said. "Write what?" "We have to thank the host for the invitation," she clarified. I was taken aback by how much middle class people were concerned with protocol when at the same time there were thirty thousand miners out of work and who knows how many more people unemployed.

The tea table was nicely set with silver cutlery and porcelain cups. It was also full of wonderful delicacies, including home-made cakes and biscuits. At about five in the afternoon we were all asked to sit around it for tea which the maids were serving to all the guests. I was sitting between my mother and another lady. The hostess, who was a very outspoken and sophisticated lady, fluttered around making sure all the dishes were on the table. As we were about to have tea she decided to make a small speech. Her experience as a writer meant that she had the ability to choose the appropriate words; it came as second nature to her. It was all about me and how wonderful and clever I was to have finished my studies in the U.K. Everybody clapped and wished me all the best.

A few minutes later, the lady next to me asked what I had been studying. "English," I replied, and taking advantage of the fact that all the ladies were looking at me I could not stop myself from spoiling the speech and the tea party. "I also cleaned toilets in London," I said. They all looked at me in astonishment. My mother kicked me under the table to shut me up, but it was too late. I had said it loud enough for everybody to hear. "Cleaning toilets?" one of them asked with a look of disgust on her face while taking a sip of hot tea that burnt her lips. Another lady choked on the cake she was eating, possibly trying to say something at the same time. Somebody had to slap her

The Illegal Dance

on the back so she could regain her bearing. They had not expected that the daughter of a distinguished friend was a servant in Europe. I left the party happy to have said little, but enough to make them think that life in England was not about eating caviar every day.

My love life continued to be in constant turmoil. I always thought that love was a simple matter, but as I grew older I realised there was nothing simple about it at all. In La Paz I met a guy I liked. He was nice, respectable and well-educated. He believed he was in love with me, but he was also in love with his childhood sweetheart. He couldn't make up his mind about which one of us suited him better. As I never saw him again I assume he tossed a coin and she won!

My relationship with my school friends had changed after years of living abroad. Everybody seemed to have moved on to other things. Most of them had finished university and were now working, or were married with children. In many ways I felt left far behind; I wasn't married, I had no children and I had not studied for a career just yet. So as the days passed my feelings of not belonging to the group of people I knew and to Bolivia in general, increased. But I felt I had seen more of the world and this undoubtedly had changed me. Besides, the Bolivian way of life wasn't changing for the better. On the contrary, it had stayed the same for the last seven years. It was just as racist, unequal and as unfair as ever; a greatly divided society between rich and poor. Nobody seemed to be able to do much about it, least of all in the circles in which I was moving.

One day my father, tired of his constant headaches and insomnia, asked me to treat him with all the natural therapies that I had been learning about in London. As soon as I started acupressure treatment he went to sleep. I worked for a couple of minutes and I left him to relax. Fourteen hours later he woke up totally revitalised and he never complained of headaches or insomnia again. It may have been this small incident, or the fact that I had still achieved so little while living in England that made me decide to go back to London with my father's recommendation that I should continue to study natural medicine.

I flew to Sweden before returning to London because my Uncle Hector's family was still living there, and because of his political status I had been given permission to live there, as long as I renewed my visa every year. On my arrival in Sweden, I went straight to the Home Office to have my visa extended for another year. When I left the building I realised that I had been given permanent residence in Sweden instead of yearly residence. A few days later I received a letter from Tom, an Irish guy I had dated in London before I went to Bolivia. He was the son of a working class Irish family who came to London in the 1950s. His father worked in construction and his mother in a hotel. In spite of his father's insistence that he should follow his father's trade, Tom went on to study economics and sociology at the London School of Economics. His letter said he wanted to come to Sweden to visit me and he expressed the wish for us to renew the relationship and to return together to England.

A few weeks later Tom arrived in Lund, but soon after this I got a letter from the Swedish Immigration Office saying they wanted to see me urgently with my passport. I went there immediately and a clerk explained that they had made a mistake with my brother's passport. Jose had arrived in Sweden a year earlier than me and it was he who should have been given the permanent residence in the country. However I was still entitled to the yearly residence. They corrected the mistake by scribbling something in my passport and stamping "cancelled" in it. They told me I could travel with it and they added a yellow piece of paper to rectify the mistake. I thought my problem was over; I had my passport and visa back, and a week later Tom and I left for London by train.

The Illegal Dance

But I spoke too soon. It must have been about midnight when we arrived at a town called Flensburg on the border between Denmark and Germany. We were fast asleep when the train stopped and a German officer woke us up for passport control. He glanced at the cover of Tom's British passport, very quickly checked the picture and returned it with a smile, no questions asked. Then he looked at my passport and with surprise asked me if I was from Bolivia. "Yes," I replied. I was used to this question. Every time I travelled anywhere my Bolivian passport was always a cause for concern. I used to have the impression that instead of holding a formal identity document I was carrying a bad luck amulet. The in-depth questioning sometimes led to a full physical examination, in case I was carrying drugs.

On one occasion when I was returning to the U.K. from Bolivia, I bought a small packet of coca tea at La Paz airport. When I got to London the customs officers searched me. When they found the coca tea in my hand luggage they called the police immediately. A full physical examination took place in one of their offices and then they read me my rights. They would not accept that what I had with me was only herbal tea and not cocaine. Even though I argued my case, they still confiscated the packet and warned me that the next time I offended I would be prosecuted.

The German officer checked my passport thoroughly, page by page, asking me questions like: "Where are you going? Why? How long for?" Then he stopped studying my passport and looked at Tom again. "Are you together?" he asked. Taken aback, Tom answered that yes we were travelling together. The German officer had spotted two of the many visas I had. "I see you've been to East Germany and Cuba," he said, in a sarcastic tone, shaking his head slightly in disapproval. Before going back to Bolivia I had been to Cuba on holiday and had also travelled with Tom to East Germany and Ireland. In those days people thought that going to a communist country was like going to hell and coming back with two horns on your head. Some people still think this way.

Tom and I looked at each other in silence. His beautiful blue but worried eyes seemed to wonder what the hell I had been doing in Cuba without him, I was sure he would have loved to have gone there, too.

Then the official spoke sarcastically again. "So your passport has been cancelled in Sweden, has it?" "No, well, no, it's not cancelled," I tried to explain what had actually happened. Then I remembered the yellow piece of paper that immigration had given me in Sweden. "I have something else to show you. It explains what happened," I said to the officer hoping this would clarify the situation. I looked for the yellow document in my handbag, but couldn't find it. The officer became impatient and asked me to leave the train immediately. He made a quick radio telephone call and two minutes later another two officers arrived. "Out of the train!" they ordered. I was surprised and scared.

Tom tried to persuade the officers that it was a misunderstanding. He attempted to explain that the passport had not been cancelled and that I still had residence in Sweden, but they wouldn't let him get involved. "It is nothing to do with you, sir. You can continue your journey," the man replied with a thick German accent. Tom helped me to bring the suitcase down from the luggage rack and also took his own. "I'm going with her," he insisted. The German officers said it was not necessary, but Tom insisted that he was coming with me. We left the train escorted by the armed officers. The night was cold and the train station was empty and silent. A few passengers looked at us through the train windows, perhaps wondering if we were two criminals on the run. We got to an office in that isolated place where more immigration police sat half asleep at their desks with nothing to do. They looked bored and tired. Empty cups and unfinished sandwiches were all around.

The Illegal Dance

They asked me to open my luggage. Four hands went through all my clothes, anxious to find something more serious than the cancelled passport. I tried again to explain what had happened with my visa, but they shouted at me to keep quiet. They didn't want to hear any more explanations, behaving like two irrational, spoiled schoolboys about to go into a tantrum if I tried to say anything. But they seemed well trained and equipped to hunt out any illegal immigrant and crush them to death like an insect; even better if this insect had been on communist soil.

"Open your handbag!" one of them yelled at me, when he had finished rifling through my suitcase. I obeyed immediately without argument. He was tall, with a stony faced, impassive gaze and an authoritarian and despotic attitude. His fine sharp pointed nose reminded me of the German soldiers in World War II that I had seen in many films. One of them emptied everything that was in my handbag on to the table. He found my wallet with all my money and put it aside. They went through all my most intimate possessions carefully and orderly and then put them all back into the bag carelessly.

They told me to go into a room and take all my clothes off. A woman officer arrived a few minutes later and examined me thoroughly wearing a pair of plastic gloves. They didn't find anything incriminating on me either. I dressed quickly, feeling ashamed. I was shivering with cold, anger and helplessness. They gave me a small board with a number to hold near my chest and then took photos of me in every position. I wanted to ask them what the hell they thought they were doing, but I couldn't; I was too scared. I was already under their psychological control, too petrified and intimidated to dare open my mouth. Their ruthlessness made me forget all the English I had learned during the years I had lived in London. No words escaped from my lips to argue my case. I was completely at their mercy, guilty of no crime but treated like a common criminal; for them I was just a number.

They seemed to be enjoying their power over me, reviving echoes of the Nazi period. With leering and distrustful looks on their faces they pushed me into a cell, threw me a blanket and locked the door. I sat down on a bench that served as a bed, in that dark, little room, totally humiliated, stripped of any dignity. Waves of revulsion and confusion went through me and I broke down crying, thinking how little Germany had changed. I thought about the millions of Jews who had perished under Nazi Germany. How terrible it must have been for them under that evil, irrational power without any hope of escape. I also meditated on all those hundreds of women and men who were arrested, tortured and many of them killed by the military dictatorships in countries like Argentina, Chile, Bolivia and others in Central America.

The next day, they let me out of the cell at about ten in the morning. Although new officers were on duty their faces expressed the same arrogance heightened by cold, expressionless eyes. At that stage I was not sure what my future was. Was I going to be taken to a larger prison? Was I going to be set free? I asked for my boyfriend, Tom. They said he had gone because he wasn't feeling well. Tom was a diabetic and he needed to eat every three hours to avoid a drop in blood sugar levels. He also needed his insulin, so may have decided to continue his journey as he probably didn't have enough with him and he wouldn't have known how long I would be kept in custody. Now I felt even more afraid and alone. I had hoped to see him, so he could help me out of this situation, but he wasn't there anymore. There was nothing I could do.

One of the officers produced a document. "Sign here," he ordered, putting a cross where I had to put my signature. I looked at the paper trying to understand what it meant, but it was all written in German. I thought for a minute or two, should I sign it? I didn't know what to do. I could have been signing for life imprisonment or my death warrant, I wouldn't have known. The immigration policeman noticed my hesitation and pointed his finger, "sign or you won't get out of here." I signed it as quickly as I could.

In retrospect I suppose I should not have obeyed them. Perhaps I should have asked for a lawyer, but I couldn't think straight. I was in total shock and hadn't slept all night. I was too tired and scared to have a clear mind. I hoped that if I signed the document without complaint they might let me go.

Then the officer spoke again. "We called Sweden, your passport is fine." They gave me back my bags, but I noticed that all my money had disappeared, a total of two thousand dollars in cash. "Where is my money?" I asked timidly, but they pretended they didn't understand my question. I insisted that I wanted my money back, but with the same attitude of the night before they shut me up. "Do you want to continue your journey?" "No," I said as I didn't have any money. I did not want to go anywhere at that moment, but home to Bolivia. I just wanted to be at my mother's bosom. "I want to go back to Sweden," I replied eventually. I sat on the train thinking that the money that these bastards had stolen from me was the money my father had saved risking his life every week on the Death Road. Those German officers robbed me of what little I had, with the same cynicism they had done to the Jews years earlier.

I stayed in Sweden for about a year before I recovered from this awful ordeal. Although I had only been one night with the German police it was enough for me to realise how difficult it must be to be in prison for a long time irrespective of the crime.

Once in Sweden I went to the police with an interpreter to ask if I had any chance of getting my money back. They thought it would be difficult. When I told them what had happened they seemed not to care either.

I went back to studying Swedish and found myself a cleaning job in a school. The work was easy and stress free. The only rule was that I couldn't start before six o'clock in the morning as the school alarm would go off if I opened the door too early. Every morning I would get to the school at five minutes past six, after the alarm had been switched off. I would clean for two hours before the children arrived and then I had the rest of the day free to study.

One day I got up early as usual, went to work and opened the door. To my surprise the alarm started ringing. I looked at my watch, which read one minute before six o'clock. I couldn't believe I had made a mistake. I went into the school and closed the door, hoping in vain that the deafening sound would stop. Ten minutes later I heard police sirens. "Here we go again, I'm in trouble. For Goodness sake, not again! I don't want more problems with the police," I said to myself, shaking my head in disbelief. They found me cleaning, holding my broom and ordered me to put my hands up and broom down. The armed officers turned off the alarm and took me to the police station to make a statement to explain who I was and what I was doing at the school. When they found out I was simply a stupid cleaner rather than a burglar, they let me go. A few days later I was sacked from the job because the school had to pay a fine of five hundred kronor to the police for wasting their time.

CHAPTER SEVENTEEN

"A bad day in London is still better than a good day anywhere else"

Unknown

"I am going back to England," I said to myself, defiantly. When I told my family in Sweden about my plans, they were horrified. "It is madness," they said. "You are much better off here. You will soon be speaking Swedish and then you will be able to study whatever you want. You could get a student loan from the government and pay it back when you start working." They were probably right, but I also knew that if I did what they suggested I would have to stay in the country for a long time and this was not what I wanted. Sweden was not for me and I was not for Sweden, though I admired it for all its good points. In the field of education, for example, the facilities students enjoy are beyond the dreams of most Bolivians. University students are provided with bank loans, comfortable flats, and all the academic support they need. This is not the case in Bolivia; however, in spite of there being comparatively less educational infrastructure, it is admirable to see that many youngsters from poor backgrounds without much economic help in fact manage to complete their education to university level.

My family continued to try to persuade me to stay in Sweden. They said it was a safe country; that it was a place where nobody had to struggle much to get by and, more than anything, I would be near family and friends. Sweden was a little oasis compared with England. However, I often felt like I was living in a very comfortable prison; a well-organised society, with little room for spontaneity. Everything was practically put on a plate for you. We were like little Bolivian robots behaving and doing exactly as the Swedes did, so we could fit in and not look odd.

Maybe I should have stayed there, but I thought an easy life never helps you to succeed. Also, the idea of returning to London was always on my mind. London was like an addictive drug, and after living for a year in Sweden, I was beginning to feel withdrawal symptoms. I missed the place, but I wasn't sure why. It had been a tough, expensive and risky life over there. It was often difficult to find a decent job and reasonable accommodation. I had memories of its cold, wet climate and the time it takes to get anywhere. But, perhaps I felt there was something out there for me if I only kept trying. Someone said to me once: "London will either make you or break you." Somehow I hoped that London would make me one day.

A few months later I returned to London, but this time I flew direct to the U.K. to avoid any more problems in Germany. I soon found out that this extraordinary and mysterious city had more surprises for me. That same year, 1988, my parents moved to Madrid, my brother José went to study at the Academy of Jazz and Contemporary Music in Barcelona, and my younger brother Marcelo was about to start dental school in La Paz.

Soon after my arrival in London I found myself a place to live in Bayswater, a job as a barmaid in a wine bar in the West End and a school where I started to study osteopathy. In those days, this was considered unorthodox therapy and was not well accepted by the medical profession. It was not generally taught at universities and was sometimes derided as "bone setting;" but this new approach to health interested me. Even though I knew I was going against convention, with the encouragement of my father I decided to go for it.

My pay as a barmaid wasn't exactly like working as a personal assistant to a top banking executive. In fact it barely covered my expenses, so I had to get yet another cleaning job in a private house for a couple of hours in the morning as well. The job at the bar was from six in the evening until about midnight during the week; at weekends I sometimes had to stay until two in the morning. I would always take a minicab to get home. Minicabs are supposed to be cheaper than the famous London black cabs because the drivers do not have the "Knowledge of London," unlike the black cabs. You have to tell the drivers carefully where you are going and often have to give them directions about how to get to your destination. They are also known for not being as safe as black cabs that were strictly regulated by the police at the time. However, our bar staff always used the same minicab company, situated around the corner from the wine bar and the drivers knew most of the people who worked in the bars and restaurants in the neighbourhood.

One Saturday evening we finished work around two in the morning, so I ordered a minicab. I left work, got into the car without looking at the driver, who turned out to be new to the company and told him my address. I must have been really tired as I dozed off and when I woke up I realised we were speeding on a motorway. I was living not far from the wine bar and in the early hours of the morning with no traffic, it should have taken him no more than fifteen minutes to take me home and we certainly didn't have to go via the motorway.

"Where are we? Where are you going?" I asked the driver, confused and scared. "Cambrish," he replied. His English wasn't good. "I beg your pardon, do you mean Cambridge? I don't live in Cambridge," I said irritated and very concerned. The driver didn't answer and didn't seem to care as he carried on driving. "Take me home, where are we going?" I shouted at him. "Yes madam, take home, home," he replied. I could feel my heart pounding rapidly in my chest. "Take me home please, please!" I began to plead with him, but the driver was concentrating on the motorway and he limited his answers to just a few mumbles, which I didn't understand. His hands were firmly stuck to the steering wheel and without looking at me through his rear view mirror, he increased his speed. "Stop, stop, please!" I started begging desperately. "You are going the wrong way, please stop." "Home, we go home," the man replied, going even faster.

I cleaned the misty window of the car with my hand and looked through it trying to distinguish something familiar in the distance, but at night you could only appreciate a few bright spots that passed by quickly, looking like Christmas lights. I did not recognise where we were, but it seemed that we had left London long ago. I felt a cold sweat running through my body and I panicked. I began to attack the driver frantically from behind, screaming madly at him, "let me out, let me out of the car." The man moved forwards and sideways to avoid me hitting him. I got hold of his hair and pulled it with all my strength in an attempt to stop him going any further. I heard him saying, "Cambrish, we go Cambrish. It is home madam, home." He would try to say something in English, but then he would end up mumbling words in his own language.

The Illegal Dance

My despair increased when I recalled stories I had read in the newspapers about rapes and even murders of women by minicab drivers and for a minute, I thought that the only thing to do was to jump out of the car. I placed my hand on the handle of the back door and began to threaten him. "Stop the car, you bastard or I'll jump." "No, no madam please," the driver pleaded without slowing down and held the steering wheel near to his chest. I continued screaming like a deranged woman totally out of control, and ready to open the door and jump. "I live in Bayswater! Bayswater!" Whether it was the movement of the car and the lights passing quickly by or the realisation that if I jumped out I would be killed instantly, I suddenly felt sick and started vomiting. I was crying and throwing up all over his car, but still the driver wouldn't stop. We finally reached a motorway exit which he took. "We go London, madam London," he said in a voice, which sounded as scared as I was; I calmed down a bit. I had a blinding headache and felt too sick to even sit up straight. From time to time, I would see the man looking at me through his mirror. His eyes had a look of horror and sorrow. It was then that I began to think that perhaps he wasn't taking me away to rape me or anything like that. Perhaps he had made a genuine mistake. I lay down on the seat feeling unwell and just hoped we were going back to London. Eventually the car stopped. It must have been around four in the morning when we finally got to Bayswater, an area where the shops were open until the early hours of the morning. It was a place I knew well because I lived there.

The driver got out, opened the back door and said, "please madam, come." I sat up like a zombie, my head felt as if it was going to explode. He helped me out of the car and took me to a café. I took the first table I saw, near the front door. My headache didn't ease; I could hardly open my eyes with the pain. The driver talked in a foreign language to the coffee shop attendant who came to my table and asked me if I wanted to drink anything. "Hot chocolate, please," I said lifting my head slightly to look at him. "My friend says sorry," the man said. "He misunderstood you; he thought you wanted to go to Cambridge." "No," I said. "It's Pembridge, not Cambridge; Pembridge Villas is where I live." A few minutes later I had my hot drink with the driver sitting in front of me and the waiter translating and laughing about the mistake he had made and the beating up I had given him.

Soon it was winter again; the cold, dark days ahead made me feel like a hedgehog preparing for hibernation. My feelings of emptiness and solitude increased. In the summer people seem to take things at a slow pace, going for walks in the countryside, or lying in the sun in the parks. But in winter there is more of a rush to achieve small, daily goals in a big city that moves faster than you do and where being ignored is practically an advantage, because you don't have to explain yourself. A Bolivian friend who was visiting London said to me that he would rather be in La Paz known as a crook and being chased by his enemies than living in London in total anonymity. However, my anonymity felt comfortable; no demands, no obligations, just the cold weather to deal with.

One rainy day, I left home for central London. I was walking along the Strand towards Charing Cross well wrapped up in winter clothes, but still feeling the cold, the annoying drizzle, and the indifference of strangers passing by. I had just been to the City Lit, an adult education college, to enrol on a new course. I got to the traffic lights and was just about to cross the road when, to my amazement, my ex-boyfriend Rafael was on the other side of the street. I could see him between the umbrellas that people were holding to protect themselves from the driving rain. He was looking left and right, not sure which direction the traffic was coming from. This takes a while to get

The Illegal Dance

used to in England since in most parts of the world vehicles are driven on the right.

From a few metres away I could see he was wearing blue jeans, a blue raincoat with a hood over his head and a black rucksack on his back. I could just see half of his rounded face and moustache. I rushed forward, crossed the road and walked rapidly behind him trying to catch him up. I didn't want to shout out his name in the middle of the street, so I just hurried behind trying not to lose him. I knew he had come to look for me but probably had my old address and couldn't find me. He reached Charing Cross Underground station and went in. There were so many people I needed to hurry so as not to lose sight of him. I ran quickly like a footballer zigzagging from one side to another to avoid bumping into people who were going in and out of the station. I got to the escalator and stood in line to go down on the right side along with the other passengers. From time to time I stepped ahead on the left side of the stairs, trying not to get in the way of anybody rushing down the stairs. I would advance one or two steps and again position myself on the right, until I finally reached him. Rafael was one step in front of me on the right of the escalator with the rest of the passengers moving down calmly to get to the trains.

I continued down the stairs to get ahead of him; I wanted to surprise him before he got on to his train. I went down one step more; I turned around and faced him. He had an empty look on his face, totally lost in his own world. I am sure he wasn't even aware that I had followed him. Our eyes met and it meant nothing for either of us. It wasn't the man I thought it was; it wasn't Rafael. I felt embarrassed and angry with myself. Nearly ten years had passed since I had left Bolivia and I was still thinking that one day Rafael might come looking for me.

During Christmas 1989, I went to visit my parents in Madrid, the least romantic city I had ever visited. It had great monuments and buildings, but an air of mistrust and foreboding infested the place. I always felt that London was for everyone, but I had many reservations about Madrid.

My parents were happy living in Spain. Dad had a good job thanks to a Bolivian doctor who employed him in his clinic. They had become good friends and enjoyed travelling around Spain and other parts of Europe whenever they wanted. They took me to visit little villages and typical Spanish cities, such as Oviedo and Avila. These were places that my mother had always wanted to see, as her maiden names were Oviedo and Avila and she believed her ancestors came from there. The Spanish background has always been of great significance to many Bolivians who cling to it to make themselves feel superior.

After a couple of weeks in Madrid, my holiday came to an end. The night before I was about to go back to London, Mum and I were in my bedroom talking when she began an unexpected conversation. She suddenly remembered something that had happened ten years before and mentioned it as if it had happened yesterday. "Rafael went to visit your father at his surgery in La Paz," she said. "What for?" I asked, puzzled, thinking he had gone for dental treatment. "Well, he wanted your father to bring you back home so he could marry you," she said. This news sent painful shock waves to my heart. "When was this, Mum?" I asked with a lump in my throat. "This happened about ten months after you left Bolivia," she explained. Mum was perhaps expecting an outburst of happiness on my part or perhaps she thought I would pack my things and go back to Bolivia. However, none of that happened. As a matter of fact her revelation just left me frozen, angry and speechless.

Ten years had passed since this had happened and this was the first time I had heard about this mysterious visit. Neither Rafael nor my parents had ever mentioned this to me before. Rafael had stopped writing many years before and although

Mum and Dad were in regular contact with me, they had never told me about Rafael's intentions. I should have asked my mother more questions that evening, but I didn't, perhaps because I didn't want to hear answers that were more painful. Mum left my bedroom and I flung myself on to the bed, crying, trying to comprehend why Rafael and my parents had never asked my opinion.

I left Madrid without mentioning the subject again, but it was clear to me that from now on things were going to change. I was going to leave behind the bitter memories of the past and make a fresh start once and for all. I never thought at the time that a few months later I would come across a stranger with an odd but interesting proposition.

It was early evening on a Tuesday, I remember well. I was working at the wine bar on my normal shift, six o'clock until midnight. The place was not busy, the music fairly loud. An Italian guy called Fabrizio and I were working behind the bar that evening. At around seven thirty a young man came in and ordered a drink. Fabrizio jumped up to serve him a glass of white wine. When the customer went to sit on a stool at the corner of the bar I realised I had seen this man before. In fact, I had seen him the previous week, sitting in exactly the same place with a cigarette between his fingers as his only company. He didn't talk to anyone that evening or the week before. He was casual but smartly dressed and had an unusual look in his eyes, observant but not inquisitive. It seemed as though nothing in the world was important enough for him to be bothered with; I felt he was just a loner. He would drink one or two glasses of wine and leave a large tip before he left. That was the reason Fabrizio had hurried to serve him.

That evening he had only one glass of Chardonnay. It was almost eleven and he was still sitting in the same place, smoking one cigarette after another. He showed no signs of lack of confidence, but did not interact with anybody all evening. On the contrary he had almost an air of arrogance.

Suddenly I yawned, a combination of tiredness and boredom. "Tired?" he asked me with a peculiar smile. "Very," I replied looking at my watch. "Why don't you work during the day time?" I heard him asking. "I go to college," I replied, still looking at my watch. I was quite surprised by his sudden interest. "You should get a grant and stop working," he suggested. "I can't, I haven't got residence in this country." "Marry me then and you will have the residence," he said looking at me with a teasing smile on his face. "What a stupid comment," I thought, without answering. I just walked away to serve somebody else. He paid for his glass of wine, but before he left, he approached me again and said, "I'm going to France tomorrow, but I will be back next week and I will come to see you again. Let me know then if you want to be my wife."

The days passed without any major incident and I forgot all about the man with the ridiculous proposition until the Tuesday a week later when he came into the wine bar again. He ordered a glass of wine as usual, lit up a cigarette and sat in the same place. Without wasting any time, he started the conversation. "What's your name?" "Ivanna." I had given him my full name, which was unusual. "Ivanna," he repeated. "Nice name, are you going to be my wife Ivanna?" He had that same mocking smile again; I laughed. "I have never encountered anyone as crazy as this guy," I thought.

At about ten o'clock and after he had finished his glass of wine, he stood up to go, but before he did he wrote his telephone number without a name on a piece of paper. "Call me tomorrow at twelve noon sharp. Don't be late because by five minutes past twelve I will be out of my flat," he said before leaving the bar.

The next day at about ten in the morning, I called Bonita my Spanish friend, the girl who had taught me how to fiddle the electricity meter. I told her about the strange guy who had come to the bar and offered to marry me. She was quite intrigued.

"Phone him," she said. "You can't lose anything. Find out what he really wants and who he really is." My friend was a risk taker and good at encouraging me to take risks, too. "She who dares, wins," she said. In any case I thought there was no harm in finding out more about him.

At noon sharp, I made the call. He answered the phone in a cheerful voice. "Hello Ivanna, so you decided to be my wife after all." he said "Well, no, I was just calling to…" He interrupted. "Don't worry, girl, meet me in half an hour in the Maida Vale cafe. I'm going for breakfast, we will talk then." I lived quite near that area so I quickly got ready and took a taxi to meet him at the coffee shop he had mentioned.

It was early spring so we sat outside enjoying the warm sunshine. "So Ivanna, tell me more about yourself. How old are you? What do you do in your free time? Why are you living in this horrible country?" He seemed so laid back and talked as if he had known me all his life. "I'm thirty years old and I think we are going to make a very good couple," he said, laughing and lighting a cigarette. "I'd like to know your name at least," I replied. 'You can call me Tom, Billy, John or Perry." "Can I call you Billy? Is that your real name?" I asked him. "No, but it doesn't matter, Billy is fine, I like it." "What about if we go to the county court to see when we can get married?" he suggested. "Why do you want to marry me?" I asked him, bewildered by his behaviour. "I think you're a nice girl and I imagine you would rather be legal in this country, wouldn't you?" he said, as if it was the most natural thing to do.

He was right, that was exactly what I wanted, to be a legal citizen, to be able to work freely and contribute to the society I was now living in, but to get married to a man I didn't love, in fact I didn't even know, was crazy and not part of my plans. I had often heard of people who did it and had to pay lots of money for it. My friend Bonita had married an English guy for three thousand pounds a few years before but the man had disappeared and she couldn't get a divorce. She had met another guy from Nigeria and she wanted to marry him for love.

This episode reminds me of a time years later when a friend of mine invited me to her wedding. She was from Brazil, the groom was from Spain. During the wedding ceremony the county clerk, known as the Justice of the Peace, asked the Spanish guy to repeat after him the words. "I, Roberto Arcos, accept Alzira Albertina da Conceição Abreu Santos Almeida as my loving wife..." The Spanish guy started to repeat the names but he stopped in the middle of the long surname. He started again, and when he got to the surname he stopped again. He couldn't pronounce the girl's surname. The hall was spacious and there were just a few people invited, so for some reason his mistake felt bigger than it was. He tried once more to say the bride's full name correctly, but without success.

I started laughing, as did the rest of the guests. Some of them coughed to calm themselves down. The atmosphere became tense, the county clerk got angry and threatened to halt the wedding if we did not take it seriously. We all pulled ourselves together; the Spanish guy managed to say the name correctly on the third attempt and the wedding continued. The county clerk pronounced them husband and wife and we all left the registry office. Later on I was told that the wedding was just to get residence for the girl. The couple didn't know each other, so it was no wonder he couldn't pronounce her surname.

I often imagined getting married, but I always saw myself as being in love and having my parents' blessing. The way Billy proposed to me seemed absurd. "Billy, getting married for just the papers is illegal, isn't it?" I said. "There are worse crimes, girl, don't worry about it." We walked to the county court in Marylebone to reserve a date for the wedding. Two weeks later, I was married to a perfect stranger with a big heart. Billy did not want a penny. Fabio, my Colombian friend and Bonita were my witnesses.

The Illegal Dance

During the two weeks prior to the wedding, I got to know Billy a bit more. He was the only son of a wealthy Jewish couple. His parents divorced when he was very young and his father had practically disappeared from Billy's life. The sporadic meetings between father and son were very unpleasant and things usually got worse when Billy asked his father for money. The relationship with his mother and grandparents had been better, but this changed when Billy turned twenty one and his mother died of cancer. A few years later, his grandfather passed away. The only other person left in Billy's life at the time I met him was his old grandmother, but not for long; she died a year later, after we got married.

Billy had ended up living on his own in a fantastic mansion flat in Maida Vale, with everything one could want. He had a good home in an expensive area; he had money, good health and all the freedom to do what he wanted, which was exactly what he did. I soon discovered that Billy was a gambler. He spent most of his time playing backgammon and poker in London, Paris, Monte Carlo, Las Vegas and the Bahamas. He was like an owl, solitary and nocturnal, active between dusk and dawn, but restless, unsettled and bored during daylight hours. The smoky casinos were his second home, where the thrill and euphoria of winning would be followed inevitably by the frustration and hopelessness of losing.

To be in a casino was something I wanted to experience. One night Billy invited me to go to the Ritz Hotel. The gambling room was small and before we starting playing he took me from table to table explaining each game. One of them was craps, a dice game where players bet on the combinations produced by throwing the two dice. These combinations are diagrammed on the table and are possible bets. Roulette was another game. Thirty seven numbers from zero to thirty six are on the table. The players have to bet on one or more of the numbers. The croupier spins the roulette wheel then throws a small white ball in. After many laps the ball stops at one of the numbers and with luck there are one or more winners. I put five pounds on the number six, but minutes later I lost. Billy then bet five pounds on each of four numbers; in total he bet twenty pounds, which he lost. He gave me fifty pounds to do the same and I told him I would go to look around the tables. I put the fifty pounds in my handbag. My week's rent was fifty pounds and I did not want to lose it. After a while I returned to Billy's table; he was still betting, totally engrossed in the game. I didn't ask him whether he was winning or losing, I just told him I wanted to go home as I was overwhelmed by the madness of the casino. He didn't try to stop me. He called one of the employees who was wandering around and asked him to get me a cab. He paid for the taxi, gave the employee a tip and I went home to my bedsit in Kilburn.

Billy had some excellent qualities to become a good husband. He was kind, generous, caring and good looking, but being the wife of a gambler scared me off. I found myself in a marriage of convenience which became very convenient for me, because my life changed. I continued living alone as before, keeping myself busy with my studies and work, but Billy and I kept in touch. Every time he was back in London after a gambling trip to one of his favourite countries, he would take me out for dinner to a posh restaurant or send me flowers if he couldn't see me. Somehow, we managed to maintain a good friendship, even though my uncomplicated life and more relaxed nature didn't go along with his frantic existence and complex personality. But how true it is what people say, that you marry for better or for worse and when naivety is a major ingredient of a marriage it can have catastrophic consequences. A year later, I realised that I had been sailing in turbulent waters, but before this happened the marriage changed my status. The permanent residence and work permit for the U.K. allowed me to continue with my studies and find two excellent jobs.

I started to work in the afternoons at a health club in St. James's. It was not a place for the "have nots." Politicians, top lawyers and wealthy business people were among our clients. At the same time, I also got a chance to practise my clinical osteopathic skills in one of the best clinics in Harley Street. My boss there, used to tell everybody that years earlier she had treated members of the royal family and she hung two framed newspaper articles about it on one of the walls of the clinic. Publicising this fact attracted more famous people to the clinic, but ironically it then kept the royal family away.

My boss at the clinic was married to an American actor and she had lots of connections within the world of acting. Many famous faces came regularly to the clinic. This was the time when I began to discover some of the rich cultural life that London has to offer: theatre, ballet, art galleries and other attractions I had never dreamed I would see. It was through the clinic and the club in St. James's that I got to know a lot of well-known and important people.

At the clinic in Harley Street I also met a young, attractive blonde woman called Annie. She was their very efficient manageress but after work she loved to get lost in the good life and from time to time she would take me along to expensive night clubs, such as Tramp and Annabel's or to private parties with wealthy people. The combination was perfect; the attractive, sexy blonde full of life and fun and the foreign brunette with a strange accent ready to discover the mysteries of life.

Every time we were out and about, we would attract men. When drunk, Annie would dance on the tables and end up in the arms of any man who offered her love and affection. It was never long before I would join her in her crazy antics and we would both end up being the main attraction and centre of attention. Any reason was a good reason to have fun and I was more than happy to be part of it. Those were the days of champagne, men and parties. My life was wild and busy, one that any young person would want; far away from parental control and the conventions of a conservative country. I forgot I was a girl from a good respectable family. I didn't want to be respectable. Life was great and I wanted to enjoy it!

One summer Annie went on holiday, invited by one of the handsome men she met during our evenings out. Yassir took her to Islamabad the capital of Pakistan, the place where he came from. They arrived at the Islamabad Serena Hotel, a fantastic place, luxurious, relaxing and friendly. It was the place where East meets West. The couple enjoyed the first night with dinner, champagne and fantastic surrounding views of the city.

The next day Yassir told Annie he was married and had to go and see his wife and children. Annie, a carefree girl and a woman of the world understood the situation and waited for him the rest of the day in the hotel. Two days later Yassir returned, stayed with her another night and off he went again to see his family the next day. But before the week ended Annie met a man from Dubai by the swimming pool. He took her for a drink at the bar and later on invited her for dinner at the hotel restaurant. As Yassir didn't return to the hotel that evening or the next, the new friend invited Annie to Dubai. She accepted gladly and off they went. Presumably, Yassir turned up sometime after Annie had left the hotel to find a huge bill and discover that his lovely English girlfriend had gone. When I asked Annie if she liked Pakistan, she simply said, "I never left the hotel!"

One evening, the same summer that Annie was enjoying the delights of the East, I went to a jazz club in London with a Bolivian friend. Here we met a black guy from Zambia called Joseph. He had a sophisticated English accent and had been educated as an architect in the U.K. Joseph was the son of a businessman in Africa and his sister was married to the then Vice President of Nigeria. He lived and worked in Floral Street, Covent Garden

The Illegal Dance

and was the perfect yuppie: young, professional, ambitious and living the high life at an exclusive address. Joseph was not good looking, but he was a very charismatic kind of guy. He had long dreadlocks which made him look very informal but original. He often wore expensive three-piece tailored suits with silk shirts and Italian ties. He was a lot of fun, a great conversationalist and liked to discuss the meaning of life and read poems to me. His friends used to call him "Joseph the Legend," because apart from being an architect, he was a musician and a complete romantic. He also had an extravagant and sophisticated life style. He and I hit it off and a few weeks later we became very close. Going out with him was always amusing. Even though he lived in the heart of London, he transported my imagination to the remotest parts of Africa with his stories and romantic poems. We spent a lot of time together, eating at good restaurants and going to jazz and funk clubs until the small hours of the morning.

One evening we were out having dinner at a restaurant in Covent Garden. I asked Joseph where he got the money from to support his affluent way of life. "My bank manager pays for it," he replied with a naughty smile. "Great," I said, "cheers to your bank manager, then!" I lifted my delicious, fruity Sauvignon wine for a toast and we celebrated the bank manager's generosity all evening.

Joseph was an eternal womaniser. He called all his girlfriends "Princess" so as not to get their names mixed up. A few months later his lifestyle, including his comfortable home in Covent Garden, his job and our relationship, came to an end. The bank manager left Joseph in the streets. All the business that Joseph was doing collapsed. Joseph the legend ended up living in his car and busking in the Underground but without his Italian ties. He was a capable man, but he had been seduced by the competitive, consumer society in which we were living, where the borrowing of capital from the banks was a necessary evil to make more money. When he didn't make the profits he expected from his deals, his lavish lifestyle ended as quickly as it had started. A few months later he had to return to his homeland.

The desire to make instant money caused many young people to get into serious financial trouble. I had clients who were working as bankers and stock brokers, making lots of money in bonuses, and with this, buying expensive flats to let. It was also the time when it seemed even the air we breathed had been privatised by Margaret Thatcher. One of her policies I never understood was the sale of 1.5 million council flats built for the poor who rented them at low prices. But due to Thatcher's new policies many people borrowed money to invest in these cheap properties and then collected the rental. Her right-to-buy policy triggered an upward spiral in house prices, which encouraged householders to take on more and more debt. The result of all this later on was a severe shortage of housing in general, but especially in London.

In the early 1990s, the U.K. found itself in an economic recession which often comes after an economic boom. Unemployment rose to 7.4% compared to the 1960s unemployment of 1.6%. So a lot of people lost their homes and the flats bought with their bonuses, because they couldn't pay their mortgages. Others ended up in negative equity on "buy to let" flats. Later on house prices collapsed, speculators surfaced to buy houses and apartments at low prices and then rented them out at high prices. Low income people suffered the consequences.

Towards the end of her time in office, Margaret Thatcher introduced the Poll Tax. This meant that every person who lived in a house had to pay for the services received from the council. It was a head tax instead of tax for the entire house. People on a low income reacted to this unfair tax and started violent riots in central London. The confrontation with police was fierce. Each passing hour the violence increased. For security reasons train

The Illegal Dance

stations, pubs and shops had to be closed because angry people were causing damage on a massive scale. More than one hundred police officers were injured and over three hundred people arrested. About the same time London was experiencing a wave of bomb attacks by the Irish Republican Army (IRA). Margaret Thatcher's actions often came with a high human and moral cost. In 1971 she was called "Margaret Thatcher Milk Snatcher" for removing school children's milk. Finally her position as Prime Minister was threatened and her tenure weakened by her own party members. The "Iron Lady" was finally forced out of office in 1990; John Major was her successor.

Early one evening in June 1990 I was working in St James's when the whole building shook; it felt like an earthquake. I hurried out into the street but a cloud of dust blinded my view. Seconds later I was quickly joined by my work colleagues who hurried out behind me. The atmosphere was tense and surreal. Someone came out from a building across the road shouting that a bomb had exploded. It turned out that it was a terrorist attack directed at the Carlton Club, the oldest, most elite and prestigious Conservative Club for gentlemen. Margaret Thatcher was its only female member.

Five minutes after the explosion the police, fire brigade and press filled the streets. Ambulances began to arrive at the scene of the bomb blast and the whole scene looked like a war film. The explosion had caused severe damage to the building and seven people were badly hurt. The police closed the street. The injured people were taken to the nearest hospitals and the rest were evacuated. The next day I bought a newspaper and saw myself dressed in my white overall on the front page, standing outside the St James's Health Club opposite the Carlton Club.

At the same time some news from Bolivia hit me like a bomb. We had had elections again and among the many candidates were former dictator Banzer Suarez, former Minister of Planning,

Sanchez de Lozada and former Vice President Paz Zamora. Eight years earlier, in 1982, Paz Zamora, who was then the vice president under Hernan Siles Suazo abandoned ship and left Siles Suazo trying to restore democracy. Paz Zamora had studied in Belgium and became a passionate advocate for social justice. He was a founder of the Revolutionary Left Movement (MIR) and was exiled during the military dictatorship of Banzer Suarez. In these new elections, none of the candidates gained a clear majority. Disappointed by such a defeat, Paz Zamora made a pact with the devil, his pursuer and bloodthirsty persecutor of his party, Banzer Suarez. This alliance somehow allowed him to be proclaimed President by Congress (1989-1993). Paz Zamora's deal with the ex-dictator disappointed thousands of young people who had trusted him. Many gave up their hopes for the future and stopped dreaming about a change in Bolivia.

A week after the Carlton Club bombing, I arranged to meet my friend Tina at her college, the British School of Naturopathy and Osteopathy. We were going to have lunch together and then use the college library. Tina was the most sensible friend I had, serious, studious and kind. She was one year ahead of me and used to help me with the osteopathy techniques we both were learning. She was the daughter of a prominent Nigerian lawyer who had married an Irish lady in the late 1950s when mixed marriages were not very common. They had five children, all of them graduated from top universities, including Columbia in New York.

Tina and I had met a few years before when we were both working in the sauna at Swiss Cottage, the same place where the police stormed in early that morning and arrested the Colombian cleaner who was dealing drugs. We were going down the stairs of her college when a handsome man passed by, carrying a pile of books and papers. He went right to the top of the stairs and came down again quickly. "Hello Tina, have you got

The Illegal Dance

a class today?" he asked, looking surprised to see her at the college at that time. Tina explained to him that we were there just to use the library. Then he looked at me as though he was trying to work out whether he knew me or not. "Have I met you before? Are you studying at this college?" he asked. "No," I replied. "I'm studying at a college in Durham and I work at the Stone Clinic in Harley Street." I thought that he may have been a patient at the clinic. "The Stone Clinic?" he asked again. "Yes, that's right and I also work in St James's Street, near the Carlton Club," I replied.

He looked at me from head to toe as though he was trying to remember something. "I have the feeling I've seen you somewhere before. Where are you from?" he asked, looking even more curious. "Bolivia," I replied, expecting him to ask me where the hell that was. This was common; many people would confuse Bolivia with somewhere like Libya or perhaps think it was part of Colombia. But he nodded his head and gave me a knowing look. "Pleased to meet you," he said politely, then he excused himself and left. Tina later explained to me that he was her physiology lecturer.

The next morning I was busy working at the clinic when the manageress called me from reception. "There's a telephone call for you," she said. I picked up the phone. "Hello, who is it?" I asked. A deep, mature and refined voice spoke. "This is Alan, Tina's lecturer. It was nice meeting you yesterday." "Oh! Is that you?" I said, surprised. "You found me too quickly!" I replied. There was a brief silence at the other end of the line and then this lovely voice spoke again. "It would be a pleasure to see you again sometime." "I can't speak at the moment," I said, "I'm rather busy. Call me tomorrow at home." I gave him my number quickly and put the phone down.

Alan told me later how he found out the telephone number of the clinic and the mistake I made in English when I answered his call. He said that after he had met me at the School of

Osteopathy he went immediately to the college reception to look up the phone number of the Stone Clinic; then he phoned it to make sure I worked there. When the receptionist at the clinic told him I was going to be working the next day he relaxed. But when I said, "oh, you found me too quickly," he thought it had been a mistake to have phoned me so soon, but later he realised I had made a mistake with the language. I had meant to say, "you found me so quickly."

My mistake with the language did not deter Alan's pursuit of me; our first date was full of adventure. We went for a walk on Hampstead Heath, the area where I lived many years earlier at the Bartons' house. This was followed by a visit to the English poet, John Keats's house and then on to the final home of Sigmund Freud. After this he took me to see where the pop singer Boy George lived. We went on to an old pub called the Magdala, where in 1955, a woman called Ruth Ellis shot her lover dead and was hanged three months later. She was the last woman to be executed in England. The death penalty was abolished ten years later. This fascinating story of passion sounded more like a Latin drama than something from the phlegmatic English.

Alan was full of interesting stories. He was an extrovert, made me laugh and would talk to me as if we were old friends. There was no convention or formality with him, nor did he seem to want to impress me. He wasn't bourgeois but he was full of substance. That day we met for the first time, he brought a newspaper with him. "This is for you," he said. "I knew I'd seen you before." It was an old newspaper with the story and picture of the bomb attack at the Carlton Club. I was standing there wearing my white uniform.

In a busy and noisy wine bar that evening, Alan seduced me with his stories of adventurous journeys around the world. He had travelled extensively around South and Central America and lived in North America and Asia. He had been to Africa, India,

Australia and all over Europe. This intriguing man amused me with his passion for birds and his capacity for telling jokes, one after the other.

Fascinated by his stories I began to talk about the colourful butterflies that had followed me when I went to school in Coroico and the other peculiar insects that I used to catch for my collection. I also told him about my trips to the cemetery searching for open graves to learn about bones, swimming in the jungle rivers and dancing and playing with my black friends from Tocaña. That night I spoke of a life which I thought I had put behind me and forgotten; a life that I thought would never come back again. But, I realised that evening, talking to Alan, that this was not the case; in fact, that life was still with me in my heart and it was practically my entire existence. Alan listened to me with as much fascination as I listened to his stories. My anecdotes were simple; there was no travelling to lots of foreign countries. I had not seen the world like he had, but my childhood in Coroico was enough to impress this Englishman who loved nature. That night I started my long and unpredictable life with Alan.

I soon learned, however, that this interesting and attractive man, who had encouraged me to talk about my life in Coroico for the first time in fifteen years, seemed to be a tortured soul. "We live in an age of incompetence," he would say. "We won't be able to save the tiger in India. Governments haven't got a clue about what to do to save this planet." He would sit in the pub for hours holding a glass of wine, cracking jokes at first but later on feeling powerless and frustrated. Then he would suddenly decide to do something crazy and illogical, like the time when England was playing football against Colombia. He left the pub, went to the betting shop and put two hundred pounds on Colombia. Unfortunately, Alan lost all his money and when I asked him why he had bet on the opposition rather than England, he replied, "darling you know I don't like football, but I love Colombian birds. That's the only reason why I wanted Colombia to win."

Alan's hobbies seemed odd to me. One night he took me trainspotting at King's Cross Station. "You have to see the steam locomotive Bittern. It's arriving at eight this evening." His knowledge of steam locomotives and enthusiasm to see them in action was to be admired. Two older men with their grandsons were also awaiting the arrival of this fantastic machine of the A4 streamlined class, designed in the 1930s by the legendary Sir Nigel Gresley of the London and North Eastern Railway Company.

It was a bitterly cold night, like many in London, but they didn't seem to care. We all walked to the end of the platform so we could catch the best view of its arrival at the station. While waiting for the famous locomotive and pointing to one of the boys, who was probably about thirteen years old, Alan said, "I was his age when I started trainspotting." I could see Alan's enthusiasm as he went over to talk to the boy, who recalled with excitement the names of some of the locomotives he had already seen.

Alan began to compare notes with the boy and told him about his adventures while trainspotting around the country. He also told him about the British engineers who built the railway in Bolivia in the 1870s, to transport tin and silver extracted from the mines. "Oh, how I would love to see those steam locomotives going along the Andes," Alan said in a dreamy voice. An hour later, one of the old men started shouting. "It's coming, I can smell the coal burning!" The young boy yelled, jumping around. "Yes, yes it's coming. I also smell the burning coal." Although I couldn't smell anything, I was jumping anyway, but I think I was jumping to keep the cold away. However, I was also keen to see the powerful machine charging into the station to the sound of its chime whistle.

Another hour passed and still nothing had happened. The men, young boys and Alan were still determined to see it anyway. "It was advertised in the newspaper that the steam locomotive called Bittern was to arrive at eight this evening," Alan said when he noticed my patience was wearing thin. It was very cold and even if they had told me that the train was coming filled with gold I would not have stayed there a minute longer. Finally, to the disappointment of everybody, an insignificant diesel-electric locomotive built in 1962 emerged slowly from the tunnel. The driver said that Bittern had failed at Stevenage on its way back from York. I didn't care anymore; all I wanted was to go home to drink a hot cup of tea.

Alan came from a middle class family in the Midlands region of England. His father had been a college principal and died when Alan was just starting university. His mother was a lovely and lively woman, a true lady. Alan had a beautiful sister and two brothers. His sister emigrated to the U.S.A. and graduated from the University of Texas. The two brothers graduated from Oxford and Cambridge. His older brother, an actuary, played bridge with the Egyptian actor Omar Sharif and his younger brother was an actor.

I was getting to know Alan well and the more I knew him, the more I liked him. I wanted him to know about all aspects of my life and culture. So one day I took him to a South American festival. We were watching some dancers when we met a young, indigenous-looking Bolivian man. Alan began a conversation with him, fascinated to have met another Bolivian in London and even more curious about the country's Indian culture. "Are you an Indian?" he asked him, waiting for a proud affirmative. "No," the man replied, curtly, "I am not an Indian." He looked annoyed and moved away to avoid further conversation. 'What happened? Have I said something wrong?' asked Alan. It was the first time since I had been in London that I found myself having to explain why this man did not like to be considered an Indian. I explained to Alan that the word "Indian" in Bolivia is an insult and that Bolivians are generally racist and class conscious, due to our long standing and unresolved national identity problem.

Alan didn't understand; the more I tried to explain, the angrier he became. "What are you talking about?" he said. "The guy had an Indian look, why would he feel insulted? What on earth is wrong with being an Indian?" he said, not understanding my country's racial problems. I tried again; "you see Alan, in Bolivia we see being an Indian as the worst thing that you can be. It is synonymous with ugliness, ignorance and poverty." "Are you joking? Who sees them that way?" he asked. "People," I replied. "Which people?" he insisted. "Middle class Bolivians, I suppose," I replied, not really sure that what I was saying was totally correct. "Come on Anita, stop pulling my leg," he said. "Please explain to me this Bolivian logic before I die. Why is it so terrible to be an Indian?"

Alan kept on talking about the incident for the rest of the day, trying to make sense of what he had witnessed. He was the sort of man who, when he thought something was ridiculous, would go on and on until he got a fair explanation. To avoid more arguments I didn't tell him that day what many Bolivians think about black people. He became increasingly keen to see Bolivia as soon as possible, so we began to plan a trip. But a few weeks before we were due to depart something totally unexpected and disturbing happened.

CHAPTER EIGHTEEN

"One's real life is so often the life that one does not lead"

Oscar Wilde

I was living in north west London in a tiny studio flat. To make it look cheerful and welcoming I bought bright, flowery curtains in a street market and hung them in the tall, wide, bay window. As well as a kitchenette, the room had a small shower cubicle and a sitting area where I slept. When the sofa bed was extended it almost filled the room. The sitting area was furnished with a small, unstable wardrobe and a table and two chairs at the bay window, where I ate and did my college work. I had a few books that I used to keep the Jehovah's Witnesses and other Christians away with. Every time they knocked on my door trying to persuade me I should be reading the Bible I would bring out a big book on anatomy and physiology and excuse myself by telling them that I was going to start with the Bible as soon as I had finished the medical book. The Jehovah's Witnesses would leave happily without putting any more pressure on me. I also owned a small black and white TV that somebody had left behind.

Alan and I spent some weekends in the bedsit, as we didn't always have money to go out. On those days we would watch old films and wildlife programs. We would also read books about fascinating true crime stories on subjects like serial killers who lived in London. One such murderer was Dennis Nilsen, a man who killed at least fifteen young men in the eighties. He kept the corpses for sexual purposes. This killer used to operate near where I lived. Alan and I would sometimes go to see the house and speculate on how Nilsen could have carried out his crimes undetected for so long. We also read about gangsters such as the Krays and the Richardsons, who terrorised London in the 1960s. Alan would take me to the pubs where they used to drink.

Alan often says that it was love at first sight the day he saw me at the British School of Naturopathy and Osteopathy. We could not bear to be out of each other's sight for a single moment. Alan abandoned his flat in Wembley and came to stay with me in my little bedsit. He would say that life then was so uncomplicated and easy going that it was as relaxing as being in the country. I did not think my place was particularly special, but perhaps he loved it because every time he came home I cooked him a Bolivian dish with salsa music playing in the background.

One day in my kitchenette he found a Spanish recipe, "*Pollo a la Valenciana*." Alan repeated the word *pollo* (chicken) a few times and said, "what a lovely word and smells good too!" This was the first word he learned in Spanish and ever since then Alan would bring *pollo* for me to cook. I'm still unsure whether he preferred the food or the sound of the word.

Early one morning, I was sleeping soundly, when at about four o'clock, I heard the doorbell ring together with loud knocking

The Illegal Dance

on the front door and persistent rattling of the letterbox. My studio flat was on the ground floor and as I was the nearest to the front door, I got up half asleep to see who it was. "Who is it?" I asked. "Police, open the door please." "Just a second please," I said, going back to my room to put on my dressing gown; Alan was not with me that night. As I went back to open the door, the girl who lived in the room next to mine came out to see what was going on. "Don't open the door," she said, scared, but the knocks began again, even louder. "Open the door!" We both stood in the corridor looking at each other, not knowing what to do. Another lodger, a gay man from Australia whose room was on the first floor, woke up and wearing a colourful dressing gown spoke from the landing in an effeminate voice. "What are you doing standing out there? Come on, open the door girls." He sounded annoyed to have been woken up that early. The girl replied, "what if it's not the police?" The Australian raised his eyes in exasperation and came down the stairs, wiggling his body as if he had feathers in his arse; he opened the front door. Three police officers with a dog were standing outside; one of them spoke. "We are looking for Mrs Levitt." "There is nobody with that name in the building," the gay guy answered. "Sorry sir, but we understand that Mrs Levitt lives at this address." The Australian guy turned back and looked at us suspiciously. I was just about to confirm to the police that there was definitely nobody with that name living in the house, when suddenly, with a jolt, I remembered that Mrs Levitt was me!

"I am Mrs Levitt," I said, taking one step forward. The other two tenants stared at me, bewildered. I never used that name, so they probably thought I must have committed some terrible crime for the police to be knocking at the front door in the early hours of the morning. "Can we come in Mrs Levitt?" the policeman asked. Before I could answer, he walked into the hall with his dog beside him. The other tenants went back to their rooms and I opened the door of my studio flat and let them in. The policeman started to look around with the help of the dog, sniffing all over for evidence of God knows what. Two other officers also came in, a woman and a man. They began to question me gently with a series of requests for information, such as how long I had lived in London, where I was from, and what I did for a living. They looked at me suspiciously as though they did not believe a word I was saying. While they listened to my answers, they carried on searching the flat, hoping to find something which would implicate me in whatever this was all about.

The woman officer took a deep breath and began to explain why they needed to talk to me. "Did you know your husband has committed a crime?" Her question sounded as terrifying as the true crime stories I read with Alan. I imagined dead bodies and blood all over the place. The serious tone of her voice worried me, especially as her body language and expression showed real contempt. I felt she was exerting her position of authority over me. I felt like a rat, trapped in a corner with no way out. Her look was defiant and intimidating. My eyes turned toward the male officers, for sympathy. "A crime? What sort of crime?" I asked, terrified about what I was going to learn. "Burglary," she replied, with a look of satisfaction, almost pleased to be the one giving me the bad news. "We also know he's been on the heavy stuff, Mrs Levitt," she continued, without giving me time to react. I knew Billy used heroin; I had seen him a few days before. He looked awful and seemed to have withdrawal symptoms as he was sweating, shaking and feeling depressed. He said his whole body ached and he looked like he had not slept for days. That day he had come to my flat to borrow money and had stolen Alan's piggy bank without me noticing; he told me he was taking methadone to help fight his drug addiction.

"We are going to look around," one of the male officers said in a softer voice. They started to look in my kitchenette and shower room and the dog sniffed all over my bed and everything around it including me. I realised I had got myself into a lot of trouble by marrying somebody I didn't know. What else was coming? Would I have to go to prison too? I thought of my Bolivian friend, Doña Asuncion. She often told me to go back to Bolivia because England was not the right place for a young, inexperienced and single woman like me. What would I tell my parents? They didn't know I was married to a man who was a gambler, a heroin addict and now a thief. Not only I am sure they would not have approved of my situation, I'm certain they would have forced me to go back home immediately.

I was so angry that I felt like screaming at the woman officer that I only married this man to get my stupid residence and I had nothing to do with him, the burglary or the drugs. But, I bit my tongue instead, keeping calm and humble, while I collected my thoughts. I lowered my head and spoke to them politely and calmly, articulating the words as best I could. I told them how sorry I was about Billy's behaviour and then I began to try and explain his actions. "He is a very nice man," I said. "I'm sure what he did was under the influence of the drug he was taking. As a matter of fact, he is taking methadone; he is trying very hard to come off heroin." I was trying to alter their view of him. I went on to say that he didn't deserve to go to prison, but rather to a rehabilitation clinic instead. They looked at me with pity, probably thinking I was a real idiot to defend such a lost cause.

Neither the police nor the dog found anything in my room, not even cigarettes. Before they left the flat, they told me I could go to see Billy at Tottenham Court Road police station, where he was being detained. They also told me that I could pay bail of five hundred pounds for him the next day if I wanted to and that his court case was due in a few weeks.

The next day I went to see him at the police station. I had the bail money with me but suddenly I had a change of heart. I explained to the police I did not want to take the responsibility for his freedom, but at the same time I didn't want him to know that. The police understood the situation perfectly. Billy was called and in front of me they told him they did not consider me responsible enough to act as bail bondsperson. I left the police station feeling like Judas. I called my brother José in Barcelona and asked him to come to London for the court case. I felt that I needed moral support; Billy was going to be charged with burglary, so I had to play the loyal and dutiful wife. I wasn't sure whether I could do it as I was so angry with him for putting me through this ordeal and furious with myself for being stupid enough to get into such a messy situation. Alan, perhaps remembering what Billy had done for me, made me promise not to jeopardise the situation for Billy and promised to be with me the day of the court case.

In the days before the hearing I was in contact with Billy over the phone and I realised that I was his only friend. Thanks to his addictions he had lost everything: money, his lovely flat in Maida Vale and his friends. His father had given up on him long before. He was penniless, lonely and facing the prospect of going to prison for at least two years. He made me promise that I would attend the court case. I reassured him that whatever happened I was going to help him come through this ordeal. On the day before the trial, I received a telephone call from Billy's barrister. "Mrs Levitt, please meet me two hours before the hearing starts, we have to talk."

Alan, my brother and I arrived at Horseferry Road Magistrate's Court on time. Billy's young Chinese barrister Mr Tang, was already there, looking through his notes. We introduced ourselves and Alan asked him what exactly Billy had done. The barrister told us that he had stolen a briefcase from a businessman at Victoria Station, tried to cash a cheque and then burgled the man's house using the address in the briefcase. The man had reported the theft of the briefcase to the police immediately, who predicted that Billy would attempt to rob the man's home. They waited for him to show up at the house and caught him red-handed. Mr Tang also explained that Billy had previous convictions that would come up in court; he told us he had been in prison in Germany for smuggling drugs and had jumped bail and left the country before he had been tried. We stood there in silence without knowing what to do or what to say. I had not been aware that Billy had a criminal record, or that he was practically a fugitive.

The barrister then asked me to follow him to a room at the end of the corridor. He wanted to ask me some private questions. I looked at Alan for reassurance. He restored my confidence with a brief clasp of my hand so I followed Mr Tang. The room he wanted to use was occupied, so we stood at the end of the corridor and talked informally. He asked me a few questions about myself, then about Billy and me as a couple. He listened with great interest, scribbled a few notes and looked at me confused. "Forgive me if this sounds rude," he said. "But why does a woman like you marry a man like my client?" Before I had time to respond, he answered his own question with a friendly look in his eyes. "I suppose opposites attract, don't they? Well, it's time to go in now," he said, walking towards Alan and my brother.

We entered the courtroom and sat in the gallery so that we could see all the proceedings. After a few minutes, we were all told to stand. The judge entered with pomp and ceremony, wearing a grey wig and long black gown and sat on a chair on a raised platform. It is said that Charles II was the one who adopted the custom of wigs, when he returned from exile in France in 1630, to restore the English monarchy. So since 1635 wigs were used among English nobles and professionals of law as a sign of dignity and justice. The barristers for the prosecution and defence, also wearing wigs and gowns, faced the judge, bowed and sat down in front of him. A few other court officials took their seats. It all looked extremely formal but elegant. In Bolivia at that time, we did not have such open court procedures. If a man was accused of a crime similar to Billy's in my country he would be sent to prison first; if he was lucky enough, a few years later his case would be dealt with by a lawyer if he could afford one. A long drawn out process would follow with legal documents to-ing and fro-ing between solicitor and judge. The result would depend largely on how much money had changed hands.

A few minutes later, Billy was brought into the courtroom accompanied by two policemen. He looked crestfallen and lost, not a bit like the confident and charming man that I had happily married a year earlier. He looked around, trying to catch sight of me, but I was not clearly visible from the dock; the trial started. Billy's barrister began, "your honour, Mr Levitt's wife, Mrs Ivanna Levitt, is here in court today in support of my client. She came to this country from Bolivia eleven years ago with nothing. She took work as a humble cleaner to pay for her education. She studied English first and then went on to become an osteopath. She is currently employed at the prestigious Stone Clinic in Harley Street. She is an honest, studious and giving person, always putting other people first. She..." Bang! Bang! The judge interrupted with his hammer, clearly irritated. "I am sure that Mrs Levitt is a fine upstanding member of the community, without a stain on her character. However, it is not Mrs Levitt who is on trial here today, it is Mr Levitt. Can we move on please?" Alan looked perplexed and turned to my brother and me. "Do you understand what's going on?" he asked. "Billy's barrister has messed it up. He's been trying to use Ana as a character reference to deflect attention from Billy and the judge hasn't gone for it."

Mr Tang started his defence again, but he was largely defeated later by the prosecuting lawyer who went into great detail about Billy's bad character. However, one final thing happened that may have helped Billy. The prosecutor told the court that when the police arrested Billy inside the businessman's house,

The Illegal Dance

he had raised his hands and said, "that's all right governor, you won't get any trouble from me. I'm not violent." The prosecutor went on to say he thought this was Billy's way of saying "it's a fair cop." The judge sentenced Billy to eighteen months in prison.

We left the court, feeling sorry for Billy. Once again he had to pay for his stupid behaviour. During those months that he was in prison, Alan and I went to visit him many times, taking with us a few things that he needed to make his life a little easier. Ten months later he was released for good conduct.

I took the opportunity then to do the paperwork for our divorce. The procedure was simple and inexpensive, because both sides agreed. We didn't need a solicitor and the divorce was finalised in the county court.

Billy left England and went to live in Thailand, where he ended up in prison again for trying to smuggle drugs. A few years later, he received a pardon from Bhumibol Adulyadej, the King of Thailand and was a free man again, this time for good. In total he spent nine years in prison in different countries, until finally one day he met a nice, beautiful Asian girl and married her. He is now the wonderful husband I always thought he would become one day; we still keep in touch.

CHAPTER NINETEEN

"I do not know any country in the world where the poor exploit the rich"

Juan Carlos Rodríguez Ibarra

In 1993, Alan and I finally made it to Bolivia. On arrival in La Paz, we discovered that the newly elected vice president, Victor Cárdenas and his wife, had been on the same flight as us from Miami. Alan went over to have a photo taken with them and was surprised to see that their security was not nearly as tight as it would have been in the U.K., U.S.A., or other European countries.

Once in Bolivia again, I soon realised that the political soap opera was alive and well. There was the usual power struggle between the different party factions with ongoing squabbling and a never ending blame game. We now had a new president,

Gonzalo Sánchez de Lozada, of the Nationalist Revolutionary Movement Party. Despite his party not getting enough votes to win the general election in 1993, he was confirmed as President by the Congress thanks to the alliances he had made with smaller political parties. Lozada chose Victor Cárdenas, the man we had met at the airport, as his vice president.

I was surprised to learn that these two men were going to run the country together; they were so different. Cárdenas, an indigenous man, was more towards the left, while Lozada, educated in the U.S.A., had more globalised right wing ideas. However, this situation was not surprising in a country like Bolivia. The previous president, Jaime Paz Zamora, a leftist leader made a political alliance with a dictator and ruled the country for four years, until 1993.

Our new president, Sánchez de Lozada, the Chicago boy, was a wealthy man who had already begun to implement some of his plans for privatisation in 1985, when he was Minister of Planning. Although many left wing parties disagreed with these radical policies, he continued with his free market ideas. The most notable achievement of his government was to redefine Bolivia as a multi-ethnic and multi-cultural country. An important new law was Popular Participation, which decentralised the country, giving the local councils more power to govern themselves. But during this period the management of four major state-owned companies was handed over to foreign interests, under the excuse of preventing corruption. These were the national telecommunications company, the national electricity company, the national airline and the national railway.

On arrival in Bolivia the first thing Alan and I did was to go birdwatching in Coroico around the area where my family's maid used to live. While looking through his telescope Alan saw a little house and some black children running around. When I looked through the telescope I started shouting, "Pastusa,

Pastusa!" hoping it was the same person I had known. A black woman came out of a hut, looking around. I shouted again. "It's Ana, it's Ana!" She called out, "Ana, where are you?" "I'm here, up on the road." She couldn't see me but she knew who I was and came running up to meet me. It was a wonderful moment. I introduced her to Alan and she invited us to her home, producing a basket full of fruit for us to eat. We spent the afternoon sitting under the shade of a coffee tree, talking to her and playing with five children, four of whom were hers. She had adopted the youngest one after her friend died while giving birth.

We then went on to see Lake Titicaca on the Altiplano, located north west of La Paz. It straddles the Peru-Bolivia border and at nearly four thousand metres above sea level, is the world's highest navigable lake. We bought tickets for the front seats of a bus so we could see as much of the scenery as possible and take pictures. But on the way to Copacabana, the village situated on the southern shore of Lake Titicaca, the driver allowed more and more people with big bags to get on the bus. This was a dangerous decision, as all the passengers were squashed together like sardines. The bus eventually became so full, we could hardly move, let alone take photographs.

The overloading of the bus was so extreme I thought an accident could happen at any moment. I was so furious with the driver that I threatened to report him to the transport police if he picked up any more people. But of course he took no notice of me, and continued to pick up locals for cash. The other passengers seemed happy with the situation. They shouted at me, "if you don't like it, you should get off the bus. This is how we travel here." Somehow the bus arrived safely at Copacabana. We went straight to the transport police to fill out a complaint form. The officer wanted to show us how efficient he was. He left the building and brought the driver to the police station straight away. He reprimanded him severely in front of us, saying that he was going to prison for a few days for endangering the lives of his passengers. The policeman confirmed it was forbidden to travel with excess passengers and that he was grateful to us for bringing such gross irregularity to his attention. We left the police station with mixed feelings. We were pleased the police had taken us seriously enough to take action, but we also felt guilty that the punishment given to the driver was too severe.

That same evening, a few hours later, we went for a walk to the village plaza, where most of the buses were parked around the square. Alan, being an observant man, recognised our driver immediately, sitting in his bus. Perhaps he had paid a bribe to the policeman to be released from custody within a few hours.

Bolivia is a place where unusual things happen. We were travelling deep in the Bolivian rainforest, when Alan began to suffer from an appalling earache that made us cut short the trip. We managed to get to Guayaramerin, a city on the border with Brazil where my brother Marcelo lived and worked as dentist. Alan immediately told Marcelo about his problem. Before taking Alan to see a doctor Marcelo examined his ear with a torch. To his horror, he found his ear was full of maggots! He recommended to Alan that he should travel to Riberalta, a town in the north of Bolivia, where the Beni river meets the Madre de Dios, a tributary of the Amazon. "There is an ear specialist from Cuba temporarily working at the hospital," he said

Alan and I took a taxi to Riberalta. After a long wait at the local hospital, the doctor was finally able to see us. He was startled when he saw the infestation in Alan's ear. A fly had laid its eggs there and they had hatched. Unsurprisingly, we were both shocked. The doctor advised us to fly to the nearest city, Santa Cruz de la Sierra, immediately because he didn't have access to the equipment necessary to operate on Alan's ear to remove the maggots.

We rushed to the small airport at Riberalta, hoping to book seats on a plane that day. Flights that connect this remote region to local cities are not frequent, perhaps just two or three times a week, but we were lucky. We found a plane that was about to depart. Alan tried to pay a man standing next to the plane by using his credit card. "I'm sorry sir," he said. "We only take cash." Alan asked for the location of the nearest cash machine. "There are none around here, sir," said the ticket vendor. Alan panicked; neither of us had enough cash to pay for the tickets. He was bent over in agony. He looked around frantically and spotted the pilot. Alan ran over to him and tried to explain what was going on. Luckily, the pilot spoke fluent English and was very helpful. He told us to board the plane and pay for the flight at our destination. He also promised to arrange for us to see an ear specialist in Santa Cruz as soon as we arrived. An argument then broke out between the man selling the tickets and the pilot. The problem was that the pilot's neat solution to the problem would cheat the ticket man out of his commission. We left the two men to their argument and jumped on to the plane, very relieved.

A few minutes later another argument flared up between two women. Both of them had bought their tickets to fly, but there were not enough seats. Neither woman wanted to give way. The pilot's assistant tried to explain politely that a mistake had been made and that one of the women had to get off the plane and her money would be fully refunded. But neither woman was prepared to leave the plane and both of them had excellent reasons why they had to be in Santa Cruz that day. As the argument raged I could see Alan closing his eyes, cringing with pain. The women's row with the pilot's assistant showed no sign of abating and take off was already half an hour late. By now, the other passengers had become involved, shouting to no avail that one of the women should leave the plane. At last, the pilot marched to the back of the plane, sat one woman on the lap of the other, fastened the seat belt around both of them, and solved the problem. Alan opened his eyes, sat up straight and looked bewildered

The Illegal Dance

at what the pilot had done. On his way to the cockpit the pilot reassured Alan, "don't worry, sir. I'll fly very low and skim the tree tops, so the altitude won't affect your ear." Alan managed to smile and off we went.

One week later Alan felt much better, so we went to La Paz and while walking in the centre, we bumped into a friend who apologised to us for the city looking so ugly because of all the Indians who were living there, when they should be in the countryside.

Alan found Bolivia a culture shock. For the first time he witnessed the reality of life in my country. He began to understand why the man we met in London at the South American festival was so keen for us not to see him as an "Indian". Alan was even more amazed when he found out that Vice President Cárdenas's original surname was Choquehuanca, a native name, but his parents had changed it when he was young. This was because "Cárdenas" sounded more Spanish and they felt it would be less of an obstacle to his future.

For Alan, this was his first taste of how Spanish colonisation had influenced all aspects of Bolivian life. The economic and social problems that we inherited from our colonial past were still evident. Spanish occupation had not only influenced our way of life, behaviour and national character, but it had even changed our spiritual beliefs and attitudes. We no longer worshipped as our ancestors did. Particularly the middle classes had no belief in gods such as Viracocha, the creator of other deities, or Pachamama, the Mother Earth. But our worldview has changed. Now we combine some native rituals with Catholic ceremonies or attend other Christian churches. People spend much of their hard earned money on carnivals or parties wearing traditional Bolivian clothes, dancing to traditional music but end up in churches offering their dancing to the Virgin. Also they continue to dress up statues of saints and carry out ceremonies and have fiestas called *"prestes"*, in honour of these saints. Alan first experienced this when we visited a church in Copacabana village that had a little museum exhibiting all the expensive dresses that the serfs had brought to the Virgin. In religious festivals there is now a symbiosis between the ancestral and the Spanish culture.

We travelled around various parts of Bolivia, observing the country. In some places, the resistance to colonisation was more obvious than in others; but these people were considered ignorant by the middle classes. Another aspect that Alan found striking was the marked divisions between the social classes. This was not a division based on knowledge or money, it was based entirely on looks; the whiter your skin, the more western you looked and the better your chances of succeeding in Bolivia. Alan was amused by an advertisement in a newspaper that said: "Woman with a good presence is needed for a law firm as a telephonist. No experience necessary." Alan asked if a *chola* could apply for the job, a *chola* being a typical indigenous woman dressed in long voluminous skirts and a bowler hat. He was joking, as he had learned by then that this could never happen.

After the end of the Second World War the U.S.A. began to exert great influence over many countries, including Bolivia and so we began to be part of the inevitable globalisation. McDonald's was introduced but for some curious reason it only lasted fourteen years in Bolivia. However, the fast food industry was creeping into every corner of the main cities. The middle class started to adopt North American customs, such as holding baby shower parties, celebrating Halloween and singing Happy Birthday in English. Whenever Alan asked middle class Bolivians whether or not they spoke an indigenous language or had a relative of Indian origin, they took offence. Such people were always proud to tell us about their Spanish origins or that they had once lived in the United States or Europe. Middle class people were always happy to speak to Alan in English if they could.

Our travels around Bolivia gave us the opportunity to meet people from every social stratum. We met country people who told us they were totally resigned to the fact that the authorities were doing nothing for them, and Bolivia would never change. We met professionals and intellectuals who were tired of what was going on and felt helpless because they believed that the new government was experimenting with the economy. They said that no administration in Bolivia had spent a minute of its time on arts, sports, or other creative activities for youngsters. They believed the politicians were using the indigenous people as pawns to win elections by making false promises.

Even though he came across a few things that he found strange in Bolivia, Alan enjoyed the country immensely. More than anything else he enjoyed the wonderful birds he found in the exotic places we visited. "Do you know how many species of bird are only found in Bolivia?" "No idea," I replied. I knew nothing about birds. "About twenty. Isn't that amazing?"

During our flight back to London, he began to wonder about my country and if privatisation of public companies was going to work out for us. "I can understand these economic measures in a country like mine," he said. "We are a wealthy nation with many people who want to live and invest in the United Kingdom. We are a country that can cope with economic change." He was referring to Thatcherite ideas of neoliberalism and privatisation. "The government tax revenue from big private companies in U.K. is high," he continued. 'We have a much more fluid economy so we can afford to become an individualistic, selfish and speculative society. In contrast to Bolivia, which is landlocked, we are surrounded by the sea to facilitate trade. We are also situated in a strategic position as the Channel Tunnel links us to mainland Europe. I hope we shall continue to be in a good economic position. There should always be ways of increasing revenue for my country, such as from tourism, even better if there is a royal wedding or divorce going on," he said, laughing.

Alan continued talking, "we allow rich Arab oil sheikhs to come to the U.K. and spend their money on expensive London property, driving prices up to the disadvantage of working Londoners. Some even pay politicians for favours; but Bolivia is another matter," he said. "You are leaving yourselves in a very vulnerable position. Privatisation will make your country unstable." "Why?" I asked, curious to hear his views. "First, private corporations and the Bolivian Government must invest heavily in your country. They need to build roads, install electricity, gas and communications; and open up job opportunities in all the villages. If they don't take action, people who are treated as second class citizens at the moment are going to resent privatisation. If middle class people who have always been in power don't take them into account, this could end up in a civil war. I feel that nobody really cares about them. Come on, Anita, you should know better," he said, upset. "Do you think those private companies will do anything for Bolivia?" he asked. "No, they won't. They will take the goods and run, as they did in Ecuador, Brazil, Venezuela and several African countries," he continued. "I have the feeling that those foreign investors, Americans and Europeans who took your natural resources to live more comfortably are going to tear your country's dignity apart. A nation that does not look after its natural wealth, a country without pride in its own people, culture and language doesn't deserve to exist," he said, with feeling.

I wanted to alleviate his worries and show that the situation was not as bad as he thought. So I said, "well, it seems that this government is making some positive changes and we have a vice president from an indigenous group."

Alan interrupted me and carried on talking as though he hadn't heard me. "What really upsets me, Ana, is that you are a society that is totally ashamed of itself. You don't want to speak your native languages; you don't want to be related to the natives. You change your surnames to be accepted as respectable middle class citizens. You would rather be Spanish or anything rather than accept your real roots. You don't mind having an Indian vice president as long as you have a president who is practically North American," he said.

"You should consider the example of India. The British colonised India, but somehow Indian people retained their identity. They come to England or travel around the world wearing their traditional clothes and following their ancient customs. Their food culture is so strong that curry is now the favourite food of the British. We left them a good technological infrastructure, which allowed Indian private companies to prosper under the British parliamentary system. I once read an article by a journalist named Nirpal Dhaliwal. He is British but his parents are Indian. He wrote that the U.K. does not have to apologise for imperialism in India, the British should not feel guilty about it either, because the two countries have mutually benefited. He writes that the use of the English language has contributed to the boom of call centres and software industries; I think that's why we respect each other. But they don't want to look or sound like the British. They are proud people; they speak their own languages as well as English. My trips to India were magical even though the poverty seemed far worse than Bolivia. By the way, I've never seen a *chola* drinking Coca-Cola in Piccadilly Circus, have you?"

While Alan was sharing reflections and jokes at the same time, I thought about how silly some of my people are in many ways. A Bolivian friend of mine who was living in London came to mind. Her mum was a *chola* and was planning to visit my friend in London. My friend told her mum on the phone that she must dress like a European if she wanted to come to London. I also remember during my time at school in La Paz, the mother of one of my classmates was an indigenous woman. She worked as a maid for a rich family, but her daughter, my school friend never introduced her as her mum. Every time we visited her home she tried to hide her mother from us. In retrospect I don't blame her, as we were so racist that my friend probably felt we would not accept her mother for who she was. I remembered my grandmother who had white skin. She used to wash the grandchildren's faces with bran so we could be as white as she was. I also thought about how pretentious and ridiculous some Bolivians sounded when they went to live in another Spanish speaking country for a couple of years. They would come back with an Argentinian accent for example. A Bolivian woman I met once at a wedding in the U.S.A. told me that the best thing we Bolivians could do was to marry a white American to better our race, it was really sad how little pride we had left.

Alan continued with his observations. "Let's take another example," he said. "In the U.K., there are people from all over the world. They live in my country as though they were still living in their own but are perhaps better off. They are generally accepted for who they are. They speak English as well as their own languages. They dress how they like, and are usually well-integrated into society. For example, my doctor is black, my accountant is Greek and Billy's barrister was Chinese. You see Indians working in post offices or running their own businesses, and so on. If all the foreigners left the U.K. at once, the National Health Service, for example, would collapse overnight. Why is it, darling, that middle class Bolivians find it so difficult to accept indigenous people from their own country?" he asked me, confused.

Alan kept talking, "you see, your country is not known for its film industry like India or the U.S.A. It is not known for its football, or any other sports, unlike Brazil, Italy, Spain or even Cuba. It is not known for its great art, literature or its contribution to science. Your country is not even known for its women," he said, with irony in his voice. "In my opinion the best thing about Bolivia is its incredibly rich wildlife, which your government is doing little to protect. They allow wild birds to be caught and caged to be sold on the streets; it's a disgrace," he said, annoyed.

The Illegal Dance

"You have a precious resource that could generate income via ecotourism, but nobody seems to realise this. In England, of course, we have lost most of our wildlife."

A few minutes passed, Alan then noticed my silence, sadness and restlessness. I knew he was right, but I felt uncomfortable about him noticing all these things about Bolivia. I had taken him to my country to show him the lovely place where I grew up, but he also saw all the things that had bothered me when I was young. I had ignored them because I thought there was nothing I could do to change anything.

A few minutes later he apologised to me. "I'm sorry, darling, but I've travelled around this world a little and seen some terrible things. To be honest, I'm sick and tired of the continual exploitation of wildlife and local people; the native lands are taken and habitat is destroyed for people and wildlife alike. I feel very strongly about Bolivia, because I feel I already belong to it."

Months later Alan told me that the combination of the high altitude in La Paz and the general strangeness of the Bolivian way of life were difficult to deal with at first because of his close bond with me.

A few weeks after we returned from Bolivia to our hectic lifestyle in London I began to feel unwell. I had morning sickness and felt nauseous on buses and in stuffy trains, so I went to see a doctor, who recommended blood and urine tests.

CHAPTER TWENTY

*"To find you, son, I cross the seas
The kindly waves take me to you
Fresh breezes cleanse my flesh of the city worms
But I am sad, since on the seas, I cannot shed my blood
for anyone"*

José Marti

A few days later, I received the best news of my life; I was pregnant. Alan and I were over the moon. He suggested that we should take another holiday before the baby was born. When I asked him about getting married first, he thought that since I got pregnant first, we should have the honeymoon second and third the wedding; so this is what we did.

We went to Israel for an Easter vacation. If Bolivia was a country full of contradictions, Israel, this part of the Holy Land, was even more so. Instead of Israel being an example of peace, love and harmony to the world, it was a country constantly at war. Israeli civilians walked in the streets armed for self-protection. Palestinian suicide bombers blew themselves and other people up out of pent up accumulated frustration due to their territories being occupied by the Israelis. The Holy Land houses three faiths: Christianity, Islam and Judaism; unfortunately it seemed that these three ways of thinking was also the cause of so much intolerance and violence.

One day we were in a restaurant, when a group of Israeli soldiers arrived. They sat down at a table, ordered their meal and put their guns on the table. This disconcerting behaviour made us shiver, so we quickly left. Later on when we arrived at the hotel we found that the concierge was anxiously waiting for us. We had parked our hire car outside the hotel. But we had rented this vehicle from a Jewish company. So as soon as the concierge saw us he rushed out to warn us that we had parked in a Muslim area. He advised us to move it straight away, as the week before some Palestinian boys had set fire to a Jewish company car like ours in the same place.

We travelled around Israel for two weeks, visiting all the holy places where Jesus had supposedly been, but I found the contrast between the religion and the reality to be a mockery. Despite all the sublime history of Jesus of Nazareth dying for our sins, hatred, distrust, resentment and fear existed everywhere between the Jews and the Palestinians. The atmosphere was suffocating and Alan and I could not relax. We were always conscious of the danger of being in the wrong place at the wrong time because tourists like us had been blown up.

Something dramatic happened on our last day when we arrived at Tel Aviv airport. There were long queues of people waiting to check in. Security was so tight we had to queue for many hours before they allowed us on to the plane. People were impatient and began to get bored and tired; some of them were sitting on their luggage, others lying on the floor; children were restless and crying. To save time, Alan decided to leave me queuing while he returned the car to the rental company. As soon as he had left the airport, an alarm went off. The noise was deafening, we all became tense, not knowing what to do. Instinctively some people began to pick up their children; others were looking around to find out what was going on. Seconds later, loudspeakers ordered us to leave our luggage on the floor and immediately get out of the airport; there was a bomb scare. Suddenly panic reigned; people pushed one another out of the way and ran everywhere like crazy; many fell on top of each other.

An orthodox Jewish man in front of me picked his two children up in his arms and ran out with them, but on the way he lost his hat. Behind them was his pregnant wife, carrying their youngest son. An old lady lost her glasses in the confusion; it was total chaos, with the alarm ringing incessantly. I ran out of the airport like everybody else, afraid of losing Alan and my luggage, which I had left where I had been queuing. But more than anything else I was afraid to lose my life, in a place which was so foreign to me. Minutes later the police surrounded the airport and organised the process of evacuation.

On the street the chaos was as bad as inside the airport, many cars were left abandoned. I ran away as far as I could from the terminal and waited almost half an hour, without knowing where Alan was or what had happened. Fortunately, the explosion never happened, but it took a while to get back to normality and to meet up with Alan again. The conflict between Israelis and Palestinians is very sad. Although it all seems to be a conflict over territory, I am sure religion also plays an important part, as it does in many other disputes in other countries too.

On our return from the Holy Land, I received a letter from the hospital inviting me to have my first scan. It was a cold morning but I was blessed with joy, so I got up early, without grumbling. I wanted to get to the hospital on time. Even though the morning sickness had lessened, I felt very unwell; but it didn't matter, it was a special day for me. I showered, had a good breakfast and put on the best and most comfortable dress I found in my wardrobe; I wore makeup as I wanted to look pretty. That morning I was going to see my baby for the first time on a screen. I went on my own as Alan was at work.

I arrived at the hospital on time; the doctor let me into her surgery and after asking me a few routine questions, told me to lie down on the couch next to some modern equipment that was placed near a window. She sat down next to me, put gel on my naked belly and with a small device began exploring. Looking at her notes she confirmed, "you are fifteen weeks pregnant, aren't you?" "Yes, that is correct," I replied, excited and proud.

After a few minutes of silent observation, she spoke. "The foetus is fully developed." She began to explain to me in detail the foetus's position in my uterus, pointing out where the head, arms and legs were. She examined me carefully, sometimes in silence and at other times making short comments about the baby. She moved the device up and down my stomach. Finally, with a forced, but kind smile on her lips, she said, "I would like you to see Dr Best on Monday morning at St Mary's Hospital." She didn't sound alarmed or worried, but she was sure that I needed to see a specialist and she made certain I understood that I should not miss the appointment. She then phoned the hospital to book it. I thanked her and as I was about to leave her surgery, she suggested that my partner should go with me.

On the Monday morning, Alan and I went to St Mary's Hospital. Dr Best was not alone; there were at least five other people waiting for us. Dr Best introduced the rest of the people as medical students. He asked me to lie on the couch and explained to us that they were expecting one more person. "Mr Henderson is coming by bicycle from another hospital," he said. I asked Alan quietly, "why is he a "mister" and not a doctor?" "A mister is a surgeon, darling," he replied. "A top surgeon coming by bike?" I thought to myself. Bolivian doctors would never ride a bike, as they would lose credibility. Later on I found out that in the 16th century in England, surgeons did not have formal qualifications and were effectively glorified barbers. They used their scissors and sharp-bladed razors for hair cutting as well as surgery, so were just referred to as mister instead of doctor, but with advances in medicine these two professions split. So by the beginning of the 19th century barber surgeons had disappeared with real surgeons retaining the title "mister" as a mark of status. A few minutes later the other specialist arrived, sweaty and apologetic for the delay. The medical team began the meticulous observation of the baby that I was already longing to hold. They discussed their findings, showing the students the position of the baby's heart, head and legs. They repeated exactly what the first doctor I saw had done. They ran a medical instrument up and down my stomach and talked amongst themselves using medical language that I didn't understand. They stopped in some places longer than in others and discussed what the images meant, while Alan and I were kept in the dark about the whole process. "Are there two babies or maybe more?" I thought to myself, looking at Alan, but I guessed he wasn't reading my thoughts. He was staring at the screen, perhaps also trying to figure out what was so different about my case that needed the involvement of five students and two specialists. The situation was so surreal that I imagined I must be carrying a Bolivian alien in my stomach.

Dr Best eventually put an end to the examination and asked us politely to wait for him in his consulting room. The other medics looked at us with weak smiles. Doctors are good at hiding emotions. They are serene, controlled and inhibited. You can never guess what they are really thinking. They are "technical" people who seem to be able to hide their feelings behind their white professional uniforms. I got dressed and then Alan and I left for the other room.

We sat down in his consulting room for a few minutes, which seemed an eternity. Alan seemed uneasy; he sat down for a minute or so and then got up, walked a few steps and then sat down again. The room was painfully silent; neither of us spoke. This had never happened before. We always had things to say to each other, but that day Alan was silent, thoughtful and nervous. Perhaps he sensed bad news or already knew what was going on. Perhaps he didn't want to speculate, or come to any conclusions before talking with the doctor. Personally, I didn't really know what to think or expect. There was something very odd about our predicament, but I thought that any problem in a modern English hospital would be easy to solve.

Dr Best opened the door at last. He had a decisive look in his eyes. It seemed as though he had worked out the problem and had the solution for us. "Mr and Mrs Green," he said, looking us straight in the eye, taking a deep breath and sitting down in his chair to face us. "The baby's condition is not good." He paused, still looking at us. "I am very sorry to tell you that your child has spina bifida myelomeningocele; I am afraid it is a very severe form of spina bifida." He continued speaking as if he didn't want to be interrupted with any silly questions. "It is the incomplete closure of the embryonic neural tube and in severe cases the spinal cord protrudes through the opening. The baby will be born with hydrocephalus, possible brain damage and other severe abnormalities. It will be paralysed, incontinent and it may have a very short life. In some cases they die six months after they are born."

Alan looked stunned, totally shocked. I did not understand the enormity of Dr Best's words. "What can cause it?" he asked, totally crushed. Dr Best was careful with his words to avoid putting the blame on anybody. "There are many reasons," he said. "It could be genetic, or due to nutritional deficiency such as lack of folic acid. It is not possible to say for sure." He paused, took a breath again and then continued; but his voice sounded a bit more sympathetic, as if he was trying to alleviate the pain he had already caused us. "Mr and Mrs Green, I can only advise you about two options you have. Option one is that if you decide to continue with the pregnancy we will try to assist in every way possible so you as parents can look after a disabled child. Option two I'm afraid, is termination of the pregnancy, that is if there are not any religious grounds or anything else that may be an obstacle of course." He continued talking while Alan and I looked at each other in total disbelief that we had to be the ones to choose. "I know this is not an easy decision to make. The medical implications are...." I broke down and sobbed hysterically; I was inconsolable. I didn't want to hear anything else; I didn't want any more explanations or reasons. I asked myself, "why me? What have I done wrong? I've just been to Jerusalem in the Holy Land; I have been to the Mount of Olives where Christ went to pray before he was arrested. I have been going to all the sites of Jesus's crucifixion, burial, resurrection and to all the churches; the Catholic Church, the mosque, the synagogue. Why did this happen to me? Why me? What have I done to deserve it?"

Alan quietly helped me to get up from the chair; it was time to go. There was nothing more to say or ask. Whatever we said or did, it wasn't going to make the baby better. The doctor walked forward and opened the door for us and said gently and attentively, "please let me know your decision; you have until Monday next week. If you decide to terminate the pregnancy we cannot wait much longer, it may be risky." The rest one can only imagine; consolation from Alan, my parents and friends didn't help my grief. I felt a failure for being unable to have a healthy child.

The Illegal Dance

The fact that I had to go back to hospital in a week's time was too painful to contemplate.

For a week I carried a baby that I knew was going to be born dead or if I waited a couple of months more it was going to be born totally handicapped. Any decision scared me and wrapped me in a mass of emotion; I felt guilty, lonely and empty. I felt like a sinner and questioned God in all his dimensions. I blamed him for putting me in this terrible situation. I became religious and prayed to change my circumstances and hated religion at the same time. I hated doctors for giving me such terrible news. I hated life and anything that crossed my path. I hated Alan for being part of my misery and at the same time I felt that he was the only one who could possibly understand my pain, anger and feeling of helplessness.

Seven days later, Alan and I decided to go back to the hospital, but this visit was to be a decisive and tragic one. The nurses were sympathetic and understanding. One of them told me that I had a nice room waiting for me; my own TV and a telephone on the bedside table. This was a luxury I wasn't expecting in an NHS hospital. They told us that Alan could stay overnight with me, which he did. They explained the procedure I was going to go through the next day. They were going to inject a drug to induce a normal delivery, but the child was going to die in the process. I chose not to dwell much on what was going to happen; all my thoughts, beliefs and feelings were frozen.

When in great difficulty one loses touch with time and the outside world. Being in hospital, there is no difference between day and night; it all seems the same, it doesn't matter. It is the nearest you can be to being with your own self, with your pain, with your sorrows. You question your strengths, your weaknesses and your mortality. You feel totally vulnerable and the universe out there seems even bigger and more unreachable. Once the medical staff takes control of the situation, you realise that your body doesn't belong to you anymore. You lose the capacity to make decisions, but in fact you don't want to make any decisions because you don't know what decisions to make; you just go with the flow.

An injection into the vein in one of my arms marked the beginning of a slow process to end our dreams. The pain of what was supposed to be a delivery increased throughout the day and night and continued the next day. A few medical students, nurses and friends came from time to time to see how I was doing, but not even my parents' anxious and loving telephone calls from Spain helped relieve my pain. It was a pain that travelled all over my body and stopped right in my heart like a deep stab. But the feeling of not being sure that what I was doing was the right thing was worse than the pain itself. I had to concentrate on what the doctor had said and the few words I had with my father over the phone. My options were limited and both choices were going to end in misery anyway.

As time passed during the night the pain would increase, reaching a peak where it seemed that the baby was going to be delivered and in the process break my back in two. But after a few minutes the pain would cease, as if the baby was trying to survive and stay with me. Alan stayed throughout the day and night without moving from my side, trying his best to help. The painful contractions of the uterus continued through the afternoon of the next day, but there was little dilation of the cervix. But now it was time to deliver the baby. A medical student arrived and introduced some forceps into my cervix to try to extract the foetus. I felt an excruciating pain as if all my organs were being pulled out. But the foetus wouldn't leave my uterus. It held on to a mother who had given up on it a long time ago. Eventually a senior doctor came to my rescue; she introduced the forceps again and with the best possible medical experience and skill she asked me to push as much as possible. "Push, push, push," she said as she snatched the baby out in just one go.

The Illegal Dance

I had heard so many times from mothers that the experience of having a baby is unique. From the first moment you conceive, this sublime act becomes a great period of anticipation, even though you are experiencing sickness. Later on and during the act of delivery, although traumatic and painful for some, it is eventually a great joyful and unforgettable episode. You hold a crying baby in your arms, a baby that comes with hope for the future. It establishes you in this world, giving you a real purpose in life. We didn't have any of that; our hopeful future ended as soon as it had started, leaving us with no strength for the future.

After the delivery they took me to the operating theatre to make sure the placenta was also removed hygienically. They injected an anaesthetic which sent me to sleep; a bit later I woke up in my room again. A nurse arrived with a small basket, inside it a tiny well-formed dead baby; it was a boy. Alan gently turned him over and saw the little gap in his back. It was the proof that he had spina bifida; I was too groggy, sleepy and numb to care. The anaesthetic was still working. Neither of us held the baby at that moment, we were too distressed and upset, still in shock for such a painful fate. Instead Alan and I held each other and cried like two children who had just damaged their most precious toy and couldn't play with it anymore. The nurse came back and took the basket with the baby away.

The next day I woke up to a new reality. I called the nurse and asked her to bring me my dead baby again. I needed to hold him for a little while, give him a name and whisper my love for him. I also wanted to kiss his little, already cold forehead and look at him and imagine him as a little boy going to school. I wanted to say goodbye to him. The nurse entered the room with a picture of the baby in her hand and was very apologetic, "I am very sorry, but this is all I have. It has been taken to a laboratory for investigation." My heart sank; I wanted to yell that she should have asked for my permission to take the dead child away! I wanted to demand that she bring the little body of my son to my side, so I could start my grieving period by holding him, but I didn't, I just cried alone inconsolably. We never named the baby, never held him, even for a minute and we never even had the chance to bury him. He was probably dumped in a cold laboratory and maybe later put in a rubbish bin.

I left hospital the following day feeling empty, childless and broken hearted, carrying with me a heavy and painful burden of guilt and frustration. A deep and dark depression followed. My Mum arrived from Spain to keep me company and to give me moral support. Alan tried in vain to help me, with promises that we would try again to have a child. My grief and depression continued for a few months until the doctor felt sorry for me and sent me to a counsellor, to hear my cries and understand my sorrow.

CHAPTER TWENTY-ONE

"The job of the artist is always to deepen the mystery"

Francis Bacon

Alan and I now flung ourselves into a busy regime; work became our best therapy. We were still living in the bedsit and we began to dream of having a big house, with a nice garden and a large kitchen to cook my *pollo* dishes. But property prices seemed very high. Even though there was an economic downturn at the time, every metre of residential space in London cost a lot of money. To buy a house was out of the question, so we finally bought a two bedroom garden flat in a very nice residential area of north west London. From now on we became totally committed to the demands of a consumer society. We had to work long hours to pay the bills that arrived regularly through our letterbox.

Thanks to Alan's discipline, we kept ahead of our financial responsibilities, but we had little time to actually see each other. When he was in, I was out working and when he was out working, I was in. My cousin Liz in La Paz came to stay with us for a while and she was surprised by our busy lifestyle and the little time we had left for each other, or for a social life.

In those days London was still resisting a wave of terrorist attacks by the IRA. This movement was aimed at creating a unified independent Ireland. During the 1980s England had suffered a series of terrorist attacks from this organisation. But from 1993 to 1997, the attacks increased in London. One of them was in January 1993 at Harrods, one of the most famous department stores in London, where four people died. Another explosion that I remember well was when the IRA detonated a huge truck bomb at Bishopsgate, killing the photojournalist Edward Henty and wounding more than forty people. This attack almost destroyed St. Ethelburga's church, and Liverpool Street Station, causing approximately three hundred and fifty million pounds worth of damage. But what most troubled me was that for eight days a series of bombs were left in different parts of the city and every explosion was getting closer and closer to the neighbourhood where we lived. In February 1993, a bomb exploded at the McDonalds restaurant in Camden Town causing many casualties. A few months later in October 1993, four more bombs exploded. These were at Highgate, Staples Corner, our area West Hampstead and finally in the Finchley Road, practically around the corner from where Alan and I had bought our flat. These desperate and deadly attacks were because when Margaret Thatcher was Prime Minister, she was not able to solve the problem of Northern Ireland. Many historians accuse her of having a simplistic approach to the great Irish dilemma. They also criticised her lack of the tolerance necessary to find solutions to the problems of a divided society. However the radical, violent approach of the IRA and Thatcher's ways of dealing with it served as an example to others to finally end the conflict in 1998 with the Good Friday Agreement. The Prime Minister, Tony Blair was to sign it.

One day in the 90s something unexpected happened. We were in the sitting room of our new flat watching television, when we heard a terrible tearing sound above us and suddenly found ourselves covered in plaster; a bomb we thought! As we looked up, a leg was coming through a newly formed hole in the ceiling. It turned out to be the leg of our Irish neighbour upstairs and this was our first introduction to him. He had bought the flat above in the same week that we had bought ours and was renovating it. But that evening he had drunk a few pints too many and had misjudged his step while walking on the rafters. As his floor was not yet laid, he came straight through the ceiling. Alan introduced himself. "Are you all right, mate? My name's Alan". "I'm ever so sorry about this, my name's Ronan," the guy said. After we had accepted his profuse apologies, Alan and Ronan went to the pub for a drink. This was the start of a lifelong friendship and was the first of their endless, funny stories.

In the same year we bought the flat, Alan and I decided to get married. I wanted a salsa party, he wanted a rock party. I wanted a small wedding, he wanted a big one. I wanted a sit down dinner, he wanted a buffet. I wanted to invite just family and close friends, he wanted as many people as possible. In the end we had guests from all over the world. During the party, instead of dancing the waltz with my groom, I danced the salsa with Fabio, my Colombian best friend. When Alan gave his speech, instead of talking about his bride, he talked about his best drinking partner, Ronan, who would go out drinking first thing in the morning so that he could then concentrate on his work later. The reception was held near Piccadilly Circus in a restaurant called Down Mexico Way.

The celebrations were going well, but I noticed that all the friends I had invited from work were very quiet. I approached them to get them to dance and they reluctantly tried to join in, but there were forced smiles on their faces. This was very unusual as they were normally a noisy and happy crowd of people. One of the girls in the group was missing, they explained she couldn't take time off work and that was the reason she wasn't at the party.

After the wedding we went on honeymoon to the West Indies for a week before going back to work. I was then told some unexpected, tragic news. The girl who was missing at our wedding had died the night before the ceremony; she and her boyfriend had spent a romantic candlelit evening having dinner and drinking wine. After a while they went to bed, and fell asleep. A few hours later the boy woke up to see the blankets on fire. He managed to get out of the room in time but couldn't help his girlfriend. Chantal was only twenty four years old when she died. Still feeling vulnerable after my own loss, I was deeply upset at her funeral.

Soon after the marriage, I decided to become my own boss. With the help of my local doctor, I started my own practice on his premises. I also enrolled on a four year nutrition course to follow my father's advice to keep learning more about natural therapies. The course was so demanding that I was constantly asking Alan for help.

My obligations and responsibilities grew massively and I felt under constant stress. Apart from studying nutrition I also had to deal with the new technology, as Alan had bought a computer. I had only used a typewriter until then, but when this state of the art machine arrived in my home I had to learn to use it and this occupied even more of my time.

Those days as a student in England reminded me of my education in Bolivia. In order to pass exams I would ask my cousin Patricia for help. This would not have been a problem had it only been Patricia teaching me, but every time her sister Liz joined the study group quarrels started. Liz would get angry and throw a tantrum when she did not understand something. Patricia was patiently trying her best to make us understand maths and physics, but whenever Liz exploded with rage, Patricia would storm out of the room and shout that she was sick of such ungrateful behaviour. As I was eager to learn, I would get up from my chair and follow her everywhere begging her to continue the lesson. This scenario would repeat itself every time she agreed to teach us both.

My whole school life was like that; I would often ask one of my clever cousins or friends for help so that I could succeed in exams. I still have nightmares about those school days in Bolivia. When I began studying in England the experience seemed to repeat itself. Alan, my friend Catherine, or somebody else was helping me with one thing or another. Sometimes I paid for private tuition so that I could do well at university.

Apart from my struggles with the course, married life was full of interesting surprises. Alan's peculiarities were more noticeable than ever. He was not only a fanatical birdwatcher and train spotter, but I soon found out that he was "star struck". Often he would come home with the news that he had met some celebrity, which is not too difficult if you live in London.

One night we went to the well-known nightclub, Tramp, with some friends. Alan soon spotted a famous actor, the late Leslie Nielsen, who was with a young, blonde and beautiful woman at a table a short distance away from us. Without hesitation, and before I could stop him, Alan walked straight up and greeted him as if he had known him forever. "Hello Mr Nielsen, you've just been working with my brother Andy in a television commercial." Alan's younger brother is an actor and had apparently been doing some filming with the star. Nielsen stared at Alan, bemused by his opening line. He may have been trying to remember the actor Alan was talking about. His eyes scanned Alan carefully trying to see in him a resemblance to someone he had just worked with. After a few minutes, Mr Nielsen replied, "I'm terribly sorry, but I don't know him." "Oh well, it doesn't matter. It was nice to meet you anyway," Alan said, shrugging his shoulders and walking away. This was typical of him. Every time he saw somebody famous, he would approach them, engage them in conversation and if I wasn't with him, he would phone me at home immediately and either ask me to talk to the celebrity or encourage me to join him so I would meet the star in person.

I used to study at home in silence, but my concentration would often be interrupted by a telephone call from Alan. "Hi darling, take a taxi and come to meet Louis Mahoney. Do you remember him? Fawlty Towers; he played the doctor. Well, I'm here having a drink with him in Hampstead." Or at other times he would come in very excited. "Guess who I just met in the street. Oh God, I can't believe it. It was Paul McCartney! We shook hands and I talked to him. You see, darling, he is part of my youth; I grew up with the Beatles music. I always wanted to meet Paul." Like a small child he would talk incessantly about his brief, chance encounters.

My Colombian friend Fabio, was goalkeeper for an amateur South American football team in London. Out of the blue the South Americans were invited to play against Rod Stewart. Rod's team was made up of former professional footballers from Chelsea, Arsenal, Sheffield, and Nottingham. The game was going to be at Rod's mansion in Essex and Alan was invited to go with them. Rod Stewart is known for his love of football and he played for his team in the first half. The result was catastrophic for the South American team; they lost badly. After the game, Rod's guys gathered to enjoy a few beers. The South Americans stood there without being offered even a glass of water!

Before leaving the house Alan asked Rod if he could take his picture with the South American players and he was happy to do so. But by then most of the team had left, as they were annoyed at the complete lack of hospitality. Alan returned home upset and disappointed about Rod's behaviour and said, "this would never have happened in South America. Rod would have been treated like a king by the poorest people."

A year later Alan found out that Hugh Grant was filming a scene of About a Boy at a friend's restaurant. Eager to go and meet him, he insisted I should call my friend to ask him if we could go to the restaurant while they were filming, but I declined because I was too busy.

One evening I was at home working on the computer as usual when the telephone rang; it was Alan. "Hi darling, is everything all right? Are you studying? How's it going?" he asked. "Yes, I am studying," I replied, annoyed that he wasn't home yet. "What time are you coming home?" "Soon darling soon, listen, Tony Blair, the Prime Minister is here with me at the moment and wants to talk to you; I'll pass him the phone." "What? The Prime Minister? Are you joking?" I shouted. "Alan, please, I don't want to talk to anybody."

However, before putting the phone down on Alan, who was often interrupting me with stupid calls, the well-known voice on the phone said, "Hello, Ana. This is Tony Blair." "Tony Blair?" I asked in disbelief. "Yes, that's right." His voice sounded so familiar that I began to stammer. "Where are you from Ana? You seem to have a foreign accent," he said. "I'm from Bolivia," I replied, not knowing what else to say to the Prime Minister. "Oh yes, I met Hugo Chavez a few years ago." "Oh! No. I'm sorry sir, Chavez is the President of Venezuela." "Oh, forgive me Ana, I'm not very good on foreign policy, I'll pass you to Alan now, very nice talking to you." Alan came to the phone bursting with laughter and revealed that "Tony Blair" was in fact the famous TV impersonator, Rory Bremner. His foreign policy joke was spot on, as a year earlier the war against Iraq had started and unfortunately for Mr Blair no weapons of mass destruction were found.

One day we were out with friends from Bolivia touring London when suddenly Alan saw the famous boxer Chris Eubank driving his huge American truck cab. Alan could not resist; we chased him in our car, finally getting his autograph and introducing him to the Bolivian couple.

After work Alan spent part of his time having fun meeting actors, comedians, or pop stars. One day it was Gary Barlow, another time David Tomlinson, Jude Law, David Cassidy, or somebody else who meant nothing to me at all! So my married life continued, me with my studies and my new job and Alan with his encounters with famous people. One Saturday afternoon Alan's elder brother and his wife were coming to visit so I hurried to do some shopping. On my return and to my surprise, there was also a new guest. This was the famous actor from the television series Starsky and Hutch, David Soul. My mouth fell open, I couldn't believe it. I used to watch him on the screen when I was living in Bolivia and now here he was sitting in my living room, drinking a beer with Alan's family. Alan had met him a few weeks before, in a coffee shop. He'd approached him, as he usually did, to talk about his latest play and they had become friends.

Alan's endless stories about famous people kept me entertained, especially while I was busy studying. One day he came home excited. "I have some news for you darling," he said. Whenever, Alan had to announce anything, whether it was trivial or interesting, he would often put on an act and use his ability to tell stories in a theatrical way. On the lips of Alan, any insignificant tale would sound fantastic and seductive. He also made the story last to keep you in suspense and entertain you as long as possible. On this occasion he spoke solemnly. "You are going to meet one of the best English actors. Actually, as a matter of fact you are going to have lunch with one of the best English actors, if

The Illegal Dance

not the best," he said, insisting I should guess the identity of the celebrity. I didn't have a clue and didn't try very hard because I wasn't all that interested.

"Come on Alan, I haven't got time to guess, who is it?' I asked. But he wouldn't tell me. He wanted to prolong his fun and my irritation. "Come on, please try and guess. You know him," he tried to remind me. "You used to watch him on television a few years ago, when you could hardly speak English." I thought I knew who he was talking about, but I couldn't remember his name. Before I had the chance to guess the famous actor's name, Alan enjoyed announcing him, as if he was introducing the start of a play. "This is Pauuul Eddingtoooon…, the man himself, here with you tonight…."

Alan's younger brother, Andy, the actor was getting married to Paul Eddington's daughter! The wedding was to be celebrated at the Garrick Club. Its name comes from the great 18th century actor, writer, producer and theatre manager David Garrick. I didn't know anything about this fascinating place until the day of the wedding.

The elegantly dressed guests began to arrive. Alan and his older brother John stood at the top of the red carpeted stairs to receive them ceremoniously. I watched fascinated and delighted to have been invited to a wedding in such a cultural place. While waiting for the whole party to arrive, I decided to walk around looking at the pictures of some of the most important members of the club, such as the novelist Charles Dickens, the famous British actor, director and producer Sir Laurence Olivier and many more. I imagined the discussions on literature and politics that would have taken place in this club. I thought of Uncle Hector and how much he would have enjoyed the opportunity to visit such a prestigious place.

The wedding lunch took place in a large, stylish hall where the dark red walls were hung with famous paintings and beautiful crystal chandeliers were suspended from the ceiling. All the guests sat at delicately decorated tables. It was a surreal day for a woman from the Andes. While the speeches were taking place, my mind wandered through the vast expanse of the Bolivian Altiplano. It is here in the arid landscape and cold air where the dry whistling wind picks up suffocating dust and envelopes the llamas which move slowly, eating sparse and coarse grass. The Altiplano is unchanging and almost infertile, where a humble, dirty peasant shepherds his flock of sheep, where dogs bark with hunger and where poverty does not allow us to dream of fame.

A couple of years later we went back to the Garrick Club, but this time it was a sad occasion. Paul Eddington had passed away and all his family, friends and work colleagues gathered for a memorial service. To my surprise all the actors and actresses that I had enjoyed watching on television many years before were there in the flesh. It was like a real life soap opera where I also had a part to play. Penelope Keith was just in front of me, surrounded by other famous British actors such as Nigel Hawthorne, Richard Briers and the writer David Storey. I really wanted to talk to her as she was part of my lonely time in London when I moved to Kilburn, separated from my Colombian friends. It was the time when I had nothing to say to myself, and watching television was my only source of company. A waiter passed by holding a tray of glasses of white wine. I took one to give me Dutch courage. I wanted to approach Penelope, but wasn't sure what to say. What do you say to somebody who you have only seen on television? "Hi, nice to meet you, I like your acting." This sounded horribly cold. Or maybe: "Hi, I think you are a wonderful actress, I like your facial expressions;" this sounded stupid. Or even: "Hi, I used to see you on television. You made me laugh although I couldn't understand you as I couldn't speak English very well at the time." She would have probably told me to get lost. So I just stood there, holding my glass of wine with my two hands, thinking that I didn't have anything to say to her.

The Illegal Dance

Noticing my indecision, Alan came to the rescue. "You want to talk to her, don't you?" he said in an encouraging tone. The smile on Penelope Keith's face was enough to tell me she was sharing a joke with her friends and I didn't want to interrupt. I would probably have said "goodbye" instead of "hello," or something else totally inappropriate. When one does not have a good command of the language one tends to feel insecure and look and sound stupid. This is especially true in England where people tend to ignore you if they don't understand you. This doesn't matter in Bolivia; if a foreign person tries to speak Spanish, it sounds cute, as Bolivians love to hear foreign accents for some reason. Alan was determined that I should talk to her. He held my hand and we approached the group. He explained to her that she was my favourite actress. That day I got my first autograph.

How ephemeral life is, after all! One day the actor is out there making the fans laugh and the next day, making them cry with the same intensity. The memorial service of Paul Eddington ended with lots of laughs, but with plenty of tears, too.

CHAPTER TWENTY-TWO

"God has no religion"

Mahatma Gandhi

Many historic events have taken place in the U.K. since Alan and I got married. Tony Blair became Prime Minister after almost fifteen years of Thatcherism, Princess Diana was killed and the Northern Ireland Peace Process was successfully negotiated.

Bolivia has also seen some seismic changes. Hugo Banzer Suarez, the old dictator, who in 1971 killed thousands of people and sent others into exile, (including my Uncle Hector) had amazingly become the constitutionally-elected democratic president. This happened due to the bad memories of many Bolivians, a coalition with other political parties and as often occurs, the involvement of the U.S. Government.

The policy of privatisation continued. The World Bank made an announcement. "Poor governments are often plagued by local corruption and are not capable of running public services, such as water, electricity and telecommunications efficiently. Therefore it is necessary to open the doors to much needed foreign private investment and skilled management..." This message was received by Hugo Banzer with great enthusiasm. He agreed to privatise SEMAPA, the state controlled water company in Cochabamba, with the intention of paying off its $30 million debt. This was to be paid with a loan from the International Monetary Fund, as long as SEMAPA was privatised. The North American firm Bechtel Enterprise Holdings with its subsidiary, a British firm, took over from SEMAPA. This immediately resulted in a twenty times increase in the price of water for the city of Cochabamba. Poor people were most affected of course, so violent demonstrations broke out and hundreds of people were injured. A general strike brought the city to a standstill for many days until the contract was cancelled and the private consortium had to leave the country. The award winning Spanish film, *También la Lluvia*, (Even the Rain), directed by Icíar Bollaín, is based on these true events.

One year later, in 2001, an event that shocked the world of course, was the horrific attack on the World Trade Centre in New York; this preceded the controversial war in Iraq. We witnessed on TV the unfolding scenes of death and suffering caused by British and American bombs raining down on Baghdad. This put Alan completely off politics and politicians. The little hope we had for a better world when Tony Blair signed the peace process with Ireland vanished completely when he blindly agreed to support George Bush in his decision to invade Iraq.

That same summer we decided to go Thailand looking for a friend. We arrived in Pattaya, a beach resort on the east coast of the Gulf of Thailand. During the day we would walk long distances looking for the address that years earlier our friend had sent us, but although we found the house there was no sign of him. The neighbours told us they hadn't seen him for years. During the evening we would go to the bars around the beach and talk to people and barmaids. After a few nights in Pattaya we realised that the whole place was practically a whore house. The resort was full of Americans, German, English and Dutch tourists picking up very young girls for sex. Whichever bar we went to, there were old men sitting holding hands or kissing girls who looked fifteen or sixteen years old. It was sad and degrading. One evening, we were talking to a barmaid. She had met a German tourist who told her he was very interested in her. He invited her for romantic dinners, promised her a proper relationship and a future with him. He took her on holiday for a week around the coast. On the last day he coldly paid her for her time and left her. Her story brought tears to her eyes as she said, "I thought my life was going to change forever with him."

It was Christmas the next day and Alan woke up visibly upset. "We must leave this whore place today. I can't stand to see and not be able to do anything about the exploitation of women by us Europeans just because we have more money."

When at home, Alan refused to watch the news on television or listen to it on the radio, but whenever we went on holiday he took a small short wave radio to pick up the BBC World Service at night. It is a peculiar feeling listening to the news when in remote places. One has a glorious feeling of escape, but the radio connects you with the rest of the world. I had this feeling of escape and connection when Alan and I were travelling by bus through the dramatic countryside in Thailand and Cambodia. We heard the news on the radio about the execution of Saddam Hussein, hanged like a common criminal. I thought this killing was tragic because no one expects a president of a significant nation to die in such circumstances.

Alan told me that Saddam Hussein not only murdered thousands of Kurds in the north of Iraq, but he also drained the wetlands of the Maysan region of eastern Iraq to destroy the Marsh Arabs who had lived there for five thousand years. The result was an environmental disaster. Saddam spent a fortune building a huge causeway to divert the river Euphrates thus destroying the largest wetland ecosystem in the Middle East. Even though this evil act was inexcusable as far as Alan was concerned, he was appalled about the Iraq war. He despised Bush and Blair for starting it in the first place. "I don't want to hear any more news. Turn off that bloody radio," he would say in frustration. Even though Alan didn't like to talk about politics, occasionally some political episode would trigger his anger and he would start to discuss it.

During the trip to Cambodia he told me how the American Government had largely eliminated the native Americans by deliberately killing the bison, their primary source of food and clothing. "The Indians followed the bison everywhere, the animals were their livelihood," he said. "But the U.S. Federal Government wanted the Indians largely removed and any remaining survivors made to live on reservations. They were also protecting the ranchers who had cattle and didn't want competition from other bovines. That wonderful animal, the bison, had nearly been exterminated by the end of the 19th century; and with it, the American Indians. Something similar happened in Australia," he remembered. "And in South America," I replied.

The lovely scenery and tropical climate on the way to Cambodia inspired Alan's thoughts again. "The Americans and the whole world make such a fuss about the World Trade Centre," he said. "Don't get me wrong. It was a terrible tragedy. Three thousand people died, but let's put this into perspective, nearly three thousand people, mainly children, die unnecessarily of malaria every day and very few people talk about it. The poverty in Africa is such that in some places they can't even afford mosquito nets to protect their children when sleeping. Spending too much money on skyscrapers when it's not really necessary; or wasting a fortune on sending people to the Moon or to explore outer space is eventually going to piss people off, because of the colossal cost of it. We have immense problems that have to be solved on this planet first, not on the Moon or Mars," he said with a melancholic air as he looked out through the bus window.

We arrived in Siem Reap, an extraordinary place, by late afternoon. Before the evening was over, we had visited several bars to drink Cambodian beer and listen to local music. We spent the rest of the night sleeping in a good hotel before visiting the Angkor Wat ruins the next day. This fascinating place built with human genius did not prepare us for what we saw next in Phnom Penh, the capital.

The Killing Fields Museum and the former school that was used as a torture chamber were full of horrible memories. About two million Cambodians were murdered during the time of Pol Pot. This triggered further reflections in our minds. Sitting in a small unpretentious restaurant in front of the mighty Mekong River, Alan reflected, "all governments have skeletons in their cupboards and some have more than others. This world is full of incomprehensible wickedness and remorse is rarely shown." He paused briefly to taste a spoonful of a lovely soup called prahok, cooked with coconut milk, fermented fish and lemon grass paste.

"The atrocities that the Khmer Rouge regime committed in the 1970s against its own people are almost beyond belief," he continued. "But, before this occurred, do you know what happened?" he asked me. "The Americans, who were at war with Vietnam, bombed Cambodia. This took place because the Vietnamese took refuge there in the 1960s, so the Vietnam War spilled over into Cambodia. As you can imagine, thousands of innocent Cambodians died and do you know what Nixon said at the time, when Kissinger warned him that he was going to be in trouble over this?" "They can't impeach me for bombing Cambodia; the President can bomb anybody he likes." Following the bombing, many peasants were so outraged at the United States and their puppet leader in Cambodia that they chose to join the Khmer Rouge. Don't you think it's ironic? The American bombarding resulted in more people joining the communist Pol Pot regime. So one year later the communists entered Cambodia with what they thought was a good reason.

That lunchtime we also talked about Ronald Reagan and how in 1986 his administration sold arms to Iran secretly in exchange for hostages. The whole transaction was brokered through Israel. With the money the Americans made out of the deal, they financed the *contra guerillas* in Nicaragua, where so many died unnecessarily. Alan also mentioned how during the 1980s the CIA, together with the contras were involved in drug trafficking from Nicaragua, to finance the contra guerrillas again. Alan rarely talked politics but when he did it made me see the world totally differently. It reminded me of my trip to Stockholm many years before with Uncle Hector, Aunt Betty and the ex-guerrilla fighters from Argentina and Uruguay. They told me so much about South American politics which largely involved dictatorships that one could not help but get depressed by it all.

A refreshing breeze stroked our faces and a deep sigh from Alan ended the conversation. Some local birds, bulbuls, began calling from the nearby trees distracting Alan's attention. He said more cheerfully, "let's go birdwatching for the rest of the afternoon, shall we?"

Alan and I decided to hire a guide so we could see as much as possible in a short time and be more in touch with the Cambodian people. We met Chann, a young man who spoke excellent English. On the first evening he took us for a night out at a plaza in an area called Mok Vaeng with his friends, two beautiful Cambodian girls and two guys. Mok Vaeng is near Preah Sisovath Boulevard by the Mekong River, which begins in Tibet and runs for five thousand kilometres before draining into the South China Sea in Vietnam.

We drank Scotch whisky and Alan ate strange Cambodian delicacies, such as fried cockroaches and tarantulas. The Cambodian guys and Alan enjoyed their crunchy appetisers. I couldn't eat them, not even after a few glasses of whisky. The next day we went to eat fresh Cambodian food in the market stalls. Later in the afternoon Chann took us to visit an orphanage and in the evening we went to have a massage from the blind masseurs.

Chann was an orphan; both his parents had died of enforced starvation working in the fields during the Pol Pot regime. He was only three years old when he was left in a Buddhist temple in Phnom Penh where he had lived for most of his life. When Chann grew up he went to live and work in Siem Reap at the Angkor Wat ruins as a guide. He told us proudly that it was whilst working there that he met ex-President Bill Clinton, who was visiting the ruins.

On the last day in Phnom Penh, we went with Chann to visit people who lived on their boats along the river; we passed by the shore of Boeung Kak Lake, located in the heart of the capital. Chann told us that all the people living around the lake would have to move in a few months. The Cambodian Government was evicting them, forcing them to sell their homes for a few riels to rich European, Chinese and Indian investors so that the newcomers could build luxury homes with a beautiful view of the Mekong River.

Chann took us to visit his former home, the temple where he had lived, and to meet his teacher, a Buddhist monk. We spent time with the holy man, who spoke to us about the things he had taught Chann when he was a young boy. He told us that every action we take in our lives has a consequence. Even when we think, we create an emotion which generates a wish and an intention and thus a consequence which can be positive or negative according to our intentions. He talked about how to appease the angry man with love, how to master the ill-natured man with goodness, how to overcome misery with generosity and how to conquer the liar with truth. He told us that one of the greatest achievements in life is selflessness and the greatest quality is seeking to serve others.

The old monk chanted for us and before we left, two women arrived at the temple. They both looked worried. Chann explained to us that one of them told the monk about a dream she remembered from the night before. The holy man revealed that the dream was a revelation of something bad that was going to happen, so he suggested a "cleansing." The anguished woman stood there with her clothes on, and the monk poured a few buckets of cold water over her while chanting away her bad luck.

We went to relax at the hotel, happy to have spent the afternoon with such an interesting old man. Alan had with him a book about Cambodia and before going to bed he read a paragraph for me which said: In the 16th century, the Portuguese friar, Gaspar da Cruz was the first missionary in Cambodia to try to convert the people to Christianity. He had limited success however, only managing to convert one man to the faith and he was actually deceased at the time!

It was soon time to fly back to London. We arrived at the airport and stood in a queue to check in. Behind us there was a group of young North Americans; they started talking to Alan, saying they were Christian missionaries. When I asked them what they thought of Cambodia, they said they loved it. Then I asked if they had been to Angkor Wat or the Killing Fields Museum and they said they hadn't. I asked them if they had tried typical Cambodian food in the market; they said they hadn't. The missionaries said they had been well looked after by Cambodians who cooked American food for them. "Do you mean you only ate hamburgers and fries and drank Coca Cola every day?" I asked in disbelief. "Yes, that's correct," one of them said, smiling. "What have you been doing in Cambodia, then?" I asked, curious about their visit. "We were giving seminars teaching Christianity," one of the American women replied, proud of what she was doing.

That moment I thought of the monk and everything he had told us. I thought of those things he had taught Chann when he was just a child. I remembered what Alan read for me the night before and I lost my cool. I began to shout angrily at them. "What the hell do you think you're doing? Cambodia is a Buddhist country! Don't you know its history? Didn't you know that the French already tried to introduce Catholicism and Pol Pot's insane Khmer Rouge killed three million Cambodians and tried to destroy their philosophy? Now when there is peace, people like you try to confuse them with an irrelevant religion! Don't you think you should leave the Cambodians alone?"

Alan stared at me, surprised by my reaction. The Christians were shocked and could not answer back. I was also amazed by my sudden outburst; why should I feel so angry? Why should these missionaries' activities or attitudes bother me? It was not my country. I don't really know, but perhaps in the back of my mind I was not only thinking of the Cambodian people; I was also mindful of Bolivia. In past centuries, people like these preachers had cleverly and quickly imposed different and incompatible faiths on us and brainwashed us into how to run our country. That day I realised that we have not had the chance to be completely free since the Spanish colonised Bolivia in 1532. These Christian missionaries were only interested in themselves and their own agenda, not in Cambodian culture or history. They were mimicking the strategies of big corporations on a massive scale; they were taking what was good for them and leaving in their wake more poverty, confusion and uncertainty.

The Illegal Dance

A few years after we left Cambodia, the inevitable evictions that Chann had predicted took place. Alan and I watched the news on television about how people tried to defend their homes. We watched the fighting and empathised with their frustration and loss as their simple houses were pulled down. Following orders from the Cambodian Government, armed construction workers used heavy machinery to wipe out a community's long established way of life in a matter of minutes. But what affected Alan and I even more was to find out that the Cambodian Government had signed an apparently illegal contract with a private company, Shukaku Inc. to fill in Boeung Lake with sand, so it could be used to build prime real estate. The social and environmental impact this is going to cause is unimaginable.

I went to bed that night thinking of the complex and tragic life of the people in that wonderful country.

CHAPTER TWENTY-THREE

"It is important to review the past and evaluate the present, to project the future"

Evo Morales Ayma

After working for seven years in Madrid, Dad retired and returned to Bolivia. He was hoping my brother Marcelo would take over his dental surgery in Spain, but after a year's holiday in Europe, Marcelo decided there was nothing better than home, so he went back to Bolivia to work as a dentist. Once more my telephone calls to my family changed direction.

Cochabamba was the city where my parents decided to settle, partly because of the wonderful climate and they bought a comfortable house with a beautiful little garden. Mum spent most of her time pottering around. Dad kept busy by teaching dentistry for a couple of hours a week in one of the local universities and so life went on for them. My older brother, José, established himself in Barcelona, Spain, first opening a bar and later a restaurant.

I found great joy in calling my parents from time to time. I loved listening to their enthusiastic and loving voices. Like most mothers, my Mum was always concerned about my wellbeing, constantly telling me to look after myself as if I was still a young girl. "You don't seem to be afraid of anything," she would often say. I would reply that it was safer to live in England than Bolivia.

Dad was by nature more relaxed and trusting than my mother. He often had a joke to tell and enjoyed his children's adventures, even when the stories were trivial. Over time, he became our best friend and confidant. My brothers and I would share with him everything that happened to us, good and bad. He would listen patiently and always had positive and encouraging advice. He never judged us; it seemed that age had softened him in the most extraordinary way. Although when we were young he was tight on discipline, he was also a caring and loving father. Once he realised that we had matured I think he began to relax more and concentrated on giving us all the affection and support he could.

My father became a modern man, growing in character in tune with us. He enjoyed all that was left of his youthful, fulfilled life. The changes in Mum were also interesting, but slower to materialise. She had become more adventurous and took life more philosophically. The social restrictions she grew up with in Bolivia were not as important to her as they once had been, especially when we were younger. She was still very much a lady however and in her old age she remained as concerned about her looks as she was when she was young. My brother José often said that he loved going out with Mum because she looked so beautiful and distinguished that everybody noticed her.

The same year that my parents returned to Bolivia, 2002, new elections were called and yet again the same politicians were candidates. Among them was the ex-President Gonzalo Sánchez de

Lozada, the wealthy businessman. He hired an expensive U.S. political consulting firm to try to secure his position in power and to run his election campaign. At first the polls looked good for him; he was the favourite to win. However Sánchez de Lozada and his party were already talking about possible alliances with other parties if his victory was not consolidated with 51% of the vote.

However, something unexpected happened. A new face appeared on the scene as a candidate for the presidency. This was a young peasant who used to work in the coca plantations. He started his political career as a union leader opposing the U.S. total eradication of the coca leaf. He vehemently opposed the violence and abuse carried out by the U.S. Drug Enforcement Agency (DEA) stationed in the Chapare, Department of Cochabamba. This young man, Evo Morales, with other activists, formed a new political party, called the Movement towards Socialism (MAS) and he soon became a member of the Bolivian Congress. A few days before the elections, Manuel Rocha, the U.S. Ambassador to Bolivia made a big mistake. He warned the country publicly that if they voted for the "Coca Leader," American aid would stop. His comments came out of the blue and provoked an unforeseen reaction from the electorate. Evo Morales got more votes than anyone expected. However, Sánchez de Lozada won the presidency thanks to the coalition he formed with other political parties.

One day in October 2003 I phoned my parents as usual. Dad mentioned that there were civil disturbances in La Paz. He went on to say that ever since Sánchez de Lozada had started his second term as president there had been waves of protest and street demonstrations. What had triggered much public anger was the fact that his government wanted to export Bolivian gas through Chile to sell to Mexico and the U.S.A. This natural resource was in the hands of foreign companies, who probably put on pressure to use the most convenient way of getting the gas out of Bolivia.

The Illegal Dance

This idea was condemned by the Bolivians because of our long and unresolved problem with Chile concerning the loss of our coastline to them. As mentioned before we had lost territory in the Pacific (Saltpetre) War, over a dispute involving potassium nitrate. In those days there was a Chilean potassium nitrate company with British investors. War broke out when Chile invaded Bolivia with the help of arms provided by Great Britain. The end result was the loss of four hundred km of Bolivian coast to Chile; a situation which still prevails today and hurts us deeply.

The inhabitants of El Alto, the city above La Paz arose in anger against the proposed gas exportation through Chile. At the same time details about contracts that foreign companies had made with the Bolivian Government began to emerge. The foreign investors had purchased access to 50% of the gas profits and they had been given full administrative control. The income produced from gas did not enter the national treasury, but instead, the contract stated it had to be invested in further exploration. The Bolivian state was going to benefit from only 18% of the profits from future gas and nothing from the existing gas reserves.

Since 1992 fifty three state companies have been privatised. Following this, many of them went bankrupt. These include the airline, Lloyd Aéreo Boliviano, which was given to a Brazilian consortium, while others, such as the Bolivian State Railway, disappeared.

Later on that year Sánchez de Lozada was found to be acquiring state owned mines and large areas of prime land near Coroico. Dad said to me, "people are tired of seeing politicians accumulating assets for themselves and are fed up waiting for serious economic improvements in this country. Loans from the World Bank are not being used appropriately. The government has not invested much of the money, not even in roads that are so important for people to export their products and they are not creating any new jobs." Listening to Dad I realised that the lack of employment was causing a flood of emigration and family strife. Parents were leaving their children with relatives and then travelling abroad to work. Family structures were being disrupted and were breaking down. I had noticed more and more Bolivians arriving in London.

When Alan and I were in Bolivia a few years earlier, he pointed out that total privatisation of all state companies was perhaps not a clever move. The hypothetical thought of paying a small fortune to warm my London flat with Bolivian gas, exported from Bolivia by a British gas company whilst most Bolivians still used firewood for heating and cooking did not appeal to me. So, I wasn't surprised that peasants, miners and impoverished urban people had taken over La Paz. They surrounded the city with a human wall and demanded President Sánchez de Lozada's resignation.

During this period I phoned my parents more frequently to keep up with the social and political developments. The demands of the people increased every day. They now wanted a new political constitution to be written. The protesters argued that the original constitution was made law with the participation of leaders of only 40% of the population and that the indigenous people had not been taken into consideration.

The demonstrations became violent, so the president sent in armed troops to maintain order. As a result, about sixty civilians were killed, including some children and hundreds of people were injured. This was yet another brutal massacre in the history of Bolivia.

During one of my calls Dad said, "these things happen when the people's patience has been exhausted." He told me a story about an event that had happened years before when they were still living in Coroico and I was already living abroad. One warm evening, my parents were chatting with Doña Justa, the woman who lived for a hundred years. A group of youngsters came running to tell them that a mob of thousands of peasants was heading towards Coroico from the nearby villages Arapata and Coripata, armed with machetes, sticks and clubs. Everybody ran in fear to their houses and locked their doors to protect themselves and their homes. My parents and my younger brother did the same; they ran home immediately. Dad said, "I had two weapons, one was a .22 revolver that I gave to your brother to defend himself and the other was an M1 Garand rifle, which was greased with Vaseline so it didn't rust. I got my rifle, cleaned and loaded it and waited in the dark for the horde that was coming to intimidate the village. I was not going to allow them to come into the house and destroy everything; I was prepared to fight. My plan was to scare them at first by shooting in the air, but if this did not persuade them to leave, I would fire at them if necessary to defend your mother and your brother." "Oh how terrible!" I was stunned by his story. "Half an hour later we started hearing the noise of pututus; do you know what they are?" he asked. Before I had the chance to reply, he said, "they are instruments made of cow horn. The sound was loud and liberating and the closer the crowd came to the village the more powerful the sound of war was heard. A swarm of peasants attacked the village and began to destroy shops, such as the butcher and the pharmacy. They vandalised the police station and town hall. It sounded as if a troop of soldiers was marching out there to the sound of pututus which would not stop. It seemed as though the sound gave them the strength to destroy everything and anyone who crossed their path. Your mum, brother and I waited quietly and in fear. We heard a commotion and screams from the people outside, but an hour later everything went back to normal. I looked through the window and saw two peasants standing outside the front door. I opened the window and asked them what was going on. The men answered, "don't worry Don Fernando, nothing is going to happen to you. We are here to protect you." "The next day we realised the magnitude of what they had done; luckily nobody died." "Why did they vandalise those shops and the police station?" I interrupted. "Because those shop owners and the police took advantage of them," he replied. "How?" "The butcher, for example, would sell them the worst meat at high prices and even steal from them by cheating over the weight. The pharmacist would ignore frantic requests for help after serious road accidents at night. The police were abusive to them and never helped if they were burgled. The peasants are decent people like everybody else. If you treat them well and with respect, they will be kind to you," he said. "But Dad, many people who live in the village are also peasants and are very likely to have relatives working in the fields." My father replied, "yes, you are right, but you are a bit naïve. People who go up socially even just a rung are the most likely to hurt their own people, because they feel better or superior." Dad's anecdote reminded me of one of my school friends, the guy who died due to injuries inflicted on him by peasants in Coroico. The police, who were generally from the lower social strata took no interest in the peasants who consequently felt they had to take the law into their own hands.

The riots lasted for several days until Sanchez de Lozada finally left the country. He and his family flew by helicopter to Santa Cruz and then on to the U.S.A. It is believed he took suitcases full of money with him. Ever since, Gonzalo Sánchez de Lozada has been a wanted man. The Bolivian authorities have requested his extradition from the U.S.A, but no progress has been made so far.

Carlos Mesa, his vice president, took over the top job. Mesa was a journalist and historian, a man known for his integrity and intellect. Unfortunately he was representing a government that did not have enough of the people's support. In his role as President, Carlos Mesa was caught between the two stools of multinational corporations and the Bolivian people. These companies expected favourable treatment with respect to the use of natural gas reserves whereas the Bolivian people wanted the policy of privatisation to be reversed. This weak president was unable to balance these conflicting demands. Under pressure from the resumption of general social unrest including road blocks, Carlos Mesa was forced to resign when civil war became a real threat. An agreement to remove the president was negotiated through the intervention of the Chief Justice of the Supreme Court, who became interim President and called for a general election immediately.

I called my parents again at Christmas in 2005. Dad answered the phone and sounded very cheerful. He asked me if I had heard about the election result that had installed Evo Morales Ayma as President. "Yes, I have," I said, showing interest in what was going on in Bolivia. He continued, "it's about time we had a president who represented the majority of the people in this country." The peasant who had worked in the coca plantations and who was opposed by the U.S. Government won the election with 54% of the popular vote. Such a majority was unprecedented in Bolivian politics. I was amazed to hear this news, after all, he had no experience of government and he was opposed by the powerful class that had prospered under previous regimes. The Establishment was not going to accept this change easily.

The presidential inauguration of Evo Morales was due to take place in January 2006 and I was not going to miss this historic event. I rushed to buy a plane ticket. Alan, meanwhile, decided to fulfil a lifelong ambition to see mountain gorillas. Instead of Bolivia, he went to the Bwindi Impenetrable Forest in south west Uganda, on the border with the Democratic Republic of Congo.

On my arrival, La Paz was in festive mood. Dressed in colourful clothes, people from all over the country and abroad gathered together in the highest administrative capital city in the world. Guests such as the Prince of Asturias, heir to the Spanish throne and presidents from many different parts of the world, together with hundreds of journalists, attended the ceremony. Everyone had come to witness the inauguration of the first Latin American indigenous president. Here was a man who used to herd llamas with his father when he was a young boy; a man who spent his youth running behind passing buses on the arid plateau of the Altiplano, hoping to pick up scraps of food that passengers would throw out on the road. He had worked as a bricklayer, a baker and a trumpet player, before eventually becoming the leader of the coca farmers. Morales had had little formal education and had been moulded by his early life experience of severe deprivation.

I walked the streets of La Paz feeling as though this was all a dream from which I was going to wake up at any moment. My thoughts went back to my childhood in Coroico, to our maid, the black woman who almost died due to lack of medical care. I thought of the many children who walked for hours to the nearest school, many of them without shoes. I thought of the racism that was ingrained in Bolivian culture. Was it now going to end at last? Was this going to be our big opportunity to really change?

Whilst walking towards the Parliament building in the Plaza Murillo, where the solemn ceremony was going to take place, I felt increasingly joyful and excited. For a few precious hours I believed I belonged to a new, proud and wonderful country, where everything was possible. I arrived in the plaza, which was crowded with happy people singing and shouting slogans. There were visitors from Peru, Chile, Ecuador and other neighbouring countries. I positioned myself in a convenient place to view the ceremony. A big screen in front of us was going to help the crowd outside follow the full emotional ceremony, step by step. Next to me was a woman who had arrived with her husband and two children from Argentina; we started talking. "I came to Bolivia just for this special occasion," she said.

Evo Morales was about to be sworn in to lead a corrupt country which was devastated economically, spiritually and morally. It had been run by no more than forty wealthy Bolivian families as well as foreign companies. 60% of the indigenous population lived in poverty, most being illiterate. Morales was taking over a nation where many adults and children still worked in slave conditions for wealthy landlords, where fifty infants in every thousand live births died within their first year. It was a country in which nobody stood up for the poor because the previous ruling classes were devoid of any interest in changing the status quo.

The newly appointed president started his speech. There was total silence as the crowd listened attentively. He talked for almost two hours, recalling hundreds of years of national frustration, exploitation and anger. Not only did he remind us of the wounds left by the Spanish, but also the damage Bolivian people had inflicted on each other by not taking action at the right time. He reminded us that the uprising against the Spanish had not made the indigenous people free people, but rather, people dominated by the descendants of the conquistadors who later became the second masters of their land. Morales stressed that not even the 1952 revolution had freed them, because although they then had the right to vote, they remained on the fringes of society and had no say in political decisions. This meant that anyone could occupy their land and take their natural resources for a few dollars. "That is all over now," he continued. "All Bolivians, with all our differences must work together to recover our natural resources. Many middle class professional Bolivians are joining this indigenous movement; my admiration to all of them. This new parliament will be the army to achieve our second independence. I invite the international community to join us too." He also talked about his hopes and dreams for a new Bolivia, with opportunities for all.

I felt a nudge from the Argentinian woman who was standing next to me. "Look at that man," she said; I turned to the right. A few steps away from us, a man, perhaps in his late sixties, was standing alone, his dark skin damaged by years of exposure to strong sunlight at high altitude. He looked old, worn out and lonely, wearing his alpaca poncho, a *ch'ulu*, a warm woollen hat worn by men in the Andes and a sun hat on top. He also wore sandals made out of rubber tyres, similar to the ones the children at my school in Coroico had worn. The man was crying like a child. He took off his sun hat and his *ch'ulu*, which he used to dry his tears. As the new president spoke, the man may have felt that the promise of change had arrived too late for him. The Argentinian woman and I just looked at each other. We both understood how much this moment meant to so many people in my country and other countries in Latin America. I thought of a poem that Uncle Hector wrote:

Poor things,
tossed aside like rotten fruit in the gutter,
pissed on by dogs, freezing to death on the street corner,
stalked by hunger and curled over in pain.

Poor things,
lice-ridden, suppurating and spat on,
solemnly pursued by the sneering pity
of the bourgeois women returning home from mass,
stinking of the semen deposited during a tryst.

Poor things,
drunk, hungry, gnarled,
enshrouded in centuries-old grime,
dripping in the stench inherited from all those who came from
    afar,

*bringing a blond whip, a gringo dollar and a gringo-made bag
in which to take home the clotted blood of miners in gringo "lobonite"
   bags.*

*Poor things,
shuffling across squares, through markets,
across the dusty paths of this stinking America,
dragging their feet with their children slung over their shoulder,
their wife pregnant again,
their daughters pregnant too young,
too young and hungry, too young.*

*Poor things,
alone among the crowd,
so strangely alone among all these decent men
that fuck their servant girls under the stairs with steadfast anxiety,
yet in ostentatious churches marry pretty maidens
who have been properly wooed, caressed, kissed and tricked.
Poor things,
so far from the whisky, so far from the high teas,
just looking for some bread, a piece of meat, some milk for the
   children,
an aspirin to ease the toothache,
some clean rags to wrap up the newborn screamed into life on the
   street corner.*

*Poor things,
too far from God, too close to sin
to ignore the fact that the gods have given up,
that the gods have left their work
to those who trade in wafers and sacraments,
with no interest in compassion or pity,
so incredibly far from sainthood and defeat.
Poor things.....*

The following day I went to visit Uncle Hector. He looked old, tired and could hardly walk. The problem with his feet was getting worse and he spent most of his time sitting in a chair in front of the television. His mind, however, was as sharp as ever, and he was delighted to witness scenes for which he had fought for most of his life. He told me with a big smile, "at last, we have won the first battle." I sat down on his bed to talk more about the recent events. He read me another poem that he had written many years previously when he was living in exile in Sweden. The poem predicted the takeover of La Paz by the indigenous population; it was like a premonition. I suggested we should go to the Café La Paz for a coffee, the same place where Klaus Barbie would go in the 1970s when he worked as an adviser to Banzer, the former dictator. "Let's go to meet your friends," I said. "I can't even walk, darling, my feet hurt so much!" I convinced him that we should try to go anyway. I phoned for a taxi and we set off for the café, to listen to the concerns and fears of others.

CHAPTER TWENTY-FOUR

"There are no secrets that time does not reveal"

Jean Racine

A few days later, before I flew back to London, I was tidying up my bedroom in my parents' flat. I looked inside a wardrobe and found an old handbag of mine. Inside were an old photograph and a business card. I looked at the picture long and hard for several minutes. I hadn't seen this photograph for twenty six years and I had forgotten all about it. The photo showed Rafael, but the image had been cut in half. I looked for the other half in the handbag, but it wasn't there. I tried to remember where it was taken; perhaps at a party. "But which party?" I thought. Then I remembered the picture may have been taken at my cousin's wedding. This was the only wedding I had attended with Rafael before I left Bolivia. "Where could the other half be? And why had it been cut into two? It would have been nice to see how I looked then," I said to myself.

Examining the photograph more carefully, I thought Rafael looked handsome and serious in his suit and I began to wonder what had happened to him in the intervening years. I then picked up the card, which read: "Rafael Del Monte, Architect." His address and telephone number were still clearly visible. Then I remembered how the card came to be in my possession. My school friend, Eli, had given it to me innocently on one of my visits to Bolivia about fifteen years previously. I recalled her telling me that she had met Rafael in the street in La Paz. They had exchanged greetings and small talk and Rafael gave Eli his business card before they parted company. She put the card in her handbag without giving it a second thought. So many years had passed since the last time I saw him. "Rafael, I would like to find out how you are," I thought to myself, looking at the photo.

I placed the business card and torn photograph in my new handbag and left home. As I walked around the busy streets of La Paz, flashes of memories of my time with Rafael came back to me. I wondered what he thought of our new president and the dramatic change in Bolivian politics. More than anything else, I had a question that I would have loved to ask him; to finally close a chapter in my life, so I decided to call him…

By the end of the following day, I still had not found the courage to call the number on the business card. I was not sure whether or not it would be a good thing to do. There was also the possibility that he might have changed his office telephone number or that he was no longer living in the city. I went to bed convinced that it was better to forget all about it.

The next day however, I woke up feeling even more ambivalent about my decision. The prospect of talking to Rafael after so many years was something that was still in my mind; the thought of hearing his voice again sent a tremor of excitement to

The Illegal Dance

my heart. I worried about what I would say to him and just how much he would remember of me after so many years.

I met a friend in town that evening. We went to a café near El Prado, the main street in La Paz. We talked for a while about old times at school and things unrelated to my thoughts about Rafael. After a while, she excused herself and went to the ladies. Now that I was alone I seized the opportunity to dial the number on the card without giving it any further thought. Somebody answered, but I immediately put the phone down; I wasn't sure what I was doing. I asked the waiter for a glass of orange juice. Mistake! I called him back and ordered a double vodka and orange juice.

I took a large swig of the drink and tried the number again, this time determined to talk. "Can I speak to Rafael Del Monte, please," I asked. "This is Rafael," he answered, in a hard and domineering tone. "Nothing seems to have changed," I thought to myself, pleased to hear his voice and realising that he was still living in La Paz.

"This is Ana....Kiwi?" I said, in a questioning tone with the hope that he would recognise my voice and nickname that he gave me when we were young. "Kiwi!" he exclaimed. "What a lovely surprise!" he said, almost laughing with joy. I felt pleased and relieved that I had phoned. His voice sounded so familiar to me, like the old days: stubborn, grumpy, jealous, distrustful, bossy, demanding, thoughtful and loving. All the things that I used to love and hate about him at the same time. I told him I was in La Paz for two more days and I asked if he wanted to meet me. He didn't reply straight away, but seemed to be in a state of shock as he repeated a few times how delighted he was to hear from me. After a few minutes on the phone we agreed to meet up the next day at seven in the evening near the University. My girlfriend came back and appeared to notice a change in my face. "Are you ok?" she asked. "I'm fine, I just had a strong drink for the cold," I replied without giving her any more details.

The following day I arrived on time, like a good English lady, as I had already learned their ways of doing things; there was no sign of Rafael. La Paz can be cold at night so I knew I couldn't wait outside for long. After a while I looked at my watch, it was seven fifteen. The street was full of people walking briskly, but none of them was Rafael. I thought of the old days when he would often arrive late to meet me. He was always in a hurry, whether going to a political meeting, to the university, or to some social event. I would wait for him for as long as it was necessary, whether it was cold, rainy or hot; I smiled thinking of those years.

My Chilean friend, Roberto, came to mind. He was the guy who lost contact with his girlfriend during the Pinochet period. I remembered his feelings of enthusiasm and confusion when he met his ex-girlfriend in London after so many years. I remembered his sad eyes a few years later, as he knew he had no hope of a future with her, even though she had divorced by then.

I thought about my own situation during my first ten years in London when I hoped and wished to be with Rafael again one day. How silly I was! Why did I wait that long? I remembered my hesitation and insecurity just two days previously before I contacted him. I anticipated that my meeting with Rafael might take me to places and scenarios that I hadn't considered before. I imagined our encounter might be difficult, or uncomfortable, but perhaps comforting, too? What I wasn't sure about was where and how this tale would end. While I waited for him I also thought about the many people who have love stories of their own to tell.

At around seven thirty, he turned up at last, looking as stressed and apologetic as ever; his behaviour and looks had not changed. His hair looked unkempt, as if he had just got out of bed and had had no time to comb it. He was dressed in jeans, a shirt, no tie and a light jacket, not suitable for a cold evening in La Paz. But he never felt the cold, as he was always in a rush, often agitated and late. He carried books under his arm, just as

I had remembered him. We greeted each other with a big and affectionate hug, and went looking for a warm place where we could talk and have a coffee.

When we got to the small, quiet cafe, I ordered a glass of wine instead of a coffee and he ordered the same. We sat down impatiently to talk about twenty six years of absence. We were eager to know what had happened to each other, but neither of us knew how or where to start.

The year I thought I was going to spend abroad when I left Bolivia had turned into so many years, in no time at all. Time is something that unfortunately we cannot hold on to; we just keep the memories that time cannot erase. At that moment it felt as if not a single day had passed since I first left the country. It was like that day, so many years ago when Rafael demanded that I tear up my plane ticket and not leave Bolivia at all. It seemed that the clock had not moved, that we had not aged, that I had never left and that nothing in the world had changed.

Rafael, at that moment seemed unchanged, with that same dishevelled hair, maybe with a bit more grey. His voice was no different either, with the familiar critical and demanding way of asking questions. He had that unforgettable penetrating look in his eyes as though he wanted to know your innermost thoughts. And his smile was the same sarcastic one, framed by his moustache. He even smelled as I remembered him, clean and manly. I looked down to examine his hands, which had taken my ring away that crazy evening while the bush crickets were mating. I felt a small jump in my heart. The waiter interrupted my thoughts when he arrived with the two glasses of wine. I took a sip to bring myself back to reality.

"You look as lovely as ever," he said tenderly. "How are things with you, Anita?" Rafael took great interest in learning what had happened in my life during those long years. For his part, he told me all about the political difficulties Bolivia had been through over the years. He told me about the constant struggle to maintain a weak democracy due to the fact that none of the candidates ever got more than twenty to thirty per cent of the vote. "Democracy in Bolivia has been like an old woman dragging her feet," he said laughing. He also talked about the precarious and fragile economy.

He talked about the new president and the reasons for his victory; how people had tolerated and finally tired of the looting of Bolivia. He spoke of the privatisation policies that had almost led to the country's economic and moral bankruptcy. "I am delighted; I'm going to support the new government and the changes we are going to have from now on. I will be totally committed to it," he confirmed. I was so pleased to hear that; it couldn't be otherwise. "You left at the right time, in those days I was totally involved in politics, it was hard and dangerous. But now I have become just a boring academic." He told me he got a PhD and was teaching post-graduate courses at the University.

As we chatted, I began to notice some changes in him. He had become a more placid man, less adventurous, less aggressive and I even noticed signs of a man inclined to religion. We also talked about his life and his family. "I am a lucky man, happily married," he said, nodding his head in a positive way. "I have a lovely wife and three beautiful daughters, I couldn't ask for more." I was honestly pleased to know that he had a fulfilled life.

We talked a bit about my life too. I told him that I had a wonderful husband and that I was happily married too. I told him that I didn't have any children, but that I had the time and freedom to travel around a bit. I told him that I had completed a degree and that London had given me the opportunity to learn many interesting things.

Almost two hours passed with neither of us wanting to move. We ordered another glass of wine and continued to talk. He asked me about my parents and made a point of saying that he remembered them well. "Your parents were so loving to each other, it was something that I admired. It is so rare to find couples like that nowadays." It was then that I took the opportunity to ask him about what had been on my mind. I held my glass of wine carefully and took a sip of the strong alcohol to give me courage. I put the glass back down on the table, holding it with my two shaking hands to avoid spilling the wine.

"Rafael," I said looking into his eyes without blinking. "Is it true that you asked my Dad to bring me back home?" My question didn't disconcert him; he wasn't expecting it but he wasn't surprised by it either. He knew straight away what I was talking about. Before I even finished speaking he replied with the same seriousness that I had put the question forward, "yes, it is true." He then began to explain what had really happened.

Sixteen years earlier, Mum had told me her side of the story. At that time I didn't want to hear it. I wasn't interested in what had happened, but now I was ready. He began his version of events. "About ten months after your departure, I plucked up courage and visited your Dad at his surgery. I went to ask him if he could bring you back home. I told him I missed you desperately and I wanted to marry you." Rafael was now looking lost in his thoughts as he was trying to remember the detail sequence of that day. His eyes were fixed in space. He looked serious and sad as if remembering was causing pain.

He went on. "My visit to his surgery didn't change his mind. He was adamant; it was all in vain." He took a deep breath and said, "I remember leaving his surgery totally discouraged and convinced that you were never ever coming back. Your father told me that it was his decision that you should study abroad and he had no intention of changing it."

I took another sip of my red wine. "But not only that," Rafael continued. "Before you had the abortion, the night I went to talk to your Dad, I asked him to let me marry you." "Did you change your mind about the abortion?" I asked him? "Yes, I did," he said looking me straight in the eyes and nodding his head. "I did, but your Dad had already made the decision that the abortion was going to happen anyway because you were too young and your future could not be jeopardised."

My lips quivered for a minute as I tried to articulate a word. I thought I was going to scream in anger and frustration. I never knew Rafael wanted to marry me when I was still pregnant. But I contained myself thanks to the wine that was still left in my glass. I wanted to ask him, why he had asked Dad and not me? But I didn't dare to open my mouth in case bitter and angry words spoiled the evening.

A few tears ran from my eyes, I wiped them delicately with my handkerchief. He placed his hand on mine as if to comfort me. I wanted to tell him that I had waited for him for ten long years in London. I wanted to tell him how much I had missed him and that many times I thought I saw him in the streets because I had wished he would come looking for me. I wanted to tell him that I had hoped one day we would be together again; but I didn't. I stayed quiet, paralysed and unable to say or do anything. There was no point in sharing my feelings anyway; it was much too late. We had both got on with our lives as best we could.

It was now time to go. I didn't want to stay sitting in front of him any longer. We exchanged email addresses before we said goodbye. He leaned across to give me a kiss, the same gentle and delicate kiss he had given me for the first time twenty seven years earlier in Coroico.

I walked away briskly and lost myself in the dark, cold night without wanting to look back. It was disconcerting to realise that two men, my father and Rafael, had loved me and wrestled over me. I was bewildered when I learned how this chapter of my life had really ended. On the one hand, I felt happy to know that Rafael had tried to convince my Dad to bring me home. On the other hand, I had a sour taste in my mouth because had I known the truth I may have come back to Bolivia long before to be with him, and I would not have been heartbroken for so many years.

The next day I was on my way back to London. The long flight gave me plenty of time to collect my thoughts and go through in my mind everything that was said the night before. I felt pleased and happy to know that Rafael had found love with a woman who loved him and understood him well. I was also pleased and grateful that in my journey through life I had met my husband, Alan, who is such a rock to me.

CHAPTER TWENTY-FIVE

"Democracy is when the indigent, and not the men of property, are the rulers"

Aristotle

I returned to my daily activities in London, but I began to do something I had never done before. I would get up early in the morning to read the Bolivian newspapers on the internet. I was intrigued by how the Morales Government was going to unfold and how long it would last.

The day I took my Uncle Hector to the Café La Paz, where his politician friends met to discuss current affairs over cups of coffee, they had shown no enthusiasm or optimism for the new government and were already predicting a grim future. "We are not really prepared for a left-wing government," they said. "We are going to antagonise the Americans who will reduce trade with us and with the excuse of Bolivia's coca leaf production, take away aid. The country is going to end up in total economic collapse, just like in the 1980s." They were also very concerned about Morales's ability to govern. He was a peasant with little academic education and had only been a union leader and parliamentarian for a short period in 2002, before he was expelled for accusing politicians of accepting money to pass laws in Parliament. He had also been accused of being a "narcoterrorist" and had organised confrontations between the coca farmers and the U.S. Drug Enforcement Agency.

While the politicians were negative about the future of Bolivia, Uncle Hector's predisposition towards the new government was the opposite. He was sure that the one person who could deal with such a problematic country as Bolivia, was Evo Morales, the peasant; only he would be able to understand its many difficulties and ethnic diversity.

Hector thought it was pointless to have a president who was brought up in North America, spoke English and had academic qualifications, someone like Gonzalo Sánchez de Lozada. "We all know Bolivia in theory, but not in practice," he would say. "Most of us don't seem to understand the idiosyncrasies of this country." After trying in vain that day to explain the logic behind having an indigenous president to begin a possible transition in Bolivian politics, he grew bored and began to make fun of his friends instead.

There was no doubt that his friends were predicting what they unconsciously wanted to happen, the fall of Morales as soon as possible. But Uncle Hector was not the type who tolerated listening to what he regarded as nonsense. He soon became angry and spoke to them in a confrontational manner, which he often did when he felt he was right or losing an argument. "If Morales makes mistakes running this country he has every right to do so! Didn't we make mistake after mistake when we were in government? What good have the middle and upper classes done in this country? What good have the people imposed on us by the U.S.A. done? Not even with all our knowledge and qualifications have we governed successfully. Haven't we done enough damage already? Haven't we created a country riddled with corruption, poverty, inequality and injustice? Aren't we still living in the most unfair, racist and poorest country of Latin America? Does it really matter if Morales screws up this country once more? Bolivia is already in ruins and it's thanks to our mistakes!" They all listened to Uncle Hector's passionate speech in silence, none of them daring to reply.

Morales's choice of vice president was an upper middle class man called Álvaro García Linera. The extreme socialist ideas García Linera held in his youth caused him to end up in prison. While incarcerated he wrote several books on Bolivian socialism. Later on, after his release, he became a university lecturer and political analyst.

The combination of these two men attracted the support and vote of both the indigenous population and intellectual Bolivians with liberal ideas who were tired of traditional, old fashioned politics. These people wanted a complete change and were not afraid if the U.S.A. decided not to continue to sponsor Bolivia. Pro Morales enthusiasts wanted their country to take its own course and its own destiny at last. It was also a propitious moment in the whole of South America. Countries like Argentina, Brazil, Uruguay and Chile were all now led by politicians with social democratic ideas.

The political union of Morales and García Linera was to become an interesting partnership. Morales was the leader and communicator whereas García Linera was the intellectual and strategist. A group of people from different social strata served them in Cabinet to form the Morales Government. Morales, as a good democrat, invited men and women in equal numbers to form his administration. This decision was influenced by his indigenous culture where men and women share equal responsibilities. It was true to say that many of the newly elected representatives had no experience whatsoever when they took their important and responsible posts. Many of them were indigenous people, who had never had the opportunity before, but we had to start somewhere and at last the moment had arrived.

Morales began his job as President by calling for a period of austerity, cutting his salary by 57% to set an example. He soon became regarded as a workaholic to such an extent that even the opposition advised him to slow down.

In the first year of his presidency he introduced some fundamental changes. He cancelled contracts with those foreign companies that practically controlled the country's natural resources. With other companies, he amended contracts to give a better return for Bolivia. To make it crystal clear what he wanted to do, he learned to say in English, "fifty, fifty." But he insisted that administration of all natural resources passed to the State and Bolivia was to have partners, not landlords. He probably wanted to prevent a repeat of what happened during the period of Spanish colonisation, when most of the silver extracted from the Rich Mountain of Potosí was shipped to Spain.

A new political constitution was written by representatives of all social classes and organisations. The old one had been written by the Bolivian elite, totally excluding the indigenous population who had never had a say in how the country was run. In the first year of government nearly a million adults were taught to read and write. Morales also put Bolivia on the world map. He travelled extensively abroad, trying to attract investors, and he became an advocate for the "Mother Earth" concept of the land giving and sustaining life. He stressed the fact that we need the earth more than the earth needs us.

Among the countries Morales visited were Cuba, Venezuela and Iran; countries firmly on the U.S.A. black list. In August 2007, the American ambassador to Bolivia, Philip Goldberg, felt the need to publicly give his opinion of Morales, saying that the Bolivian Government had the right to visit and deal with other nations but they must be democratic ones. However he forgot to mention that at the same time President George Bush had a very cosy relationship with the Pakistani dictator Pervez Musharraf who gained power through a military coup against the democratically elected President Nawaz Sharif. Bush also had close relationships with the Saudi Arabian and Chinese regimes, which are totally undemocratic and have appalling human rights records. Goldberg also did not acknowledge that in the past the U.S.A. had supported many criminal dictators, such as Somoza in Nicaragua, Pinochet in Chile, Videla in Argentina, Mubarak in Egypt, Suharto in Indonesia, Batista in Cuba, Banzer in Bolivia and Saddam in Iraq. It is a long list of questionable relationships.

Based in England, I began to hear more in the media about Bolivia and the new president. Television documentaries about Bolivia had become more common and he was being written about in newspapers, magazines and books. It was clear, however, that the American administration was wary of Morales, especially due to his alliance with Castro and Chavez and his powerful speeches against U.S. imperialism. He made clear his quest to recover the Bolivian identity, which we had been losing in our fight for survival and the right to govern ourselves without constant U.S. interference.

His first years in government were difficult though. It was almost impossible to implement his policies due to constant attacks from the opposition, which came from three distinct fronts. One source was the political opposition in the Parliament; another was departmental elites, who reacted like angry hyenas to whatever change Morales wanted to make; and the last group came from the U.S.A., where right wing political opinion was set against Morales, constantly planting the seeds of doubt in people's minds.

Government sympathisers and the opposition would exchange insults every day and during this period the situation became unsustainable. President Morales was not even allowed to enter certain parts of his own country, including cities such as Santa Cruz de la Sierra, Tarija, Trinidad and even Sucre, the legal capital. The social scourge of racial harassment by the middle classes against people of indigenous origin became more overt as well as a growth in the mutual dislike between *collas* and *cambas*.

I remembered the first day I arrived in London and how Juan's mother was constantly putting down indigenous people from the region where I was born. Almost twenty six years later this attitude had worsened and it really saddened and worried me.

Powerful lobbyists, right-wing activists and businessmen from the eastern region of Bolivia, the richest part of the country, were totally opposed to Morales. They began to talk about ways of attaining independence. They demonstrated their disapproval of him by organising strikes, violent demonstrations and damage to public buildings. This group displayed their rejection of the government by attempting to blow up a gas pipeline that supplied Argentina and by taking over airports.

Their anger extended to anyone who supported Morales. It was irrelevant to them whether or not they came from the north, south, east or west of the country; it did not matter. In Sucre, a shameful assault occurred against a group of indigenous people who were waiting for the president to arrive to donate ambulances to the rural communities. A few months later there was a massacre of Morales sympathisers in the Amazon region. A few people from the opposition also died in this confrontation.

Later on, police shot and killed a group of mercenaries who had been recruited to fight for the independence of eastern Bolivia. These soldiers were foreigners and it is claimed that they were paid by the Santa Cruz elite to also assassinate the president. The opposition claimed that the mercenaries were paid by the government to cause disturbances in order to blame the opposition separatists.

Every time I phoned Dad in Bolivia, he kept me informed about the difficult political situation. "Do you think we could end up with a civil war, Dad?" I asked him, feeling apprehensive about what might happen next to my country. He was always positive and confident, totally convinced the situation would soon calm down because Morales had so much support from the majority of the population. "The opposition has to accept the new reality and negotiate their demands accordingly," he said in a confident voice. I could not see why he was so optimistic. The country seemed to be in turmoil, which seemed worse from the distance of London as I was no longer used to living with constant political instability. In England we respect the winner whether we like it or not. I felt Dad's belief that things would be resolved in the end came from the fact that he had witnessed so many appalling dictatorial governments in Bolivia when he was young.

At the same time nasty publicity from a malicious internet campaign circulated against Morales. I began to receive anti Morales emails from people I had not heard from for ages and from people I didn't even know. The campaigners used the web against him cleverly. They mocked his indigenous origins and the way he dressed; they even went as far as criticising the way he spoke Spanish, unaware that his first language was Aymara.

Many Bolivians felt embarrassed, regarding him as a joke; they wanted to disassociate themselves from Morales. "He is so ignorant that he wants to go back in time," somebody said to me once, simply because he wanted to give a voice to indigenous people. Another told me without embarrassment, "you can see lots of Evos in the zoo." Some people found it inconceivable to have a man from the lowest social class as President. They began to question their own status in society and ask what was going to happen to them. The middle and upper classes felt pushed aside and tasted for the first time what it felt like to be disregarded. Many of them fought the new government tooth and nail; others adopted a resigned attitude, gaining solace from the thought that at least they had distinguished Spanish surnames. Finally they were reduced to calling Morales a communist. "The communists are going to take away our homes! The communists are going to close the churches and ration our food!" It was a revelation to me how some Bolivians reacted. The fact that the new Head of State was an Indian with no university degree, who did not speak sophisticated Spanish and was born into a "low social class" caused resentment among the middle class. This was evidence that Morales was beginning to change the status quo. Poor people identified with this man and felt more protected. For the mass population, Morales was a brother who was going to represent them and bring them out from the margins of society.

In September 2008 I read in the press that President Morales had accused Philip Goldberg, the U.S. ambassador, of "conspiring against democracy," because he had been seen in meetings with the opposition. Morales ordered him to leave the country at once. I was not surprised at Morales's reaction; the U.S.A. was totally opposed to socialism, especially during the Cold War era. They were afraid that left wing ideas might spread and interfere with their economic interests. As part of state policy, the U.S. Government sanctioned the overthrow of democratically elected governments without hesitation. The U.S.A. backed coups organised under the UN radar in countries such as Guatemala,

Chile and Nicaragua and of course supported the 634 unsuccessful CIA assassination attempts on Fidel Castro.

The news I continually received from Bolivia was like a never ending soap opera, like EastEnders or the cheap Mexican television series I watched occasionally when I was living in my country. The only difference was that Bolivian politics had no overt love affairs or happy endings. Misunderstanding, mistrust, hatred and a complete lack of tolerance were the order of the day. Sir Ernest Benn, the British writer and political publicist, was right when he said, "politics is the art of looking for trouble, finding it whether it exists or not, diagnosing it incorrectly and applying the wrong remedy." This quote fitted Bolivia perfectly. I have never liked politics, but the subject never seemed far away from me. I was glued to the internet, looking for something good to happen. Unfortunately, all the news I read at that time sounded irrational, disturbing and in many ways, sad and pathetic.

My calls to Bolivia and Sweden became more frequent. I would call Dad, Uncle Hector or my cousins Eliana and René to discuss the news. I would talk about it with friends in London too. John, an English friend, was one of the people I talked to about the situation. I met him and his wife many years previously at the central London clinic where I used to work. We became good friends. John was a prominent corporate lawyer who had built a colossal law firm from scratch. He was a fascinating man with an amazing mind and a wonderful sense of humour. I wasn't the only one to think this. The Director of a Saudi Arabian bank, who I also met through work, said, "I told my Saudi colleagues that if they wanted to win the case they had against another bank they must use John, even though he is Jewish. They did what I told them and won the case. There is no better lawyer in London at the moment." He was proud to have met John and had a lot of respect for him.

John was born into a working class family, his father was a tailor. He had left school at sixteen and never attended university.

He worked as a messenger at a law firm and it was then that he decided to study law, which he did on his own. He only went to university to take his exams. When he finally graduated, he set up his business in a small office and gradually built up a huge firm. With great pride he would tell me that among his clients were the former Prime Minister Harold Wilson, Joan Collins and Margaret Thatcher, who offered him the title of Lord, but he strongly rejected this because he would say that he did not want to perpetuate the English upper classes.

He had a wide general knowledge and would talk to me about politics, religion, history or whatever else came up in conversation. He remembered dates, names and places with amazing precision. Every time I had the chance I would listen to his careful analyses of events taking place around the world. John, apart from having a keen intellect, was a kind and generous man.

When we discussed Bolivia, he would say that for Morales to succeed with his transformational policies he had to introduce them slowly and not be so radical, as all extremists tended to go wrong eventually. As a Bolivian, this was a concept that I could not grasp. In my view, the country had waited so long for these changes that they had to be done at once, so as not to lose momentum. Morales and his team probably thought the same way.

I would visit John on Thursday afternoons for a bit of mutual therapy. I enjoyed sampling his wife's delicious cakes and admiring her art work. She was a thought provoking artist, an expert at embroidery and a tasteful interior decorator. She was also a beautiful, sophisticated woman. It was always a joy to visit them at their stylish home and our time together never seemed to be enough.

When Evo Morales became President, many of my English friends became interested in Bolivian politics, as England was going through a period of deterioration at the political level; Peter was one of them. He was a political activist and consequently he was well informed. He would give me press clippings or, if he heard something about my country in the news, he would phone me straight away to tell me all about it. He was in many ways more radical than John when celebrating Morales's achievements. Like John, he was an avid reader and would often give me books as presents. In those days, Bolivian and other South American friends also came round to discuss politics. Some of them held anti-Morales views, but they recognised that change had to come one day.

CHAPTER TWENTY-SIX

*"We should consider every day lost on which we have
not danced at least once"*

Friedrich Nietzsche

London is a city that makes one feel young. There are so many things to do that age is immaterial. I was still enjoying my dancing. Clubs and salsa classes had opened up all over London; many of my English friends began to learn it. As dancing was not one of Alan's favourite activities I would go out with them, or I would go to salsa sessions with a group of friends from Santa Cruz. My friend Fabio and his Colombian wife would also invite me out dancing, especially if there was a salsa band coming to play in London from Colombia, Cuba or Puerto Rico.

Twenty five years before, when we were young we went out looking desperately for the warmth and sensuality of the salsa.

Those years have now gone; we have got over our old anxieties and nostalgias of living in a foreign country. Now that we have more placid and resigned lives, the salsa no longer always seeks us to invite us to dance. But one night, with Fabio and his wife we were at a club trying to get into the atmosphere, when a small Chinese man asked me to dance. I got up and followed him to the dance floor. "Me good dancer, you dancer?" he asked. "Yes," I nodded. "Ok, which style? Cuban, Puerto Rican, Miami, or New York style?" he asked in a strong Chinese accent. Wow, I didn't know so many styles existed. I could dance Cuban style because I had learned it when I went to the island. I picked up the Colombian style from Fabio, but the other ones I had never heard of until that evening. "Cuban please," I said. I was proud of my dancing skills, so I would never have said I can't do this or that style. He held me tightly then spun me round like a spinning top. I wasn't sure if he was following the beat of the music because his fast, loose movements felt like they had no rhythm. Feeling that I was in danger of collapsing, I asked him to change to Miami style, hoping this would be gentler, but he threw me away from him and then brought me back towards him like an elastic band. Then he turned me around very fast a couple of times, made a few manoeuvres and pushed me away again, to start the whole sequence once more. My head was going backwards and forwards so much I was in danger of getting whiplash. I could see Fabio looking at me, amused, he probably thought I was going to end up on the floor. In a final attempt to calm the man down I suggested we change to Puerto Rican style; unfortunately, this was worse. I remember feeling like I was in a tumble dryer and from time to time hearing him say, "me teacher, me good dancer!" I thanked God when it was all over; it took me a while to recover. I sat down wondering if I wanted to dance again. A few minutes later an Irish guy asked me to dance, but I wasn't sure what to do. It is terrible to go out to dance and end up not dancing. I accepted his invitation, but soon found out he was a beginner. I don't know which is worse, to dance with an expert who can break your back, or to salsa with a beginner who needs your continual guidance; it was like trying to control a badly behaved child. He had no rhythm at all and had difficulty with every movement. I felt as though I was trying to bend a piece of hardwood. When we had finished he asked where I was from. "Bolivia," I replied. "You South Americans dance as well as we Irish drink!" he said, holding a glass of beer.

A few weeks later, I invited a friend of mine called Rachael to go salsa dancing. I had met a very attractive man called Lenny at a party. We had made friends, exchanged telephone numbers and I promised to call him one day to go out dancing, as I wanted to introduce him to a pretty friend of mine. The day before my meeting with Rachael, I sent Lenny a text message inviting him to join us. A few hours later he called to thank me for the invite and to confirm that he was coming. It was all arranged and my friend Rachel was thrilled that she was finally to meet the guy I had talked so much about.

At precisely ten o'clock the next evening, my doorbell rang; thankfully I was almost ready to go out. I ran to the door, expecting to see Lenny, but when I opened it, to my great surprise there in front of me stood a Rastafarian black man with long dreadlocks and a big smile. It was my plumber! For a moment I thought that maybe Alan had called him to fix something in the flat, but I felt it was a bit strange him coming that late. Then I realised that I had made a big mistake. The plumber's name was also Lenny and I had texted him instead of the other guy! I called Rachael immediately to tell her we were going out with the plumber; she was already on her way. We had a wonderful evening, Rachel and I taught Lenny how to dance salsa and he promised to take us to a reggae party the following weekend. To me this was London; unlike Bolivia, it gives you more opportunities to interact with anyone regardless of social class. It is one of London's greatest attractions.

However, unpleasant things happened sometimes. One evening we were dancing at a club in Brixton. We were totally absorbed in the music, when immigration officers somehow sniffed out illegal immigrants and raided the salsa club. To the rhythm of rumba, people rushed out to hide like mice fleeing the cats, who, with a calm and disinterested air, randomly asked for documents. Illegal or not, nobody had documents of course. In a couple of seconds the dance floor was almost empty, but the music carried on playing. The cats caught about ten mice who looked more illegal than the rest. They led them out still with the sound of the rumba ringing in their ears to dance behind bars.

Salsa in London, salsa in Barcelona, salsa in Cuba, I danced wherever I went. Thanks to salsa I have been in awkward situations, I have met nice people, but strange people too. During a visit to New York with some English girlfriends for a hen party, we were staying in a posh place called the New Palace Hotel. I was sharing a room with a girl who was in the mood to do something different. We had done the Sex in the City tour of Manhattan and spent a lot of time shopping and going to restaurants. "We are in New York! We're free, let's have fun!" she said and asked me if I liked to go dancing. "I'm good at salsa," I replied. "Let's go dancing then," she got more enthusiastic. As the other girls were not interested, just the two of us went out. We asked the concierge for the address of a good place for salsa. He gave us the details of one nearby and off we went.

We got a taxi and during the journey the driver was friendly and talkative; I think he was from India or somewhere else in Asia. He asked us questions and told us about the salsa place we were going to, which he said was not good. "It's full of blacks; it's not a place for you." I imagined he was associating our hotel with people with money and that the salsa club only attracted losers.

He suggested taking us to the Holiday Inn where we could listen to "decent music."

By this time I was not interested in going anywhere but the salsa club and I found his comment about "blacks" racist and offensive. In fact, I thought the more blacks the better, as they were often the best dancers; but my roommate began to have second thoughts. I suggested we should go to see what kind of place it was to make up our own minds. But she panicked and became irrational and aggressive, pleading with the driver to take us back to the hotel; so we went without the satisfaction of having danced in New York. Some people imagine themselves on an unusual night out, but when you put them in a real situation they run away like scared squirrels.

After the trip to New York a school friend from Bolivia, married to a doctor, announced that they were coming to London for a few days. Because her husband's main interest was 60s British rock music, Alan prepared a rock music history tour of the city. So we went to see where many rock musicians, such as the Rolling Stones, Beatles and the Kinks had played their first gigs or where they used to live. On their last day with us, we took them to a football match to round off their time in London. After the game at Charlton Athletic's ground we went dancing. We were having our drinks, when suddenly the fire alarm went off. The staff started running around trying to find the fire. Alan asked one of the workers what was going on. The guy wasn't sure, he said that everything seemed to be ok, there was no fire anywhere, but the alarm continued to ring. The manager then asked everybody to leave; we left our glasses half full and were evacuated. The noise of a fire engine approaching made the situation seem serious. For a moment I thought the whole building would go up in flames. The four of us walked quickly away but the alarm seemed as loud as it was when we were inside the cafe. Because it was cold I put my hands in my pockets and felt an object inside. Guess what it was. It was my personal pocket alarm, which somehow had been activated. My Bolivian friends looked at me in astonishment. Alan said, "sorry guys, I always have to take Ana everywhere twice, the second time to apologise!"

CHAPTER TWENTY-SEVEN

"Life is not made of wishes, but of the acts of each of us"

Paulo Coelho

My friends returned to Bolivia. A few days later I checked my emails as I hadn't sat in front of a computer for several days. One message was totally unexpected; I felt uneasy when I saw who it was from. Before opening it I went to the kitchen to make myself a strong cup of English tea. I had my first sip, burnt my tongue and opened the email, which I was eager to read. It went:

Dear Anita,
The coincidences of life never seem to amaze me. My daughter is going to London for a few days and I would be delighted if you both could meet. Perhaps I never told you this, but I dreamt of

going to London one day to give you a surprise visit. I would have loved to have been with you in such a foreign world which now belongs to you. Unfortunately this didn't happen due to certain unavoidable personal reasons. I have found this very frustrating, something very close to a personal failure; but time is in charge of everything. In the beginning it provides you with blind alleys and distractions, but eventually life itself heals you and generously provides other wonderful things which give direction to your life. Somehow things again have interwoven us as my fondest daughter is going to London. She is nineteen years old, an extrovert, strong and an easy going young girl, a bit like you! Her English is fluent and she will be in London for a few days. It will give her mother and I peace of mind if you would guide her around such a big city. She knows that you were an important part of my youth and she also knows that we are now good friends.

My eternal gratitude,
Love, Rafael.

I sipped my tea intent on absorbing everything I read. For a couple of minutes I stared, bewildered by the possibility of meeting Rafael's daughter. This was something I never expected to happen. I thought I had closed the chapter with Rafael the last time I met him in Bolivia, but it seemed this sudden visit was again going to open up memories and wounds that had taken so long to close.

During the days leading up to her arrival, my mind was in turmoil, spending a few nights tossing and turning in bed. I calculated the time in my head and worked out that I could have had a child with Rafael as old as the girl who was about to visit us. I also thought of the child Alan and I had lost; he would have been ten years old. Rafael's daughter would probably bring sad memories of my past without her knowing it. I began to have doubts about this visit. I wasn't sure if I was doing the right thing by agreeing to Raphael's request and whether it was sensible for me to meet her. I wasn't sure if I could handle the situation.

I discussed it with Alan and he immediately understood my concerns. He thought I should regard this visit as a kind of apology from Rafael, for his failure to come to see me when I really needed him. He didn't mind the young girl's visit and even offered to take me to the airport to pick her up, which we did. Talking to my friend Peter, who often popped in with news about Bolivia, also helped me understand Rafael's wishes for a friendly and healing reconciliation.

One night I couldn't sleep and I lay there remembering something that happened a few years before. My friend Ashda and I were on holiday on Kos, a beautiful Greek Island. It was mid-afternoon and the stifling heat was making us feel drowsy. We were wandering around aimlessly when we heard a rough croaking voice behind us; we turned around and saw an old woman dressed in a traditional long black dress standing by her front door. She offered us some Greek coffee. We accepted gladly and sat down outside her old house while she went in to prepare it. A few minutes later she came out with two very small cups of coffee and a pleasant smile on her wrinkled face. Eager to make conversation with us, she began to ask us questions, such as where we were from and whether we liked Kos. Her English was not very good and she sounded as though she was practicing the few words she had learned maybe to get attention and perhaps some money from tourists. After a while she offered us another cup. Ashda accepted it, but as I don't normally drink such strong and bitter coffee I declined.

I was holding my almost empty cup when she leaned towards me and asked me to drink it all. I did what she said and handed the cup back to her. She began to look inside, examining the grounds carefully, turning the cup in every direction. Gesturing with her eyes and fingers she said, "me read future, do you want?" Ashda and I looked at each other and smiled, both probably thinking she was trying it on to make money from us. "Good fortune, good fortune," the woman said smiling, trying to convince us to have a reading with her. "How much?" my friend asked. "Is up to you," she replied, shrugging her shoulders as though the money didn't matter. Ashda and I looked at each other, not sure what to do. "You go first," Ashda said, encouraging me to do it. "Ok," I said, happy to waste my time and money on silly things.

The woman took me inside the house to a room cluttered with paintings of saints on the walls. The smell of incense was so strong that I began to get a headache. After asking me to sit on an old discoloured sofa, she sat in front of me. She placed the cup with the coffee grounds on a round table, where there was a deck of tarot cards. Then she began to talk, looking into the cup and said, "you have two or three children." "No, no children," I replied. Her carefully painted eyebrows moved down closer to her small eyes, showing signs of confusion; the movement wrinkled her broad forehead even more. Putting the cup aside and picking up the tarot cards, she shuffled them a couple of times and asked me to divide the pack. She picked up one half and placed the other under it. Spreading the cards skilfully on the table, she looked at me with a little smile of self-satisfaction. "Yes, you two or three children." "No, I haven't got children," I said firmly. Then she asked to see the palm of my right hand. She looked at it for a few seconds and said again, "yes, two or three children, and then with a tinge of sympathy in her eyes she asked, "they are dead?" It took me a few minutes to realise that she had probably sensed something that I had almost totally forgotten; I looked at her in amazement. I tried to explain without being sure if she understood me what had really happened. She looked at me again with those small, dark, hard eyes and said, "no matter, no matter, they children anyway." I sat down looking at her, unable to comment. She then gave me two candles to hold as she lit them. "These for children, we pray." "Why do I have to do this?" I asked her. "Their souls no resting in peace. They wander around," she replied, as best as her English would allow. We prayed for a few seconds and I left the room with the two candles in my hands, feeling confused. I walked away thinking about my losses as tricks of nature, tricks that perhaps I didn't deserve. My friend also had a reading that day, but she left the house smiling.

In London, still not being able to sleep that night, I got up from bed and walked towards a chest of drawers. I looked eagerly in one of the drawers until I found the photo that I had carefully placed there for safekeeping. It was the photo of the baby that Alan and I had never held. I lit a candle and in an act of rebirth I gave the child a name. I also thought of the other child that had not been born and I promised to go to church with a candle for it. That night I made a decision; I wanted to record my life. I moved stealthily around the flat, trying not to make any noise to wake Alan up. I turned the computer on and the first chapter of this book began.

A few days later the pretty girl arrived and she was just as her father had described; a happy, intelligent and fun girl. She was also the spitting image of him. The visit turned out to be a total success. We enjoyed each other's company and she loved what she saw of London. As we went sightseeing we even had the chance to talk about her father and me. This allowed a special friendship to develop between us, which we still have today.

CHAPTER TWENTY-EIGHT

*"The world has enough for everybody's need,
but not enough for everybody's greed"*

Mahatma Gandhi

By 2008 my life in London had become even more hectic. I was studying for an MSc. degree in nutrition that involved a lot of research, essay writing, attending conferences and travelling to Worcester University. My work was also growing, together with my knowledge.

One gloomy evening in the middle of winter, when the long dark days usually pass uneventfully, something happened to break the monotony. It was about seven o'clock, when a surprising visitor knocked the door of the clinic. Philip Gould, one of the closest advisers to Prime Minister Tony Blair at the time, ventured a visit without an appointment. After his consultation

The Illegal Dance

and treatment, he asked me to be personal therapist to himself and his wife. Weeks later a famous journalist of the Independent newspaper came recommended by a former patient. A well-known history of war author joined the list of interesting clients and so on week after week more and more people from the world of politics, business, or art were added to my list.

During the following months my social life also expanded and I was frequently invited to parties or interesting events. On one occasion I was a guest at a very unusual wedding. In fact it was the most unconventional marriage I had ever attended. The couple looked very glamorous, but one could not see the difference between the bride and the groom; it was a gay wedding. In Bolivia such a ceremony would have been scandalous. The Catholic Church would have closed its doors and gone into mourning, praying thousands of Ave Marias for the souls of these two guys and the church bells would never have rung again in protest. The Church in Bolivia would never accept this kind of love. Even though the new political constitution in Bolivia is clearly against sexual orientation discrimination, it is still too soon for gay and lesbian couples to get married and enjoy their honeymoon at Lake Titicaca.

The wedding party was made up of people of every nationality, colour and sexual orientation. Other gay couples joined in the celebration, along with relatives and friends of the grooms. One of the men getting married worked for the Blair Government, so a couple of cabinet ministers were also guests such as Peter Hain. I have always loved surprises and London was full of them.

One morning on my way to work I stopped at a café near Green Park as I had half an hour to spare. I was due to see a client to design a suitable diet for her to combat stress. It was unusual for me to be early for an appointment. Even though I had been living in London for over twenty years, I had not completely rid myself of some bad Bolivian habits such as unpunctuality.

The place was full of people on their way to work. I sat down in the only seat available and waited to be served.

Something different in the café caught my attention that morning, something I had not noticed before. Most of the people had an open computer on their table and were totally immersed in them; some of them were even talking to these machines; it seemed so bizarre. "How things have changed!" I thought. Just a few years before, one would go to a coffee bar and read a book or a newspaper. Nowadays, computers seem to be replacing everything; you can do your shopping online, book your holidays, study on courses remotely and make international calls. You can even find love on the internet, as did happen to a couple of friends of mine, who met their partners through internet dating sites and subsequently got married.

That morning I realised how much technology had transformed our lives without us even noticing. In some ways this change was for the better but in others for the worse. Technology was replacing people in an unnatural way. It felt like a new, powerful and sophisticated industrial revolution. In supermarkets, for example, self-service tills have been installed, where you pay a computer by pressing buttons. I hated these machines and refused to use them. I would rather stand in a long queue to be served by a real person. I like the chit chat that you can have with them. "Are you alright, love? Do you need anything else? Have a nice day!" that sort of thing. Nobody can talk to a machine and in big cities like London, surely lonely people would much prefer to deal with human beings.

A friend of mine, James, once said to me, "London is becoming more and more a fast-paced impersonal city, strangling its potential to be romantic." Was this really true? Were all the technological tools that we were acquiring making our lives less human? Even when we made a telephone call there was now an answering machine, with different options available to deal with our enquiries or problems. Were we becoming automatons, using devices like computers, plastic cards and other gadgets to give us more comfortable lives, but with less human contact?

While drinking my hot chocolate, I pondered on how much things had changed since the first time I arrived in London almost thirty years before. I put on my reading glasses to glance through a free newspaper I'd picked up in the Underground. The news I read was so shocking, it may have explained why people were engrossed in their computers that morning.

The newspaper headline read: "Lehman Brothers Bankrupt." I could not believe that one of the most prestigious American banks had collapsed. It was disastrous financial news that would not only affect the U.S.A. and Europe, but probably the whole world. I thought of my country whose economy was largely dependent on the state of the U.S. economy.

The bank had lost hundreds of billions of dollars; twenty five thousand people lost their jobs, five thousand based in London. The U.S. utilities company Enron, came to mind. When it went bankrupt, in 2001, the name Enron became synonymous with fraud and corruption. I also thought of the giant U.S. company Merrill Lynch that also went bust in 2008, losing billions of dollars. It is said that bonuses totalling $3.6 billion had been paid to employees, some of whom had probably contributed to this economic disaster.

But there was more to come; the same year saw similar bad news. The American investment advisor, Bernard Madoff operated a Ponzi scheme and conned $18 billion out of hundreds of wealthy people who believed they could make even larger amounts of money through him. As well as greedy individuals, unfortunately charitable foundations also lost their money. Madoff went to prison for the rest of his life

Reading the newspaper headline about Lehman Brothers reminded me that Aunt Betty had once said to me, "all empires collapse sooner or later." Was it now America's turn? Were all these businessmen, city bankers and stockbrokers the real Osama Bin Laden of North America? These men did not need aeroplanes or bombs to destroy everything, just greed, corruption and a fundamental lack of understanding of the real world.

I finished my drink quickly and walked to see my client who opened her front door with a strained smile on her face. She looked so worried and stressed it seemed as if she had not slept all night. She listened without interest to my advice about stress management. Her mind seemed to be somewhere else as she was completely silent. I felt she wanted me to finish as soon as possible and leave. After half an hour of breathing exercises however, she relaxed, opened up and told me she had lost a fortune. During that week I heard similar stories from several clients.

On the evening news that night, a soldier who had fought in the Iraq War gave an interview on his return to the U.S. He felt that the problems that America faced were not in places like Iraq, Iran or other countries, but were internal ones. He felt that Americans were committed to the pursuit of freedom, but their definition of freedom was simply false. He believed that the American people had been convinced that accumulating material goods and indulging the appetites of a consumer society was the best way to liberty and happiness. I wondered if the free capitalist world that we so much appreciate and that America is so proud of and eager to impose on everybody, was built on corruption, scams and fraud.

I remembered reading a memoir a few years earlier by a former "economic hit man," the North American, John Perkins, about the intelligent greed of American big corporations. They sent their economic hit men to persuade needy countries like Bolivia to hand over their natural resources for very little in exchange. These corporations, working together with the International Monetary Fund, trick countries like mine into borrowing money from them. The result is developing countries debts have grown to more than $2.5 trillion with the inevitable increase in poverty in Africa and South America. The Gross Domestic Product (GDP) per capita of the ten richest countries in the world doubled between 1985 and 1995, while the GDP per capita of the ten poorest countries decreased by 30%. The difference in GDP between the richest country and the poorest country in those years grew from 70 to 430 times. Twenty years later, this difference hasn't deepened, but it is still enormous.

Bolivia was one of those countries in constant debt, but without enjoying the benefits of the borrowed money. Having handed over its natural resources to big corporations, the tax revenue to the Bolivian exchequer was so little that successive administrations could not pay back the money they owed to the International Monetary Fund. Instead they had to borrow more money, to keep the country afloat. The government could not even afford to pay workers' Christmas salaries. So I did not blame Morales for taking a strong stand against imperialist nations and companies who took advantage of our weak position.

The banking crisis that started in America in 2008 was followed by equivalent calamities in the United Kingdom and across Europe. Among the banks which had to be rescued with tax payers' money were the Royal Bank of Scotland and the Northern Rock Building Society. Some economic experts believed that the lack of regulation by governments led to more greed and corruption. Others believed that too many rules would not allow the free market and private enterprise to flourish. It seemed that nobody knew what to do to resolve the problem.

In the meantime bankers were still receiving huge amounts of money in bonuses. Many of them chose to retire with fortunes in their accounts. A stockbroker friend once told me that the City and Wall Street were full of greedy, ruthless and very clever people. "It's capitalism at its worst. The truth is that our financial system is little more than a giant Ponzi scheme that is based on debt and paper promises. Every day after the collapse of Lehman Brothers, the news became more and more alarming. One night I heard that the British Government had run up debts totally 4.8 trillion pounds, roughly a third of the U.S. national debt, due to waging wars in Iraq, Afghanistan and other countries, plus general bad management of the economy. When a journalist interviewed some Members of Parliament and asked them if they knew how much the debt was, all of them apologised for their ignorance. "I'm sorry, I don't have that information," or "thanks for the question but…" They were all very polite, but none of them had an answer; they were not aware of the enormity of the situation. It all looked so surreal to me; it was clear that the country had been living beyond its means without realising it.

This reckless overspending became more evident a year later when anti-capitalist, violent demonstrations began to emerge, not only in the U.K., but also in France, Spain, Greece and Portugal. Angry people took to the streets, calling on their governments to account for the crisis and take action.

In 2009, the Daily Telegraph, a highly respected British newspaper, published details of a huge scandal involving many Members of Parliament, mostly from the House of Commons but also from the House of Lords. Articles gave details about the deliberate and gross misuse of expenses for personal gain that MPs across all parties had claimed. The reputations of U.K. politicians suffered possibly irreversible damage as a result of these disclosures. The more serious offenders were either not re-elected in the following general election, or did not stand again for office; a few politicians were sent to prison. Naively I had thought that this kind of misconduct only happened in countries like Bolivia.

I was saddened by all this. As a child in Bolivia I remember reading, "London, greatest city in the world. Home to the oldest democracy, has a worldwide reputation for its integrity and honesty, firmly based on a thousand years of the rule of law."

The expenses outrage actually started in 1983 when Margaret Thatcher was the Prime Minister. She wanted to give the MPs a pay rise. But it was felt that the general public would not tolerate it. So she solved the problem by not actually giving a pay rise, but instead she encouraged MPs to supplement their salaries through the expenses system. "Recompense would replace remuneration." This led the way to dishonest MPs claiming far more than they were entitled to as expenses.

In 2010 there was a general election in the U.K., but this major scandal contributed towards the failure of any party to obtain enough support; people felt betrayed and angry. The Labour Party, who had the chance to build a fairer society, allowed the opportunity to slip through its fingers. The Conservative Party, with a reputation damaged by fifteen years of Thatcherism, also failed to obtain enough support to win the election.

For the first time ever since I arrived in England, a coalition of two supposedly different parties was formed. This situation was very familiar to me; it was like the old days in Bolivia. It was the normal way to govern before Morales became President with more than fifty four per cent of the popular vote.

The new U.K. Prime Minister, David Cameron, began to talk of a period of austerity, just as Morales had when he started his presidency. In Bolivia the period of austerity began with the cutting of the high salaries of politicians and increasing the low salaries of the less fortunate. In the U.K., incomes were slashed in the opposite direction. The ones who suffered the cuts or frozen salaries were in the public sector, like nurses, teachers and the police. Politicians' salaries were immune from cuts, on the contrary, they even increased. This of course included Cameron, who unlike Morales, kept his high salary.

So the economic crisis was now targeting and affecting ordinary people. As time passed, it seemed that the demands and obstacles of this great country were increasing at great speed. It was difficult to find jobs and education costs, especially university fees, had shot through the roof. This made the lives of many young people very stressful, not only British students, but also those who came to study from abroad. Many South American youngsters returned to their home countries or left the U.K. to try their luck elsewhere.

I also noticed changes in British immigration policy. Over the years control over illegal foreigners had not been very tight, but now the Home Office seemed to have changed its attitude. Jointly with the police, Border Agency officers patrolled the streets in great numbers within areas of large ethnic communities to pick up illegal immigrants and send them back to their countries without even the option of packing their belongings. In many cases these deportations seemed arbitrary and unfair. One afternoon I received a call from a Bolivian friend who told me he needed help. He sounded very worried and was talking quickly. I told him to calm down and tell me what was wrong. "I've been caught by the police on my way to work," he said. "I'm in a detention centre at Gatwick Airport. Please go to my room and get as many of my things as possible. Put them in a suitcase and bring it here as quickly as you can." He gave me the address, I did as he said and a few days later he was deported.

The same day his roommate was caught. She was studying and working legally and paying tax on her part time earnings. But she was kicked out of the country because she was employed a couple of hours a week more than was allowed. They had both been doing low paid menial jobs that many English people are not prepared to do. Months earlier a Brazilian girl who helped me with the cleaning of my flat was also deported; bit by bit I was losing friends.

In the U.S.A., the attitude towards immigration also became tougher. After the collapse of the banks two million illegal immigrants were expelled, even though the U.S. economy and society in general were built on immigration, both legal and illegal. It was a similar story in the U.K.

While observing these historical events I felt that this crisis was not just an economic one but a moral one too. We were losing our sense of right and wrong. Young people lacked role models to look up to. On the contrary, people were exposed to violence and war and socially neglected youngsters in the U.K. were affected by it. Youth turned increasingly to alcohol, forming gangs that fought each other viciously for no apparent reason. In some cases they even killed to be accepted into gangs. Gang members carried out exactly what they saw on the news every day on television: violence and more violence

It was that morning, when I sat down in the Green Park café that I began to perceive things differently after so many years in London. Since I first arrived, the U.K. has been involved in at least four wars. I wonder how politicians can talk about peace in the world when arms continue to be manufactured and wars continue to be started. It is estimated that in the 20th century alone humans have killed more than two hundred million of our own species.

That day I understood that I was living in a world full of inconsistencies, which seemed greater in capitalist, progressive countries than in developing ones. The speculative, opportunistic, free market and globalisation had given some people in the West everything, but this also gave rise to an unfair distribution of wealth elsewhere. The system that we thought would make us prosperous was now turning against us. This combined with the corruption that has always existed around the world added to the many difficulties we now faced. I once heard somebody say that we are ninety nine per cent animal and one per cent human, and it is the human part that causes all the problems.

CHAPTER TWENTY-NINE

"When a man is tired of London, he is tired of life; for there is in London all that life can afford."

Samuel Johnson

A year after Rafael's daughter came to London, the political situation in Bolivia began to settle down, as the problems between the new government and the opposition subsided. With a new political constitution a new country was formed. President Morales gave up one year of his first term so that new elections could take place in 2010. He won a second term easily and his political party managed to secure a total majority in the Congress, in both upper and lower houses. I was delighted to see a multi ethnic Parliament. As well as indigenous people, the first black man in Bolivian history was elected to Congress to represent the black community in the Yungas, which was the region in which I grew up.

Soon after the elections, an anti-racism law was introduced. It was a ruling required by the UN since 1975, but which had been ignored by Bolivia as successive governments had not considered the policy to be important. I was sure then that genuine transformation had begun to occur in my country.

After Morales became President in 2006 the Bolivian economy improved considerably. This was due to a combination of good luck and political skill. The factors that helped this process were an increase in the price of minerals and gas in the international market, better administration of the profits from the country's natural resources and the implementation of a policy to crackdown on corruption. For the first time in Bolivian history the country's foreign reserves increased, from under $2 billion in 2005 to over $11 billion in 2011, providing a cushion against the global downturn. The increase in revenue and reserves allowed Bolivia to expand its macroeconomic policies and maintain a growth rate of more than 4% during the world recession. While the U.S.A. and its European allies were busy fighting wars and the economic crunch at its peak, Morales in Bolivia was fighting poverty.

On one particular morning in London I took the tube to work as usual. The carriage was not full, so I managed to get a seat. I looked in my bag for my snack. The train often did as my restaurant. The lack of time in big cities like London does not allow you to have an hour to eat your lunch in a civilised manner. I ate in a hurry and when I had finished my sandwich I raised my eyes and looked at the dark window of the train reflecting the features of a mature woman with dark lines under her eyes and pronounced cheekbones; a jaded face looked back at me. I felt a rush of heat through my body causing me great discomfort which was difficult to ignore; the first signs of middle age. While on the train I thought of my childhood in Coroico when I used to run around oblivious to the passing of time. I was also aware of just how long it had been since I had watched those beautiful butterflies fluttering around me or heard the strange gurgling of the crested oropendola, when I roamed free in the countryside. I shivered with the knowledge that I had lived outside Bolivia for over thirty years.

In the months that followed, Bolivia occupied my thoughts with a greater frequency than ever. Returning to live in my homeland began to seem like a real possibility. I would sit in my living room, contemplating the garden through the large windows of the sunny conservatory that we had built a few years before. My thoughts drifted in an attempt to reconcile my dreams with hard facts. My love of London contrasted with my longing for Bolivia and I was left feeling confused. I would sometimes share my ambivalent thoughts with my friends, who would try to comfort me by saying that I had lived away from home too long and that I would never get used to Bolivia again. I felt they were probably right; maybe I was pining for a fantasy that I would forget with time.

I had not discussed these feelings with Alan as I thought this emotional state would not last for long. I also believed that he would dismiss the possibility of ever leaving his country for good. He loved travelling, but he also loved the diverse life in London. He didn't mind going to Bolivia as many times as I wanted to, but to go and live there for good was something that we had never considered.

So life went on, until one evening, while feeding the timid fox that used to come and visit us most nights in the back garden, I felt an inexplicable desire to return to Bolivia. For no obvious reason I was suddenly seized by a yearning for my country. I decided to tell Alan what was on my mind. He looked at me flabbergasted. "Live in Bolivia?" he asked. "What are we going to do there?" "Well," I said, "I've been thinking for some time now that I should return. I've been in London for most of my life

The Illegal Dance

and…" "To do what?" he interrupted. "Aren't you happy here? We've just had the extension built, something that you insisted on and wanted so much. We now have a fantastic place to live. I'm going to retire soon and you have finished your MSc. We can travel anywhere you want to go on holiday, including Bolivia." He was right, I had always been happy living in London, making it my permanent home, but as time passed, in spite of Doctor Johnson's opinion, this inexplicable desire grew stronger in me. "No, Alan, I want to return to Bolivia for good," I replied, convinced that this was the right decision. "I don't understand you," he said. "The last time we went there you didn't even like it. You said Coroico was totally spoiled when they built the new road. You didn't like the ugly concrete buildings that didn't harmonise with nature, and made the short streets look too narrow. You said that ever since television was introduced to the village, people had stopped going for walks in the plaza. You said there were too many cars in Coroico and not enough space for pedestrians. You said there were too many tourists, too many night clubs and too much noise. You even noticed that there were fewer shrubs in the gardens of the main square, leaving the place looking naked and less romantic. You said Coroico wasn't the "magic little place you grew up in anymore." It was true; ever since the new, wider, much safer road had replaced the "Death Road," the village had changed, not necessarily for the better. "Bolivia is big," I said. "We don't have to live in Coroico." "Let's talk about it tomorrow, please," Alan went back to marking exam papers.

I didn't get anywhere that night, but I was relieved that at least I had broached the subject and it was just a matter of time before we talked the matter over again. I sat next to Alan with my head on his shoulder, the spitting image of a little girl looking for reassurance. My thoughts travelled to Bolivia; I imagined the smell of a humid forest and the inebriating scent of tropical fruit hanging from slender branches like natural baskets ready to be picked from. I thought of the virtues that nature had granted to Bolivia giving the country so much potential. I remembered my grandfather saying when I was a young girl, "we Bolivians are like beggars sitting on a throne of gold."

I remembered a conversation I had with a friend in Coroico who had become a cloistered nun many years before. I had asked her why she had become a nun. She said that she had heard the call of God. "What do you mean? I have never heard the call of God," I said. She then explained to me that it was a gradual thing and did not come overnight. "God talks to you and makes you listen to His call in the most unexpected and extraordinary ways, and sometimes He gives you a mission. This feeling may disappear, but sometimes it comes back again even stronger. It becomes a constant nagging, something that you cannot ignore." "But why have you become a cloistered nun and not just a woman with a mission?" I asked her. She replied very gently as if she was in a trance, her words coming from the deepest part of herself, her soul. "God not only wanted to give me a mission, with a beginning and an end, He wanted my whole life and I could not refuse Him." I did not understand her explanation at all, maybe because I have never been religious. I looked at her as though she had gone mad before I walked away, leaving the nun smiling.

That evening while I was sitting on the sofa watching television with Alan I thought of the nun again and I began to comprehend what she meant. "Was I in fact in the same kind of situation?" I asked myself. "Was my desire to go back to Bolivia a gradual thing? Like a warm nagging feeling as she had explained? Was I experiencing a call? Was it a call from the Andes?"

I sprang up from the sofa and went to call my parents. "Dad, I have made up my mind, I'm going back to Bolivia for good," I said all excited, even though I was not quite sure whether Alan was going to agree. Dad was delighted to hear the news. "You have made me the happiest man on Earth," he said. "I never thought the day would ever arrive when you would return home." His voice trembled with emotion, perhaps thinking that he should never have sent me away in the first place. "Your mother and I are getting old and the only thing we would like is to be near you and your brothers." My brother José had gone back two years earlier and it was clear that they were just waiting for my return.

During the months that followed I spent time planning our departure; it filled me with great expectation and hope. However, I also had moments of doubt and concern. Maybe I was too old to start again in a country that I had not lived in for so long and of which I only had childhood memories. I also thought of the various things that annoyed me about Bolivia on the few occasions I had visited since living abroad. I remembered its inefficient bureaucracy, the corruption, the chaotic traffic with the constant noise of car horns and the intrusive voices of the bus drivers' assistants shouting out the places they were going. It also irritated me to see pedestrians trying to cross the road at token zebra crossings with drivers making no attempt to stop, not even at red lights. I thought of the first time Alan and I went to Bolivia. He was talking to a group of Bolivian doctors, trying to understand from them why intelligent Bolivian people, when they drive, completely ignore the rules of the road. The doctors gave a few reasons, such as the fact that Bolivians are anarchic people who don't always like to obey the law. Alan did not find their answers reasonable and he went on asking "why?" repeatedly, like a child asking his mother a question.

They say that Bolivians are very gentle people, but wild drivers. The bus drivers stop anywhere to pick up or drop off passengers, causing terrible traffic jams. The constant strikes and road blocks, the lack of respect for the law and the authorities also troubled me. I was bothered by the thought of walking on uneven, unsafe pavements packed with street traders. A lack of punctuality in keeping appointments and poor discipline in general are national features ingrained in the culture of my beloved country and this was unlikely to change. Most of all, it concerned me that crime had increased over the last few years.

I also felt guilty about Alan. He had now generously agreed to live in Bolivia, but I was worried about taking him out of his own environment to a country where the language was going to be the first obstacle. I felt sad to leave our lovely home in London; our garden, the beautiful spring and summer flowers that I had planted carefully over the years; the blackbirds, robins and magpies that came to eat at the squirrel-proof feeder; and even the hesitant fox that visited the garden every night through the hole in the fence that we had left deliberately.

I suddenly had the feeling that I hadn't done enough in London, that there was so much more I could do. After thirty years of hard work, I was now free to enjoy the great cultural life the great city has to offer. The museums, the different types of music concerts and the theatre that I loved so much, ever since Alan took me to see *The Woman in Black* when we first met. It was my first and most unforgettable play.

I was fascinated by the capacity of the actors' ability to memorise long scripts and act in plays without making mistakes. Performing on stage is not like making a film, where the actors can repeat the same scene many times over until it is perfect. I remember Rafael's daughter's excitement when we took her to see the *Harry Potter* actor Daniel Radcliffe in a play. She couldn't believe she was so close to him, that she could almost touch him.

I also had more time now to visit the countryside, to explore the many small and beautiful English villages and to go to historic castles I still hadn't seen. I had more opportunity to frequent art galleries, exhibitions and pubs and there was also the chance of meeting more famous people like Alan used to do.

My confusion and sadness grew even more when I thought of leaving the many good friends I had made in London over the

The Illegal Dance

years. One of the closest, Fabio and I had been through thick and thin together during our first years in London. He was now well established, married to a lovely Colombian lady and father of two children to whom I had the honour of being godmother. I would also be leaving my Nicaraguan friend, Elea, whose family links with the dictator Anastasio Somoza had forced her to leave her country as a political refugee when the Sandinistas overthrew him. We had met at Doña Asuncion's bedsit the year I arrived in London and we had been good friends ever since, even though we had different political views. Doña Asuncion had returned to Bolivia a few years before. She had gone back with damaged knees after years of working, cleaning houses. But in Bolivia she felt uneasy and anxious; she missed London, so she came back. But when she returned she missed Bolivia. Would I suffer the same kind of syndrome?

There were my friends Stella from Panama and Catherine from Ireland; I had met them while studying nutrition. This started a custom of regularly meeting up to try out the best restaurants in town. One evening during one of our regular dinners we saw a mouse running under the tables. We called the restaurant manager. The embarrassed man at first didn't know what to do to keep us quiet so the rest of the customers wouldn't know that there was a mouse running around from table to table. That evening we ate and drank free to our heart's content.

Then there was Hazel from London, my unusual Jewish friend who, from the age of four, had for some reason felt a strange but strong affinity with Bolivia. Her mother was bewildered by this and thought Hazel might be a case of reincarnation! Hazel learned Spanish at school and maintained connections with South America all her life. We met when we were both working at the Latin American Health Project in North London. She was a nurse and had visited Bolivia several times. I was intrigued by her love for the country, especially as it had started at such a young age.

With my friend Rachel, a very clever lawyer and salsa dancer, we enjoyed so many nights out dancing away like two young girls without a care in the world. Rachel had a lovely daughter, who I watched grow up: would I see them again one day? Also, my sophisticated English friend, Gerry, would arrange classy trips and parties in London and glamorous places like New York. At the airport she would always convince the check in staff that we should be upgraded to first class and then on arrival have a limousine waiting for us.

Miriam, Carmen, Naomi, Teresa, Roxana and Patricia, my Bolivian friends, like me, had lived years in London. Even though we were so far away, they kept the good memories of my country alive, and the bad memories too, such as the constant racism ingrained in us Bolivians. It was hard for me to accept that meeting up with my beautiful Nigerian friend, Tina, would be very difficult, now that she had moved back to her homeland. There were also my nephews, Chris, Javier, Rodrigo, Waskar and Kantuta who kept me young and in touch with modern life. They would drift in and out of London, always bringing news or invitations to parties, concerts and art galleries; or bringing their friends to have drinks at my home. We often ended up dancing until the early hours of the morning. Our neighbours, David and Lois, always had a smile to spare when we met in the street and took me with them dancing; I would miss them, too. I will remember Nasser the Iranian shopkeeper around the corner; if I was short of money, I could always pay tomorrow. It broke my heart to leave so many friends in London. I had also met so many interesting people through my work. I was full of trepidation when I realised that I had decided to leave the city that had given me so much and where I had found true love. Why did I want to leave a place where I had had the opportunity to fulfil my dreams and where my life had been made richer? Was it because I was looking for other challenges, or for other purposes? I had no answers. My parents were a good reason, but I could always go and see them as many times and as long as I wanted, as Alan had said. Perhaps leaving the U.K. would help me to re-evaluate my life objectively and get a better understanding of what was happening in the world. To return, retread my footprints and mingle with the people of the past might be a good start.

To leave the home where you have lived most of your life is not easy; Alan and I had endless things to do before travelling. Many possessions had to be sold, some put into storage and others given away. Alan had a collection of eight hundred CDs, a library with more than a thousand books and a small museum of zoological specimens. We didn't know what to do with them. Our few fairly valuable paintings and other things with sentimental value, we decided to take with us. We had to leave our bank accounts in order, with all debts paid. My consultation room was something else I had to deal with; I needed a specialist to carry on my practice. Some days I would get up in the morning happy to organise everything in boxes, but other days I would feel a terrible depression and sadness to walk away from everything I had built.

One spring afternoon, the telephone rang with unexpected and devastating news; Dad was terminally ill. I had embraced precious memories when making plans with my parents for my return. But now those dreams were gone. My life turned upside down in just a few minutes; one call changed everything. I had not counted on this; until that moment I had everything, wonderful parents in good health, waiting for me, but now things were going to be different. I wondered if real happiness exists or whether it is just a state of mind that only lasts a short time before it is over. Happiness is so elusive and fragile. It is an apocalyptic peace. It is near and it is far and where happiness starts is exactly where it ends. Maybe happiness is just a mere illusion after all.

Dad had been a point of reference for me ever since I was a little girl. We had so many things in common. He understood me and loved me unconditionally. I always felt his immense love for me, even though sometimes his love had hurt me. That spring afternoon I felt it was the wrong time to lose him.

We decided to return to Bolivia immediately. The route was London, Brazil and Santa Cruz de la Sierra. Once in Santa Cruz the quickest way to Cochabamba where my parents lived was to take a direct flight. But I had another plan in mind; I wanted to arrive in La Paz. Alan complained about my decision because La Paz is at such a high elevation, that without prior acclimatisation, he would feel unwell. But I behaved selfishly; I was determined to land in La Paz. It was important for me as there was something waiting for me there. Many years before, when I left Bolivia for the first time, I had made a promise, a promise I always meant to keep.

We left London during a wave of demonstrations and discontent about the new government's austerity measures. On the train to the airport, through the window I saw my London, slipping past and away from me. I grabbed a pen and paper and wrote:

London, magical and vital city.
City of charms, of contrasts and adventure.
City of Kings and Queens.
Forever young, elegant and modern.
Your River Thames gives you a bohemian and theatrical aura.
London, city of dreams, desires and surprises.
You are the only one in your integrating quest.
From your moist lips spring hundreds of different languages and you are culturally rich, three hundred and sixty five days of the year.

London, eternal city, when I'm with you I want nothing that can replace your gifts,
but as time passes by I feel your constant demands, you are difficult and lonely.
I feel you more unreachable and distant every day.

CHAPTER THIRTY

"When my voice ceases to speak with death, my heart will continue talking to you"

Rabindranath Tagore

When we arrived at São Paulo we met some Bolivian guys who were returning home from Spain. At first I thought they may have been deported, like many people I had met over the years, but their relaxed attitude suggested otherwise. As we got talking I asked them the reason for their return. "We lost our jobs, so we couldn't pay for accommodation." "We ended up sleeping under a bridge," he laughed. "What are your plans when you get to Bolivia?" I asked them. "We'll probably work as builders," they said. "We've been told there are lots of jobs in construction in Bolivia at the moment. Stories like this were common in Europe; people were returning to South America.

In the previous two years fifteen thousand migrants returned to Bolivia. "It's better to be out of work in your own country than abroad. Europe and the U.S.A. are no longer the promised lands for South Americans," said one of them. They were not at all sorry for having made the decision to leave Spain. A foreigner in Europe is often seen as a needy immigrant; however a foreigner in Bolivia is seen as a respectable tourist.

From talking to these guys I hoped that the experience of working in developed capitalist countries may teach us Bolivians that relatively large quantities of money flowing in the economy do not necessarily make us wealthy. In fact we can lose sight of what is truly valuable in life; our capacity to share equally what we have in our country, without fighting between each other and where generosity, dialogue and tolerance should always prevail.

Our first stop in Bolivia was Santa Cruz de la Sierra. On stepping out of the plane, a blast of heat made us quickly strip off our warm London clothes. A deep relaxing sigh emerged from my soul as I took in the wild Amazonian vista of palm trees and rheas grazing in the fields. "Look! A burrowing owl!" shouted Alan. We had to change planes; Alan suggested once more that we should take the next flight directly to the Cochabamba Valley, but I insisted on going to La Paz first. He looked at me with inquiring eyes but as a good, polite Englishman, did not ask for any explanation.

When we checked in, I made sure our seats were on the right side of the plane. Alan seemed a little confused by my curious behaviour; first insisting that we should land in La Paz, and now making sure we sat on the right side of the plane. "Anything else, darling?" he said with a bemused expression on his face. "Yes," I said, exhausted by the long flight from London. "Please wake me up just before we land."

Half an hour later Alan shook me gently to let me know that we were about to arrive in La Paz. I looked through the window at the view of the vast sky covered in angel-like clouds. The plane began its descent towards its very high speed landing, necessary because of the thin air providing less lift at the high elevation. In the distance, I saw the omnipotent, immortal and haughty snow-capped Mount Illimani waiting patiently for my arrival, as it had awaited the return of the many others who had left Bolivia under different circumstances. My heart jumped with emotion and satisfaction. Thirty years before I had asked for the mountain's forgiveness for deserting my country; I had also invoked its protection and blessings. Now, I had fulfilled the promise I had made, to the majestic Illimani. I was coming home and this time for good.

In Bolivia as well as the U.K., there were endless demonstrations, strikes and roadblocks demanding one thing or another from the new government. This time, however, the discontent came not only from the opposition parties, but also from the people who had helped Morales to gain power.

A few months before, the Bolivian Government had tried to abolish a fuel subsidy that had been implemented thirty seven years previously, costing the country more than $1000 million a year, money that the new government thought could be better used for development projects. Even though it was widely agreed that this was a necessary change, the people were not happy. Angry crowds rallied against this radical measure, threatening the political and economic stability of the country. The possibility of the collapse of democracy forced Morales to quickly reverse the policy, claiming that he governed by listening to the people. Whether they listened to him or not was another matter.

Following this, for whatever reason, the rate of inflation rose to seven per cent. A few months later doctors, teachers and other workers went on a ten day strike to protest against the ten per cent increase in salaries that had been offered as they wanted at least fifteen per cent. Once this problem had been resolved,

The Illegal Dance

the government announced that the people who had been on strike would lose pay proportional to the days that they did not work during the strike. This triggered another strike, with the unions demanding that workers should be paid in full, whether they worked or not.

This situation reminded me of what happened in the 1980s, when we began a democratic period with Hernán Silez Suaso after so many years of dictatorship. When President Silez Suaso first encountered a difficult period, even Jaime Paz, his vice president, turned against him. The trade union federation and members of the left-wing opposition paralysed the country with constant strikes. The economy was already in poor shape, but the political turmoil damaged it further.

I thought of Uncle Hector when, in the Café La Paz a few years earlier, he told his political friends that Bolivia was a difficult country to govern and that politicians are in a constant tussling match where logic seldom prevails. It is said that in Bolivia there is a minimum of at least four strikes per week making around two hundred strikes per year. But in the last two years there have been at least a thousand strikes, with the loss of billions of dollars in productivity.

During my time in England, due to Thatcher, the trade unions had lost most of their power, whilst in Bolivia their power had grown. With Morales we had learnt about our rights, but little about our obligations. I was afraid that this might not help the country to construct a better society and that it would undermine Morales's well-meaning intentions and hard work.

Even though we had managed to take big steps towards a fairer and more tolerant society, we still had big challenges ahead. This democratic process of change in Bolivia was just the beginning; it was obvious that much more had to be done. New leaders will come in the future with more innovative ideas and will correct the mistakes that are an inevitable part of any peaceful, revolutionary process. This difficult task is not the job of one man or one government; it is every Bolivian's responsibility.

Dad could no longer eat or talk anymore; the throat cancer had put an end to those joys. I held him as gently as I could, trying not to muddle up the tubes that were giving him his oxygen and food. I reassured him that everything would be all right, even though I was very unsure of what I was saying. He nodded, trying to be positive, but tears trickled from his eyes and mine at the same time. We both knew we did not have long together. We wanted to say things to each other, perhaps even to recriminate ourselves for our long separation. We both had regrets I am sure; I should have returned to Bolivia years before, when Doña Asuncion told me to. Dad's life was coming to an end and the only thing left for me now was remorse. I wanted him to know that my life had turned out well after all and it was all thanks to him, but my tears stopped me from saying a word. I kissed his hands gently to try to lessen his pain and mine.

A few days later we realised that there was little to be done. Dad was gasping for air constantly. The cancer was destroying his lungs and any hope of recovery was gone. He had lost the ability to communicate with us through writing and he became delirious. The doctor gave Dad a small dose of morphine to try to reduce the pain and distress and because he was so weak it would be enough to induce a compassionate end. "He won't feel pain any more. This will help him to disconnect," the doctor reassured us with a caring and sympathetic voice.

My brothers, Mum and I sat around his bed and comforted him while he went to sleep. The next day, a deep sigh ended dad's life. He was the man who had shaped my life; he had been a pillar of strength and a source of vitality for us all. He passed away holding my Mum's hand, reassured by our eternal love and gratitude for all he had done for us. A few days later we found two letters in his desk, one was addressed to the three children and the other to my mother.

Dear Children,

This letter is addressed to you three, who have been, with your mother, the most important things in my life.

When I married your mother, I hoped it would bring me many gifts: a companion, children and a fulfilled life. I have had all this and much, much more; more than I ever imagined.

Now death has surprised me in the sunset of my life, when I felt safe from ambush and adversity. I want to make a recommendation to you, my children. Please maintain unity between the three of you throughout all the vicissitudes of your lives. I want nothing to distance you from one another; when one of you fails, the others will help, mediate, or comfort. This is the one request I have because I think I deserve it.

During my life I have learned that one of the most powerful forces that nature can give us is love. This love that I have for you I can summarise by saying: "I have no gold or diamonds, but enough love for you all." Ling Yutang writes: "even hate is hungry love."

Finally, do not let my body be buried between bricks and mortar. Scatter my ashes on the bountiful land of the Yungas, close to Uchumani mountain, where I can be fused with nature, the nature that I have loved.

My wish is to be reborn in the sap of plants and trees. I want to go to their leaves and feel the caress of the wind, the freshness of the rain, the warmth of the sun during the day and at night the pale light of the moon, cold as death.

And to finish I suggest having in your memory only, an epitaph that had occurred to me: "Here lies Dr. Fernando Borda, the man who knew how to laugh and love unlike any other man. The only thing that hurts me is not to have died of laughter or love, but of cancer."

My eternal love,
Dad

Letter to Mum
My Love,

I do not know where to begin, I just want to tell you that I taught you how to walk through life, but you taught me how to fly. Most importantly you taught me how noble is the heart of a woman.

If there is another place, I'll be waiting there for you, in the meantime, look ahead; enjoy the rest of your life. Love our children and all children.

My eternal love,
Ferdy

A year later, and without warning, the death of my mum hit me with the same intensity. I was holding on to her to fulfil my desire for her to spend her old age in my company, but Mum without Dad had become like a fragile leaf on a windy day. Without his love, without his company and guidance, she lost the will to live. Later on my brothers and I scattered my parents' ashes in Coroico, just as they had always wanted.

A few months after Mum's funeral Alan and I went to the main plaza in Cochabamba. The heat that day was intense, but somehow it felt like a comforting caress for our huge and irreplaceable loss. There were some people, mainly retired, enjoying their free time sitting in the shade of the coral trees. I thought of Mum and Dad, when they used to come to this plaza to read their newspaper and feel the breeze of the late afternoon.

A typical Bolivian woman dressed in a short pollera (voluminous skirt) and white bowler hat stood at the corner of the square, selling fresh orange juice. A group of people surrounded a man talking about herbal remedies and selling ointments to treat arthritis. Another small crowd listened to a man talking politics, trying to convince everybody that the only way to change things

The Illegal Dance

was an armed revolution. Someone else held a Bible, preaching about God being the only way to salvation.

This all reminded me of Speaker's Corner in Hyde Park, London; a place where people traditionally go every Sunday morning to freely express their opinions. Alan and I sat down on a bench to enjoy the afternoon. A small boy approached us carrying an old wooden box. "Can I clean your shoes, sir?" Alan accepted at once. The boy sat on the ground in dirty, shabby clothes and took from his box small bottles of dye, a dirty cloth and two brushes. He was ready to start his everyday ritual to make enough money to buy himself something to eat.

Suddenly he made a clumsy movement and all the liquid in the bottles was spilt on the ground. The anguished child looked up at us forlornly. Not only had he lost the polish to clean Alan's shoes, but he had also wasted the chance to clean probably ten more pairs. The boy tried to salvage some of the dye, but it was now filthy and unusable.

"Perdón, señor," he said dejectedly, his sad eyes begging forgiveness. Alan spoke in English, in an indifferent voice. "Oh well, it doesn't matter, such is life." He looked for some small change in his pocket to give to the boy but he didn't have any. Then, to the boy's surprise and mine, he took fifty bolivianos from his wallet and gave the cash to him. This was the equivalent to about twenty shoe shines.

The boy looked at the money in disbelief. His dark, doubtful eyes scrutinised Alan for a few moments, as if to give him the chance to change his mind. Then he put the cloth and brushes back into his wooden box and got up slowly. He took some steps backwards with the box hanging from his small shoulder. He glanced back as though he was looking for someone. With a timid, but delightful smile he looked at us once more. Then he turned around and ran away, jumping and bounding, looking for his friends to share his luck with.

A noise like castanets came from high in the trees. Alan got up suddenly from the bench and looked through his binoculars; it was a flock of large, noisy green parakeets with red faces. "Oh my God!" he shouted. "Mitred conures! I can't believe my luck!" The lovely, raucous flock took off with rapid wing beats, curving towards the setting sun. Alan turned to me and said, "I love your country." I replied with a smile, "So do I."

Made in the USA
Monee, IL
21 November 2022